The Official Autism 101 Manual: Autism Today

The Official Autism 101 Manual ©2006 Autism Today

Autism Today
2016 Sherwood Dr., Suite 3,
Sherwood Park, Alberta
Canada T8A 3X3.

<www.autismtoday.com>

Cover design: Dunn + Associates Design
Interior design & typesetting: Folio Bookworks

ISBN: 0-9724682-8-5
ISBN-13: 978-0-9724682-8-2

Publisher's Cataloging-in-Publication Data

The official autism 101 manual / [created and compiled by] Karen L. Simmons. -- Alberta, Canada : Autism Today, c2006.

p. ; cm.

ISBN-13: 978-0-9724682-8-2
ISBN-10: 0-9724682-8-5
Contains contributions from professionals in the autism community.
Also available in electronic book format.
Includes bibliographical references.

1. Autism. 2. Autism--Diagnosis. 3. Autism--Treatment. 4. Autism--Psychological aspects. I. Simmons, Karen L. II. Autism 101 manual.

RC553.A88 S56 2006
616.85/882--dc22   0604

The Official Autism 101 Manual Contents

James B. Adams, Ph.D.
Anne Addison, MBA, NHA
Anthony Attwood, Ph.D.
Jed E. Baker, Ph.D.
Laurence A. Becker, Ph.D.
Barry Bettman, PCC Professional Certified Coach
Teresa Bolick, Ph.D.
Sally Brockett, MS
Jennifer Buchanan, BMT, MTA
Diane D. Burns
Laura Cook
Stephen M. Edelson, Ph.D.
Lori Ernsperger, Ph.D.
Karen Siff Exkorn, BA., MA
Toni Flowers
Temple Grandin, Ph.D.
Michelle M. Guppy
Sandra L. Harris, Ph.D.
Daniel Hawthorne
Lawrence P. Kaplan, Ph.D.
David Kirby, Journalist
Rebecca Landa, Ph.D., CCC-SLP
Lisa S. Lewis, Ph.D.
Nicholas Martin, MA
Keith McAfee, MD
Thomas A. McKean
Arnold Miller, Ph.D.
Sharon Mitchell, BA, BEd, MA
Ellen Notbohm
Barry M. Prizant, Ph.D.
Gwen Randall-Young, MEd Cpsych
Bernard Rimland, Ph.D.
William Shaw, Ph.D.
Stephen Shore, AbD
Lisa Simmons
Karen L. Simmons, CEO, Author
Jessica "Jazz" Summers
Sherri Tenpenny, DO
Darold A. Treffert, MD
Terrylynn M. Tyrell, Med
Mary Wrobel, CCC, SLP
Pat Wyman, MA
Veronica York

Dedication
To the real stars of autism

I dedicate this resource first and foremost to my children, Kimberly, Matthew, Christina, Jonathan, Stephen and Alex. They are all my favourites! This book sets out to share the wealth of information and resources I have found and used to help my two special needs children, Jonathan and Alex. Though there have been many challenges over the years, I wouldn't have my children any other way. They are who they are—whole, loving and complete, exactly as they are. Jonny's humour and wit make me laugh. His ability to focus and concentrate enables him to hone in on what he enjoys most while offering him hope for the future. Alex's persistence will carry him far in life and certainly keeps us all on our toes! So much for growing old quickly!

I also dedicate this resource to all of Jonny and Alex's peers with Attention Deficit Hyperactivity Disorder (ADHD) or autism. You are the real shining stars of autism and you offer a unique perspective that enriches the fabric of human kind. I like to say we must all "discover the awesome in autism," and this is what Autism Today is all about. In fact, many leading individuals may have had high functioning autism, including Albert Einstein, Marie Curie and Thomas Jefferson, to mention a few. Our world is much better because of your contributions.

A great big thank you goes out to all the wonderful authors and presenters who have contributed to this resource. Your commitment and perseverance in discovering help for this special group of people is what is moving the entire field forward. One of my goals is to facilitate the change of views and attitudes that people have about autism around the world. It is important to help people see that autism is a unique condition, with many symptoms that can be overcome through intervention, rather than as a negative affliction, as it was viewed in days past. Regardless of our circumstances, we can choose to see peace within it. By doing so, the quality of everyone's lives will become more positive and loving.

The person with autism is in your life for a reason. Perhaps this person is there to teach you love, patience and understanding. If you are the person with autism, you also have your lessons to learn. Maybe they are to accept yourself, explore your strengths and learn to love and laugh more easily. No matter what we are all here to experience, I challenge each and every one of you to look into your hearts and ponder what you are here to learn and then seek to fulfill your true gifts and strengths. Thank you for being you!

Introduction
Why Autism Today is providing this manual

The purpose of this "first of a kind" publication is to help people, no matter what their role is in the autism field, to find the resources they need. Parents, family members, educators, professionals and people on the autism spectrum can learn to understand this condition and what they can do to reach for the best possible outcome for the person with autism. In this book you will learn about where to start, what interventions are available and even glimpse the future by hearing what people on the autism spectrum have to say.

This book aims to provide current, relevant information in a way that is easy to understand and user friendly. The e-book format gives us an ability to update the book's content. As a "living book," this one will always be alive with current information, providing or directing you to critical resources describing new discoveries, treatments, scientific updates and personal accounts—all while helping to raise awareness of this mysterious condition and bring its mysteries to light.

We welcome your feedback, suggestions and comments. They will help us keep this book a vital, easy-to-use reference for those with autism, their families, professionals, educators and anyone else interested in learning more about autism and some attention deficit disorders.

As a parent of a child with autism, author and educator of sorts, I have hosted many conferences with world-class speakers in North America and have travelled to other conferences gathering a great deal of information. I have sold copies of leading publications in the autism field, while gaining knowledge along the way. At many of the conferences I have hosted, I am asked to recommend resources for behavior, social skills, communication and sensory issues.

Throughout this book I will be doing just that, from my own personal experience, of course, and from the recommendation of many Autism Today members. I feel my unique perspective can help many parents, educators and professionals find what, in my viewpoint, are the true gems of knowledge and understanding that they are seeking. I hope this book helps each and every one of you tremendously.

— *Karen L. Simmons,*
Founder of Autism Today

What exactly are autism spectrum disorders?

CHAPTER 1

What is autism?

Autism refers to neurologic disorders involving serious impairment of abilities to interact and communicate socially, and repetitive and restricted interests and activities. Classic autism is at one end of the autism spectrum. This is associated with delayed or absent spoken language, and sometimes with cognitive delay. Asperger's Syndrome is at the other end of the autism spectrum. It is not associated with delayed language, cognitive development or self-help skills.

Generally, people on the autism spectrum have great difficulty making friends and understanding social rules. They typically have one or a few interests, activities or physical movements, which they engage in repeatedly. They may or may not have mental retardation and/or a marked delay in language, although even those using superficially "normal" language will have problems using language in a socially fluent and appropriate way.

What is the cause of autism?

Researchers worldwide are devoting considerable time and energy to find an answer to this critical question. Medical researchers are exploring various explanations for the forms of autism. Although a single specific cause of autism is not known, current research links autism to biological or neurological differences in the brain. In many families there appears to be a pattern of autism or related disabilities. This suggests there is a genetic basis to the disorder, although at this time no gene has been directly linked to autism. The genetic basis is believed by researchers to be highly complex, probably involving several genes acting together.

Several outdated theories about the cause of autism have been proved false. Autism is not a mental illness. Children with autism are not unruly kids who choose not to behave. Bad parenting does not cause autism. Furthermore, no known psychological factors in the development of the child have been shown to cause autism.

How is autism diagnosed?

There are no medical tests for diagnosing autism. An accurate diagnosis must be based on observation of the individual's communication, behavior and developmental levels. However, because many of the behaviors associated with autism are shared by other disorders, various medical tests may be used to rule out or identify other possible causes of the symptoms being exhibited.

Diagnosis of autism is difficult for a practitioner with limited training or exposure to it. Since the symptoms of autism vary so much, a child should ideally be evaluated by a multidisciplinary team that may include a neurologist, psychologist, developmental pediatrician, speech/language therapist, learning consultant or another professional knowledgeable about autism.

A brief observation in a single setting cannot present a true picture of an individual's abilities and behaviors. Parental (and other caregivers') input and developmental history are very important components of an accurate diagnosis. At first glance, some people with autism may appear to have mental retardation, a behavior disorder, problems with hearing, or even odd and eccentric behavior. To complicate matters further, these conditions can co-occur with autism.

Sometimes professionals who are not knowledgeable about the needs and opportunities for early intervention in autism do not offer an autism diagnosis even if it is appropriate. This hesitation may be due to a misguided wish to spare the family. Other times, well-meaning professionals have misdiagnosed autism.

Difficulties in the recognition and acknowledgment of autism often lead to inadequate provision of the services required to meet the complex needs of individuals with autism. An accurate diagnosis and early identification of autism provide the best basis for building an appropriate and effective educational and treatment program.

What is Asperger's Disorder (Asperger's Syndrome)?

Asperger's Disorder—also known as Asperger's Syndrome—is one of five Pervasive Development Disorders (PDDs) that also include autism, Rett's Syndrome, Childhood Disintegrative Disorder, and PDD-Not Otherwise Specified (PDD-NOS). PDDs are a category of neurologically-based disorders characterized by a range of delays in various developmental stages.

Asperger's Disorder was first described in the 1940s by Viennese pediatrician Hans Asperger, who observed autistic-like behaviors and difficulties with social and communication skills in boys who had normal intelligence and language development.

Many professionals felt Asperger's Disorder was simply a milder form of autism and used the term "high functioning autism" to refer to it. Professor Uta Frith, with the Institute of Cognitive Neuroscience, of University College London, and author of *Autism and Asperger Syndrome*, describes individuals with Asperger's Disorder as "having a dash of autism." Asperger's Disorder was added to the American Psychiatric Association's *Diagnostic and Statistical Manual of Mental Disorders* (DSM-IV) in 1994 as a separate disorder from autism. However, many professionals still consider Asperger's Disorder to be a less severe form of autism.

What distinguishes Asperger's Disorder from autism is the severity of the symptoms and the absence of language delay. Children with Asperger's Disorder may be only mildly affected and frequently have good language and cognitive skills. To the untrained observer, a child with Asperger's Disorder may just seem different.

Children with autism are frequently seen as aloof and uninterested in others. This is not the case with those with Asperger's Disorder. Individuals with Asperger's Disorder usually want to fit in and have interaction with others; they simply don't know how to do it. They may be socially awkward, because they do not understand conventional social rules, or may show a lack of empathy. They may engage in limited eye contact, seem to be unengaged in a conversation and not understand the use of gestures.

Interests in a particular subject may border on the obsessive. Children with Asperger's Disorder frequently like to collect categories of things, such as rocks or bottle caps. They may be proficient in knowing categories of information, such as baseball statistics or the Latin names of flowers. While they may have good rote memory skills, they have difficulty with abstract concepts.

One of the major differences between Asperger's Disorder and autism is that, by definition, there is no speech delay in Asperger's Disorder. In fact, children with Asperger's Disorder frequently have good language skills; they simply use language in different ways. Speech patterns may be unusual, lacking inflection or having a rhythmic nature. Speech may be formal and too loud or high pitched. Children with Asperger's Disorder may not understand the subtleties of language, such as irony and humor, or may not understand the natural give and take of a conversation.

Another distinction between Asperger's Disorder and autism concerns cognitive ability. While some individuals with autism experience mental retardation, by definition a person with Asperger's Disorder cannot possess a "clinically significant" cognitive delay. This does not imply that all individuals with autism have mental retardation. Some do and some do not, but a person with Asperger's Disorder possesses average to above-average intelligence.

While motor difficulties are not a specific criteria for Asperger's Disorder, children affected by it frequently have motor skill delays and may appear clumsy or awkward.

How is Asperger's Disorder diagnosed?

Diagnosis of Asperger's Disorder is on the increase, although it is unclear whether it is more prevalent or whether more professionals are detecting it.

The symptoms for Asperger's Disorder are the same at those listed for autism in the DSM-IV. However, children with Asperger's Disorder do not have delays in the area of communication and language. In fact, to be diagnosed with Asperger's Disorder a child must have had normal language development as well as normal intelligence. The DSM-IV criteria for Asperger's Disorder specifies that the individual must have "severe and sustained impairment in social interaction, and the development of restricted, repetitive patterns of behavior, interests and activities," that must "cause clinically significant impairment in social occupational or other important areas of functioning."

The first step to diagnosis is an assessment, including a developmental history and observation. This should be done by medical professionals experienced with autism and PDDs. If Asperger's Disorder or high functioning autism is suspected, the diagnosis of autism will generally be ruled out first. Early diagnosis is important. Children with Asperger's Disorder who are diagnosed and treated early in life have a better chance of being successful in school and eventually living independently.

What is Asperger's Syndrome?

Contributing Author Dr. Tony Attwood is a Clinical Psychologist who has specialized in autism for over 20 years. As a practicing clinician with special interest in early diagnosis, severe challenging behavior and Asperger's Syndrome, his experience covers the full range of the spectrum, from the profoundly disabled to the most highly functioning.

Resources and links—Tony Attwood, Ph.D. suggests visiting his Autism Today website to learn about his other products and services: Visit <http://attwood.autismtoday.com> today! (*Please note, don't put in the www*)

Dr. Hans Asperger, an Austrian paediatrician, originally described Asperger's Syndrome in 1944. The syndrome has more recently been classified as an autistic spectrum disorder. Children and adults with Asperger's Syndrome have an intellectual capacity within the normal range, but have a distinct profile of abilities that has been apparent since early childhood. The profile of abilities includes the following characteristics:

A qualitative impairment in social interaction:
- Failure to develop friendships that are appropriate to the child's developmental level.
- Impaired use of non-verbal behaviour such as eye gaze, facial expression and body language to regulate a social interaction.
- Lack of social and emotional reciprocity and empathy.
- Impaired ability to identify social cues and conventions.

A qualitative impairment in subtle communication skills:
- Fluent speech but difficulties with conversation skills and a tendency to be pedantic, have an unusual prosody and to make a literal interpretation.

Restrictive Interests:
- The development of special interests that is unusual in their intensity and focus.
- Preference for routine and consistency.

The disorder can also include motor clumsiness and problems with handwriting and being hypersensitive to specific auditory and tactile experiences. There can also be problems with organisational and time management skills and explaining thoughts and ideas using speech. The exact prevalence rates have yet to be determined, but research suggests that it may be as common as one in 250. The aetiology is probably due to factors that affect brain development and not due to emotional deprivation or other psychogenic factors.

The characteristics of Asperger's Syndrome described above are based on the diagnostic criteria and current research and have also been modified as a result of my extensive clinical experience. I would like to provide a personalised description of Asperger's Syndrome that also incorporates the person's qualities as well as their difficulties.

From my clinical experience I consider that children and adults with Asperger's Syndrome have a different, not defective, way of thinking. The person usually has a strong desire to seek knowledge, truth and perfection with a different set of priorities than would be expected with other people. There is also a different perception of situations and sensory experiences. The overriding priority may be to solve a problem rather than satisfy the social or emotional needs of others. The person values being creative rather than co-operative. The person with Asperger's syndrome may perceive errors that are not apparent to others, giving considerable attention to detail, rather than noticing the 'big picture'. The person is usually renowned for being direct, speaking their mind and being honest and determined and having

a strong sense of social justice. The person may
actively seek and enjoy solitude, be a loyal friend
and have a distinct sense of humour. However, the
person with Asperger's Syndrome can have difficulty
with the management and expression of emotions.
Children and adults with Asperger's syndrome may
have levels of anxiety, sadness or anger that indicate a
secondary mood disorder. There may also be problems
expressing the degree of love and affection expected
by others. Fortunately, we now have successful
psychological treatment programs to help manage and
express emotions.

Savant syndrome

Contributing Author Darold A. Treffert, MD—Dr. Treffert is a clinical professor at the University of Wisconsin Medical School, in Madison, WI, and a member of the Behavioral Health Department at St. Agnes Hospital, in Fond du Lac, WI.

Resources and links— Darold A. Treffert, MD suggests visiting his Autism Today website to learn about his other products and services: Visit <http://treffert.autismtoday.com> today! (*Please note, don't put in the www*) You can contact Dr. Treffert by visiting <www.daroldtreffert.com> or calling (920) 921-9381. For more information, visit <www.savantsyndrome.com>.

Introduction

George can tell you, almost instantly, which years in the next 50 that Easter falls on March 25. He can tell you the day of the week of any date over a 40,000-year span backward or forward. He and his identical twin brother trade 20-digit prime numbers for amusement, notes Oliver Sacks.[1] Yet George cannot multiply the simplest of numbers. George also remembers the weather for every day of his adult life. Unable to explain his incredible talents, George is content to say "It's fantastic I can do that!" And it truly is.

Richard's swiss-oil crayon drawings are collected internationally. He has had no formal art training and is classified as legally blind. He began drawing at age three. At age 12 an art critic was "thunderstruck" by Richard's drawings, which he described as an "incredible phenomenon rendered with the precision of a mechanic and the vision of a poet." Some of Richard's drawings are in the collections of Margaret Thatcher and The Vatican. One, presented to Pope John Paul II, depicts thousands of pilgrims in Vatican Square. You can almost single out each of the persons on the drawing.

Tony is blind and autistic. He is also an incredible musician. He won a jazz contest as a teenager and was admitted to the prestigious Berklee College of Music in Boston from which he then graduated *Magna Cum Laude*. He now plays 20 instruments and has produced four CDs that include many of his own compositions.

Joseph is a lightning calculator. He can multiply 341 by 927 in his head and quickly give you the answer: 316,107. He is fascinated with license plate numbers and remembers myriads of them only glimpsed at years earlier. His memory is so good that he can study a 36-number grid for less than two minutes and tell you what was in the grid, without making a mistake, in 43 seconds. He uses his memory in his work as a librarian. Joseph was one of the people Dustin Hoffman spent many hours with learning about autism and savant skills for his portrayal of an autistic savant, Raymond Babbitt, in the movie Rain Man.

Ellen is a musical virtuoso. A lover of opera, she memorized Evita within a week of hearing it. She also has a superior spatial sense and can keep time precisely without referring to a clock or other time piece. Since she is blind, she has never seen a clock. Her superior spatial sense is demonstrated by her ability to walk in any unfamiliar setting without running into objects, as if using some type of personal radar. She also has an extremely accurate memory and a preoccupation with rhythm that has been present since childhood.

These five remarkable individuals are persons with savant syndrome. They typify the musical, artistic, calendar calculating, lightning calculating, and spatial and mechanical skills that are so characteristically seen in savant syndrome, superimposed on autistic disorder, and always coupled with extraordinary memory. These special skills, linked with massive memory in persons with developmental disorders, including autistic disorder, is savant syndrome. And, just as these five individuals demonstrate the typical range of savant skills, they also demonstrate the 5:1 male–female ratio seen in savant syndrome.

More information about these special persons, and their equally special families, can be found in *Extraordinary People: Understanding Savant Syndrome,* a book first published 1988 and then re-issued in an updated version in 2000.[2] There is more about these special persons as well on the savant web site at <www.savantsyndrome.com>.

Each story documents the emergence of special skills in a child, often at about age three or four, superimposed on symptoms and behaviors of autistic disorder. The special skills of these individuals are often in the areas of art, music, calendar calculating, mathematics, or mechanical and spatial skills. All are combined with prodigious memory. But the savant skills, rather than being frivolous, are in fact the child's way of communicating from their otherwise relative isolation, and the savant abilities become, by "training the talent," a conduit toward better language development, increased social and daily living skills, and overall independence.

What follows is a summary of where we are in understanding savant syndrome, today, where we've been in the past, the research directions in which we are proceeding and, most important, how the special talents in the twice exceptional child can be worked with and channeled toward fully actualizing a-bilities while at the same time lessening dis-abilities. Beyond that, a closer look at savant syndrome triggers a closer look at human potential overall; however, especially as the so-called "acquired savants" more recently described provide some hints at the hidden potential that may lie within us all.

Until we can understand and explain savant syndrome, we cannot fully understand and explain ourselves. And no model of brain function will be complete until it can fully incorporate and account for this remarkable juxtaposition of ability and disability in these extraordinary people. Beyond synapses and neurons, though, these stories also tell of the incredible power of the belief, determination, persistence, optimism and love of family members for these special people and how this propels their potential. The stories provide uplifting examples of how it is not enough to care for the savant, and his or her mind. We must care about them, and their world, as well.

Where we have been

Savant syndrome, with its "islands of genius," has a long history. Benjamin Rush provided one of the earliest reports in 1789 when he described the lightning calculating ability of Thomas Fuller, "who could comprehend scarcely anything, either theoretical or practical, more complex than counting."[3] However, when Fuller was asked how many seconds a man had lived who was 70 years, 17 days and 12 hours old, he gave the correct answer of 2,210,500,800 in 90 seconds, even correcting for the 17 leap years included. Actually, however, the first description of savant syndrome in a scientific paper appeared in the German psychology journal, *Gnothi Sauton,* in 1783. It described the case of Jedediah Buxton, a lightning calculator with extraordinary memory.[4]

The now regrettable term idiot savant was coined by Down in 1887 when he presented 10 cases in colorful detail from his 30-year experience at the Earlswood Asylum.[5] These cases demonstrated the typical musical, artistic, mathematical and mechanical skills, coupled with phenomenal memory, that have so unfailingly reoccurred in savant syndrome to the present day. Down meant no harm by that term. At that time "idiot" was an accepted classification for persons with an IQ below 25, and "savant," or "knowledgeable person" was derived from the French word savoir meaning "to know." While descriptive, the term was actually a misnomer since almost all cases occur in persons with an IQ higher than 40. In the interest of accuracy and dignity, savant syndrome has been substituted and is now widely used. Savant syndrome is preferable to "autistic savant" since only about 50% of persons with savant syndrome have autistic spectrum disorder and the other 50% have some other form of CNS injury or disease.

The first definitive work on savant syndrome was a chapter by Tredgold in his 1914 textbook, *Mental Deficiency.*[6] In 1978 Hill provided a review of the literature between 1890 and 1978 that included 60 reports involving over 100 savants.[7] That year Rimland provided a summary of his data on "special abilities" in 531 cases from a survey population of 5,400 children with autism.[8] Treffert provided an updated review in 1988, which contained more detail on all of those earlier cases.[2] Since that time there have been six books on the topic and several review articles with extensive bibliographies.[9]

What we do know

The condition is rare but one in 10 autistic persons show some savant skills

In Rimland's 1978 survey of 5,400 children with autism 531 were reported by parents to have special abilities and a 10% incidence of savant syndrome has become the generally accepted figure in autistic disorder.(8) Hermelin, however, estimates that figure to be as low as "one or two in 200."[10] The presence of savant syndrome is not limited to autism however. In a survey of an institutionalized population with a diagnosis of mental retardation, the incidence of savant skills was 1:2,000 (0.06%)[11] A more recent study surveyed 583 facilities, and found a prevalence rate of 1.4 per 1,000, or approximately double the Hill estimate.[12]

Whatever the exact figures, mental retardation and other forms of developmental disability are more common than autistic disorder. So it turns out that about 50% of persons with savant syndrome have autistic disorder and the other 50% have other forms of developmental disability, mental retardation or other CNS injury or disease. Thus not all autistic persons have savant syndrome, and not all persons with savant syndrome have autistic disorder.

Males outnumber females in autism and savant syndrome

In explaining this finding, Geschwind and Galaburda, in their work on cerebral lateralization, point out that the left hemisphere normally completes its development later than the right hemisphere and is thus subjected to prenatal influences, some of which can be detrimental, for a longer period of time.[13] In the male fetus particularly, circulating testosterone, which can reach very high levels, can slow growth and impair neuronal function in the more vulnerably exposed left hemisphere, with actual enlargement and shift of dominance favoring skills associated with the right hemisphere. A "pathology of superiority" was postulated, with compensatory growth in the right

brain as a result of impaired development or actual injury to the left brain.

This finding may account as well for the high male–female ratio in other disorders, including autism itself since left hemisphere dysfunction is often seen in autism as will be explained below. Other conditions, such as dyslexia, delayed speech and stuttering, also with male predominance in incidence, may be manifestations of this same left hemisphere interference in the prenatal period.

Savant skills typically occur in an intriguingly narrow range of special abilities

Considering all the abilities in the human repertoire, it is interesting that savant skills generally narrow to five general categories: music, usually performance, most often piano, with perfect pitch, although composing in the absence of performing has been reported as has been playing multiple instruments (as many as 20); art, usually drawing, painting or sculpting; calendar calculating (curiously an obscure skill in most persons); mathematics, including lightning calculating or the ability to compute prime numbers for example, in the absence of other simple arithmetic abilities; mechanical or spatial skills, including the capacity to measure distances precisely without benefit of instruments, the ability to construct complex models or structures with painstaking accuracy or the mastery of map making and direction finding.

Other skills have been reported less often, including: prodigious language (polyglot) facility; unusual sensory discrimination in smell, touch or vision, including synesthesia; perfect appreciation of passing time without benefit of a clock; and outstanding knowledge in specific fields such as neurophysiology, statistics or navigation.[14] In Rimland's sample of 543 children with special skills, musical ability was the most frequently reported skill followed by memory, art, pseudo-verbal abilities, mathematics, maps and directions, coordination and calendar calculating.[8]

Generally a single special skill exists, but in some instances several skills exist simultaneously. Rimland and Fein noted that the incidence of multiple skills appeared to be higher in savants with autism than in savants with other developmental disabilities.[15]

Whatever the special skill, it is always associated with prodigious memory. Some observers list memory as a separate special skill, however prodigious memory is an ability all savants possess, cutting across all of the skill areas as a shared, integral part of the syndrome itself.

There is a spectrum of savant skills

The most common are splinter skills, which include obsessive preoccupation with, and memorization of, music and sports trivia, license plate numbers, maps, historical facts or obscure items such as vacuum cleaner motor sounds, for example. Talented savants are those cognitively impaired persons in whom the musical, artistic or other special abilities are more prominent and finely honed, usually within an area of single expertise, and are very conspicuous when viewed in contrast to overall disability. Prodigious savant is a term reserved for those extraordinarily rare individuals for whom the special skill is so outstanding that it would be spectacular even if it were to occur in a non-impaired person. There are probably fewer than 50 prodigious savants known to be living worldwide at the present time who would meet that very high threshold of savant ability.

The skills tend to be right hemisphere in type

These (right hemisphere) skills can be characterized as non-symbolic, artistic, concrete and directly perceived, in contrast with left hemisphere skills, which are more sequential, logical and symbolic, and include language specialization.

The special skills are always accompanied by prodigious memory

Whatever the special abilities, a remarkable memory of a unique and uniform type welds the condition together. Terms such as automatic, mechanical, concrete and habit-like have been applied to this extraordinary memory. Down used the term "verbal adhesion";[5] Critchley used the terms "exultation of memory" or "memory without reckoning";[16] Tredgold used the term "automatic";(6) and Barr characterized his patient with prodigious memory as "an exaggerated form of habit."[17] Such unconscious memory suggests what Mishkin and Petri referred to as non-conscious "habit" formation rather than a "semantic" memory

system.[18] They proposed two different neural circuits for these two different types of memory: a higher level cortico-limbic circuit for semantic memory and a lower level, cortico-striatal circuit for the more primitive habit memory which is sometimes referred to as procedural or implicit memory. Savant memory is characteristically very deep, but exceedingly narrow, within the confines of the accompanying special skill.

Savant syndrome can be congenital or it can be acquired following brain injury or disease later in infancy, childhood or adult life

Recent reports of savant-type abilities emerging in previously healthy elderly persons with fronto-temporal dementia are particularly intriguing.(19,20)

Savant skills characteristically continue, rather than disappear, and with continued use the special abilities either persist at the same level or actually increase

In almost all cases, unlike the case of Nadia, there is no trade-off of special skills with exposure to more traditional schooling.[21] Instead, the special skills often serve as a conduit toward normalization with an actual improvement in language acquisition, socialization and daily living skills.

No single theory has emerged thus far that can explain all savants

An important basic question surrounding savant syndrome is how do they do it? Numerous theories have been put forth, but no single over-arching theory can explain all savants. The theories have included: eidetic imagery or the related but separate phenomenon generally called photographic memory; inherited skills; sensory deprivation and sensory isolation; highly developed rote memory; and compensation and reinforcement to offset lack of more general capacity or intelligence.[2]

There are problems with each of these theories. For example, formal testing for eidetic imagery shows that phenomenon to be present in some but certainly not in all savants and when present it may be more a marker of brain damage than an agent of savant abilities.[22, 23] Two studies, one with 25 savants and another with 51 subjects showed relatives with special skills in some but certainly not all cases; another study of 23 relatives of carefully studied savants found only one family member with special skills.[24–26] Several investigators have shown that memory alone cannot fully account for savant abilities, particularly calendar calculating and musical skills.[10, 27]

In recent years several neuropsychological theories have also directly addressed the abundant reports of splinter and savant skills in the autistic population. "Weak central coherence" theory (WCC) cites a particular cognitive and perception style—focusing on details rather than the whole—as being present in persons with autism and postulates that such a style of information processing could be an important part of those persons with savant abilities. Not being distracted by more global patterns, the savant can focus on a single item or skill and perfect it.[28] Simon Baron-Cohen has advanced the "extreme male brain" theory of autism. This proposes that attributes of the male brain, systematizing and spatial skills, produce a special predilection for autism in males.[29–30] He finds such special systematizing skills and lack of social abilities and empathizing in persons with Asperger's Disorder particularly.[31]

However, the newer neuro-psychiatric theories seem more to describe the autistic person than to explain him or her, and they do not account for the fact that of those with savant syndrome only 50% are autistic while the remainder have other developmental disabilities, CNS disorders or disease.

New findings

Left brain injury and right brain compensation
One theory that does provide an increasingly plausible explanation for savant abilities in many cases is left brain injury with right brain compensation. As pointed out above, the skills most often seen in savant syndrome are those associated with the right hemisphere, as described by Tanguay.[32] Rimland commented that in the autistic savant simultaneous, high-fidelity imagery and processing—right hemisphere functions—tend to be more prominent than the verbal, logical and sequential processing more typically associated with the left hemisphere.[8, 33]

In autism, left brain dysfunction has been demonstrated in a number of studies. As early as 1975, pneumoencephalograms demonstrated left hemisphere abnormalities, particularly in the temporal lobe areas in 15 of 17 patients with autism, four of whom had savant skills. Investigators in this study concluded that motor and language functions were "taken over" by the right hemisphere because of deficits in the left hemisphere.[34] A 1999 PET study showed low serotonin synthesis in the left hemisphere of persons with autistic disorder, and other studies have confirmed such left hemisphere deficits as well.[35] Boddaert and co-workers demonstrated that five children with autism when at rest and when listening to speech-like sounds displayed a volume of activation that was greater on the right side and diminished on the left. The reverse was found among the eight children in the control group.[36] Escalante and colleagues demonstrated an atypical pattern of cerebral dominance and a history of early language disorder among individuals with autism when compared to both healthy participants and persons with normal acquisition of early language skills.[37]

With respect to savant syndrome, in 1980 Brink presented a case of a typically developing nine-year-old boy who was left mute, deaf and paralyzed by a gunshot wound to the left hemisphere.[38] Following that injury an unusual savant mechanical skill emerged, presumably from the undamaged right hemisphere. Subsequent reports have likewise implicated left hemisphere injury, such as those in a musical savant, and a mathematical savant with left hemisphere damage documented in both on neuropsychological tests and neuro-imaging studies.[39, 40] Likewise CT scans and neuropsychological test results for a prodigious musical savant described by Treffert showed left brain damage.[2] Munoz-Yunta and co-workers report similar findings of left hemisphere damage and dysfunction in savant syndrome based on PET and magnetoencephalography techniques.[41]

A significant new discovery: the "acquired" savant
However, the most powerful confirmation of the left brain dysfunction/right brain compensation theory in savant syndrome comes from a 1998 report by Miller and co-workers. They described five previously

non-disabled patients with fronto-temporal dementia (FTD) who acquired new artistic skills with the onset and progression of FTD.[19] Several of these individuals had no previous history of particular artistic ability. Yet prodigious art skills emerged as the dementia proceeded. Consistent with characteristics and traits of savants, the modality of skill expression in these five, older adults was visual, not verbal; the images were meticulous copies that lacked abstract or symbolic qualities; episodic memory was preserved but semantic memory was devastated; and there was intense, obsessive preoccupation with the artwork. Neuro-imaging studies showed dominant (left) hemisphere injury and dysfunction.

The authors hypothesized that selective degeneration of the (particularly left) anterior temporal and orbitofrontal cortices decreased inhibition of visual systems involved with perception, thereby enhancing artistic interest and abilities. Kapur called this process "paradoxical functional facilitation" and speculated that this process accounts for unexpected behavioral improvement in discrete domains following brain injury.[42]

In an expansion of that work, Miller described seven additional FTD patients who acquired new visual or musical talents despite the progression of their dementia.[20] The 12 FTD patients with these newly emerged savant-type talents were compared on SPECT imaging and neuropsychological testing to FTD patients without such talent. Nine of the 12 showed asymmetric left-sided SPECT deficits; one demonstrated bilateral abnormalities (left on MRI, right on SPECT), while two had asymmetric right-sided dysfunction (one of whom was left-handed). The talented group performed better on tasks assessing right frontal lobe functions, but worse on verbal abilities. The authors conclude: "Loss of function in the left anterior temporal lobe may lead to the 'paradoxical functional facilitation' of artistic and musical skills. Patients with the left-sided temporal lobe variant of FTD offer an unexpected window into the neurological mediation of visual and musical talent."

These FTD cases are interesting additions to the earlier cases of newly "acquired" savant abilities such as Brink's case, already noted, following a gunshot wound to the left hemisphere.[38] An internationally known, now adult, savant sculptor had his remarkable talent emerge following a childhood fall.[2] Lythgoe and co-workers describe a 51-year-old male whose prolific drawing and sculpting skills unexpectedly emerged following a subarachnoid hemorrhage that affected principally frontal areas.[43]

SPECT Imaging in a nine-year-old artistic savant with autism

After finding left hemisphere dysfunction, particularly left anterior temporal dysfunction in the 12 patients with fronto-temporal dementia, Miller and co-workers performed neuropsychological and neuro-imaging studies on a newly diagnosed nine-year-old artistic savant with autism.[44] This childhood artistic, autistic savant showed "striking parallels" to other artistic savants, particularly Nadia, with an obsession for one art medium (felt-tipped pen) and one type of subject (cartoon figures), and with extraordinary drawing skills and exceptional visual memory. MRI scan was normal. SPECT showed bilateral increased frontal perfusion with bilateral anterior temporal lobe hypo-perfusion, which was worse on the left than on the right. This is the same site of dysfunction noted in the 12 elderly FTD patients with savant-type skills. These researchers conclude: "The anatomic substrate for the savant syndrome may involve loss of function in the left temporal lobe with enhanced function of the posterior cortex."

A gene for savant syndrome?

In the search for subgroups within the aggregate autism spectrum disorders, Nurmi and colleagues identified (among 94 multiplex families) 21 families as "savant skills positive" and 73 families as "savant skill negative."[45] The subset study of savant-skills positive families yielded significantly increased evidence for linkage to 15q11-q13 compared to savant-skills negative families. Interestingly, the presence of savant skills was the only factor that isolated a subgroup from the larger autistic spectrum disorders group. The authors note that Prader-Willi syndrome is due to a deletion on this same region of chromosome 15 (i.e. 15q11-13) and that some features (including puzzle skills for example) of PWS and autism overlap. The researchers conclude that it is possible that a gene, or genes, in the chromosome 15q11-13 region, "when perturbed contributes to predisposition to a particular cognitive style or pattern on intellectual impairments and relative strengths. Precisely how those skills are manifested in a given individual may be influenced by a variety of environmental, and possibly, genetic factors."

Prodigies and savant syndrome

There is emerging evidence that prodigies and savants may share certain underlying mental processes when carrying out their specialized, expert tasks. Event-related potentials (ERPs) can measure very early components of brain activity reflecting initial, "preconscious" stages of mental processing. This fast, low-level "preconscious" mental activity contrasts sharply with that seen when higher level, "executive" functions are accessed during typical information processing. Birbaumer compared ERPs of a "human calculator"—a non-autistic arithmetic whiz—to same age, IQ matched, healthy controls.[46] Compared to controls, early on in the calculating process, the expert calculator showed evidence of "enhanced automatic low-level processing." Studies are now underway with autistic savant calculators to see whether this particular type of early, lower level processing ("without reckoning") is the same as that used by the non-autistic "expert" calculator.

In a similar effort using PET, Pesenti and his team examined differences between a calculating prodigy and normal control subjects in the neural basis of mental calculations.[47] When completing less complex calculations in a typical manner, both the expert and non-expert persons showed activation in the brain bilaterally but with a clear left-sided predominance for select regions. However when the "expert" completed complex calculations much more accurately and swiftly than controls, he "recruited" a system of brain areas implicated in episodic memory including right medial frontal and parahippocampal areas. Moreover, the expert utilized a unique method of exploiting the seemingly unlimited storage capacity of long-term memory in order to maintain the sequence of steps and intermediate results needed for the more complex calculations. On the contrary, the normal control group relied on the more limited span working memory system. Therefore unique brain mechanisms are utilized by the expert when demonstrating this special skill. And, when doing these special skills, the prodigy is perhaps relying on some right brain capacities and some special memory recruitment as may be the case for the savant.

An article by Kalbfleisch further explores the functional neural anatomy of exceptional talent and interfaces between talent, intelligence and creativity in prodigies and savants.[48]

Repetitive Transcranial Magnetic Stimulation (rTMS)

Several investigators are exploring the use of rTMS to temporarily immobilize portions of left hemisphere function to see if, given Miller's work and some of the other left-sided findings summarized above, savant-type abilities emerge in healthy volunteers.

Snyder and Mitchell argue that savant brain processes occur in each of us but are overwhelmed by more sophisticated conceptual cognition.[49] They conclude that autistic savants "have privileged access to lower levels of information not normally available through introspection." Snyder and co-workers tested that hypothesis in 11 male volunteers using rTMS applied to the left fronto-temporal region while carrying out two drawing tests and two proofreading tests.[50] rTMS did not lead to any systematic improvement in naturalistic drawing ability but it did lead to "a major change in the schema or convention of the drawings of four of the eleven participants." Two of the participants noted improvement in their ability to proofread and recognize duplicated words. In a similar study Young and colleagues, using a wide variety of standard psychological tests and tasks specifically designed to test savant skills and abilities, showed that savant-type skills improved in five out of 17 participants during rTMS stimulation.[51] They conclude that savant-type skill expressions may be possible for some, not all, individuals just as it appears to be the case in the disabled population. This group intends to carry out further studies using more efficacious and targeted stimulation.

These new studies suggest that savant syndrome may be due, at least in part, to "paradoxical functional facilitation" of the right hemisphere, allowing for new skills as a compensatory process. Increasingly, however, an alternative theory is advanced wherein these right brain skills are not necessarily newly developed but instead represent latent but dormant skills that are released from the "tyranny of the left hemisphere," or what is, more simply, left cerebral dominance in most persons.

Savants: past and present

Dr. Down's original 10 cases of savant syndrome

In his 1887 Lettsomian Lectures before the Medical Society of London, Down presented 10 cases encountered in his 30 years in practice that had particularly caught his attention.[5] Each of these were individuals who, while mentally retarded, exhibited remarkable "special faculties." Down did not identify any of these special persons as autistic; that designation did not occur until Kanner's paper over 50 years later.[52] But in closely reviewing Down's entire lecture series, he did, interestingly, specifically mention a group of individuals who differed in many ways from those with more typical mental retardation, a group he identified as "developmental" in origin. That is a term—developmental disability—now applied to autistic persons a century after Down's observations. Down's astute observations regarding this group of "developmental" cases is described in detail on the savant syndrome web site at <http://www.savantsyndrome.com> in the articles section under the title of *Dr. J. Langdon Down* and *Developmental' Disorders.*

Down's description of his 10 cases of "special faculties" in those 1887 lectures reads like descriptions of many savants over a century later. Each of his cases of developmental disability demonstrated some special skills combined with prodigious memory. That is savant syndrome. One of his patients, for example, had memorized verbatim *The Rise and Fall of the Roman Empire.* Other children drew with remarkable skill "but had a comparative blank in all the other higher faculties of mind." Still other children remembered dates and past events. Arithmetical genius was evident in some children, including lightning calculating. Music and musical memory was also described among the special abilities. And there was yet another boy

who was unable to use a clock or tell time in any conventional manner, yet had perfect appreciation of past or passing time.

While not identified as such, in reading Down's careful and colorful accounts of his cases of "special faculties," it is clear that among the children were some with what would now be identified as autistic disorder, in which savant syndrome occurs with a distinctive frequency as noted above. Among his cases one finds the typical artistic, musical, mathematical and other enhanced abilities noted so often in the literature in the 118 years since Down's original observations.

Later cases, including those of Dr. Leo Kanner

Tredgold presented 20 additional cases 27 years later.[6] His cases are a catalogue of the categories and skills—musical, artistic, mechanical, calendar and mechanical/spatial—that are repeated so strikingly in all the subsequent cases to date.

The several hundred cases in the literature since Tredgold are summarized in a 1988 review article.[53] The 2000 edition of *Extraordinary People: Understanding Savant Syndrome* added additional cases.[2] And the web site <www.savantsyndrome.com> has added many new cases worldwide as well.

Six of Kanner's original cases of Early Infantile Autism had specific musical abilities, and Kanner was struck by the overall heightened memory capacity of all 10 of these individuals.[52] The identical twin calendar calculators first described by Horwitz have been extensively studied since that time.[54] The brothers have a calendar calculating range of 40,000 years and they also remember the weather for each day of their adult life. Their ability to compute 20-digit prime numbers, inability to do simple arithmetic and special abilities were described by Sacks and incorporated into some scenes in Rain Man.[1]

Some well-known savants

Without doubt the best-known autistic savant is a fictional one—Raymond Babbitt—as portrayed by Dustin Hoffman in the Academy Award-winning movie Rain Man. The original inspiration for the savant portrayed in Rain Man is a 53-year-old male who has memorized over 8,600 books and has encyclopedic knowledge of geography, music, literature, history, sports and nine other areas of expertise.[55, 56] He can name all the U.S. area codes and major city zip codes. He has also memorized the maps in the front of telephone books and can tell you precisely how to get from one U.S. city to another and then how to get around in that city street by street. He also has calendar calculating abilities and more recently rather advanced musical talent has surfaced. Of unique interest is his ability to read extremely rapidly, simultaneously scanning one page with the left eye, the other page with the right. An MRI shows absence of the corpus callosum along with substantial other CNS damage. His history and savant abilities are described in detail on the savant web site.

The phenomenal drawing ability of a British savant with autism has resulted in several popular art books published by him.[57, 58] His extraordinary memory is illustrated in a documentary film clip: after a 12-minute helicopter ride over London, he completes, in three hours, an impeccably accurate sketch that encompasses four square miles, 12 major landmarks and 200 other buildings, all drawn to scale and perspective. A rather marked musical ability has surprisingly surfaced in this artist as well.[59] Recently an 11-year-old's artwork from the U.S. has gained international attention.[60]

The triad of blindness, autism and musical genius continues to be conspicuously over-represented and prominent throughout the history of savant syndrome, including Blind Tom at the time of the Civil War, Tredgold's case at the Salpetriere and several well known present day musical savants.[2, 61] A Japanese musical savant's ability as a composer demonstrates decisively that savants can be creative; his 40 original pieces on two internationally popular CDs forcefully document that ability.[62] Smith describes in detail a remarkable language (polyglot) savant in *The Mind of the Savant*.[63]

However female savants continue to be few. Self described the case of Nadia which has triggered considerable debate about the possible "trade-off" of special skills for language and social skills acquisition.[21] Viscott documented in detail, including psychodynamic formulations, a female musical savant whom he followed for many years.[64] Treffert described a blind, autistic musical savant who, along with her musical ability, demonstrated very precise spatial location abilities and precise time-keeping skills without access to a clock face or other time instruments.[2]

Most reports continue to be anecdotal, single cases. However, Young traveled to a number of countries and met with 59 savants and their families, completing the largest study done on savants to date using uniform history taking and standardized psychological testing.[25] Forty-one savants carried a diagnosis of autism and the remainder some other type of intellectual disability. Twenty were rated as prodigious savants; 20 were rated as talented; the remaining 19 had splinter skills. The savants in this series of cases had the following elements in common: neurological impairment with idiosyncratic and divergent intellectual ability; language and intellectual impairments consistent with autism; intense interest and preoccupation with particular areas of ability; rule-based, rigid and highly structured skills lacking critical aspects of creativity and cognitive flexibility; preserved neurological capacity to process information relating to the particular skills; a well-developed declarative memory; a familial predisposition toward high achievement; and a climate of support, encouragement and reinforcement from families, case workers, teachers, caretakers and others.

In a recent summary of work with savants, Nettlebeck and Young conclude that rote memory does not provide sufficient basis for savant skills; instead such savant skills are based on extensive, rule-based knowledge confined to narrowly defined abilities that are imitative and inflexible.[27] They conclude that savant skills do not represent separate forms of intelligence (outside the concept of overall intelligence) and that these skills depend on modular processing and memory structures that have been spared damage affecting other areas of the brain.

Rain Man the movie/Rain Man real life

Raymond Babbitt, the main character in the movie Rain Man, has become the world's best known savant due to Dustin Hoffman's remarkably accurate and sensitive portrayal of savant syndrome in that film. That 1988 movie, in its first 101 days, accomplished more toward bringing savant syndrome to public attention than all the efforts in the 101 years following

Dr. Down's 1887 description of the disorder. A detailed description of the background and chronology of the movie, including the people Dustin Hoffman studied with as he prepared for his role, is described elsewhere.[2] But several things warrant mention here.

First, the movie is not a documentary. Yet its accuracy added to its value as an informative and entertaining film. One indicator of that accuracy is that there was no six-day, cross-country "cure" of autism. The real change of character occurred in the brother, Charlie. This conveys the important message that in dealing with persons with disabilities it is often we who need to accommodate their needs and special qualities—and not they who need to make all the changes required for them to live with us, side-by-side, in our communities. Third, as a gentle caveat, the audience needs to realize that Raymond Babbitt is a high functioning autistic person, and not all autistic persons function at that high level; it is a spectrum disorder. Fourth, as a second caveat, the audience needs to realize that not all autistic persons are savants, and not all savants have autistic disorder.

The major message in the movie concerning the special qualities of the autistic savant is a welcome and positive one. The message raised public interest in both autism and savant syndrome. Few disabilities will receive the public focus and heightened visibility as autism and savant syndrome received as a result of Rain Man.

Training the Talent:
successful education approaches

Etiologic considerations aside, what is the best approach to the savant and his or her special skills? Phillips framed the controversy in 1930 when he wrote: "The problem of treatment comes next. . . . Is it better to eliminate the defects or train the talent?"[65] Experience has given the answer—train the talent and some of the "defect" disappears. The special talent, in fact, becomes a conduit toward normalization: the unique savant skills promote better socialization, language acquisition and independence. The special skills can be used to engage the attention of the savant. They can be used to help the savant express him- or herself. They can be used as channels for the expression of more useful abilities.

Clark developed a Savant Skill Curriculum using a combination of successful strategies currently employed in the education of gifted children (enrichment, acceleration and mentorship) and autism education (visual supports and social stories), in an attempt to channel and apply in useful ways the often non-functional obsessive savant and splinter skills of a group of students with autism.[66] This special curriculum proved highly successful in the functional application of savant skills and an overall reduction in the level of autistic behaviors in many subjects. Improvements in behavior, social skills and academic self-efficacy were reported, along with gain in the communication skills of some subjects.

Donnelly and Altman note that increasing numbers of "gifted students with autism" are now being included in gifted and talented classrooms with non-disabled, gifted peers.[67] Discussing this, they outline some of the special approaches that are effective with gifted student with autism, including the use of an adult mentor in the field of their talent, individual counseling and small group social skills training.

Some specialized schools are emerging as well. For example, Soundscape Centre in London recently began operating as the only specialized educational facility in the world uniquely dedicated to the needs and potential of persons with sight loss and special musical abilities, including musical savants.[68] Orion Academy <www.orionacademy.org> in Moraga, California, specializes in providing a positive educational experience for high school students with Asperger's Syndrome. Hope University <www.hopeu.com> in Anaheim, California, is a fine arts facility for adults with developmental disabilities. Its mission is to "train the talents and diminish the disability" through the use of fine arts therapy, including visual arts, music, dance, drama and storytelling.

The Savant Academy <www.savantacademy.org> in Los Angeles, California, was established in 2003 to support the education of people with savant syndrome, including linguistic, mathematical, musical and artistic savants. David Mehnert, the musician and teacher who established the Savant Academy, suggests specialized techniques to unlock hidden savant abilities, using music particularly as a pathway to special abilities. On the web site, Mr. Mehnert provides more information about those techniques and provides, as well, some useful information about "myths" surrounding savant syndrome and about perfect pitch, an extremely important consideration when dealing with musical savants. More information about perfect pitch and teaching musical savants is also contained in a booklet by Susan Rancer, a Registered Music Therapist.[69]

Dr. Temple Grandin is well known as an international authority in her field of animal science. She is also well known for her books including *Thinking in Pictures* and *Animals in Translation*.[70, 71] She is also autistic. Her recent book, with Kate Duffy, *Developing Talents: Careers for Individuals with Asperger Syndrome and High-Functioning Autism,* is an excellent practical resource for discovering, nurturing and "training the talent," so that many persons on the autistic spectrum can experience the important experience of work and "the satisfaction of contributing to their families and their communities, of being independent and economically self-sufficient."[72] This book outlines methods of helping children "develop their natural talents" using "drawing, writing, building models, programming computers" and similar skills to help build a "portfolio" of skills they can apply in their search for a meaningful work experience. The book helps people on the autistic spectrum and their family members, teachers, counsellors and others better understand and develop the career planning process for these special persons with special skills.

Future directions

No model of brain function, including memory, will be complete until it can account for, and fully incorporate, the rare but spectacular condition of savant syndrome. While in the past decade, particularly, much progress has been made toward explaining this jarring juxtaposition of ability and disability, many unanswered questions remain. However, interest in this fascinating condition is accelerating, especially since the discovery of savant-type skills in previously unimpaired older persons with FTD and other "acquired" savant instances. This finding has far-reaching implications regarding buried

potential in some, or perhaps, all of us.

Advanced technologies will help in those investigations. Images of brain structure are now integrated with studies of brain function using PET, SPECT and fMRI. Diffusion Tensor Imaging (DTI) and direct Fiber Tracking now permit non-invasive tracking of white matter pathways within and between brain regions, better delineating the under-connectivity and over-connectivity problems perhaps causal in autism and savant syndrome itself.[73] Findings from all these newer techniques can then be correlated with detailed neuropsychological testing in larger samples of savants, comparing and contrasting those findings with data from both impaired and non-impaired control groups, including prodigies. The interface between genius, prodigies and savants is especially intriguing, and these studies can shed light on the debate regarding general intelligence *versus* separate intelligences. Some researchers suggest that savants provide a unique window into the creative process itself. From studies already completed important information has emerged regarding brain function, brain plasticity, CNS compensation, recruitment and repair.

But there is more to savant syndrome than genes, circuitry and the brain's marvellous intricacy. Scientific interest aside, those with savant syndrome and their families, caregivers, teachers and therapists have a great deal to teach us. Human potential consists of more than neurons and synapses. It also includes, and is propelled by, the vital forces of encouragement and reinforcement that flow from the unconditional love, belief, support and determination of families and friends who not only care for the savant, but care about him or her as well.

Savant syndrome remains a "challenge to our capabilities," as one person described it in an American Psychiatric Association paper in 1964, concluding that the real significance of savant syndrome lies in our inability to explain it.[54] But savant syndrome is less now a "landmark to our ignorance" than at that APA meeting 41 years ago. More progress has been made in the past 15 years in better understanding and explaining savant syndrome than in the previous 100. And that important inquiry continues, with the prospect of us advancing further than ever before as we unravel the mysteries

of these extraordinary people and their remarkable
abilities and, in the process, learn more about ourselves,
our hidden potential and our possibilities.

1. Sacks O: The Twins New York Review of Books. 1987; 32:16–20.
2. Treffert D: Extraordinary People: Understanding Savant Syndrome. Omaha, NE IUniverse.com, 2000 (originally published 1989, New York, Harper & Row.
3. Scripture, E.W. Arithmetical prodigies Am J Psychol 1891; 4:1–59.
4. Gnothi Sauton oder Magazin der Erfahrungsseelenkunde als ein Lesebuch fur Gelehrte und Ungelehrte Edited by Mortiz, KP, Berlin, Mylius, 1783–1793.
5. Down JL: On Some of the Mental Affections of Childhood and Youth. London, Churchill, 1887.
6. Tredgold, AF: Mental Deficiency. New York, William Wood, 1914.
7. Hill, AL: Savants: mentally retarded individuals with special skills, in International Review of Research in Mental Retardation, vol 9, Edited by Ellis NR. New York Academic Press, 1978.
8. Rimland B: Savant capabilities of autistic children and their cognitive implications, in Cognitive Defects in the Development of Mental Illness. Edited by Serban, G. New York, Brunner/Mazel, 1978.
9. Nettlebeck T, Young, R: Savant Syndrome. International Review of Research in Mental Retardation 1999 22:137–173.
10. Hermelin B: Bright Splinters of the Mind. London Jessica Kingsley Publishers, 2001.
11. Hill AL: Idiot savants: rate of incidence Percept. Mot Skills 1977; 44:161–162.
12. Saloviita T, Ruusila L, Ruusila U: Incidence of savant skills in Finland Percept. Mot Skills 2000; 91:120–122.
13. Geschwind N, Galaburda AM: Cerebral Lateralization:Biological Mechanisms, Associations, and Pathology. Cambridge, Mass, MIT Press, 1987.
14. Kehrer HE: Savant capabilities of autistic persons. ACTA Paedopsychiatrica 1992; 55:151–155.
15. Rimland B, Fein DA: Special talents of autistic savants, in The Exceptional Brain: Neuropsychology of Talent and Special Abilities. Edited by Obler LK, Fein, DA New York, Guilford Press, 1988.
16. Critchley M: The Divine Banquet of the Brain. New York, Raven Press, 1979.
17. Barr MW: Some notes on echolalia, with the report of an extraordinary case J. Nerv Ment Dis 1898; 25:20–30.
18. Mishkin M., Petri H.L.: Memories and habits; some implications for the analysis of learning and retention, in Neuropsychology of Memory. Edited by Squire L.R., Butters N. New York, Guilford Press, 1984.

19. Miller BL., Cummings J., Mishkin F,. Boone K., Prince F., Ponton M., Cotman C.: Emergence of artistic talent in fronto-temporal dementia. Neurology 1998; 51:978–982.

20. Miller B.L., Boone K., Cummings L.R., Mishkin F.: Functional correlates of musical and visual ability in frontotemporal dementia. British Journal of Psychiatry 2000; 176:458–463.

21. Selfe L: Nadia: A Case of Extraordinary Drawing Ability in an Autistic Child. New York, Academic Press, 1978.

22. Giray E.F., Barclay AG.: Eidetic imagery: longitudinal results in brain-damaged children. Am J Ment Defic 1977; 82:311–314.

23. Bender M.B., Feldman M., Sobin A.J.: Palinopsia. Brain 1968; 91:321–338.

24. Duckett J.: Idiot-savants: Superspecialization in mentally retarded persons. Doctoral Dissertation, University of Texas in Austin; Department of Special Education, 1976.

25. Young R.: Savant Syndrome: Processes underlying extraordinary abilities. Unpublished doctoral dissertation, University of Adelaide, South Australia 1995.

26. LaFontaine L.: Divergent abilities in the idiot savant. Doctoral Dissertation, Boston University in Boston, School of Education, 1974.

27. Nettlebeck T., Young R.: Savant Syndrome in International Review of Research in Mental Retardation, ed. C.M. Glidden New York, Academic Press, 1999.

28. Frith U., Happe F.: Autism: Beyond 'theory of mind.' Cognition 1994; 50:115–132.

29. Jolliffe T., Baron-Cohen S.: Are people with autism and Asperger syndrome faster than normal on the Embedded Figures Test? Journal of Child Psychology & Psychiatry 1997; 24:613–620.

30. Heaton P., Hermelin B., Pring L.: Autism and pitch processing: A precursor for savant musical ability? Music Perception 1998; 15:291–305.

31. Baron-Cohen S.: The extreme male brain theory of autism. Trends in Cognitive Sciences 2002; 6:248–254.

32. Tanguay P.: A tentative hypothesis regarding the role of hemispheric specialization in early infantile autism. Paper presented at UCLA Conference on Cerebral Dominance, Los Angeles 1973.

33. Rimland B.: Infantile Autism: The Syndrome and its implications for a neural theory of behavior. New York, Appleton-Century-Crofts, 1978.

34. Hauser S., DeLong G., Rosman N.: Pneumographic findings in the infantile autism syndrome. Brain 1975; 98:667–688.

35. DeLong R.: Autism: New data suggest a new hypothesis. Neurology 1999; 52:911–916.

36. Boddaert N.: Perception of complex sounds: abnormal pattern of cortical activation in autism. Am J Psychiatry 2003; 160:2057–2060.

37. Escalant-Mead P., Minshew N., Sweeney J.: Abnormal brain lateralization in high-functioning autism. J Autism and Developmental Disorders 2003; 33:539–543.

38. Brink T.: Idiot savant with unusual mechanical ability. Am J Psychiatry 1980; 137:250–251.

39. Steel, J., Gorman R., Flaxman, J.: Neuropsychiatric testing in an autistic mathematical idiot-savant: Evidence for nonverbal abstract capacity. Journal of the American Academy of Child Psychiatry, 1984 3:469–487.

40. Charness N., Clifton J., MacDonald L.: Case study of a musical "mono-savant:" A cognitive-psychological focus in The Exceptional Brain, eds. L. Obler and D. A. Fine, New York, Guilford, 1988.

41. Munoz-Yunta J., Ortiz-Alonso T.: Savant or Idiot Savant Syndrome Rev. Neurol 2003 Feb; 36 Suppl 1:157–161.

42. Kapur N.: Paradoxical functional facilitation in brain-behavior research: A critical review. Brain 1996; 119:1775–1790.

43. Lythgoe M., Pollak T., Kalmas M., de Hann M., Chong W.K.: Obsessive, prolific artistic output following subarachnoid hemorrhage. Neurology 2005; 64:397–398.

44. Hou C., Miller B., Cummings J., Goldberg M., Mychack P., Bottino, B., Benson F.: Artistic Savants Neuropsychiatry, Neuropsychology and Behavioral Neurology 2000; 13:29–38.

45. Nurmi E.L., Dowd M., Tadevosyan-Leyfer O., Haines J., Folstein S., Sutcliffe J.S.: Exploratory sub-setting of autism families based on savant skills improves evidence of genetic linkage to 15q11–q13. Journal of the Academy of Child Adolescent Psychiatry 2003; 42:856–863.

46. Birbaumer N.: Rain Man's Revelations. Nature 1999; 399:211–212.

47. Pesenti M., Zago L., Crivello F.: Mental Calculation in a prodigy is sustained by right prefrontal and medial temporal areas. 2001 Nature Neuroscience; 4:103–107.

48. Kalbfleisch, M.: Functional neural anatomy of talent. Anatomical Record 2004; 277B:21–36.

49. Snyder A., Mitchell D.: Is interger arithmetic fundamental to mental processing? Proceedings of the Royal Society of London Biological Science 1999; 266:587–592.

50. Snyder A.W., Mulcahy E., Taylor J.L., Mitchell D., Sachdev P., Gandevia S.C.: Savant-like skills exposed in normal people by suppressing the left fronto-temporal lobe. Journal of Integrative Neuroscience 2003; 2:149–158.

51. Young R.L., Ridding M.C., Morrell T.L.: Switching skills by turning off part of the brain. 2004 Neurocase 10:215–222.

52. Kanner L.: Early Infantile Autism. Journal of Pediatrics 1944; 25:200–217

53. Treffert D.A.: The 'idiot savant': a review of the syndrome. Am Journal of Psychiatry 1988; 145:563–572.

54. Horwitz W.A., Kestenbaum C., Person E., Jarvik L.: Identical twins—idiot savants—Calendar calculators. Am J Psychiatry 1965; 121:1075–1079.

55. Peek F.: The Real Rain Man. Salt Lake City, Utah, Harkness Publishers, 1996.

56. Treffert D., Wallace G.: Islands of Genius. Scientific American 2002; 286:76–85.

57. Wiltshire S.: Drawings. London, J.M. Dent and Sons, 1987.

58. Wiltshire S.: Floating Cities. New York, Summit Books, 1991.

59. Sacks O.: An Anthropologist on Mars. New York, Alfred Knopf.

60. Lehrman J.: Drawings by an Artist with Autism. George Braziller, Inc. New York, 2002.

61. Miller L.: Musical Savants: Exceptional Skill in the Mentally Retarded. Lawrence Erlbaum Associates, Hillsdale NJ, 1989.

62. Cameron L.: The Music of Light: The Extraordinary Story of Hikari and Kenzaburo Oe. The Free Press, New York, 1998.

63. Smith N., Tsimpli I.: The Mind of the Savant: Language, Learning and Modularity. Oxford, Blackwell, 1995.

64. Viscott D.: A musical idiot-savant. Psychiatry 1970; 33:494–515.

65. Phillips A.: Talented Imbeciles. 1930 Psychological Clinics 18:246–255.

66. Clark T.: The Application of Savant and Splinter Skills in the Autistic Population Through Curriculum Design: A Longitudinal Multiple-Replication Study. Unpublished Doctoral Thesis, The University of South Wales, School of Education Studies.

67. Donnelly J.A., Altman R.: The Autistic Savant: Recognizing and serving the gifted student with autism. Roeper Review 1994; 16:252-–255.

68. Ockelford A.: Sound Moves: Music in the education of children and young people who are visually impaired and have learning disabilities. London, Royal Institute for the Blind, 1988.

69. Rancer S.: Perfect Pitch and Relative Pitch: How to identify & test for the phenomena: a guide for music teachers, music therapists and parents. Self-published. SusanRMT@aol.com.

70. Grandin T.: Thinking in Pictures And Other Reports From My Life With Autism. Vintage Books, New York, 1995.

71. Grandin T.: Animals in Translation: Using the Mysteries of Autism to Decode Animal Behavior. Scribner, New York, 2005.

72. Grandin T., Duffy K.: Developing Talents: Careers for Individuals with Asperger Syndrome and High Functioning Autism. Autism Asperger Publishing Company, Shawnee Mission, KS 2004.

73. Conturo, T., Nicolas E., Cull T., Akbudak E., Snyder A.Z., Shimony J.S., McKinstry R.C., Burton, H., Raichle E.: Tracking neuronal fiber pathways in the living human brain. Proc. Natl. Acad. Sci 1999; 10422–101427.

REFERENCES

Early diagnosis and best outcomes

CHAPTER 2

Early detection of autism spectrum disorders

(This article is reprinted with permission from the January–February 2004 issue of the Autism Asperger's Digest, a 52-page bimonthly magazine on autism spectrum disorders. For more information, write <www.autismdigest.com> or call 1-800-489-0727. The publisher, Future Horizons Inc., is a world leader in autism/Asperger's/PDD publications.)

Contributing Author Rebecca Landa, Ph.D., University of Washington, CCC-SLP—A speech-language pathologist, Dr. Landa directs the Center for Autism and Related Disorders at Kennedy Krieger Institute, at The Johns Hopkins School of Medicine, Baltimore, MD, and is the principal investigator on several NIH- and CDC-funded studies of autism. She authored the Pragmatic Rating Scale, which is used internationally in autism research.

Resources and links— Rebecca Landa, Ph.D., CCC-SLP suggests visiting her Autism Today website to learn about her other products and services: Visit <http://landa.autismtoday.com> today! (*Please note, don't put in the www*) You can write to Dr. Landa at <landa@kennedykrieger.org>.

Children with autism are typically diagnosed after three years of age. Yet parents typically expressed their first concern to their pediatrician when their child was 18 to 20 months of age (Stone et al., 1999). Many times, parents indicate that they had some concern about their child with autism even before telling their pediatrician.

These concerns were often "soft" signs of a problem. For example, some parents remember that their baby became very upset when riding in a car or when their feet touched grass, that their baby infrequently looked into their eyes, or that their baby was unusually content or quiet. What is a parent to make of these characteristics? The picture becomes a bit more complicated as the baby ages and new developmental features are supposed to appear. Skills may emerge, but may be qualitatively different from that seen in most children. For example, first words may emerge but sound like they were taken from a Disney video, or they are produced once and then rarely heard again. Parents watch their infants' development carefully, but most parents rely on experts to guide them about whether the developmental process is coming along as expected.

This article addresses: (a) Why is early detection of an autism spectrum disorder (ASD) important? (b) If early diagnosis is so important, why are so few children with an ASD identified early? (c) What "red flags" might signal that development is not coming along in a typical fashion? Our research has focused on these questions, and more. We address these questions through the longitudinal assessment of infant siblings of children with autism (6–36 months of age), children who are late talkers but have no family history of autism (18–36 months of age), and children who have no family history of autism and appear to be developing typically (6–36 months of age).

Why is early detection of an ASD important?

Fundamentally, early detection is important because earlier intervention appears to drive better outcomes than later onset intervention (Harris & Handleman, 2000). Why would this be? The answer is that brain development occurs through interplay between external stimulation and neurobiological processes. Consider the following neurodevelopmental phenomena and their implications for early intervention.

(a) In normal development, infants have more neurons than they need, and these extra neurons must be selectively "pruned" or eliminated. If they are not, there could be an excess of excitation in the brain that could negatively impact learning and development.

Treatment implication: Intervene early while this pruning process is underway. Guided input of stimulation may assist with this pruning process. For example, babies who are not prone to looking at faces can be "tricked" into or enticed to look at faces. For babies who are prone to exploring objects only through mouthing them, guided experience coordinating information across sensory domains can be provided by helping the babies look at a nubby ball, touch it, squeeze it and so forth.

(b) Pathways (forming a "communication system") must develop in the brain whereby signals carrying information can travel from one area of the brain to another. For example, a structure deep in the brain may help babies look at faces, but it is not until connections are made between that structure and the cortex of the brain that babies are capable of a more sophisticated analysis of facial information. There is evidence that this connection process occurs through extensive experience with looking at faces and the brain's neurobiological program to make neural connections.

Treatment implication: Intervene early when these pathways are scheduled to make their connections. (Scientists have defined the timeframe for the formation of some of these connections) The same examples given above apply here. If babies are not prone to explore or pay attention to certain types of input, they may require more exaggerated input (such as exaggerated smiles paired with vocalization, balls that light up when handled).

(c) There are sensitive periods in brain development wherein "learning" occurs quickly, without the baby having to really "focus" attention on the incoming information. For example, early in development, babies are able to "hear" all the differences in the speech sounds they hear, even sounds that are not in their native language. Japanese babies can "hear" the difference between "r" and "l", even though these sounds are not distinguished in their language. At about 6 months of age, babies begin to categorize speech sounds into the different phonetic classes that characterize their native language. At this time, Japanese babies stop discriminating "r" and "l", and

begin to hear these as one speech sound. This helps them because they don't get confused if one speaker of the language pronounces a speech sound slightly differently than another speaker of the language. This process occurs just as babies begin to comprehend language. Babies do not have to be taught to do this, it just happens through exposure of speech input at the right time in development.

Treatment implication: Intervene early, as close to the timing of the sensitive period as possible. Give enriched input, in formats that attract the infant's attention.

(d) The brain is able to "compensate" for problems that it has, such that a skill can be learned by an "alternate" region if the region typically responsible for learning that skill is disabled in some way. This is called neuroplasticity. Neuroplasticity timeframes differ from brain region to brain region but it is most powerful in the young brain.

Treatment implication: Intervene early, during periods of maximal neuroplasticity. Development of each skill or part of a skill will facilitate development of associated skills (e.g., as visual spatial skills develop, object knowledge develops, which enhances language development, which enhances social development).

(e) An untreated disruption in one brain region could have "downstream" effects on brain regions that would have otherwise been normal or minimally impaired.

Treatment implication: Intervene early and treat areas of deficit that most affect social and communication development. Social development, for example, has many component or sub-skills. Helping babies develop each of those sub-skills can help prevent or reduce the effect of social impairment. An infant with low social responsiveness will elicit less input from those around him, and this is just the type of infant who cannot afford to have reduced social learning opportunities.

If early diagnosis is so important, why are so few children with an ASD identified early?

One of the reasons that ASD is not identified early

is that the signs of ASD in infants and toddlers have not been clearly defined. In addition, we know very little about whether the presence of certain "red flags" actually signals a true developmental disorder. Some professionals feel that discussing concerns with parents may cause them to be upset, and so they elect to wait until development is more clearly disrupted or delayed before they make a referral for further assessment.

The first concern that parents generally raise is that their child is not talking as expected. Many "late talkers" go on to have typical development. Prospective, longitudinal research (such as that being conducted in our lab) is needed to identify early signs of risk for autism and how reliably those signs actually predict the onset of a disorder. Since the developmental disruption in autism is probably present before the expected onset of first words, we need to develop an eye for these non-linguistic signs of ASD in infants and toddlers. We will be looking at things far more subtle than a spoken word. Late onset of language is too general a "red flag" to serve us well in identifying children who are likely to manifest an ASD. Guidelines and characterized developmental patterns across time are needed to help professionals identify infants and toddlers at risk for an ASD.

What "red flags" might signal that development is not coming along in a typical fashion?

The "red flags" will change as new skills are expected. Based on our longitudinal research with infant siblings of children with autism, we propose the following "red flags" as signs that a screening should be conducted by an expert in infant and toddler development as well as in autism.

6 months of age

- Infrequent babbling.
- Infrequent vocalization in response to caregiver vocalization (Remember that typically developing infants require a little time to coordinate their responses. So caregivers should provide some silent moments between the vocalizations that they direct to their infant.

This gives the infant time to coordinate a response.)
- Infrequent looking at the face of the interactive partner.
- Infrequent matching of the facial expression of the caregiver; infants should smile when their caregiver smiles at them (not every single time, but consistently enough to be noticeable); parents should expect their infant to be synchronized with them, in emotional expression, vocalization patterns and so on.
- Odd or unusual movement patterns (e.g., method of grasping an object, rolling over and, in older infants, crawling; odd transitions in movement from one position to another).

9–12 months of age

- Reduced or absent non-verbal intentional communication (waving bye-bye, pointing).
- Reduced or absent social communication (showing, pointing things out, sharing, giving you a bite of their snack, "calling" you from the crib).
- Reduced complexity of babbling or reduced variety in the types of sounds produced by the infant during babbling.
- Reduced use of vocalizations in interactions or during intentional communicative attempts (trying to get you to give him a Cheerio, or trying to get you to pick her up).
- Reduced comprehension of your nonverbal gestures (your hand out as you ask for him to "give it to me").
- Reduced response to his/her name being called.
- Being overly "fixated" on objects or movement patterns.
- Reduced imitation of simple movement patterns that the child can already perform on his or her own.
- Reduced attempts to make you laugh. (Typically developing infants enjoy attention and do things to seek it out. If they see that they have made you laugh, they are likely to perform the behavior again to get you to laugh again or to keep your attention.)

14–16 months of age

(We chose 14 months instead of 12 months because first words and the ability to walk are expected by this age.)

- Reduced looking to the caregiver when the caregiver is talking but not necessarily to the child.
- Lack of the onset of first words.
- The primary way that you can consistently get and keep the child's attention is when you perform a favorite routine (peek-a-boo, sing a certain song, etc.).
- Fixated on videotapes.
- Echoing what others say without social and communicative intention.
- Lack of teasing. (Toddlers of this age have ways of signalling when they are initiating a social game. They will give a coy look, offer you a toy and then retract it as they smile, and so forth. The absence of this teasing behavior is a "red flag.")
- Infrequent coordination of looking at you, smiling and producing some form of communication (a word or vocalization or gesture).
- Imitation that is reduced in frequency, atypical in form or unpaired with social connection (e.g., eye contact and/or a smile).
- Reduced frequency or length of turn-taking exchanges (with or without objects).
- Repetitive behaviors or sensory seeking (e.g., pressing head against caregiver, peering at the edge of a table).
- Reduced number of play sequences (put spoon in cup and stir; put spoon in bowl then to teddy bear's mouth) or range of behaviors that are exhibited in play. (A child who engages only with cause-effect toys or stacking blocks, to the exclusion of functional play with objects and emerging pretend play (e.g., putting a phone to her ear) should be watched to see whether there are other "red flags" present.).

Early diagnosis and intervention provides a child with optimum opportunities for enhanced growth and development. If an infant or toddler's actions mimic several of these "red flags," someone has concerns about the infant's development, or there is a family history of an autism spectrum disorder, the infant should be seen by a developmental expert (psychologist or speech language pathologist).

References

Harris, S., & Handleman, J. (2000). *Age and IQ at intake as predictors of placement for young children with autism: A four to six year follow-up.* Journal of Autism and Developmental Disorders. 30, 137–142.

Stone, W., Lee, E., Ashford, L., Brissie, J., Hepburn, S., Coorod, E., & Weiss, B. (1999). *Can autism be diagnosed accurately in children under three years of age?* Journal of Child Psychology and Psychiatry, 40, 219–226.

Are you wondering whether a child you know may have autism or Asperger's Syndrome?

If you are wondering if a child may have autism or Asperger's Syndrome, take the following quiz, answering "yes" or "no" to the questions.

1. Do they spin objects around and around?
2. Is their speech repetitive, like an echo?
3. Are they attracted to shows like Wheel of Fortune or Jeopardy?
4. Do they like to watch the same movie over and over again?
5. Are they fascinated with numbers and letters?
6. Do they seem unafraid of things that they should be afraid of?
7. Is it hard for them to make eye contact?
8. Do they shy away from being touched?
9. Do they like to line objects in a row?
10. Do they lack the ability to play "with" other children?

If you answer "yes" to three or more of the questions, consider the following steps, not necessarily in the order provided:

1. Call your local autism support group for a doctor referral, and to learn about local available services and parent support group.
2. Research available behavioural, educational, and sensory interventions for autism.
3. Research your child's biomedical needs, including those of nutrition.
4. Check your insurance policy, to find out if it covers autism.
5. Find out about early intervention services for autism in your community and begin to take advantage of them as soon as possible after diagnosis.

Early detection of autism spectrum disorders

Contributing Author Terrylynn Tyrell is completing a doctoral degree in severe disabilities at the Johns Hopkins University. Her dissertation topic involves training pediatric practitioners to utilize autism screening tools. In 2004 she co-authored a legislative bill entitled, "Pilot Program to Study and Improve Screening Practices for Autism Spectrum Disorders". This bill was passed in the state of Maryland in April 2005.

Ms. Tyrell received her undergraduate degree with honors in psychology from the University of East London and her master's degree in educational psychology and counseling from McGill University. Terrylynn started working as an educational therapist for the Bermuda Department of Education in 1998. During this time she developed an intervention database for children with behavior and emotional disorders. She also served as a trainer for active parenting sessions.

While pursuing her doctoral degree, Ms. Tyrell worked at the Kennedy Krieger Research Institute as a research coordinator on a center grant: Studies to Advance Autism Research and Training (STAART). During this time she was an active participant of the Johns Hopkins University Autism Network and the Early Detection and Intervention Network at the Kennedy Krieger Research Institute. She has also served as a program consultant and evaluator for the United States District court in review of instructional and inclusion services in the Baltimore city public school system.

Ms. Tyrell is an associate of the Johns Hopkins University teaching faculty for students in the Department of Special Education. Ms. Tyrell is also a member of the American Educational Research Association, the American Public Health Association, and the Council for Exceptional Children.

Ms. Tyrell is the recipient of a Bermuda Government Further Education Award, a McGill University Graduate Studies and Recipient Award and the Johns Hopkins University Buchaner Scholarship and Schiffman Scholarship.

Ms. Tyrell has worked with families and children with disabilities for 15 years.

Resources and links—Terrylynn M. Tyrell, M.Ed. suggests visiting her Autism Today website to learn about her other products and services: Visit <http://tyrell.autismtoday.com> today! (*Please note, don't put in the www*)

Introduction

Autism is at the forefront of local, national, and international educational and political agendas. Autism is currently receiving major attention because over the past decade there has been an explosion in worldwide prevalence rates (Fombonne, 2000). Epidemiological research indicates a vast increase in the incidence of autism (Bryson, Clark, & Smith, 1988; Fombonne, 1999). In addition, there has been a considerable rise in the number of people receiving services for autism spectrum disorders (Newchaffer & Curran, 2003; Rice, Schendel, Cunniff, & Doernberg, 2004). These factors have resulted in an amplified awareness about this disability.

Autism is considered a major health issue (Newschaffer & Curran, 2003; Tebruegge, Nandini, & Ritchie, 2004). According to Johnson (2004), a member of the American Academy of Pediatrics (AAP) Autism Panel, a primary care physician that cares for

1,000 children in general practice should anticipate that 3-7 of his/ her patients will exhibit signs of autism spectrum disorder. Some researchers indicate that the prevalence of autism spectrum disorders is comparable to Alzheimer's disease and, as a result, represents a clear medical need (Gerlai & Gerlai, 2003). Pediatric practitioners need to be prepared to meet the needs of their patients with autism spectrum disorders.

Although autism is a life-long disability, treatment can make a significant difference. The DSM-IV-TR (2000) states that the age of onset of symptoms occurs prior to age 3, therefore people with autism and their families live with this disability for the majority of their life. Retrospective studies show that infants with early onset of autism spectrum disorders can be identified at 8 – 10 months of age (Werner, Dawson, Osterling, & Dinno, 2000). Current research indicates that a reliable diagnosis can be made as early as 24 months of age and this diagnosis remains stable over time (Moore & Goodson, 2003). Autism should be detected prior to the age of 3 as research demonstrates that there are early signs that can help with early identification.

The major benefit of early detection is timely access to early intervention services (King & Glascoe, 2003). Many studies demonstrate that early detection and early intervention leads to improved outcomes (Committee on Children with Disabilities, 2001; Howlin & Moore, 1997; Woods & Wetherby, 2003). Early intervention can assist with educational preparation, family supports, counseling, and medical treatment (Filipek et al, 2000). In addition, Prater and Zylstra (2002) estimate that one third of people with autism live independently. It is evident that early detection of autism is desirable and imperative (Baird et al., 2001).

The purpose of this is to demonstrate the importance of early detection in children with autism spectrum disorder. First, the nature and possible cause of autism are reviewed. Recent epidemiological findings about autism and the response to this public health concern are addressed. Finally, current pediatric practices regarding developmental screening are described. This review will also highlight the importance (need) of developmental screening in early childhood. It will also provide recommendations (solutions) for increasing earlier identification through early developmental screening. This proposal concludes with future considerations for the early identification of autism spectrum disorders.

What is Autism?

Autism is a life-long pervasive developmental disorder that affects normal development of the brain in areas that impact communication and social interaction combined with restricted patterns of behaviors (Baird, et al, 2001; Nash & Coury, 2003; Tidmarsh & Volkmar, 2003). Impairments in these areas range from mild to profound. A high-functioning individual with autism can have a high IQ, can be verbal and may socially interact with others while a low-functioning individual with autism may have mental retardation, be completely non-verbal and

may not interact with others. This extensive range represents many autism conditions that are known as Autism Spectrum Disorders (ASD). The Diagnostic and Statistical manual of Mental Disorders, IV, Text Revision (DSM-IV-TR, 2000) notes that autistic disorder is one of five disorders that fall in the category of pervasive developmental disorder.

Cause of Autism

At this time there is no single known cause of autism. Past theories about the cause of autism have proven incorrect. Originally, deviant parenting was considered to be a cause of autism (Bettelheim, 1967). Recently genetics was considered a significant factor in autism and other pervasive developmental disorders (Bespalova & Buxbaum, 2003; Constantino & Todd, 2003; Rutter, Bailey, Simonoff, & Pickles, 1997; Shastry, 2003). Studies show that siblings of a child with autism have a higher risk of autism than siblings of children without autism (Bespalova & Buxbaum, 2003; Bolton et al., 1994). Research has also indicated that vaccines and thimerosal are not associated with the rise in autism prevalence (Johnson, 2004 ; Hviid, Stellfeld, Wohlfahrt, & Melbye; Madsen et al., 2003). Investigators are still searching for a definitive cause of autism. At this time there is no biological marker for autism (First Signs, 2003).

Epidemiological Research Studies on Autism Spectrum Disorders

Epidemiological research has demonstrated a vast increase in the rate of autism. Epidemiology is the study that relates to patterns of disease incidence in human populations and the causes that affect them (Fombonne, 1999). In Atlanta, Georgia the rate of autism spectrum disorder increased from 4 to 5 per 10,000 in the 1980's to 34 per 10,000 in 1996 (Yeargin-Allsopp et al., 2003). Recent epidemiological surveys have been conducted in several countries and numerous researchers have discovered an increase in the prevalence of autism (Fombonne, 2003). *International studies.* There have been several international studies on the prevalence rate of autism spectrum disorders. Autism was reported 10 per

10,000 in a Canadian study of the epidemiology of autism (Bryson, Clark, & Smith, 1988). Population studies of children in Goteborg, Sweden revealed an increase in autism from 4 per 10,000 in 1980 to, 7.5 per 10,000 in 1984, and 11.6 per 10,000 in 1988 (Gillberg, Steffenburg, & Schaumann, 1991). In Cambridgeshire, United Kingdom (U.K.), the prevalence rate of autism spectrum condition in 5 to 11 year olds was 57 in 10,000 (Scott, Baron-Cohen, Bolton, & Brayne, 2002). Lower rates were reported in Kent, U.K. as 23.7 per 10,000 and in a North East population in London, U.K. as 14.9 per 10,000 in children age 5-14 years (Lingam et al., 2003). These studies indicate an inconsistency in the rate of autism.

US studies. A study in the Brick township of New Jersey reported the prevalence of autism spectrum disorders as 67 per 10,000 children (Betrand et al., 2001). An assessment of prevalence of autism spectrum disorder in California revealed a rate of 12.3 per 10,000, a much lower rate than New Jersey (Croen, Grether, & Selvin, 2003). An Atlanta, Georgia study of autism prevalence revealed a rate of 3.4 per 1,000 (34 per 10,000), which is half the rate of the Brick township study (Yeargin-Allsopp, et al., 2003). A Minnesota evaluation of prevalence trends of autism over time discovered an increase in prevalence from 3 per 10,000 in 1991-1992 to 52 per 10,000 in 2001-2003 (Gurney et al., 2003). Although the prevalence rate of autism seems to be inconsistent within the U.S. and the U.K. it is apparent that the rate of autism is increasing and as a result communities need to be prepared to address this rise.

Public Health Response

Response from the federal government

The United States federal government publicly recognizes autism as a public health problem. Persons with developmental disabilities may need life-long services and the financial costs can be astronomical (Rice, Schendel, Cunnif, & Doernberg, 2004). The societal cost for a person with autism is estimated to be four million dollars (Newschaffer & Curran, 2003). In 1995, the US Congress mandated research programs that would detect the gaps in the knowledge-base regarding autism. The Children's Health Act

of 2000 passed by Congress, legislated many activities related to autism research (PL 106-310). The Act specifically recommended earlier screening of autism. At the request of Congress the National Institutes of Health (NIH) formed a Federal Interagency Autism Coordinating Committee (IACC), to organize and sustain autism research and services (NIH, 2004). This committee includes representatives from five NIH institutes, the Center for Disease Control (CDC) and Prevention the Food and Drug Administration (FDA), and the US Department of Education, which hopefully enables and encourages dialogue between these organizations.

The IACC responded to the request from Congress by developing two major research studies related to autism spectrum disorders that are funded by the NIH. In 1997, a five-year, $42 million, ten international networks (Britain, Canada, France, Germany, and the U.S.) of Collaborative Programs of Excellence in Autism (CPEA) was created to study possible genetic, environmental, and immune causes of autism. Another activity that resulted from the Children's Health Act of 2000 was the creation of Studies to Advance Autism Research and Treatment (STAART), a new NIH program, to examine the effects of treatment on children with autism. There are eight STAART centers across the country and the NIH provides millions of dollars in funding for these studies. In 2002, the total support for autism research was 74 million dollars.

The CDC is another federal agency that supports research in autism spectrum disorders in several states. There are several projects that the CDC is currently funding. The Autism and Developmental Disabilities Monitoring network (ADDM) is creating and advancing programs to monitor the number of children with autism and related disorders in ten states. The Centers of Excellence for Autism and Developmental Disabilities Research and Epidemiology (CADDRE) work with the ADDM to monitor the number of children with ASD. CADDRE also aims to increase awareness about ASD, to expand access to services for children with ASD, and to direct epidemiologic research associated with ASD, and other developmental disabilities. The CDC currently funds five CADDRE networks. Other federal activities include annual reports to congress to review the provision of the Children's Health Act of 2000 and a two-day Autism Summit Conference. It is evident that the federal government has responded positively to the increased prevalence of autism.

Response from the scientific community

The AAP has responded with a multitude of autism resources for professionals, parents, and the community. The AAP has also developed a policy regarding the pediatrician's role in the diagnosis and management of autistic spectrum disorder (Committee on Children with Disabilities, 2001). The CDC has launched a campaign, "Learn the Signs. Act Early, to improve childhood developmental screening (CDC, 2004). Free resources have been distributed to pediatric practices throughout the United States. Moreover, researchers in the autism field are currently working on a Baby Sibs Project that is searching for signs of early indicators of autism in infants as young as 6 months (Johnson, 2004).

US Department of Education

In 1990, Autism became a federal category for special education. According to the Maryland State Department of Education (2004) 260 children with autism ages 3 to 21 were served in federally supported programs in 1993. This figure increased to 4,804 in the year 2003. There is a 25% increase per year in the number of children classified with autism across the country (Newschaffer & Curran, 2003). In response to this escalation, educators and researchers have promoted early intervention services for children with autism. Early intervention is offered to infants and toddlers with disabilities, at no cost, through Part C of the Individuals with Disabilities Act of 1997 (U.S.C. §1400). Several research studies have demonstrated the benefits of early intervention. Early intervention can enhance language, develop social and academic skills in children with ASD (Butter, Wynn, & Mulick, 2003; Jensen & Sinclair; 2002; Ozonoff & Cathcart, 1998; Volkmar, Lord, Bailey, Schultz, & Klin, 2004).

Current Pediatric Practice

Based on the recent epidemiological studies of autism we can expect a large number of children to be identified with autism. A pediatrician should expect to provide a medical service for at least one child with autism (Committee on Children with Disabilities, 2001). There may be more than 500,000 people with autism in the USA with an average lifespan of 76 years representing 44 million patient years (Gerlai & Gerlai, 2003). Parents typically indicate concerns as early as 18 months (Committee on Children with Disabilities, 2000; Filipek et al., 2000; Gray & Tonge, 2001). Unfortunately children with autism are typically diagnosed between the ages of 4 and 6, years after parents first ask for professional help regarding their children (Howlin & Moore, 1997; Siegel, Pliner, Eschler, & Elliott, 1998). The delay between a parent's preliminary concern and the ultimate diagnosis can defer early intervention and diminish the impact that early intervention has on early brain neuroplasticity. This is an issue that needs to be addressed.

Screening for Autism

Screening is the process of identifying an unrecognized disorder by using specific tests or examinations (Baird et al., 2001). Although autism is more common than once thought it is often recognized and diagnosed at a very late stage (Filipek et al., 2000; King & Glascoe, 2003). Less than 30% of pediatricians perform standardized screening tests at well-child visits according to the Quality Standards Subcommittee of the American Academy of Neurology and the Child Neurology Society (2000). A recent survey discovered that 7 out of 10 pediatricians detect children with developmental problems using clinical judgment, without the use of a screening instrument or checklist (King & Glascoe, 2003). Unfortunately research shows that pediatricians identify few children with disabilities when they rely solely on clinical judgment (Glascoe & VanDervoort, 1985; Regaldo & Halfon, 2001; Silverstein, Grossman, Koepsell, & Rivaram, 2003).

The CDC (2004) recently highlighted several barriers to early screening by pediatricians, including (a) a focus of physical development as opposed to cognitive and social development; (b) a lack of training to conduct screening, and (c) an inclination to support a "wait and see" approach. It is apparent that early and accurate screening for autism is an existing problem in pediatric practice that needs to be addressed.

Parental Role in Early Screening for Autism

Parents first recognize problems in their children between 12 and 20 months of age (De Giacomo & Fombonne, 1998). Research suggests that parental concerns about their child's attention span, hearing, and language are sound predictors of developmental concerns (California Department of Developmental Services, 2002; Glascoe, 2003). Unfortunately there is an indication that pediatricians do not routinely inquire about parental concerns and when parents do raise concerns they are often discounted by professionals. Moreover parents believe that health professionals need more knowledge about autism in relation to their child (Kerrell, 2001).

Recommendations for Changing Pediatric Practice

The AAP recommends that the primary pediatrician familiarize himself or herself with "at least one autism screening tool and perform it on all children" (Committee on Children with Disabilities, 2001 page 6; Johnson, 2004). Moreover, studies indicate that screening combined with parental observations increases the effectiveness of screening tools (Baird, et al, 2001). Screening for autism should occur for all children who do not meet specific milestones such as "babbling by 12 months, . . . single words by 16 months, and . . . two-word spontaneous phrases by 24 months" (Filipek et al., 2000 p 471). The American Academy of Child and Adolescent Psychiatry, the American Academy of Neurology, and the Child Neurology Society have issued practice parameters regarding regular developmental surveillance and screening. These professional entities absolutely recommend the use of developmental screening with particular screening for autism during all well child visits (California Department of Developmental Services, 2002; Committee on Children with Disabilities, 2001; Filipek et al., 2000; First Signs; 2003).

Screening Methodology

Screening methods specific to the identification of autism have recently been developed (Baird et al., 2001). Several tools are used to screen for autism including the (a) Autism Behavior Checklist (Krug, Arick, & Almond, 1980), (b) the Autism Diagnostic Interview-Revised (Lord, Rutter, & LeCouteur, 1994), (c) the Autism Diagnostic Observation Schedule-Generic (Lord, Rutter, & DiLavore, 1997), (d) the Behavior Rating Instrument for Autistic and Atypical Children (Ruttenberg, Dratman, Faknoi, & Wener, 1966), (e) the Behaviour Observation Scale for Autism (Freeman, Ritvo, Guthrie, Schroth, & Ball, 1978), (f) the Childhood Autism Rating Scale (Schopler, Riechler, DeVellis, & Daly, 1980), and (g) the Screening Test for Autism in Two-Year-Olds (Stone & Ousley, 1997). There are benefits to each of these tools but in terms of pediatric practice these screening tools are extremely long, are for older children, require the administrator to be specialized in autism, and do not consider parental input.

Autism screening methods that can be easily used in pediatric practice include the (a) the Checklist for Autism in Toddlers (CHAT), and (b) the Modified Checklist for Autism in Toddlers (M-CHAT). These tools are quick to administer, do not require special training, and consider parental input. The CHAT (Baron-Cohen, Allen, & Gillberg, 1992) was the first attempt to create a general population screen. It was developed to prospectively identify autism at 18 months. This screening tool has 9 statements about infants that are related to joint attention, social orienting, language, symbolic play, and social interaction. The physician asks the parent the first 9 test items. There are also 5 separate items that a home health visitor observes the child in the home setting. The CHAT was used to screen 16,000 children and 12 children were considered at risk for autism. Although the CHAT has a high predictive value it has poor sensitivity towards children with mild symptoms of autism (Baird et al., 2000; Filipek et al., 2000). This lack of sensitivity failed to identify 4 of 5 children that were later recognized as having signs of autism (Baird et al., 2001). To date, there have been limited published studies on the effectiveness and reliability of other autism screens.

The MCHAT is an extended version of the CHAT. It using the first nine items from the CHAT and has the same layout. The M-Chat (Robins, Fein, Barton, & Green, 2001), a 23- item checklist, is an autism screen that is used at ages of 18 months and 24 months. The M-CHAT includes more developmental areas than the CHAT such as motor abnormalities, social referencing, imitation, and orientation. This checklist is a modified version of the Checklist for Autism in Toddlers. Additional items were developed based on research regarding early symptoms of ASD that are present in infants and toddlers. The checklist is completed by parents and scored by clinicians.

Guidelines for Developing Screening Methodology

The autism field is appealing for the development of appropriate screening tools with acceptable sensitivity and specificity in young children and the tool should be accessible to use by a variety of practitioners (Filipek et al., 2000). Early detection of autism requires screening tools that are quick to use, sensitive, specific, reliable, and relevant to the population for which they are used. An autism screen should address language, joint attention, play, repetitive behavior, and regression (Stewart, Challman, & Myers, 2004).

Current Pediatric Practice

Presently, pediatric practice is not prepared to screen and identify children that exhibit the signs of autism. There is a need for pediatric practitioners to develop clinical expertise to recognize the signs of developmental disorders, particularly ASD. Practitioners need to be trained in the screening of children with social and developmental disorders. Moreover, the feasibility of early systematic surveillance in all aspects of development must be demonstrated as important. In addition, pediatric practitioners need a resource that they can be easily used as an early screen for ASD.

Ongoing Research Study

A training proposal entitled Early Developmental Screening is currently being implemented by the author 1) to educate pediatric practitioners about the importance of early detection and screening for autism and 2) to train how to recognize the early indicators of autism.

How and where is autism currently detected?

Parental Detection

Autism spectrum disorders are often detected by parents. The diagnosis is usually acknowledged or confirmed by an expert clinician or developmental pediatrician (not a family practitioner or normal pediatrician). The diagnosis usually requires a specialized medical visit which may or may not be covered by insurance. Experts usually use several assessments to determine whether or not there is a diagnosis ASD – Autism Diagnostic Interview, Autism Diagnostic Observation Schedule, and the Mullen. These tests can take 2 days to complete.

Detection at Well-Child Visits

The well-child visit is the optimal opportunity to detect or screen for ASD. Often, the pediatrician has the chance to obtain a developmental picture of an infant or a toddler. A 10–20 minute period of screening for ASD can be conducted if practitioners know 1) how to use and screen, and 2) know what signs to look for. It has been noted that "well-child care is a core service of pediatrics, but it receives little emphasis in pediatric training, reluctant consideration by insurers and rare attention by researchers" (Schor, E.L. 2004).

Pediatricians conduct surveillance in their practice to glean a developmental picture. This picture needs to embrace the possibility of ASD. Many practitioners can be trained to use an autism screening tool including, pediatricians, family practitioners, physician assistants, pediatric nurse practitioners, public health clinics, and parents. Other essential and often overlooked professionals that can learn how to screen are early interventions, day-care providers, and psychologists.

Autism Screening

There are certain signs to look for when conducting a screen for spectrum disorders. Based on the DSM IV TR and expert research the indicators of autism include impaired communication, impaired social interaction, and restricted repetitive and stereotyped patterns of behavior. These global concepts can be separated into specific signs of ASD in infants and toddlers:

Lack of Typical Behaviors

- Showing
- Appropriate gaze
- Warm, joyful expression
- Sharing interest / enjoyment
- Response to name
- Coordination of nonverbal communication
- Exhibition of Atypical Behaviors
- Repetitive movements with objects
- Repetitive movements or posturing of body

(Wetherby, Woods, Allen, Cleary, Dickinson, & Lord, 2004)

Clues: Early Identification of ASD

- Limited gaze shifts
- Lack of shared affect
- Lack of conventional and symbolic gestures
- Limited use of speech
- Lack of pretend play and limited conventional use of objects
- Unconventional means of communication (using a person's hand as a tool; SIB; echolalia)

(Stone, Ousley, Yoder, Hogan, & Hepburn, 1997; Wetherby, Prizant, & Hutchinson, 1998)

Absolute Indicators of Referral

- No babbling by 12 months;
- No gesturing by 12 months;
- No single words by 16 months;
- No 2 spontaneous word phrases by 24 months;
- ANY loss of ANY language or social skills at ANY age.

(American Academy of Neurology)

<http://www.neurology.org/cgi/reprint/55/4/468.pdf>

Autism Screening Clinical Guidelines

Level 1
- General Surveillance in relation to the above diagnostic criteria and / or early indicators.

Level 2
- Assessment and Diagnosis of Autism

Referral

Once children are identified as being at risk for ASD or any developmental disability, the child should be referred to the local Infants and Toddlers Program. The local Infants and Toddlers program is legally required to provide intervention services to children and their families. The main purpose of early identification of ASD is to increase the chance of the best prognosis and to enable better access to services, treatment, and intervention.

Future Consideration to Enhance Early Identification

- Continue to educate professionals and the general public about the importance of early identification.
- Encourage all pediatric practitioners to continue with general surveillance with the addition of an autism screen.
- Target all professionals who interact with infants and toddlers, including nurse practitioners, early intervention workers, and psychologists.
- Provide free training sessions that are comprehensive yet brief.
- Include "support staff" in planning.
- Provide incentives for professionals to participate in training sessions such as reimbursement for time or credit towards their continuing medical education.
- Advocate for reimbursement by insurance providers for conducting autism screening in medical practice.
- Advocate collaboration between experts in the field of early detection and professionals that work with infants and toddlers.

<http://www.neurology.org/cgi/reprint/55/4/468.pdf>*(page 3)*

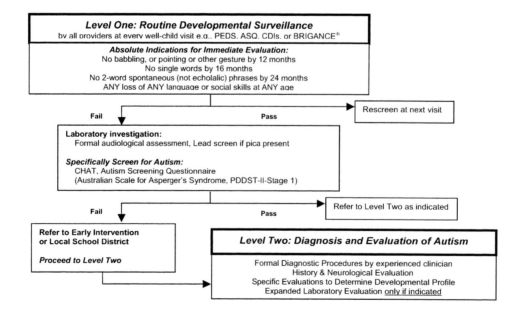

Medical testing for autism, Asperger's Syndrome and PDD

(This article is reprinted with permission from the July–August 2004 issue of the Autism Asperger's Digest, a 52-page bimonthly magazine on autism spectrum disorders. For more information, write <www.autismdigest.com> or call 1-800-489-0727. The publisher, Future Horizons Inc., is a world leader in autism/Asperger's/PDD publications.)

Contributing Author William Shaw, Ph.D., Biochemistry, Genetics and Human Physiology, Medical University of South Carolina—Dr. Shaw is the Director of The Great Plains Laboratory, Inc., which specializes in metabolic and nutritional testing, especially in autism. He is board certified in the fields of Clinical Chemistry and Toxicology by the American Board of Clinical Chemistry. He has supervised large endocrinology, nutritional biochemistry, toxicology and immunology departments in positions at the Center for Disease Control and Smith Kline Clinical Laboratories in Atlanta, Georgia. He was Director of Clinical Chemistry, Endocrinology and Toxicology at Children's Mercy Hospital, the teaching hospital of the University of Missouri at the Kansas City School of Medicine.

Resources and links— William Shaw, Ph.D. suggests visiting his Autism Today website to learn about his other products and services: Visit: http://shaw.autismtoday.com today! (*Please note, don't put in the www) For more information, contact Dr. Shaw by calling (913) 341-8949, writing to him at <GPL4U@aol.com> or visiting <www.greatplainslaboratory.com>.

It is generally accepted within the autism community by parents and professionals alike that autism is a behaviorally-based disorder. That is, diagnosis is based on observation of behavior and treatment focuses on alleviating challenging behaviors. However, a growing number of individuals within this expanding community also acknowledge that there exists an equally relevant biomedical component to the disorder that should not be overlooked in planning treatment programs for individuals with autism spectrum disorders. While recognizing the need for biomedical testing, both parents and medical professionals can be at a loss in understanding the array of tests available and how to determine which test(s) are most appropriate for a child or adult with an ASD.

The recommendations for testing that follow are based on my 10 years experience as a Laboratory Director of The Great Plains Laboratory, a medical laboratory that has performed more testing for people on the autism spectrum than any other place in the world. My recommendations are now also based on experience with my own 14-year-old stepdaughter, Paulina, who has severe autism.

Food allergy testing

The single most useful test for people on the autism spectrum is the comprehensive IgG food allergy test. The most common foods prompting an abnormal reaction in children and adults on the spectrum are cow's milk, cheese, yogurt, wheat, barley, rye, spelt and soy. We have documented these allergies at The Great Plains Laboratory by testing thousands of blood samples from people on the spectrum throughout the world. Multiple articles in the medical journals report similar abnormalities.

The incidence of high IgG antibodies to wheat and milk is approximately 90% in people on the autistic spectrum. Most individuals with IgG allergy or sensitivity to cow's milk are also allergic to goat's milk. Other common allergies include peanuts, eggs, citrus fruit, corn, sugar and baking yeast. There are various allergy tests available. So it is very important to check which type of allergy test is being offered. Although helpful in some cases, I have not seen IgE food allergy testing to be as valuable for individuals with ASD. Unfortunately, this is the only kind of food allergy test that most laboratories offer.

Determining whether or not IgG food allergies are present is important. These allergies or sensitivities are associated with the reaction of foods with certain white blood cells that release powerful cytokines, protein substances like gamma-interferon that can cause profound behavioral changes and even psychosis. IgG allergies are found in children and adults on the entire autistic spectrum, including autism, PDD and Asperger's Syndrome. These abnormalities are also very common in attention deficit disorder.

Wheat and milk restriction has been one of the most successful treatments for individuals on the spectrum. Prior to initiation of the gluten and casein free diet, Paulina spent most of the day screaming, crying, throwing tantrums and pulling things off the shelves. She could not go to dinner at a restaurant because she was so hyperactive that she would squirm out of her seat and wander around the restaurant. All of these difficult behaviors ceased after implementation of the gluten free and casein free diet (as well as an antifungal treatment).

Testing for Celiac disease

Celiac disease is another common disorder of wheat intolerance with an incidence of about 1:150 among people of European descent. The incidence of this disorder does not appear to be higher in those on the autism spectrum than in the general population, although people on the spectrum occasionally have celiac disease also. Celiac disease can be confirmed by the presence of antibodies to the intestinal enzyme transglutaminase, which is involved in the biochemical processing of gluten.

Inhalant allergy testing

Allergies to things in the air are termed inhalant allergies. In contrast to food allergies, these allergies do need to be tested with IgE tests. Some of the most common allergies are mold, mildew, pollen, cats, dogs, birds and dust. One child with autism had a severe behavioral reaction whenever a certain special teacher entered the classroom. After testing for inhalant allergies, we found that the child had severe cat allergies. The teacher was a cat lover and had several at home. The cat hair would get on the teacher's clothes and trigger allergic reactions in the child. The child was transferred to another teacher and the severe behavioral reactions ceased.

Testing for yeast

Another very common abnormality in autism is a gastrointestinal overgrowth of Candida. Candida is a member of the yeast family—a type of fungus. Drugs that kill yeast or fungus are called antifungal drugs. The greatest bulk of Candida is present in the intestinal tract, although it may occasionally enter the bloodstream and has been detected in the blood of children with autism by a highly sensitive test called PCR that measures the Candida DNA. There are about a dozen species of Candida but three of the most common are Candida albicans, Candida parapsilosis and Candida krusei.

There are many reasons for controlling Candida overgrowth. Excessive Candida can inhibit normal digestion and absorption of nutrients into the bloodstream, as well as prevent the production of important vitamins needed for optimal health. Candida produces many toxic by-products, including gliotoxins, which can impair the immune system. In addition, large portions of a Candida cell wall protein (HWP1) have a structure that is virtually identical to the wheat protein gluten. Because of this similarity, Candida binds to the enzyme transglutaminase, which is present in the intestinal lining. This binding to transglutaminase anchors long strands of the yeast cells to the intestine like ivy vines climbing a brick wall. This anchoring inhibits the yeast from being mechanically dislodged as digested food passes by. The binding of Candida to transglutaminase also interferes with the normal function of this enzyme in the digestion of gluten. If pieces of the Candida cell wall protein (which is similar to gluten) enter the bloodstream, they may react with one of the blood clotting factors that also has transglutaminase activity, leading to interference in the blood clotting mechanism. These modified proteins may not be recognized by the immune system, which can lead to autoimmune diseases. Lastly, the Candida cells can also produce digestive enzymes like proteases and phospholipase that actually eat away the intestinal lining, allowing undigested food molecules to pass through into the bloodstream, and as a result, cause more food allergies.

Candida can be detected by culturing the stool on Petri dishes or by measuring the amount of chemicals produced in the intestinal tract. These by-products can be measured in the urine organic acid test (OAT), which also checks for inborn errors of metabolism, nutritional deficiencies and other factors. These chemicals or fermentation products are absorbed from the intestinal tract by the blood vessels that are called the portal veins. These blood vessels carry these fermentation products to the liver where they are distributed throughout the bloodstream. The blood containing these fermentation products is filtered through the kidney, and they are excreted in the urine.

It is important to know that stool testing can frequently miss the presence of Candida when there are high amounts of antibodies called IgA in the intestine. These IgA antibodies may coat the yeast cells and inhibit their growth enough to prevent them from growing in the Petri dish even though they may still be able to grow enough in the intestine to cause problems. Such a situation can lead to a false negative result.

By testing the yeast fermentation products in urine, this problem can usually be overcome. However, about 10% of yeast do not produce the common fermentation products. We have resolved this problem by offering a COMBO test for both the yeast fermentation products—the urine organic acid test (OAT)—as well as the yeast culture from stool. If the yeast can be cultured, there is the added advantage that the sensitivity of the yeast to various drugs or natural agents can be determined. Many yeasts have developed resistance to various antifungal drugs because of the widespread use of these drugs in people with human immunodeficiency virus (HIV) infection. Like people with HIV, many people on the autism spectrum have a serious lack of immunity to Candida. One possible reason that people with autism have this problem is that the measles vaccine virus can severely impair the ability of the cellular immune system (Vaccine Jan 8, 2001) to control Candida. We have found this same lack of cellular immunity in people with autism. The Great Plains Laboratory

expects to have a test for this defect available shortly and a possible treatment as well.

Alongside the GF/CF diet, reducing or eliminating yeast overgrowth has been one of the more effective methods of reducing autistic symptoms. Paulina had been on antifungal treatment (Nystatin) for several years, but her behavior began to deteriorate markedly. Testing showed that her yeast had developed resistance to Nystatin. With this change, she had become extremely hyperactive and unco-operative. She spent much of the time crying and whining, had difficulty sleeping and pulled things off the table. Within six hours of starting the antifungal drug Diflucan, her normal smiling behavior returned. Unfortunately, with prolonged use, Diflucan can sometimes cause liver damage. So we implemented a limited carbohydrate diet to help control the yeast after we discontinued the Diflucan. With successful antifungal treatment, parents have reported reduced aggressive and self-hurtful behaviors, improved learning at school, improved focus and concentration, better sleep and reduced hyperactivity. Many parents don't realize that antifungal treatment is a long-term issue in autism; others treat it with antifungal drugs that are ineffective. It's important that antifungal treatment be done under the supervision of a qualified medical professional. A less expensive microbial organic acid test can be done regularly to make sure that the yeast or harmful bacteria have not returned.

Testing for Clostridia

Several years ago, I began a collaborative study with Dr. Walter Gattaz, a Research Psychiatrist at the Central Mental Health Institute of Germany, in Mannheim, to evaluate urine samples of patients with schizophrenia. These samples were very valuable since they were obtained from patients who were drug-free. Thus, any biochemical abnormalities would be due to their disease and not a drug effect. Five of the 12 samples contained a very high concentration of a compound identified as a derivative of the amino acid tyrosine, which is very similar, but not identical, to 3,4-dihydroxyphenylpropionic acid. I have since identified this compound as 3-(3-hydroxyphenyl)-3-hydroxypropionic acid or HPHPA. This particular

39

compound has been linked to colonization of the intestinal tract with Clostridia bacteria.

How is this important to autism? HPHPA is found to be much higher in the urine of autistic children than in normal children. People with autism who have high values of this compound may have extremely abnormal or even psychotic behavior. One child with high amounts of HPHPA in urine kicked out the windows of the family car while being transported to school. Clostridia can be treated with the antibiotics Vancomycin or Flagyl. The first patient in a medical study improved after Flagyl treatment but then regressed when the drug was discontinued. The same child was retreated with a six-week course of Vancomycin. A developmental specialist estimated that the child had gained six months of development after the six weeks of therapy. Again, the child regressed after discontinuation of therapy. The use of beneficial bacteria, Lactobacillus acidophilus GG, whose brand name is Culturelle, is very useful in controlling Clostridia species in most cases and can be safely used for years if necessary. This product has about a millionth of a gram of the milk protein casein in each capsule but such a small amount is unlikely to have a significant effect in most milk-sensitive people.

Testing for HPHPA is also included on the full organic acid test or microbial organic acid test of the Great Plains Laboratory. It is important to be aware that some laboratories incorrectly measure DHPPA as a marker for Clostridia. DHPPA is a byproduct of chlorogenic acid, a common substance found in beverages and in fruits and vegetables such as apples, pears, tea, coffee, sunflower seeds, carrots, blueberries, cherries, potatoes, tomatoes, eggplant, sweet potatoes and peaches. In addition, it is a chemical by-product of the good bacteria E-coli and Lactobacillus.

The toxicity of mercury

Mercury is a naturally occurring metal found throughout the environment. Mercury can enter the environment from deposits of ore containing mercury due to wind or rain or from the actions of humans. In addition to mercury from the vaccine preservative Thimerisol, major sources of mercury that contaminate humans include dental fillings, which are about 50% mercury, and large fish such as tuna and swordfish.

Mercury exists in two major forms, inorganic and organic. Inorganic mercury consists of metallic mercury and inorganic mercury compounds called salts. Metallic mercury is a liquid at room temperature. It is the shiny silver material in thermometers and is commonly combined with silver as an alloy for dental fillings. Liquid mercury from thermometers can give off vapor if a thermometer breaks, which could then be absorbed through the lungs. Mercury is also used in alkaline batteries. Organic mercury compounds include methylmercury, ethylmercury and phenylmercury. Methylmercury is produced from inorganic mercury by microorganisms in the environment and perhaps by the microorganisms in the intestinal tract. Methylmercury is extremely toxic. Exposure to three drops of methylmercury to the gloved hands of a researcher was fatal. Mercury exposure should be avoided at all costs.

It is important to note that the symptoms of mercury toxicity closely mirror the clinical symptoms of autism. Parents of a child who had developmental delays and a muscle disorder contacted me because the child's tests had revealed high levels of mercury in the hair and blood. They reported that their child ate salmon or tuna five or six times a week. Although fish are an excellent source of essential fatty acids, most large fish have significant amounts of methylmercury. The FDA has recommended that pregnant women abstain from certain fish high in mercury. Since methylmercury is fat soluble, it might also contaminate supplements derived from fish oils. In addition, mercury was used as an antifungal agent in paint prior to 1992. Therefore, anyone in an older house needs to be aware that peeling paint or sanding off existing paint could lead to mercury exposure. Mercury in the fillings of pregnant women may be a significant source of exposure to developing infants in utero. Ethyl mercury, the most common preservative found in vaccines, has been present as a preservative in other products as well: contact lens solutions, nasal sprays, and in ear and eye drops.

Testing for heavy metals

Heavy metals may often have combined effects, so that exposure to multiple heavy metals at low levels might be just as toxic as exposure to one metal at a high level. Heavy metals found to be elevated in children and adults with autism and PDD include uranium, mercury, cadmium, arsenic, lead, aluminum and antimony. Hair is the easiest sample to collect in most cases and is generally considered one of the best samples for screening for heavy metals since a heavy metal like mercury may be present in the hair at a level 250 times higher than in the blood. However, the use of hair metal testing is controversial. The State of New York bans hair testing for heavy metals, while the Environmental Protection Agency (EPA) of the U.S. Government promotes hair screening for mercury as a very useful method. In New York State tests for heavy metals in blood or urine may have to be used instead of hair. Chelation treatment with the chelating agent DMSA is probably the most effective treatment at this time for those people with abnormal values.

Multiple tests can be very useful to pinpoint the most significant biochemical abnormalities and to focus treatment on the most important issues. Although each autistic child will experience varying levels of success with biomedical testing and treatments, I would like to share one success story that outlines what can happen in some cases. Three years ago, a family came to visit from Turkey with their four-year-old son with severe autism. They insisted that they wanted every single test offered by the laboratory. I tried to convince them to reduce the financial burden by suggesting which tests might be delayed to a later time. They would not listen and insisted firmly that they get every test available. Two years later I received a letter from the parents who had implemented all the therapies indicated by the testing. Their son had completely recovered and was successfully attending a regular school classroom without an aide.

The tests emphasized in this article have been useful to people with autism of every degree of severity. Parents and treating professionals who want to embark on biomedical testing should first start with this group. Many other tests may be useful to people with autism of every age. Most tests are covered by insurance, but HMOs generally do not pay unless the physician gets advance approval from a review committee.

As concerned parents and professionals, it is vitally important that we be holistic in our approach to treatment and investigate whether or not biomedical/biochemical agents are contributing to autistic symptoms. Only then will we be best able to successfully reduce or eliminate the behavioral challenges associated with ASDs.

Study: Pediatricians do not always recognize ASD symptoms in infants

Contributing Author Lawrence P. Kaplan, Ph.D., Health Administration and Research with an emphasis in autism spectrum disorders, Kennedy-Western University—Dr. Kaplan is the Executive Director of US Autism and Asperger Association, Inc., a national association dedicated to enhancing the quality of life of individuals and their families/caregivers touched by autism spectrum disorders by providing educational and family support through conferences/seminars and published and electronic mediums. Dr. Kaplan is the author of *Diagnosis Autism: Now What? 10 Steps to Improve Treatment Outcomes.*

Resources and links— Lawrence P. Kaplan, Ph.D. suggests visiting his Autism Today website to learn about his other products and services: Visit <http://kaplan.autismtoday.com> today! (*Please note, don't put in the www.*) You can reach Dr. Kaplan at US Autism and Asperger Association by calling 1-888-9AUTISM or by writing <drlkaplan@usautism.org>.

According to a new study by Special Abilities, Inc., pediatricians do not always recognize the symptoms of ASD in infants, potentially delaying the benefits of intervention and therapy.

Autism is a complex neurological disorder that may be characterized by profound delays in communication and social interaction and that affects over 1.7 million individuals in the United States.

"This is an important issue," says Lawrence P. Kaplan, Ph.D., chief investigator for the study on early diagnosis of ASD. "This research shows that although pediatricians are given sufficient clinical diagnostic protocols to identify developmental delays in infants, there (can be) a significant delay of the early diagnosis of ASD."

In a response from over 500 parents whose children were diagnosed with ASD, only 2.7% of pediatricians diagnosed any degree of autism. The diagnosis was made by developmental pediatricians in 20.4% of cases, psychiatrists in 35.4% of cases, neurologists in 20.4% of cases and others, including psychologists and neuropsychologists in 36% of cases.

Nearly 50% of the children were diagnosed after the age of three. About 10% of the children were diagnosed with autism during the 12–24 month age period, while none were diagnosed before age one. Half of the children were diagnosed after age three. Some 58% of pediatricians did not notice any developmental delay in children who were eventually diagnosed with ASD.

There is compelling evidence in medical literature that intensive behavioral therapy, beginning before age three and targeted toward speech and language development is successful both in improving language capacity and later social functioning.

"It is imperative to recognize the symptoms of ASD in a timely manner, preferably in the first two years of a child's life," says Dr. Kaplan. "Providing an appropriate early diagnosis, whether it be of autism or even developmental delay, means that an early treatment program can be started for the child."

As a parent of a child with ASD, and the author of *Diagnosis Autism: Now What? 10 Steps to Improve Treatment Outcomes,* Dr. Kaplan says that intervention before age two is extremely effective. "It's just trying to get the pediatrician to identify some type of developmental delay as soon as possible," says Dr. Kaplan.

Dr. Kaplan says that his goal is to get more pediatricians to reach the diagnosis of autism earlier. This may help thousands of children take advantage of the earlier intervention treatment programs that have proven successful for other children with ASD.

The research was funded by Special Abilities, Inc., a 501(c)(3) not-for-profit organization that was founded in 1995 and is dedicated to improving outcomes for children with autism spectrum disorders by promoting public awareness, and providing educational programs for parents and assistance to special education schools.

Historical perspectives on autism

CHAPTER 3

How autism has been understood

Contributing Author Lawrence P. Kaplan, Ph.D., Health Administration and Research with an emphasis in autism spectrum disorders, Kennedy-Western University—Dr. Kaplan is the Executive Director of US Autism and Asperger Association, Inc., a national association dedicated to enhancing the quality of life of individuals and their families/caregivers touched by autism spectrum disorders by providing educational and family support through conferences/seminars and published and electronic mediums. Dr. Kaplan is the author of *Diagnosis Autism: Now What? 10 Steps to Improve Treatment Outcomes.*

Resources and links— Lawrence P. Kaplan, Ph.D. suggests visiting his Autism Today website to learn about his other products and services: Visit <http://kaplan.autismtoday.com> today! (*Please note, don't put in the www.*) You can reach Dr. Kaplan at US Autism and Asperger Association by calling 1-888-9AUTISM or by writing <drlkaplan@usautism.org>.

Introduction

It would be an understatement to say that a wide range of hypotheses are used to account for autism-related disorders. Historically, the disorders have been understood mainly through psychoanalytical, neurobiological, genetic and executive function approaches. There have, however, also been combinations of unrelated approaches.

Historical definition of autism

Bleuler defined the concept of autism in 1911, believing it was not a separate condition but one of the secondary effects of schizophrenia.

Thirty-two years later, in 1943, Leo Kanner described autism as a rare psychiatric disorder with onset before age two-and-a-half years of age. Kanner's definition and his subsequent description of its main distinguishing characteristics made autism a medical entity (Kozloff, 1998). As a new psychiatric medical entity, the practitioners of the day offered as treatment psychoanalytic forms of therapy.

By the late 1950s, current thinking about autism was changing. In 1959, for example, Bender characterized autism not as an inborn impairment of the central nervous system, but as a defensive reaction to one—a disorder whose basis is an inability to shield self from unbearable anxiety. A year later, C.E. Benda wrote that the autistic child is "not mentally retarded in the ordinary sense of the word, but rather is a child with an inadequate form of mentation which manifests itself in the inability to handle symbolic forms and assume an abstract attitude."

During the mid-1960s, understanding of autism continued to shift. In 1964 Bernard Rimland published a biogenic theory of autism: "The basis of the autism syndrome is the child's impaired ability to relate new stimuli to remembered experience. Hence, the child does not use speech to communicate because he cannot symbolize or abstract from concrete particulars. And he is unresponsive to his parents because he does not associate them with previous pleasurable experiences." Rimland thought that the underlying cause of autism was an impairment in the brain's reticular formation—the part of the brain felt by many to link sensory input and prior content.

During the 1960s and into the 1970s researchers offered biogenic explanations of autism—theories focusing on biochemical and metabolic anomalies in people with autism, or on the role in the development of autism of various problems of the central nervous system. Autism was beginning to be viewed as a neurological disorder.

This viewpoint is still very much with us. Speaking at the 1999 National Conference of Autism, James Ball referred to autism as a complex developmental disability resulting from a neurological disorder that affects the functioning of the brain.

That year, clinical practice guidelines on autism published by New York State referred to it as a part of a clinical spectrum of pervasive developmental disorders. "Autism is a neurobehavioral syndrome caused by dysfunction in the central nervous system, which leads to disordered development."

Beginning in the mid-1960s and carrying forward through the 1980s to 2000, researchers have turned to genetics, searching for the genetic error, perhaps inherited, underlying the development of autism. The roles of several candidate genes are being studied.

In the 1990s, other approaches to autism were described, including the executive functions approach, the hypothesis that autism results from early life brain damage, the theory that autism is the result of neuro-immune dysfunction, and that it is the result of autistic enterocolotitis, which may be linked with the measles, mumps and rubella vaccination.

Dealing with autism

CHAPTER 4

Addressing behavioral challenges for individuals with ASD

Contributing Author Lori Ernsperger, Ph.D., Special Education, Indiana University—An expert in the field of autism and behavioral disorders, Dr. Ernsperger has over 21 years of experience working in the public schools as a classroom teacher, administrator, and behavioral consultant. She owns and operates Autism and Behavioral Consulting an agency that works with school district personnel and families to provide effective educational programs and best practice strategies for students with autism and behavioral disorders. Dr. Ernsperger has authored two books, *Keys to Success for Teaching Students with Autism* and *Just Take a Bite: Easy Effective Answers to Food Aversions and Eating Challenges* published by Future Horizons.

Resources and links— Lori Ernsperger, Ph.D. suggests visiting her Autism Today website to learn about her other products and services: Visit <http://ernsperger.autismtoday.com> today! (*Please note, don't put in the www.*) You can contact Dr. Ernsperger by writing <drlori@cox.net>.

Introduction

Effective teaching strategies for students with autism require development of a systematic program for addressing problem behaviors. Students with autism often exhibit a wide variety of challenging behaviors, including physical aggression, self-injury, tantrums and non-compliance. These behaviors are disconcerting to staff and parents, and should be resolved. Developing effective behavior intervention programs is often the most important step for the classroom or home. The following are important elements of an effective program:

- Reviewing the elements of a functional assessment
- Developing and writing a behavior intervention plan
- Identifying the principles of active programming
- Teaching replacement skills
- Reviewing environmental controls
- Implementing compliance training
- Planning reactive programming
- Developing a crisis management plan

An effective program for managing problem behaviors focuses on two main strategies: proactive programming and reactive programming.

Principles of proactive programming

Highly effective programs for students with autism emphasize proactive strategies for reducing problem behaviors and teaching replacement skills. Proactive programs:

- Assume the problem behavior serves a purpose for the student and attempts to teach alternative and replacement skills that serve the same function
- Modify the antecedents and environmental controls
- Begin by determining the function of the maladaptive behavior for the student
- Seek replacement behaviors for the maladaptive behavior

Principles of reactive programs

Systematic reactive programs can effectively decrease the frequency and duration of problem behaviors. Unfortunately, most classrooms for students with autism focus entirely on reactive programming. Reactive programs:

- Wait for the maladaptive behavior to occur and then respond with a punishment
- Focus on the consequences of the behavior
- May ultimately reinforce the maladaptive behavior

- Do not significantly or permanently change maladaptive behaviors

Functional assessment

A comprehensive intervention program for students with autism will provide a careful balance between both a proactive and reactive program. This involves conducting a thorough functional assessment and developing an appropriate behavior intervention plan.

A thorough functional assessment is the first step in a proactive program. It begins the process of understanding the purpose of the student's behavior and what the student is trying to communicate. The goal of a functional assessment is to identify the purpose and effect of a target behavior by examining its function for the student.

An effective functional assessment is built on several assumptions:

- That the problem behavior serves a function for the student. A student exhibiting problem behaviors is using a functional approach to communication to achieve a specific outcome. Therefore, school personnel must conduct a functional assessment to thoroughly understand function of the behavior for the student.
- That if a student is repeating a problem behavior, then the consequence of the behavior has been reinforced for that student in the past. Each of us tends to repeat behaviors that are positively reinforced.
- That a student exhibiting problem behaviors often does not know the correct adaptive skills or has not been reinforced effectively for displaying appropriate adaptive behaviors.

Functional assessment made easy

Whether mandated through an IEP team or conducted as an informal assessment by the classroom staff, a functional assessment can be conducted efficiently and easily with the right tools.

Step 1: Define target behavior

First, define an observable and measurable target behavior. The problem behavior targeted for a functional assessment will vary with the student. The team may choose to target a behavior which can be easily corrected before moving to more challenging behaviors. Targeting lesser behaviors may build success for the student and staff and make changing more challenging behaviors easier.

If, however, behaviors are harmful to the student or others, the team may choose to work on several behaviors at once. All identified target behaviors must be clearly defined and measurable to ensure consistency across settings.

Step 2: Information gathering

Collect information from a variety of sources. The team may interview teachers, parents and related service personnel who work with the student. Interview data focuses on the antecedents and consequences of the behavior. Interview adults who have a significant relationship with the student and who can contribute to defining the target behavior and function.

Information may also be collected through direct observation. Observations focus on the frequency, duration and intensity of the target behavior. Observations should occur in the natural settings where the target behavior is exhibited. Direct observations also include an analysis of environmental factors that may contribute to the maladaptive behavior.

Physiological factors are the last area of data collection which may influence problem behaviors. Students with autism often have potential medical issues that are causing an increase in maladaptive behaviors. Physiological areas to be considered in a functional assessment include:

- Diet and nutrition
- Sleep patterns and fatigue
- Medication side effects
- Sickness
- Stress outside the classroom

It is important to carefully consider how these variables influence problem behaviors. If the student is hungry or thirsty and has no functional communication system, the outcome will be irritability and an increase in problem behaviors. The classroom team can effectively address these issues and reduce further problem behaviors.

Step 3: Developing a hypothesis

In this step, review the data and identify the function of the problem behavior. The function of problem behaviors varies with each student. The following are a few common functions and applicable questions to be addressed by the team:

(a) Escape/Avoidance
- Is the task too difficult?
- Is the student bored?
- Does the behavior start when a request or demand is made?
- Does the activity take too long?
- Is the classroom too noisy?
- Does the behavior stop when the student is removed from the activity?

(b) Attention
- Is the student receiving adequate attention for NOT displaying the problem behavior?
- Are other students receiving more attention?
- Is the student alone for long periods?
- Does the student exhibit the behavior when they are alone?
- Does the behavior occur to get a reaction?

(c) Power/Control
- Is the student given choices in the classroom?
- Are there opportunities for the student to take a break?
- Does the behavior stop after the student receives a desired object?

(d) Communication
- Does the student have a functional and reliable communication system?
- Is the student provided with the necessary equipment to communicate wants and needs?
- Does the behavior seem to be a way for the student to ask for help?

(e) Stress/Frustration
- Is the student stressed?
- Does the student have adequate skills to release stress in an appropriate manner?
- Is the classroom environment chaotic?
- Does the student seem calm or relaxed after the problem behavior has stopped?

(f) Self-stimulation or sensory stimulation
- Is the behavior part of the stereotypical pattern of behaviors?
- Is the environment producing adequate stimulation?
- Does the student have frequent opportunities for sensory integration?
- Does the student repeat the behavior when alone?
- Does the student appear unaware of his surroundings?

The multidisciplinary team examines the information collected and develops a written statement regarding the function of the behavior. A clear hypothesis statement is written in a positive manner, based on facts from information gathering. The following are examples of hypothesis statements:

- Morning circle is too long for Jonathan, and he bites other students to escape the task.
- Samantha refuses to complete her morning math work because she requires additional adult assistance. When the teacher is helping other students, Samantha attempts to run out of the room to get immediate attention from the teacher.
- When Stephen goes to the cafeteria with the fifth grade class, he pushes other students and runs down the hallway to be first in line and to avoid waiting with the other students.

Each hypothesis statement identifies the target behavior and provides an "informed guess" as to the function of the behavior for the student.

Key concept: functional communication—Students with ASDs often have severe deficits in expressive language and communication skills. Therefore, there is a strong need for alternative communication systems. Augmentative and alternative communication devices allow the student to communicate and respond to the environment. Problem behaviors will only persist or increase if the student is unable to communicate basic needs.

Step 4: Developing a behavior intervention plan

The behavioral intervention plan is a written document that includes:

- An operational definition of the target behavior.
- Summary of the relevant data.
- Written hypothesis statement stating the function of the behavior.
- List of modifications to the environment.
- Teaching replacement or alternative behaviors.
- Criteria or outcome evaluation.
- Consequence strategies: crisis intervention plan and reactive programming.

Most school districts have developed appropriate forms to be used for a written behavior intervention plan. If no form is readily available, the teacher can easily create an individualized plan for use in the classroom.

The behavior intervention plan requires two main components: teaching replacement skills and modifying the environment. Teaching replacement skills or alternative behaviors assumes that the student's problem behavior is meeting a need for the student and that the student may not have the skills required for more adaptive behaviors. The replacement behavior, therefore, must be as effective and powerful as the maladaptive behavior.

For example, if Zachary receives immediate and intense attention from the teacher for biting another student, the new replacement behavior must also give Zachary the same immediate and intense attention from the teacher. Teaching Zachary to raise his hand and wait several moments for the teacher's attention will not be an effective alternative skill.

Key concept: teaching replacement skills—Teaching the desired replacement skill should result in:

- Meeting the same function or purpose for the student
- Teaching a skill that can be implemented across settings
- An efficient and effective alternative for the student

Teaching replacement behaviors to students with autism uses a variety of instructional techniques. While discrete trial instruction and incidental teaching are highly effective strategies in teaching replacement behaviors, the classroom staff can also implement other techniques including shaping, differential reinforcement and token economies.

Reinforcement strategies

Since all people are motivated by positive reinforcement, using reinforcement strategies is a key element for teaching students with autism. Most typically developing students are reinforced through task completion and teacher praise, but students with autism are not typically reinforced through these internal methods. They require external motivation to maximize their learning and increase adaptive behaviors. Therefore school personnel must identify appropriate reinforcers and use them effectively throughout the school day. Types of reinforcers include edibles (but use these seldom and only while other reinforcers are being developed), tangibles, social praise and activities.

Guidelines for selecting reinforcers

Selecting reinforcers for students with autism is a continuous process which changes throughout the school year. Not all students are motivated by the same items. Selecting appropriate high-quality reinforcement involves:

- Observing the student in the classroom;
- Completing a reinforcement survey; and/or
- Interviewing the student or other adults.

The reinforcement interests of some students may be readily apparent, while reinforcing other students requires investigation. Some students may have little experience playing with certain toys and games and therefore must be taught to enjoy specific items or activities.

Avoid bribery

Reinforcement depends on the student's completion of a task or of his exhibiting a desired behavior. Therefore reinforcement is NEVER to be used as bribery. For example, reinforcement would not be provided to a student in the middle of a tantrum. Nor would a student receive a high-quality reinforcer to entice him into working. Bribery teaches the student that he does not have to comply in order to achieve the desired outcome.

Reinforcement schedules

Reinforcement is provided to the student after the student has met the predetermined criteria for a task or has exhibited a desirable behavior. The rate of reinforcement will be based on the task and the individual skills of the student. A reinforcement schedule will assist the staff in determining the appropriate timing for reinforcement.

When first teaching a new skill or desired behavior, reinforcement will be immediate and continuous. This immediate and continuous reinforcement will insure repetition of the desired behavior. As the student progresses with a newly acquired skill or behavior, the reinforcement schedule will be thinned and become more intermittent. An intermittent schedule is like a slot machine: the student receives the payoff at varying intervals and will not know in advance when a payoff will occur.

Delayed reinforcement is used in a token economy system where the tokens are earned and can be exchanged for the reinforcement at a later time. Delayed reinforcement should be systematically scheduled to increase the desired behavior. Inconsistencies with delayed reinforcement increase student frustration and trigger problem behaviors. Again, the goal of reinforcement is to help the student become naturally self-motivating.

Environment and curriculum modifications

Although teaching replacement skills to the student is a daily activity and an integral part of the behavior intervention plan, the classroom staff must also address environmental modifications. After completing a classroom inventory, the teacher must review the needs of each student. Although the overall classroom may be arranged appropriately, some students will have specific needs that must be addressed. Additional modifications, tailored where possible to the specific needs of each student, will help ensure on-task behavior and increased independence.

Specific modifications may include:

- Level of support: The student may need more adult assistance to learn a new skill.
- Time: The student may require more or less time to complete an assigned task.Some students may need more breaks in their schedule.
- Level of difficulty: Be sure to create a curriculum that is neither too easy nor too difficult. Unchallenging repetitive tasks create boredom for the student and will likely increase maladaptive behaviors.

Reactive programming

Although the focus of teaching students with autism should be proactive programming, it is also essential to develop a reactive program. In a reactive plan, the team determines the steps that will occur after the maladaptive or problem behavior is exhibited.

There are several strategies available to school personnel to address behaviors after they have occurred. The multidisciplinary team should consider the least intrusive methods for decreasing the likelihood of problem behaviors. Response cost, extinction and punishment are a few reactive techniques which may be used in a school setting.

Reactive programming can further decrease the frequency of problem behaviors and may help the team regain control in a crisis. In a well-designed behavior program, reactive procedures will be used minimally and then only with respect for the student.

Response cost

A response cost technique reduces undesirable behavior by removing a reinforcer. A response cost program is designed to remove a reinforcer when the problem behavior occurs.

For example, the student may be highly reinforced by working on the computer. Therefore, the teacher has laminated the eight letters of the word COMPUTER and placed each individual letter on the student's desk. Each time the student exhibits the problem behavior, one letter is removed from the word COMPUTER. For every letter that remains at the end of the day, the student receives five minutes of computer time.

Other response cost programs may include point systems or marbles in a jar. Response cost systems do not teach replacement skills and they focus only on the consequence of the problem behavior.

Extinction

Another reactive technique for problem behaviors is extinction. Extinction is the gradual decrease of the problem behavior as reinforcement is discontinued. Extinction attempts to reduce the problem behavior by eliminating the reinforcement that maintains the behavior.

Many teachers try to use "planned ignoring" in order to extinguish a problem behavior. Decreasing disruptive behaviors through planned ignoring will depend on the function of the behavior and the ability of the teacher to completely eliminate reinforcement. If the function of the behavior is attention, it is imperative to remove all attention from the student. For example, a student who screams and tantrums for attention may still have his needs met if he receives attention not only from the adults, but also from the other students. Therefore, all positive attention must be removed before ignoring will extinguish the problem behavior.

Ignoring or paying little attention to problem behaviors can be an effective procedure in a reactive program. Caution must be taken not to completely ignore self-injurious behaviors and aggression because of the likelihood the behavior will escalate. In some cases, the staff must provide some minimal attention

in order to secure the environment for the student and others. Minimal attention means:

- A calm and neutral voice
- Little or no eye contact
- Minimal physical restraint
- Reduced demands

Extinction is a planned reactive intervention and should be used only when the function of the behavior is reinforced through attention from others.

Aversions and punishment

I do not recommend using or implementing averse procedures in school settings for students with autism. Aversives can be characterized as intrusive procedures requiring corporal punishment, use of water sprays, performance of exercise or the deprivation of necessary food and water. Aversives are not effective over time and may cause the student to fear the adult applying the punishment. School personnel must report any aversive treatment to the proper authorities.

Even mild forms of punishment such as verbal reprimands and simple restitution should be used cautiously. Timeout is often referred to as an effective punishment in a reactive program. Discretion must be used when implementing time out procedures. Time out means that the student receives no reinforcement. In the case of a typically developing student, being moved from the classroom to an isolated area may be considered time out from reinforcement. Unfortunately, this is not generally the case for students with autism. A student with autism will most likely perceive the time out area as reinforcing because:

- There are no demands being placed on him
- The function of his behavior is escape and avoidance
- He can initiate self-stimulatory behaviors which are highly reinforcing
- He may require a break or quiet area time

Time out from reinforcement must be carefully planned and used with caution to avoid reinforcing and increasing the problem behavior.

Crisis management

Despite careful planning and the development of active programming, school personnel may occasionally be faced with a crisis. Phases of a crisis cycle are:

- Phase 1. Calm; optimal; comfortable level; baseline
- Phase 2. Trigger
- Phase 3. Irritable; frustrated; demanding; anxious
- Phase 4. Peak
- Phase 5. De-escalation
- Phase 6. Recovery

School personnel must be very aware of the specific triggers for each student. Once a trigger has occurred for the student, it is important that appropriate and meaningful strategies be implemented to redirect the student to a preferred task. Encourage the use of previously taught stress management techniques. Also, be sure to control your own response to the trigger. Reduce any signs that you are agitated or stressed.

Practice, practice, practice

Crisis intervention is a serious undertaking. It requires multiple opportunities to practice the correct procedures. Because students are not in crisis every day, it is important for the staff to practice their crisis intervention skills. Practice role playing different crisis scenarios. Have each staff member devise a plan and discuss the steps for intervention.

Conclusion

Again, reactive programming should occupy a small portion of the overall behavior program for students with autism. These procedures are only considered after other strategies have failed. If a crises continues to occur for a particular student, teachers should re-evaluate and reassess to determine the function of the behavior. The behavior intervention program for students with autism and Asperger's Syndrome should focus on teaching replacement skills and reinforcing appropriately displayed behaviors. Because many of these maladaptive behaviors are chronic, it may take the school team and parents many months to effectively teach a new skill. Therefore, it is important to focus on the process and celebrate the small changes.

Addressing masturbation

Contributing Author Mary Wrobel, speech-language pathologist and certified teacher—Ms. Wrobel is an autism consultant, and presents at autism workshops in the U.S. (and soon in Canada). She graduated with a Master's degree from Western Illinois University in Macomb, IL in 1980. Ms. Wrobel is the author of *Taking Care of Myself*

Resources and links—Mary Wrobel, CCC, SLP suggests visiting her Autism Today website to learn about her other products and services: Visit <http://wrobel.autismtoday.com> today! (*Please note, don't put in the www.*) You can write to her at <marywrobel@aol.com>.

Masturbation is a natural, biological behavior, which humans of all ages occasionally engage in. It can be a conscious, deliberate act or it can be a behavior performed without thinking or even understanding its implications. Masturbation is regarded as a very private, sexual behavior. It's typically inappropriate to talk about it, and it's never appropriate to perform it in public. It's also not a behavior we usually think about with regards to others.

Early on we learn the social rule that it's absolutely inappropriate to touch, rub and generally stimulate our genital area in the presence of others. It's not a rule that we necessarily need to be taught. Young children may discover the pleasurable sensations that masturbation can produce, and they may continue to engage in it because they don't understand the social rules regarding masturbation. Eventually, most children correctly identify masturbation as a private matter and learn not to discuss it or perform it in public.

Students with special needs, particularly those with autism or mental impairment, are not likely to be embarrassed by masturbation or to understand the social and moral taboos attached to it. Sometimes negative attention merely exacerbates a situation and a student will continue the inappropriate behavior. The student might enjoy the shocked reaction of others, or the negative attention when he or she masturbates in front of others. Teachers and parents often mistakenly believe that a child will eventually tire of masturbating and stop on his or her own. Sometimes that is true. But masturbation is a pleasurable behavior and it's unlikely that an individual will tire of it and give it up completely. Even when punished, or given natural consequences for masturbating, many students with special needs still continue to masturbate.

Masturbation can become especially prevalent during adolescence. According to recent statistics many teenagers masturbate. Ninety-five percent of all teenage boys occasionally masturbate.

Seventy-five percent of teenage boys admit to masturbating on a regular basis. Also, twenty-five to forty-five percent of teenage girls masturbate. Most parents of teenagers are not aware of these statistics because neuro-typical teenagers understand the social taboos of masturbation. They not only perform such behaviors in private, but keep this information to themselves and often hide the fact that they do, in fact, masturbate.

We need to realize that masturbation is a behavior which might not go away. As teachers and parents, it's important to approach masturbation with a calm, mature attitude. It will not help the situation if we get upset and angry about it. We start first by learning why a student is masturbating. Surprisingly, a child/student might not be masturbating for sexual gratification. There are other reasons for masturbation, especially with pre-adolescent children.

Dealing With Young Children Who Masturbate

Young children who masturbate often do so as a self-calming, comfort response. They are often unaware they are masturbating, or that they are doing anything wrong.

If a young child is masturbating occasionally or predictably, it/s important to first determine *why* they are masturbating. For instance, they may have discovered masturbating one time when they were upset, or in need of sensory regulation, and the act of masturbating soothed them, calmed them and even helped them to sleep. After that initial self-calming, they may have come to rely on masturbating to self-calm in a variety of situations. A child could also have discovered masturbation when he or she was bored and subsequently found something to play with when putting hands into pants. So, for example, when he's bored, a young boy may find it fun and enjoyable to play with his penis. And after playing with his genitals he finds that it feels good. So perhaps every time he's bored or seeking some enjoyment his hands go down his pants.

When you know why a child is masturbating you will be able to find appropriate replacement behaviors for the inappropriate, masturbation behavior. When a young child is masturbating, it's important to redirect him or her in a calm, matter of fact manner. Establish highly motivating replacement behaviors for the masturbating, such as a large motor activity, a squeeze toy, reading a book, hugging a stuffed animal, doing an activity that requires two hands, or sensory integration activities such as applying deep pressure.

Once they are able to choose more appropriate replacement behaviors, reward them for doing a good job keeping hands on the table or other appropriate place. Realize that pre-adolescent masturbating feels good and is comforting, but it is still more of an habitual behavior rather than one for sexual release.

Dealing With Adolescents Who Masturbate

When an adolescent is masturbating on a regular basis, it is often purposeful behavior and unlikely to stop. The adolescent is very likely getting sexual gratification from the masturbation.

Because of the sexual gratification, it is not likely you will be able to find a highly motivating replacement behavior for the masturbation. But because the student is a teenager his or her masturbation will not be tolerated by society, as a young child's might, and furthermore, the masturbation behavior may risk his or her personal safety. In other words, a student may invite molesting and sexual abuse if he or she masturbates in public. In some cases, students have been physically abused if caught masturbating by other students or even other adults.

It is absolutely important that a student understand that masturbating is a very private behavior: no one should see it, no one should hear it, and no one should know about it.

Masturbating can only occur in very specific locations and conditions: when an individual is alone in his or her bedroom or bathroom with the door closed.

Parents need to accept the fact that their adolescent child is masturbating and allow him or her to masturbate in the privacy of his or her own bedroom and bathroom. If a teenager is not allowed to masturbate in appropriate, private locations such as bedroom and bathroom, then it is likely he or she will masturbate in very inappropriate places such as a playground, a public bathroom, at school, on the bus, etc.

If you know a student or child is masturbating for sexual gratification, you need to address it directly. Talk about what happens as a result of masturbation. Discuss erections and ejaculations, in the case of adolescent boys. Allow them to ask questions, and then answer them honestly. Talk about it with the adolescent until you know he or she fully understands what masturbation is and why it must be very private. The adolescent may want to establish his or her own private routine for masturbating. That's okay. But again remind them that it must be private and no one, not even mom or dad, want to know about it. The exception would be if there is pain, an unusual discharge, or something abnormal, like a lump. Pain may be the sign of an infection, such as a urinary infection; in which case the adolescent should tell parents and a doctor about the problem. We should not be private about something if there is pain and sickness.

At some point other sexual topics may come up, such as dating, sexual intercourse, sexually transmitted diseases, birth control and pregnancy. When you feel a student or child is able to understand these topics, then address them simply and directly. Let them know the facts and always ask and answer questions clearly.

Monitor and chart your child's development

(adapted from Step 1 *in Diagnosis Autism: Now What? 10 Steps to Improve Treatment Outcomes*)

Contributing Author Lawrence P. Kaplan, Ph.D., Health Administration and Research with an emphasis in autism spectrum disorders, Kennedy-Western University—Dr. Kaplan is the Executive Director of US Autism and Asperger Association, Inc., a national association dedicated to enhancing the quality of life of individuals and their families/caregivers touched by autism spectrum disorders by providing educational and family support through conferences/seminars and published and electronic mediums. Dr. Kaplan is the author of *Diagnosis Autism: Now What? 10 Steps to Improve Treatment Outcomes*.

Resources and links— Lawrence P. Kaplan, Ph.D. suggests visiting his Autism Today website to learn about his other products and services: Visit <http://kaplan.autismtoday.com> today! (*Please note, don't put in the www.*) You can reach Dr. Kaplan at US Autism and Asperger Association by calling 1-888-9AUTISM or by writing <drlkaplan@usautism.org>.

Introduction

The first step to a productive parent–physician team approach is to provide your physician with a thorough record of your child's development. Accurate, complete records of your observations and concerns are essential for accurate diagnosis and early intervention treatment. Here, we will look at tracking behaviors and traits by:

- Maintaining a Daily Log that monitors your child's development.
- Reviewing common characteristics of autism spectrum disorders.
- Developing a school activity chart to record your child's daily activities.

Charting, using a Daily Log

Monitoring your child's development, to keep track of his or her progress, involves setting up a system for describing symptoms and behaviors. You may prefer to note behaviors on a calendar or complete a computerized diary. After many weeks of charting, you will begin to note relationships and patterns of behaviors.

Charts can be kept by anyone. The more detail you document and record, the better prepared you will be when you meet with health-care practitioners. In addition to you and your spouse charting your child's daily activities, anyone in close contact with your child, such as doctors, therapists and teachers can keep a log.

Professionals frequently use charts to document progress, predict reactions and behaviors, and ensure there is a physical record of a patient's history.

Start by getting a spiral notebook and listing the issues that concern those under the "autism spectrum" label. The issues may be neurological, gastrointestinal, communicative, social, behavioral, immunologic, nutritional or metabolic, or they may be related to allergies or genetics.

For example, you may note that an autistic child is sensitive to certain lights, sounds or smells. If so, environments where these interact may pose special difficulties for the child. Places that might over-stimulate a child include swimming pools, supermarkets and fast-food restaurants." Other behaviors and reactions to chart may include:

- Little or no eye contact,
- crawling,
- eating habits (list all the foods your child eats and drinks),
- food reactions,
- frequency of urination and bowel movements,
- speech patterns,
- tantrums,
- and transitioning.

All these should be charted. Recording them in a Daily Log preserves them so that you have a record of them when you meet with your physician. (For more information on the Daily Log, visit <Diagnosis Autism: Now What?>*)*

Common characteristics of autism spectrum disorders

The following common characteristics of autism spectrum disorders, from the <Autism Society of America,> should be noted when charting your child's development for your health-care practitioner:

- Insistence on sameness; resistance to change.
- Difficulty in expressing needs; uses gestures or pointing instead of words.
- Repeating words or phrases in place of normal, responsive language.
- Laughing, crying, showing distress for reasons not apparent to others.
- Prefers to be alone; aloof manner.
- Tantrums.
- Difficulty in mixing with others.
- May not want to cuddle or be cuddled.
- Little or no eye contact.
- Unresponsive to normal teaching methods.
- Sustained odd play.
- Spins objects.
- Inappropriate attachments to objects.
- Apparent over-sensitivity or insensitivity to pain
- No real fears of danger.
- Noticeable physical overactivity or extreme underactivity.
- Uneven gross/fine motor skills.
- Not responsive to verbal cues; acts as if deaf, although hearing tests in normal range.

The <Autism Research Institute> adds: "Most autistic children are perfectly normal in appearance, but spend their time engaged in puzzling and disturbing behaviors which are markedly different from those of normal children. They may stare into space for hours, throw uncontrollable tantrums, show no interest in people (including their parents) and pursue strange, repetitive activities with no apparent purpose. They have been described as living in a world of their own.

Some autistic individuals are remarkably gifted in certain areas such as music or mathematics."

Developing a School Activity Chart

Ask all of your child's teachers to start tracking his or her behavior, cognitive skills and language. Some schools supply a form for teachers to complete daily. This is an excellent communication tool that allows continuous monitoring of your child's daily activity. Based on the input from the school, you can chart the effectiveness of various interventions you have been using over the course of a treatment program. A sample *School Activity Chart* is located at the end of Step 1 in <Diagnosis Autism: Now What?> Information from the *School Activity Chart* notifies the parent of the child's activities throughout the day.

Let's look at an example of how the School Activity Chart works. The parents are starting a new gluten-free casein-free dietary therapy program. They alert the school that the child will be starting the special diet on Monday and ask the teachers to eliminate dairy and gluten products. The parents supply appropriate snacks for the child to the school. After one month of having teachers document information on the School Activity Chart, the parents review the information to see if there are any changes or improvements during this period of time. They notice that the child has eaten most of his lunch and is very active, and his bowel movements have improved. The teachers comment that the child has shown interest in group activities and his eye contact is better. The parents identify similar improvements in the Daily Log and can now take the well-documented information to the doctor for an evaluation of the current intervention program.

Remember that every individual with an autism spectrum diagnosis is unique. No two individuals on the spectrum will have exactly the same behaviors, strengths, deficits and challenges.

Exploring the relationship between autism & ADD/ADHD

CHAPTER 5

What is the difference between Asperger's Syndrome and ADD/ADHD?

Contributing Author Sharon A. Mitchell, BA, B.Ed., MA, McMaster University, University of Saskatchewan, San Diego State University—Ms. Mitchell has been involved in the field of special education for over twenty-five years as a Resource Room teacher, counselor and consultant. She's also worked in a hospital setting doing neuropsychological assessments. Her current position is as a Special Ed Consultant and Coordinator in an amalgamated school district. As well, she is seconded by the provincial department of education to present workshops on working students with autism spectrum disorders. Parents, school personnel, social workers, day care staff, occupational therapists, speech/language pathologists, psychologists, and counselors attend these workshops.

Resources and links—Sharon Mitchell, BA, B.Ed., MA suggests visiting her Autism Today website to learn about her other products and services: Visit <http://mitchell.autismtoday.com> today! (*Please note, don't put in the www.*) You can learn about Ms. Mitchell's work by visiting her website, <http://www.sasklearningvillage.ca>. Alternatively, you can write to her at <mitchell.sharon@gmail.com>. To aid in your search for ways to help your child, Ms. Mitchell recommends a visit to <http://www.angel-images.com>, a site run by a woman whose son has Asperger's Syndrome and ADHD. For a free e-book on ASD, visit <http://www.pediatricneurology.com/autism.htm>. For a free e-book on ADHD, visit <http://www.pediatricneurology.com/adhd.htm>. For a free e-book on learning disabilities, visit <http://www.pediatricneurology.com/learning.htm>.

Often, children with ADHD find themselves in conflict with their peers. They have trouble sticking to boring, mundane tasks. Their organizational skills may be weak. They find it hard to switch their attentional focus. They benefit from structure, consistent routines and visual approaches.

Sound familiar? These statements could just as easily describe a child with Asperger's Syndrome as a child with ADHD.

In fact, many children who eventually receive the label of Asperger's Syndrome were previously diagnosed as having ADHD. Although they did display many of the characteristics of ADHD, that diagnosis didn't quite explain all the symptoms.

Did someone misdiagnose the first time around? Not necessarily. Keep in mind that Asperger's Syndrome and high functioning autism are still relatively new diagnoses. Ten years ago, it was rare to even hear the term Asperger's Syndrome. And ASD shares many characteristics with ADHD.

Part of the reason for the similarities lies in the area of executive functioning. The University of Nebraska Lincoln's site defines executive functioning as "the ability to organize thoughts and work, to create plans and successfully execute them, to manage the administrative functions of one's life. Individuals with impaired executive function may appear to live moment to moment, failing to monitor their activities or social interactions to make sure plans are carried out (or even made). With diminished ability to create strategies, to handle more than on task at a time, to be effective, reliable, and productive, the simplest job may be too challenging." (Osborn, 1998)

Click on the following link to read more about the components of executive functioning: <http://tbi.unl.edu/savedTBI/executive/characteristics.html>. When you look at the following list, you can see how ADHD and autistic tendencies overlap:

- Pragmatic deficits
- Poor reasoning
- Memory deficits
- Organizational deficits
- Poor self-awareness
- Processing weaknesses
- Impulsivity
- Inattentiveness

Dr. David Rabiner is renowned for his work in the field of attention deficit disorders. He lists the following skills as being at the heart of an ADHD person's difficulties: " . . . organization and planning skills, establishing goals and being able to use these goals to guide one's behavior, holding information in memory, selecting strategies to accomplish these goals and monitoring the effectiveness of these strategies, being able to keep emotions from overpowering one's ability to think rationally, and being able to shift efficiently from one cognitive activity to the next."

Sound much like autism? Read on.

Rabiner explains that deficiencies in these areas may cause: " . . . poor tolerance for frustration, inflexibility, and explosive outbursts that are seen in "inflexible-explosive" children. For example, if a child has difficulty shifting readily from one activity to the next because of an inherent cognitive inflexibility, it may explain why he or she becomes so frustrated when parents request that he/she stop playing and come in for dinner. Such a child may not be intentionally trying to be non-compliant, but their non-compliance may instead reflect trouble with shifting flexibly and efficiently from one mind-set to another."

You can read more about this and Dr. Rabiner's work at <http://www.help4adhd.org>.

Martin Kutsche, MD, with the Department for Pediatrics and Neurology at New York Medical College say it is probably best to consider ADHD as sometimes sharing the following symptoms with—but not being part of—Autism Spectrum Disorders:

- Poor reading of social clues ("Johnny, you're such a social klutz. Can't you see that the other children think that's weird?")

- Poor ability to utilize "self-talk" to work through a problem ("Johnny, what were you thinking?! Did you even think this through?")

- Poor sense of self-awareness (Johnny's true answer to the above question is probably, "I don't have a clue. I guess I wasn't actually thinking.")

- Do better with predictable routine.

- Poor generalization of rules ("Johnny, I told you to shake hands with your teachers. Why didn't you shake hands with the *principal*?)

Kutsche also explains this difference between ASD and ADHD: ADHDers typically have trouble with "executive functions," with subsequent difficulties in their relationship with others. Usually, though, they have adequate capacity for empathy—but may have trouble inhibiting their behavior long enough to show it. Conversely, many children with ASD may appear to have a short attention span but just aren't able to stay focused on situations they don't understand.

Learn more about Dr. Kutsche's views by visiting <http://www.pediatricneurology.com/autism.htm/>.

While ADHD and autism may be separate disorders, they share some common traits. In fact, there are many disorders with characteristics similar to those shown by people on the autism spectrum, particularly in the areas of executive functioning, social pragmatics, language processing and sensory sensitivities.

Although sometimes needed for funding purposes, does the particular label really matter? Perhaps the most important thing is finding strategies that help that child be all that she can be, no matter what the diagnosis.

The Difference Between Autism, Aspergers Syndrome, ADD and ADHD

Contributing Author Diane Burns, who lives in Dallas, Texas, has written *Autism? Aspergers? ADHD?ADD? A Parent's Roadmap to Understanding and Support!* a safe, humorous novel to guide parents to action. With advance warning, she helps readers navigate the emotional roadmap of accepting a different child, while motivating them into action.

Resources and links—Diane D. Burns suggests visiting her Autism Today website to learn about her other products and services: Visit <http://burns.autismtoday.com> today! *(*Please note, don't put in the www.)*

I'm so sorry you had to ask. Imagine being surrounded every day by family and friends, schoolmates and employers, all glowing with symptoms of autism, Asperger's syndrome, attention deficit disorder and attention deficit hyperactive disorder, and one still has to make gargantuan efforts to decipher the vocabulary. In a perfect world, parents would be able to step in to their doctor's office with a few observations and step out with an understanding. Instead, it's like playing a shell game with a different diagnosis under each cup, thus the "Let's Pick This One Today" diagnosis. On behalf of all of us who have gone before . . . .Sorry.

You've come to one of many "right" places for answers. In these chapters are parents, doctors and therapists who understand how you feel and are familiar with the behaviors you are seeing. The challenge is in looking long enough and hard enough to arrive at an acceptable diagnosis.

Stop! Acceptance does not mean Done. It doesn't mean you're necessarily happy with where you are and don't particularly worry about the future. It definitely does not mean retirement from trying new things and wanting *better* for your child.

Acceptance means no more crying binges and beating your head against the wall. Acceptance means getting your life back . . . to be able to laugh again and enjoy your family in spite of the rough spots.

When people ask if I'm done looking for treatments for my near twelve-year-old, I simply say, "We're still tweaking." I think we'll always be tweaking those little areas of the brain that do a hitch-kick instead of a round-off. Yet, it's great to be able to say I love my son's differences, now more than ever.

The most important thing to take with you from this chapter is that each one of these developmental differences are treatable. Whether it's autism or ADD, treat the child, not the diagnosis. Listen to your child for they are your best laboratory. Ask for help. And remember, always remember, there is hope. I give you a standing ovation for your efforts.

Autism, Asperger's Syndrome, ADHD and ADD

Autism is a developmental disorder and the child is delayed in several areas. Among others, they can be in areas such as language processing, social, fine or gross motor skills and verbal skills. It is diagnosed by observing certain behaviors. For example, a lack of interest in others, perseveration (unable to break away from a certain object like their finger or a spinning wheel), obsessive-compulsive behaviors, sensory issues like problems with sounds, smells, tactile things and an aversion to change.

The typical autistic child has communication delays. Either he can't, doesn't care to, or has some type of speech delay. In general, you can see that when compared to similar-aged children, he's behind. And he's not only different, he's different in ways that are hard to explain.

Autism can range from very mild to severe. Some autistics are easily identifiable because they are non-verbal or minimally verbal, self-destructive, and/or violent. Intervention could not come soon enough for these children and if you have a child exhibiting extreme behaviors, please run, don't walk to your nearest

DAN (Defeat Autism Now) doctor found through the Autism Research Institute, bookstore (Children With Starving Brains by Jacquelyn McCandless, Unraveling the Mystery of Autism and PDD by Karyn Seroussi) and other resources as presented in this book. Autism is treatable. Search for a physiological explanation which would point to behaviors resulting from pain, drug-like effects from certain foods, or the absence of some essential component of brain nutrition.

As you move away from the extreme behaviors, things begin to get a little fuzzy. Many autistics have families, good jobs and become very successful. Their differences, again, reside heavily along the need for structure (absence of change), obsessive behaviors, ticks or stimming, communication and social lines. Often they are extremely literal and generally have a hard time fitting in (though many hide it well).

In my opinion, the separation between high-functioning autism and Asperger's lies in communication. It occurs in both, sometimes easily, but there seems to be a cognitive disconnect for children with autism whereas children with Asperger's are much more at ease communicating, though frequently inappropriately.

Still under the umbrella of Autism Spectrum Disorder, those with Asperger's Syndrome often have it harder than their autistic brother who's symptoms are more severe.

Their expertise in a particular area often separates them from their peers. People think they are quirky. Children and adults can become isolated because they don't know how to fit in. They struggle to read facial expressions and verbal cues. As a result, many suffer from depression. They want friends, they just don't know how to get them. It is critical to provide educational opportunities (to learn social skills) and social support (to provide relationships) to the individual with Asperger's Syndrome.

Attention Deficit Disorder (and ADD With Hyperactivity)

ADD and ADHD are obviously diagnosed when *attention* is a key problem. Behaviors include difficulty focusing, finishing a task, paying attention, "getting it", staying on task and being easily distracted. Often, intentions are good. It is impossible for them to perform the task simply because their brain won't let them. As with ASD, this developmental difference generally benefits from an increase in protein (especially at breakfast), essential fatty acids, certain drugs, sensory integration therapy, etc. If they are ADD or ADHD, you will see an improvement with treatment.

ADHD contains the hyperactive behaviors such as constant movement, fidgeting, pacing, needing to throw things (great for those athletes), highs and lows. ADHD loves to be doing. Again, many of these behaviors aren't wrong, they're just different and when they interfere with a child's ability to do their best, they need to be addressed.

I hope this provides just enough information to get you started. Whether I've confirmed or infuriated you, if it motivates you to help your child, then I've succeeded. Remember, you are your child's greatest advocate, teacher and friend. God bless you on your way.

Why is autism on the rise?

CHAPTER 6

Why is autism on the rise?

Contributing Author Stephen M. Edelson, Ph.D., Experimental Psychology—Dr. Edelson has worked in the field of autism for 25 years. He is the Director of the Center for the Study of Autism in Salem, Oregon, which is affiliated with the Autism Research Institute in San Diego, CA. He is also on the Board of Directors of the Oregon chapter of the Autism Society of America and is on the Society's Professional Advisory Board.

Resources and links—Stephen M. Edelson, Ph.D. suggests visiting his Autism Today website to learn about his other products and services: Visit <http://edelson.autismtoday.com> today! (*Please note, don't put in the www.*) Dr. Edelson's main autism website is <www.autism.org>.

Autism is clearly an epidemic. According to the Center for Disease Control (CDC), the prevalence of autism is now 1 in 166 children. Prior to the mid-1980s, the rate of autism was estimated to be 1 in 2,000 children, a 1,200% increase! The big question: What is responsible for the dramatic increase in autism over the past 20 years?

Some people argue that the increase in autism reflects better ways to diagnose these children and an increase in awareness of the disorder. Many of them also claim that the underlying cause of autism is purely genetic. There are problems with these claims:

- There can be no epidemic of purely genetic diseases. The prevalence of genetic diseases is expected to increase only about 1% per century.

- Prior to the mid-1980s, two-thirds of the children diagnosed with autism were affected at birth (i.e., early onset), and only one-third became autistic between their first and second year of life (i.e., late onset). Today, the opposite is true. One-third have early onset autism and two-thirds have late onset autism. The notions that the increase in autism is due to better diagnosis and/or awareness and/or is genetic does not explain the huge increase in late onset autism.

- If autism has always been highly prevalent, where are the 1 in 166 autistic adults? There are still only a relatively small number of autistic adults, even though their numbers will increase enormously in the coming years.

There are many theories on why the prevalence of autism has increased over the past 20 years, including a yet-to-be identified virus. One thing is for certain: there is growing scientific evidence linking vaccines with autism. There are two aspects to the vaccine issue. One is the mercury problem. Mercury is highly neurotoxic and is used as a preservative, called thimerosal, in many vaccines. Second is the Measles-Mumps-Rubella (MMR) vaccine. Here are just a few of the arguments in support of the autism–vaccine connection:

- Research has shown that many autistic children have very high levels of mercury and other heavy metals in their bodies. Additionally, according to a survey by the Autism Research Institute, parents rated chelation, a method to detoxify the body from heavy metals, as the single most effective biomedical intervention that they have tried on their children, of the 80 biomedical interventions (including 45 drugs), they were asked to rate. (See <www.AutismResearchInstitute.com>, link Parent Ratings of Behavioral Effects of Biomedical Interventions.)

- Some critics argue that since mercury (or thimerosal) has been removed or reduced in vaccines, one should expect a decrease in the rate of autism. In 1999, the Food and Drug Administration (FDA) asked (not demanded) the drug manufacturers to remove mercury from the vaccines. We assume drug manufacturers started to comply with this request in 1999/2000 and that the mercury-containing vaccines are still being phased out. Since the average age of diagnosis of autism is four years, one would expect to see a decrease in autism in 2004. The California Department of Developmental Disabilities Service has been keeping careful track of the incidence of autism over the years, and there is some indication that the rate of autism in 2004 is starting to decrease.

- Soon after the MMR vaccine was introduced in the U.S., the rate of autism began to rise. The MMR vaccine was introduced in the United Kingdom about 10 years later, and the incidence of autism, again, soon began to rise. Note: some people claim that the increase in autism in the U.K. occurred several years prior to the introduction of the MMR. However, these critics do not take into account the "catch-up" period in which older children were also given the MMR vaccine.

- A series of studies by Dr. Andrew Wakefield, as well as several other scientists worldwide, have found live measles virus in many children who became autistic after receiving the MMR (i.e., late-onset autism).

We must rely on science to determine the true cause(s) of autism. At this point, scientific studies are providing some evidence suggesting that vaccines may be associated with autism.

Why is autism on the rise?

Contributing Author Daniel Hawthorne is a diagnosed High Functioning Autistic. He is the author of *Child of the Forest* and *Guidelines to Intervention in Autism,* and webmaster and author of the award winning site <www.autismguidelines.com>. He has degrees in Communication and Business Administration, most recently through the University of Arkansas. He does numerous speaking engagements to autism support groups and to special schools, in addition to managing an online resume posting business.

Resources and links—Daniel Hawthorne suggests visiting his Autism Today website to learn about his other products and services: Visit <http://hawthorne.autismtoday.com> today! (*Please note, don't put in the www.)* He enjoys corresponding with parents, teachers, and others in the autism community, and may be contacted at <daniel@autismguidelines.com>.

To me, the real question is whether autism truly is on the rise—or does it just seem so due to improved medical diagnosis and a greater awareness of the traits of autism?

I have always had my qualms about the diagnosis of any disorder or health condition made solely on the observation of someone's behavior, especially if that observation is brief and done by only one person. In my opinion, behavior-based diagnoses tend to be subjective, making whatever specific disorder the individual may have seem vaguely defined and ambiguous, and making any intervention for it controversial. Such diagnoses typically depend on the perspectives and knowledge of the one making the diagnosis. Too often, it is made with too little actual, one-on-one observation by the psychologist in the child's natural setting.

Personally, I would like to see the day when diagnoses of autism are made based on physiological factors, through futuristic medical brain scan techniques as well as intensive observation by skilled experts.

Also, I have no doubt that the news media has helped raise the awareness of the disorder among the general public. Unfortunately, from my observation, the media tends to use the term "autism" in its broadest possible sense, lumping together everyone within the spectrum into one big batch and without mention that these traits vary widely from one individual to the next. All too often, reporters use the same kind of sensationalism when reporting on autism as they do when describing the play-by-play action of a sporting event. I find this sad, even if it does increase viewership.

The question remains: Is the rate of autism itself really increasing or does it just seem like it? There are no shortage of theories, especially over the Internet. One I read recently especially bothers me. It seems that some anonymous individuals are claiming not only that autism is on the increase but this is so because of e-mail. They claim, in their words, that the Internet tends to bring eccentric people together, who then pass on their genes to their eccentric children, ones that society then labels as autistic. I suppose everyone has a right to an opinion and I have a right to disagree with it.

From my view point, in order to truly discern whether the rate is increasing or not, one must have a point of comparison. While much more is known about autism now than was known in 1943, when Leo Kanner first wrote about it, the basic traits that he described so well and that today are commonly known as "classic autism," have changed little. So, I would think that is the segment of the autism spectrum that should be examined. If one accepts the view that autism is on the rise, then the question then becomes the reason why. If, on the other hand, it has not risen, then why does it just seem like it?

My belief is that there must be both a genetic predisposition and an environmental trigger for autism to develop. While little can be done about the genes one inherits, I think that much can be done about limiting the factors that can tend to trigger development of a condition such as autism.

The studies I have seen do seem to indicate certain genetic factors that directly influence the immune system and indirectly cause certain groups to be more predisposed than others. Some groups are said to be more predisposed to a number of health conditions, such as high blood pressure. But the problem is this: who's to say whether genetic factors have changed so radically in just the past 70 years to have caused this sudden increase in diagnosed cases? After all, DNA identification is still a new science.

My gut feeling is that if anything has changed in the past 70 years, it is not the genes but the environment. In my own case, my mother contracted a case of Rubella during her second trimester, causing me to be born with autism. Clearly, this would have been an environmental factor triggering the disorder. I recall my Mom telling me that the doctor at the time told her it was just a mild case and probably would not cause her all that much discomfort.

Shortly before my third birthday, my family moved to a town with a paper mill and a plywood mill as its main industry. Growing up there, I did not realize what clean air smelled like until after I moved away for college then came back some months later. It was a mystery to me. I had difficulty grasping not only why I never noticed the odor before but also how permanent residents could tolerate it now. As I went around seeking answers to this question, people often just laughed and said, "It is the smell of money."

I have no way of knowing just what toxic chemicals were in the air at the time. I do know a considerable amount of recent medical evidence indicates that mercury affects how the brain functions, often causing symptoms quite similar to autism. A lot of anecdotal evidence I've seen tends to indicate the children became autistic only after they come in contact with toxic chemicals, such as mercury. While certain immunizations may well be one source of mercury, I do not doubt that there probably are many other sources as well. For so many of us, low levels of toxic chemicals are in our ground water, in the air we breathe and even the foods we eat. Being raised a Southerner, I used to love catfish, though I did wonder why I ached so much and had so much difficulty functioning for days afterward eating it. Then I learned that catfish can be a prime source of mercury poisoning.

I think hardly anyone would contend that the environment today is as clean and as pure as it was, say, a hundred years ago. An interesting study was made recently of the Amish. The study seemed to indicate a much lower incidence among that group than the general population in what can be classified as classic autism. From what I know of the Amish, they have a simple lifestyle involving much physical activity, a diet low in processed foods and a lower level of emotional stress.

It is not surprising to me that groups having a smaller amount of physical activity also tend to have the highest rates of autism. From what I have read in medical literature, the human body is in itself truly amazing. The sweat glands work to cleanse the body of toxins, much like the kidneys do. So I would think that groups such as the Amish would have a lowered rate for that one reason, if for no other.

Their diet may also be a factor. So many processed foods state, in their list of ingredients, "made with natural and artificial flavorings." I know the real reason for stating it this way is to prevent others from copying the recipe, but of course, this could encompass just about anything edible. Personally, I tend to be allergic to red food dyes and even when I read the list of ingredients, I discover only afterwards—via certain specific allergic reactions I have—that the food contained red dye.

As for how the level of stress is connected to all this, doctors often tell me that emotional health can definitely influence the immune system, and indirectly cause all kinds of health problems. So, to me, it would make sense that urban dwellers who live a fast paced life, may also have higher levels of stress in their life. Since the Amish way of life is slow paced, I would think this could also help explain their apparent lower rate.

The belief in vaccines

Contributing Author Sherri Tenpenny, DO—Dr. Tenpenny is board-certified in Emergency Medicine and currently specializes in Integrative Medicine. She is an outspoken advocate for healthcare choice, including the right to refuse vaccination. She speaks nationally and internationally on the subject of "Unspoken Risks: The Impact of Vaccines on health."

Resources and links—Sherri Tenpenny, DO suggests visiting her Autism Today website to learn about her other products and services: Visit <http://tenpenny.autismtoday.com> today! (*Please note, don't put in the www*). You can write to Dr. Tenpenny at <NMASeminars@aol.com>.

When Parents Question Vaccination

(Originally published in Dr. Tenpenny's "Vaccines: The Risks, The Benefits, The Choices — A Resource Guide for Parents")

When parents question vaccination, strong opposition from their pediatrician or family doctor often confronts them. Below is a list of commonly used arguments promoting vaccination and my suggestions for rebutting them.

Key: "S" = Statement "R" = Rebuttal

General

S: Immunization has been repeatedly demonstrated to be one of the most effective medical interventions we have to prevent disease.

R: Most of the common childhood diseases were declining both in terms or morbidity (complications) and mortality (death) prior to the introduction of vaccinations. Graphs (included in this manual) and numbers obtained directly from government documents show this evidence.

S: It has been estimated that immunizations currently save 3 million lives per year throughout the world.

R: You can't prove a negative (ex: how can you know that a vaccine saved a life? Do all people contract all infections? How do you know how many infections have been prevented by vaccines and by other means?)

S: Vaccination is one of the most cost effective health interventions.

R: We don't know the actual cost of vaccination worldwide but a few costs are known:

- The WHOLESALE price for vaccines used in the U.S. pediatric schedule is more than $170 per child. Given that there are more than 77,000 live births per week in the U.S…that is more than $13M/week to prevent a few childhood infections.

- More than $1.3B has been spent to eradicate polio from Third World Countries

- The estimated lifetime cost of caring for one autistic (possibly vaccine-injured) child is more than $4.5M. What about other illnesses possibly induced by vaccination? Therefore, WHAT IS THE REAL COST OF VACCINATION?

S: Vaccines are safe and do not cause untoward effects on the immune system.

R: Safety studies have been too short, too small and too few to consider vaccines safe. The immune system of infants has not been studied and is not fully understood. The long term consequences of vaccines on the immune systems of children under 2 years of age cannot be predicted. Worse, it is not being followed. If a child develops an autoimmune disorder, the cause is not studied; a therapy/medication is developed to treat it. Are vaccine-related immune system disruptions creating "customers for life" for the pharmaceutical industry?

S: The additives in vaccines are in small concentrations and are non-toxic.

R: Vaccines contain a combination of at least 39 different additives, preservatives, and cell types introduced during the manufacturing process. None of these are non-toxic. The cumulative effect of these toxins, particularly the heavy metals, is being hotly debated. In addition, vaccine contaminants have included bovine (cow), avian (chicken) and monkey viruses, and bacteria such as streptococcus in the DTP vaccine [Pediatrics, Vol. 75, No. 2, Feb 1985] and Serratia marcesens in the influenza vaccines [2004 influenza season].

For example, DTaP is produced using formaldehyde, aluminum hydroxide, aluminum phosphate, polysorbate 80, gelatin and, thimerosal is still used in third world countries. The polio vaccine is produced using 3 types of polio virus, and can contain formaldehyde, phenoxyethanol (antifreeze), sucrose (table sugar), neomycin, streptomycin, polymyxin B, and VERO cells, a continuous line of monkey kidney cells.

Ask your doctor this:

1. Is potential for toxicity from aluminum, formaldehyde and thimerosal from each of the vaccines cumulative, since multiple vaccines are given together?

2. At what age is a baby capable of eliminating aluminum from his body?
ANSWER: Aluminum is eliminated from the body primarily through the kidneys. Infant kidney function (glomerular filtration rate) is low at birth and doesn't reach full capacity until 1-2 years of age. *[REF: Simmer, K. Aluminum in Infancy. In: Zatta PF, Alfrey AC. (Eds) Aluminum Toxicity in Infants' Health and Disease. 1997, World Scientific Publishing.]*

3. And if you are bold enough, ask doctor if he/she would be willing to take the same dose of the additive that is in the vaccine, adjusted for his adult weight?

S: Vaccines provide high levels of protection against several diseases, and protection against disability and death.

R: Vaccines vary in efficacy, and many that have been vaccinated get the disease. Therefore, vaccines do not necessarily protect against disability and death from disease. In addition, vaccines have been documented to CAUSE certain disabilities and death.

S: Serious adverse events following immunization are rare.

R: Between mid-1999 & Jan. 4, 2004, (for all vaccines and all reactions), 128,035 adverse reactions reported to the Vaccine Adverse Event Reporting System (VAERS). It is estimated that only 10% of all reactions are actually reported to VAERS. Therefore, this may actually represent between 1.28 million (10%) and 12.8 million (1%) of all vaccine-associated adverse reactions.

In that same period, there were 2,093 deaths reported in the VAERS. This may actually represent between 20,930 (10%) and 209,300 (1%) of the DEATHS thought to be associated with vaccines.

Even though this data does not PROVE an association to vaccine-related injury and death, the magnitude of the numbers certainly takes exception to the concept of a "rare" event.

Of note: more than $1B has been paid to victims of vaccine-related injuries and death through the Vaccine Injury Compensation Program (VICP).

S: Vaccines do not cause disease they are designed to prevent.

R: This is simply not true.
From 1987 to 2001, the oral polio vaccine (OPV) was the only cause of polio in the US. OPV was removed from the market here, but is still used in massive immunization campaigns worldwide during

annual National Immunization Days (NIDs), when more than 430 million children worldwide are vaccinated with the OPV vaccine. The WHO no longer tracks vaccine-induced paralysis, even though statistically 2 cases of paralysis are caused for every 2 million doses of vaccine. (Ref: WHO documents)

The first generation HiB vaccine (PRP) was associated with a transient increased risk of invasive HiB meningitis after vaccination and therefore, is no longer used. Nearly 3% of those vaccinated with the chickenpox vaccine contract the infection. The rubella virus is known to shed from the MMR vaccine and can potentially cause congenial rubella in a woman exposed during her 1st trimester of pregnancy. The measles fraction of the MMR has been implicated in causing MINE syndrome. (Discussed below). And we all know of people who contracted the flu within days of receiving the live-virus flu vaccine. It is not possible to contract the stated disease from these vaccines: DTaP, Prevnar and Hepatitis B.

S: There is no evidence that vaccination can lead to chronic disease.

R: There is plenty of evidence to the contrary. Here are a few examples:

1. The following vaccines and vaccine additives have been associated with an increase of serum IgE the antibody associated with the development of allergies: Mercury (thimerosal); Aluminum; Gelatin in chickenpox vaccine; DT vaccine; Rubella vaccine; and Acellular Pertussis vaccine.

2. There is no doubt that the new recombinant hepatitis B vaccine has the ability to trigger autoimmunity." [REF: Cohen AD. Vaccine-induced autoimmunity. J Autoimmune. 1996 Dec; 9(6): 699-703. PMID: 9115571]

3. There has been a case report of a 35-day-old infant who developed Kawasaki disease (an autoimmune disease involving the blood vessels of the heart) one day after receiving his second dose of hepatitis B vaccine.

4. Tetanus toxoid, influenza vaccines, polio vaccine, rubella vaccines and others, have been related to phenomena ranging from auto-antibody production to full-blown illness (such as rheumatoid arthritis)." [REF: Shoenfeld Y. Vaccination and autoimmunity-'vaccinosis': a dangerous liaison? J. Autoimmune. 2000 Feb; 14(1): 1-10. PMID: 10648110]

S: The vaccine-preventable diseases of childhood are still with us and continue to cause substantial distress, disability and even death. No child should be denied the benefits of vaccination.

R: Neither should any child be subjected to vaccination until vaccines have been proven to be safe through long-term follow up studies. There is a substantial body of science in the medical literature that demonstrates that immunizations are an assault on the immune system. It is important that your doctor honestly discusses the benefits and risks of vaccination. You have a right to know and your doctor has a responsibility to be honest to maintain his credibility. The choice between the risk of the disease and the risks of the vaccines should be the Right of the Parent.

S: The arguments against immunization are irrational, based on fear of a particular injection and a resistance to authority. (i.e. they don't want the government telling them what to do.)

R: Arguments FOR vaccinations are based on fear. Arguments against vaccination are not weak and are based on a review of the medical literature that reports many complications from vaccination, including autoimmune disease, allergy, and death.

NO medical test can ensure the safety of an individual child; therefore, each shot to each child is truly "Russian Roulette"; which child will react and be the "rare" death or complication is completely unknown.

It should be the right of every parent to determine what is allowed to be injected into their children. Government mandated vaccination is no different than government mandated use of anti-depressants or anti-psychotics "for the good of the community." Would you allow that for your child?

S: Vaccine-preventable diseases of childhood can cause serious problems, even death. If you do not vaccinate your child, and your child contracts one of these illnesses, your child could die.

R: This is partially true . . . childhood illnesses can be serious in some children. However, it must be understood that the mortality (death) rate from pediatric infectious diseases had declined to very low levels even before the vaccines for those diseases had been introduced. (see Graphs in this manual.)

Even though complications from childhood diseases can occur, serious complications, including death, can also occur from the vaccines.

Here is one example from the CDC:

Chickenpox: The number of children with serious complications from chickenpox is thought to be approximately 1800 cases/year. (Note: This is a hypothetical computer generated number since Chickenpox is not a disease. Also, keep in mind that there are nearly 4 million live births in the US each year.)

The facts about Chickenpox Vaccine (Varivax)

1. Between March 1995 and July 1998, VAERS received 67.5 adverse event reports per 100,000 doses of chickenpox vaccine or a total of 6,574 reports. 82% of the adverse event cases occurred in individuals who received chickenpox vaccine only. Approximately 4% of cases (about 1 in 33,000 doses) were serious, including shock, convulsions, encephalitis, thrombocytopenia and 14 deaths.

2. Studies have shown the effectiveness of the vaccine to protect against chickenpox can be as low as 40%. And up to 20% of vaccinated children contract the disease.

3. Studies show that up to 3% of chickenpox vaccine recipients contract chickenpox from the vaccine, and that some cases of chickenpox may be contracted from recently vaccinated children.

S: Childhood diseases have a high rate of serious complication.

R: Childhood diseases have a risk of a serious complication, but not a "high rate" of complications. Most are benign to most children. The question needs to be asked: Do these complications occur in primarily healthy children, or immunocompromised children? What were the living conditions of those that died? What were the circumstances of those that died at the time they contracted the disease? Additionally, ask the question, "how many serious complications are caused by the vaccines?" Doctors do not have the answers to these questions.

S: Pertussis causes significant morbidity. Pertussis can cause seizures, encephalopathy (brain inflammation) and death. During 1992 and 1993, 23 deaths attributed to pertussis were reported to the United States Centers for Disease Control and Prevention.

R: In 15 years (from 1980 to 1995) there were 92 deaths reported from pertussis. In 1998 alone, there were 17 reported deaths the day after a pertussis vaccination.

The vaccine does not protect from the infection. In fact, most of the investigations into infection outbreaks have conclusively shown that the infections occur in vaccinated children. In November 2003, 120 cases of pertussis were reported in Fon du Lac, Wisconsin. Based on data taken directly from the state public health department, the county had a 99.9% vaccination rate. (Note: The CDC states that an 80% vaccination rate is sufficient for protection and "herd immunity.")

S: Everyone must be vaccinated for everyone to be protected.

R: This argument in support of concept referred to as "herd immunity." This concept states that if at least 80% of a population is "immune" to a disease, then the rest of the "herd" will be protected from the infection. The original concept of herd immunity here. This has been rolled over to include a vaccinated population. However, since it is well known that not 100% of persons vaccinated will develop antibodies to protect the "herd", the CDC recommends all to be vaccinated for the "good of the whole." Not all children should be vaccinated and the one-size-fits-all public health policy that becomes "sacrificing a few for the good of the whole."

Pertussis

S: The acellular pertussis vaccine (part of DTaP) is safe and effective.

R: Listed in order of increasing severity, observed adverse reactions to the pertussis vaccine include irritability, persistent, unusually high pitched crying, somnolence, seizures, a shock-like "hypotensive, hyporesponsive" state, and encephalopathy.

In evaluating side-reactions to the vaccine, the following must be kept in mind:

1. Vaccines are not standardized between manufacturers;

2. For a given manufacturer, vaccines are not standard from one batch to the next;

3. Unless the vaccine is properly prepared and refrigerated, its potency and reactivity varies with shelf life.

R: "In fact, the whole question of vaccine detoxification has never been systematically investigated." Workshop on neurologic complications of pertussis & pertussis vaccinations, by Mekes, JH, Kinsbourne, M. Neuropediatrics. Nov 1990; 2K4 171–176 DMID 1981251

Measles

S: Measles is one of the most severe and infectious diseases of childhood. In the 1990s, one of every 5-10,000 measles cases dies from the acute effects of the disease, despite the best modern medical care. One measles case in 70 requires hospital admission.

R (1): Serious consequences to measles occur in children suffering from immunocompromise or malnutri-

tion – i.e. in Third World countries. In healthy, well-nourished children, the infection is well tolerated and only rarely are there complications. There were only 13 reported cases of wild measles in the US in 2003. MMWR, April 2005/Vol.52/No.54 p.12

R (2): The death rate from measles in the US was 1 in 10,000,000 (1:10million) in 1955. The measles vaccine was not introduced until 1963. Therefore, risk of death from measles has been negligible for a very long time.

S: The more serious and potentially deadly complication of measles infection is SSPE (Subsclerosing Panencephalitis). If your child contracts measles, he may develop this complication.

R: This is true. Subacute Sclerosing PanEncephalitis (SSPE) is due to an aborted form of the wild measles virus which results from a faulty immune reaction of the human body. The individual is unable to launch a full immune response to clear the virus from the body, and parts of it remains in the central nervous system leading to a persistent infection. The aborted virus can remain quiescent for months to years, before the development of the neurological and ophthalmic symptoms of SSPE.

In the 1960s, there were approximately 60 cases of SSPE per year among the >500,000 reported cases (as many cases may not have been reported) of measles per year. There have been only 80 cases of SSPE reported in the US in the last 15 years.

Some aspects about the clinical and pathogenetic characteristics of measles infection: SSPE and MIME. Dykon, Paul. J. Ped. Neurology, 2004; 2(s); 121–124

S: There is no relationship between MMR and autism. Therefore, the MMR is completely safe and effective. If your child contracts measles, he may develop this complication.

R: The relationship between SSPE and persistent measles infection is well established, but the second syndrome, now being referred to as MINE Syndrome (Measles Induced Neuroautistic Encephalopathy, a childhood neurodegenerative disease), has been shown

77

to be related to the live measles vaccination (MMR), if not proven to be caused by it.

There is a constellation of features which make up the MINE syndrome including:

1. All children had a live-attenuated MMR vaccination between 12 and 21 months of age;

2. Prior to vaccination, none of the children showed any features of autism or any signs of enterocolitis (gut problems);

3. All of the symptoms developed many months after the measles vaccine (i.e. an interval period is characteristic of all slow viral diseases) which for the most part were autistic in nature;

4. Prior to vaccination children have had a history of severe, recurrent infection or frank allergy to eczema, suggesting that each had a pre-existing immunological problem;

5. There is a preponderance of males who demonstrate MINE syndrome, an interesting fact since male predominance also features the cousin disease, SSPE;

6. In a subset of children whose blood and spinal fluid was tested, there was enough measles antigen present to identify through sophisticated testing that this was the vaccine-related strain measles and not the wild measles virus gene.

For both syndromes (SSPE and MINE) to develop, two factors are required: an immature, defective or damaged immune system which is unable to eliminate the measles virus from the body, whether it is the wild strain in active infection, or the live-attenuated form from the MMR. Individuals can become immune to the wild measles virus when the live-attenuated (MMR) is given them, but a small portion do not completely neutralize the live-attenuated virus and the MINE syndrome can develop. *[Ref: Editorial: Some aspects about the clinical and pathogenetic characteristics of the presumed persistent measles infections: SSPE and MINE. by Paul Richard Dyken Institute for Research in Childhood Neurodegenerative Diseases, Mobile, Alabama, U.S.A.]*

Bottom Line: EVEN IF THE RISK OF SSPE IS REAL, IT IS FRACTIONAL COMPARED TO THE RISK OF MMR. THIS SHOULD NOT BE DISMISSED LIGHTLY.

Polio

S: **We must continue to vaccinate for polio until the WHO declares the infection eradicated. After all, polio is only a plane ride away.**

R: The US has had no polio cases of wild polio since at least 1991; The WHO declared the Western Hemisphere "polio free" in 1994.

There are only 7 remaining countries in the World in which polio is still being reported: Nigeria, Pakistan, Somalia Afghanistan, Niger, Egypt, and India, arguably some of the economically and hygienically poorest countries in the world. As of Oct. 15, 2003, only 414 cases of wild polio were reported in the world. And yet, we continue to give our children 5 polio injections, each containing 3 individual inactivated viruses.

As for polio "only being a plane ride away"…in 18 years, there were only 6 cases of imported polio in this country, the last being in NYC in 1993. How valid is that argument, especially when >98% of all polio virus exposures result in symptoms appearing no more serious than a short bout of diarrhea? How benign is the vaccine in the long run, especially when it is coupled with so many other live and attenuated viral vaccines? This is the question to be asked.

What is all the buzz about mercury?

CHAPTER 7

Evidence of harm

Contributing Author David Kirby has been a professional journalist for 15 years. He has contributed to The New York Times and several national magazines, writing about many subjects including health, technology and politics. He lives in Brooklyn, New York.

Resources and links—David Kirby, Journalist, suggests visiting his Autism Today website to learn about his other products and services: Visit <http://kirby.autismtoday.com> today! (*Please note, don't put in the www).* You can order *Evidence of Harm* (St. Martin's Press, ISBN: 0-312-32544-0) through <Amazon.com> or the <National Autism Association>. You can write to Mr. Kirby at <dkirby@nyc.rr.com>.

Does mercury in vaccines cause autism in children? A definitive answer has so far proven elusive. No one can say with certainty that thimerosal, the vaccine preservative made with 49.6% mercury, helped fuel the explosion in cases of autism, attention deficit disorder, speech delay and other disorders over the past decade. But no one can say for certain that it did not.

On May 18, 2004, the respected Institute of Medicine issued a much heralded report stating that the bulk of evidence "favors rejection of a causal relationship" between thimerosal and autism.[i] The independent panel, commissioned by the government to investigate alleged links between vaccines and autism, delivered a harsh blow to advocates of the thimerosal-autism hypothesis. But despite its authoritative certainty, the report failed to close the books on this simmering medical controversy. Indeed, recently published animal and test tube studies provide compelling biological evidence of harm (though certainly not proof) from thimerosal containing vaccines.

Exactly five years ago, the federal government disclosed that most American children were being exposed to levels of mercury in vaccines above federal safety limits. Since then, officials moved to phase out mercury from childhood vaccines and to determine if thimerosal exposure in infants could cause autism and other neurological developmental disorders. To date, neither goal has been fully attained.

Thimerosal has been removed from most routine vaccinations given to American children. But it is still found in the majority of flu shots, which the U.S. government now recommends for pregnant women and children between six and 23 months of age.[ii] In 2004, the Centers for Disease Control and Prevention declined to state a preference for mercury-free flu shots in infants.[iii] Mercury is also found in tetanus, diphtheria-tetanus, pertusis and meningitis vaccines, which are sometimes, though not routinely, given to children. It is also still used in many over-the-counter products, including nasal sprays, ear and eye drops, anabolic steroids and even a hemorrhoid treatment.[iv]

Meanwhile, the CDC has been unable to definitively prove or disprove the theory that thimerosal causes autism, ADD, speech delays or other disorders. Several studies funded or conducted by the agency have been published in the past year, all of them suggesting that there is no connection between the preservative and the disorder. The CDC insists that it looked into the matter thoroughly and found "no evidence of harm" from thimerosal in vaccines.

But "no evidence of harm" is not the same as proof of safety. No evidence of harm is not a definitive answer; and this is a story that cries out for answers.

Why would a trusted health agency allow a known neurotoxin to be injected into the bloodstream of small babies—in amounts that exceed federal safety exposure levels for adults by up to 50 times per shot? It's a disturbing question, and there are no satisfying answers.

But a small group of parents, aided by a handful of scientists, physicians, politicians and legal activists, spent the past five years searching for answers. Despite heavy resistance from the powerful public health lobby, the parents never abandoned their ambition to prove that mercury in vaccines is what pushed their children, most of them boys, into a hellish, lost world of autism.

Of course, there are two sides to every good story, and this one is no exception. For every shred of evidence the parents and other researchers have unearthed linking thimerosal to autism, public health authorities have produced forceful data to the contrary.

The parents and their allies accuse public health officials and the pharmaceutical industry of negligence and incompetence, at best, and malfeasance and collusion at worst.

On the other hand, the mercury-autism proponents have been greeted with contempt and counterattack by many in the American health establishment, which understandably has an interest in proving the unpleasant theory wrong.

Each side accuses the other of being irrational, overzealous, blind to evidence they find inconvenient, and subject to professional, financial or emotional conflicts of interest that cloud their judgment. In some ways, both sides are right.

Some children with autism were never exposed to thimerosal, and the vast majority of people who received mercury in vaccines show no evidence of harm whatsoever. But if thimerosal is not responsible for the apparent autism epidemic in the United States, then it is incumbent upon public health officials to mount a full-scale quest to identify the actual cause. At the very least, the thimerosal debate has compelled the scientific community, however reluctantly, to consider an environmental component to the disorder, rather than looking for a purely genetic explanation. Autism, by most accounts, is epidemic. And there is no such thing as a genetic epidemic.

Something in our modern world is apparently pushing a certain number of susceptible kids over the neurological limit and into a befuddling life of autism and other brain disorders. Several potential culprits beside thimerosal have been mentioned, though there is no hard evidence to link any of them to autism. Possible environmental "triggers" include: mercury in fish, pesticides, PCB's, flame retardants, jet fuel, live viruses in vaccines or some as-yet unidentified virus, and even rampant cell phone use. It is plausible that any combination of the above, with or without thimerosal exposure added into the mix, might cause harm to some fetuses and infant children.

But so far, only thimerosal exposure has been studied to any significant degree in children (with the exception of the Measles-Mumps-Rubella vaccine, or MMR). This book looks at evidence presented on both sides of the thimerosal controversy, but told from the parents' admittedly subjective point of view. Perhaps this story will be told one day from the opposing view, from the doctors, bureaucrats and drug company reps who claim nothing more than the laudable desire to save kids from the ravages of childhood disease.

But many of the public health officials who discount the thimerosal theory were unwilling (or prohibited by superiors) to speak on the record for this book. Readers are invited to reach their own conclusions on the evidence.

Did the injection of organic mercury directly into the developing systems of small children cause irreparable harm? It's a plausible proposition, and a hugely important question. If the answer is affirmative, someone will have to pay to pick up the pieces.

Why did the CDC and the Food and Drug Administration allow mercury exposures from childhood vaccines to more than double between 1988 and 1992, without bothering to calculate cumulative totals and their potential risks?

Why, for that matter, was there a corresponding spike in reported cases of autism spectrum disorders? Why did autism grow from a relatively rare incidence of 1 in every 5,000 births in the 1980s, to 1-in-500 in the late 1990s. Why did it continue to increase to 1-in-250 in 2000, and then 1-in-166 today?[v] Why are rates of ADD, ADHD, speech delay and other childhood disorders also rising, and why does one in every six American children have a developmental disorder or behavioral problem?[vi] And why does autism affect boys at a 4-to-1 ratio over girls?[vii]

Autism traditionally has been a disease of industrialized nations, at least until recent years. But not all Western countries have autism epidemics. Autism spectrum disorder in the United States, with 60 per 10,000 (1-in-166) kids now affected, is much more prevalent than it is in northern European countries such as Denmark, which removed thimerosal from vaccines in 1992 and now reports just 7.7 per 10,000 children (or 1-in-1,300). The U.K., meanwhile, which just announced that it will remove mercury from vaccines in September, 2004, reports exactly the same prevalence of ASD–1 in 166 children—as the United States.[viii]

This is not an anti vaccine book. Childhood immunization was perhaps one of the greatest public health achievements of the 20th Century, and vaccines will continue to play a crucial role in our lives as we enter an uncertain age of emerging diseases and potential bioterrorism.

Some parents, fearing harmful effects, have been tempted not to vaccinate their children. Most people would agree that this is foolhardy and dangerous. Few of us are old enough to remember the great epidemics of influenza, pertussis, smallpox, polio, diphtheria and measles that once swept entire populations—until the advent of vaccines reduced those maladies to abstract, unthreatening concepts, at least in America. These diseases, all of them preventable, can kill children. When vaccination rates fall, disease rates rise.

Nor should this book be regarded as politically partisan in nature. Though some people in the book do launch harsh criticisms against the Bush Administration and Republican leaders in the Senate, two leading protagonists—from these parents' point of view—are among the most conservative members of Congress. Moreover, much of the story here took place under the Administration of President Bill Clinton.

Parental fear of vaccines has threatened the viability of the U.S. National Immunization Program. But if scientists prove that mercury in vaccines was at least partly to blame for much of the autism epidemic—and that the culprit has been largely (or one day entirely) removed—then confidence in childhood immunization should return to comfortable levels.

But most health officials insist that mercury in vaccines is harmless, even as warnings go off about the toxic effects on infants and fetuses from mercury in fish.

This mixed message is doing nothing to bolster faith in the immunization program.

Many vaccines come in multi-dose vials, which cannot be sold without a preservative, such as thimerosal. Because of its mercury content, thimerosal prevents bacterial and fungal contamination in vials that undergo repeated puncturing of the seal by needles. Thimerosal is not required for single-dose vials, nor is it found in live vaccine preparations, including MMR, which contains live organisms.

Thimerosal was marketed for vaccines the 1930s and remained the preservative of choice in the U.S. throughout the 20th century. Mercury-free solutions were developed, but never widely used. The reason is thought to be economic.

Developing alternative preservatives, and having them tested and approved by the FDA is a costly proposition. Switching to single dose vials, another alternative, is viable. But it is also expensive and more cumbersome for transportation and storage. Finally, thimerosal is often used in vaccine manufacturing itself, to preserve sterility in the lab. Since it was already in vaccines, it didn't make much sense to seek out an alternative. And at any rate, the FDA and CDC never said that thimerosal might be hazardous.

Curiously, the first case of autism was not recorded until the early 1940's, a few years after thimerosal was introduced in vaccines. It was described by psychiatrists Leo Kanner and Hans Asperger, who independently coined the terms "autism" and "autistic" respectively. The term comes from the Greek word for self, autos.

In the late 1940s, Austrian-born psychologist Bruno Bettelheim proposed that autistic children came from aloof mothering; they were by-products of women who could not or would not provide the warmth and emotional support needed for the normal development of a child. He labelled these women "refrigerator mothers," a term that stuck until the 1960s.

In 1964, Bernard Rimland, a psychologist and father of an autistic son, wrote a groundbreaking book called *Infantile Autism: The Syndrome and Its Implications for a Neural Theory of Behavior.* The book is widely credited with debunking the refrigerator mother theory, which today seems both laughable and insulting to many parents. The book helped convince the psychiatric community that autism was not an emotional problem at all, but rather a biological one.

In the 1980s, suspicions began to surface among some parents of autistic children that vaccines were somehow involved in the disorder. In 1985, Barbara Loe Fisher, co-founder of the National Vaccine Information Center, co-authored a book (with H. L. Coulter) called *A Shot in the Dark.* In the course of her research she found many children who developed autism after a reaction to the diphtheria-pertussis-tetanus (DTP) shot.

Vaccines continued to remain on autism's radar screen and were raised to new notoriety when a young English doctor named Andrew Wakefield said that the Measles-Mumps-Rubella (MMR) live-virus vaccine (which does not contain thimerosal) might be contributing to regressive autism in children.

Then in July, 1999, came the U.S. government announcement about mercury levels in childhood vaccines.

Now the stakes could not be higher. Perhaps billions of dollars in litigation is pending against drug companies involved in vaccine production. . . . . Meanwhile, the reputation of American public health is on the line.

The jury is still out on thimerosal, but deliberations are well under way. One side will emerge vindicated, and the other will earn eternal scorn in the medical history books.

In November, 2003, the father of an autistic boy in North Carolina, an anti-thimerosal activist and a believer, approached a well-known pediatrician after the doctor had delivered a lecture on the safety of vaccines in general, and thimerosal in particular.

"You know something doctor?" the father said. "If it turns out that you are right, then I will personally come down to your office and apologize to you with every fibre of my being."

"But if it turns out that you are wrong," he added, "then you are going to hell."

References

[i] Immunization Safety Review: Vaccines and Autism (2004), Executive Summary, Institute of Medicine, Committee on Immunization Safety, National Academies Press.

[ii] "Prevention and Control of Influenza: Recommendations of the Advisory Committee on Immunization Practices," Morbidity and Mortality Weekly Report, Centers for Disease Control and Prevention, May 28, 2004.

[iii] Ibid.

[iv] "Mercury in Drug and Biologic Products," U.S. Food and Drug Administration, Center for Evaluation and Research (CBER), August 5, 2003; updated March 30, 2004.

[v] Sources for 1 in 5000 figure: Only two autism prevalence studies were conducted in the U.S. in the 1980's: one showed a rate of 1 case per 10,000 children, and the other showed a rate of 3.3 per 10,000, (or 1 in 3,030). This typically has been averaged out to 2 per 10,000, (or 1 in 5000). Source for 1 in 500 figure: Marie Bristol, et al, "State of the Science in Autism: Report to the National Institutes of Health," Journal of Autism and Developmental Disorders, 1996, Vol. 26, No. 2, pp. 121-157. Source for 1 in 250: In 2002, the CDC conducted a prevalence study in Brick Township, NJ, showing a rate of 4 per 10,000 (or 1 in 250), CDC, National Vaccine Program Office, Vaccine Fact Sheet on Autism. Source for 1 in 166 figure: "Autism A.L.A.R.M." – U.S. Department of Health and Human Services, CDC, The Medical Home Initiatives and First Signs.

[vi] "Autism A.L.A.R.M." – U.S. Department of Health and Human Services, CDC, The Medical Home Initiatives and First Signs.

[vii] C. Gillberg C, M. Coleman "The Biology of the Autistic Syndromes - 2nd Edition, Mac Keith Press, 1992, Page 90. (SEE: Bernard et al, 2000).

[viii] Denmark source: "A Population-Based Study of Measles, Mumps, and Rubella Vaccinations and Autism," Madsen, et al, The New England Journal of Medicine, Vol. 347, No. 9 - November 7, 2002, pp. 1481. UK source: "MRC Review of Autism Research – Epidemiology and Causes," Medical Research Council, U.K., December, 2001.

Where do I begin when autism has been diagnosed?

CHAPTER 8

Advice for parents of young autistic children: spring (2004)

Contributing Author James B. Adams, Ph.D., (Arizona State University, Tempe, Arizona) is the father of a young girl with autism and has served for several years as the President of the Greater Phoenix Chapter of the Autism Society of America. He is also a Professor of Chemical and Materials Engineering at Arizona State University, where much of his research is focused on finding the biomedical causes of autism and effective treatments for it. His website is <www.eas.asu.edu/~autism>.

James B. Adams, Ph.D. suggests visiting his Autism Today website to learn about his other products and services: Visit <http://adams.autismtoday.com> today! (*Please note, don't put in the www.)*

Contributing Author Stephen M. Edelson, Ph.D., Experimental Psychology (Autism Research Institute, San Diego, California), has worked in the field of autism for 25 years. He is the Director of the Center for the Study of Autism in Salem, Oregon, which is affiliated with the Autism Research Institute in San Diego, CA. He is also on the Board of Directors of the Oregon chapter of the Autism Society of America and is on the Society's Professional Advisory Board. His main autism website is <www.autism.org>.

Stephen M. Edelson, Ph.D. suggests visiting his Autism Today website to learn about his other products and services: Visit <http://edelson.autismtoday.com> today! (*Please note, don't put in the www.)*

Temple Grandin, Ph.D., (Colorado State University, Fort Collins, Colorado) is an Associate Professor of Animal Science at Colorado State University and a person with autism. She is the author of *Emergence: Labeled Autistic* and *Thinking in Pictures,* and a designer of livestock handling facilities. Half of the cattle in North America are handled in facilities she has designed. She is a popular speaker at colleges and autism conferences. Her website is <www.grandin.com>.

Temple Grandin, Ph.D. suggests visiting her Autism Today website to learn about her other products and services: Visit <http://grandin.autismtoday.com> today! (*Please note, don't put in the www.)*

Bernard Rimland, Ph.D., is the director of the Autism Research Institute (ARI) in San Diego, which he founded in 1967, and the founder of the Autism Society of America, which he founded in 1965. He is also the co-founder of the Defeat Autism Now! (DAN!) Project, which is sponsored by ARI. Dr. Rimland is the author of the prize-winning book, Infantile Autism: The Syndrome and Its Implications for a Neural Theory of Behavior, which is credited with debunking the "mother-blaming" theories of autism prevalent in the 20th century. He is also the father of an autistic adult. His website is <www.AutismResearchInstitute.com>.

Bernard Rimland, Ph.D. suggests visiting his Autism Today website to learn about his other products and services: Visit <http://rimland.autismtoday.com> today! (*Please note, don't put in the www.)*

Introduction

This paper is geared toward parents of newly diagnosed autistic children and parents of young autistic children who are not acquainted with many of the basic issues of autism. Our discussion is based on a large body of scientific research. Because of limited time and space, detailed explanations and references are not included.

Although for some parents a diagnosis of autism offers the relief of a label for their child's symptoms, the diagnosis can also be devastating. Many parents can be overwhelmed by fear and grief for the loss of the future they had hoped for their child.

Joining parent support groups may help. However, these strong emotions also motivate parents to find effective help for their children. The diagnosis is important because it can open the doors to many services and help parents learn about treatments that have benefited similar children.

The most important point we want to make is that autistic individuals have the potential to grow and improve. Contrary to what you may hear from outmoded professionals or read in outmoded books, **autism is treatable.** It is important to find effective services, treatments and education for autistic children as soon as possible. The earlier these children receive appropriate treatment, the better their prognosis. Their progress though life will likely be slower than others, but they can still live happy and productive lives.

What is autism?

Autism is a developmental disability that typically involves delays and impairment in social skills, language and behavior. Autism is a spectrum disorder, meaning that it affects people differently. Some children may have speech, whereas others may have little or no speech. Less severe cases may be diagnosed with PDD or with Asperger's Syndrome. These children typically have normal speech, but they have many "autistic" social and behavioral problems.

Left untreated, many autistic children will not develop effective social skills and may not learn to talk or behave appropriately. Very few individuals recover completely from autism without any intervention. The good news is that there are a wide variety of treatment options that can be very helpful. Some treatments may lead to great improvement, whereas other treatments may have little or no effect. No treatment helps everyone. A variety of effective treatment options will be discussed below.

Onset of autism: early onset versus regression

Autism develops sometime during pregnancy and the first three years of life. Some parents report that their child seemed different at birth. These children are referred to as early-onset autism. Other parents report that their child seemed to develop normally and then had a major regression resulting in autism, usually around 12–24 months. These children are referred as late-onset or regressive autism. Some researchers argue that the regression is not real or the autism was simply unnoticed by the child's parents. However, many parents report that their children were completely normal (e.g., speech, behavior, social) until sometime between one and two years of age. The possible causative role of vaccinations, many of which were added to the vaccination schedule in the 1980s, is a matter of considerable controversy at present.

One recent study, conducted by the first author, compared 53 autistic children with 48 typical peers. The parents of the early-onset autism group reported a significant delay in reaching developmental milestones, including age of crawling (two-month delay), sitting up (two-month delay), walking (four to five month delay) and talking (11 month delay or more). Thus, there appeared to be a delay in gross motor skills as well as of talking. Many children with autism also need physical therapy. In contrast, the late-onset autism group reached developmental milestones at the same time as typical children.

Prior to 1990, approximately two-thirds of autistic children were autistic from birth and one-third regressed sometime after age one year. Starting in the 1980s, the trend has reversed—fewer than one-third are now autistic from birth and two-thirds become autistic in their second year. (See figure below.) The following results are based on the responses to ARI's E-2 checklist, which has been completed by thousands of autism families. These results suggest that something happened, such as increased exposure to an environmental insult, possibly vaccine damage, between ages one and two years.

Several brain autopsy studies have indicated that brain damage occurred sometime during the first trimester of pregnancy, but many of these studies involved individuals who were born prior to 1990. Thus, these findings may not apply to what appears to be the new population of regressive autism.

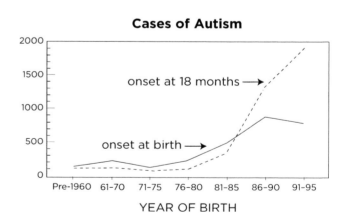

Cases of Autism

onset at 18 months →

onset at birth →

YEAR OF BIRTH

Pre-1960 61-70 71-75 76-80 81-85 86-90 91-95

Speech development

One of the most common questions parents ask is: "Will my child develop speech?"

An analysis of ARI's data involving 30,145 cases indicated that 9% never develop speech. Of those who develop speech, 43% begin to talk by the end of their first year, 35% begin to talk sometime between their first and second year, and 22% begin to talk in their third year and after. A smaller, more recent survey conducted by the first author found that only 12% were totally non-verbal by age five. So with appropriate interventions there is reason to hope that children with autism can learn to talk, at least to some extent.

There are several ways to help autistic children learn to talk, including:

- Teaching speech with sign language: It is easy for parents to learn a few simple signs and use them when talking to their child. This is referred to as "simultaneous communication" or "signed speech." Research suggests that the use of sign language increases the chance of children learning spoken language.

- Teaching with the Picture Exchange Communication System (PECS): This involves pointing to a set of pictures or symbols on a board. As with sign language, it can also be effective in teaching speech.

- Applied Behavior Analysis: This will be discussed further in this section.

- Encouraging child to sing with a videotape or audiotape.

- Vestibular stimulation, such as swinging on a swing, while teaching speech.

- Several nutritional/biomedical approaches have been associated with dramatic improvements in speech production including dimethylglycine (DMG), vitamin B6 with magnesium, and the gluten-/casein-free diet. This will be discussed further in this section.

Genetics of autism

Genetics appear to play an important role in causing some cases of autism. Several studies have shown that when one identical twin has autism, the co-twin often has autism. In contrast, when one fraternal twin has autism, the co-twin is rarely autistic. Studies trying to identify specific genes associated with autism have been inconclusive. Currently, it appears that 20 or more genes may be associated with autism. This is in contrast to other disorders, such as Fragile X or Rett's Syndrome, in which single genes have been identified.

A large number of studies have found that autistic individuals often have compromised immune systems. In fact, autism is sometimes described as an autoimmune system disorder. One working hypothesis of autism is that the child's immune system is compromised genetically and/or environmentally (e.g., exposure to chemicals). This may predispose the child to autism. Then, exposure to an (additional) environmental insult may lead to autism (e.g., the MMR vaccine) or mercury-containing vaccine preservatives (i.e., thimerosal).

If parents have a child with autism, there is an increased likelihood, estimated at 5% to 8%, that their future children will also develop autism. Many studies have identified cognitive disabilities, which sometimes go undetected, in siblings of autistic children. Siblings should be evaluated for possible developmental delays and learning disabilities, such as dyslexia.

Possible environmental causes of autism

Although genetics play an important role in autism, environmental factors are also involved. There is no general consensus on what those environmental factors are at this point in time. Since the word "autism" is only a label for people who have a certain set of symptoms, there are likely to be a number of factors that could cause those symptoms. Some of the suspected environmental causes for which there is some scientific evidence include:

- Childhood vaccinations: The increasing number of vaccines given to young children

89

might compromise their immune system. Many parents report their child was normal until vaccinations.

- MMR Vaccine: Evidence of measles virus has been detected in the gut, spinal fluid and blood. Also, the incidence of autism began rising significantly when the MMR was introduced in the U.S. (1978) and in the United Kingdom (1988).

- Thimerosal (a mercury-based preservative) in childhood vaccines: The number of vaccines given to children has risen over the last two decades, and most of those vaccines contained thimerosal, which is 50% mercury. The symptoms of mercury poisoning in children are very similar to the symptoms of autism.

- Excessive use of oral antibiotics: These can cause gut problems, such as yeast/bacterial overgrowth and prevents mercury excretion.

- Maternal exposure to mercury (e.g., consumption of seafood high in mercury, mercury dental fillings, thimerosal in RhoGam shots).

- Lack of essential minerals: Zinc, magnesium, iodine, lithium and potassium may be especially important.

- Pesticides and other environmental toxins may play roles.

- Other unknown environmental factors may play roles.

Prevalence of autism

There has been a rapid increase in the number of children diagnosed with autism. The most accurate statistics on the prevalence of autism come from California, which has an accurate and systematic centralized reporting system of all diagnoses of autism. The California data show that autism is rising rapidly, from 1 per 2,500 in 1970 to 1 per 285 in 1999. Similar results have been reported for other states by the U.S. Department of Education. Whereas autism once accounted for 3% of all developmental disabilities, in California

it now accounts for 45% of all new developmental disabilities. Other countries report similar increases.

We do not know why there has been a dramatic increase in autism over the past 15 years, but there are several reasonable hypotheses. Since there is more than one cause of autism, there may be more than one reason for the increase. A small portion of the increase of autism where speech is delayed may be due to improved diagnosis and awareness, but the report from California reveals that this only explains a minute part of the increase. However, the increase in the milder variant called Asperger's Syndrome may be due to increases in diagnosis. In Asperger's Syndrome, there is no significant speech delay, and early childhood behavior is much more normal. The major reason for the increase is certainly due to environmental factors, not genetics, since there is no such thing as a "genetic epidemic." Some *possible* environmental factors were discussed in the previous section, and an increased occurrence of one or several of those factors probably accounts for the rapid increase in autism.

Common co-occurring conditions in autism

Mental retardation

Although it has been estimated that up to 75% of people with autism have mental retardation, research studies have frequently used inappropriate IQ tests, such as verbal tests with non-verbal children and, in some cases, estimating the child's intelligence level without any objective evidence. Parents should request non-verbal intelligence tests that do not require language skills, such as the Test for Nonverbal Intelligence (TONI). Furthermore, regardless of the result, realize that autistic children will develop more skills as they grow older and that appropriate therapies and education can help them reach their true potential.

Seizures

It is estimated that 25% of autistic individuals also develop seizures, some in early childhood and others as they go through puberty. (Changes in hormone levels may trigger seizures.) These seizures can range from mild (e.g., gazing into space for a few seconds) to severe, grand mal seizures.

Many autistic individuals have subclinical seizures that are not easy to notice but can significantly affect mental function. A one- or two-hour EEG may not be able to detect any abnormal activity. So a 24-hour EEG may be necessary. Although drugs can be used to reduce seizure activity, the child's health must be checked regularly because these drugs can be harmful.

There is substantial evidence that certain nutritional supplements, especially vitamin B6 and dimethylglycine (DMG), can provide a safer and more effective alterative to drugs, for many individuals. (Write to the Autism Research Institute for publication P-16 for more information.)

Chronic constipation and/or diarrhea

An analysis of the ARI's autism database of thousands of cases show over 50% of autistic children have chronic constipation and/or diarrhea. Diarrhea may actually be due to constipation—i.e., only liquid is able to leak past a constipated stool mass in the intestine. Manual probing often fails to find an impaction. An endoscopy may be the only way to check for this problem. Consultation with a pediatric gastroenterologist is required.

Sleep problems

Many autistic individuals have sleep problems. Night waking may be due to reflux of stomach acid into the esophagus. Placing bricks under the legs at the head of the bed may help keep stomach acid from rising and provide better sleep. Melatonin has been very useful in helping many autistic individuals fall asleep. Other popular interventions include using 5-HTP and implementing a behavior modification program designed to induce sleep. Vigorous exercise will help a child sleep, and other sleep aids are a weighted blanket or tight fitting mummy-type sleeping bag.

Pica

Thirty percent of children with autism have moderate to severe pica. Pica refers to eating non-food items such as paint, sand, dirt, paper, etc. Pica can expose the child to heavy metal poisoning, especially if there is lead in the paint or in the soil.

Low muscle tone

A study conducted by the first author found that 30% of autistic children have moderate to severe loss of muscle tone, and this can limit their gross and fine motor skills. The study found that these children tend to have low potassium levels. Increased consumption of fruit may be helpful.

Sensory sensitivities

Many autistic children have unusual sensitivities to sounds, sights, touch, taste and smells. High-pitched intermittent sounds, such as fire alarms or school bells, may be painful to autistic children. Scratchy fabrics may also be intolerable, and some children have visual sensitivities. They are troubled by the flickering of fluorescent lights. If the child often has tantrums in large supermarkets, it is possible that he/she has severe sensory over-sensitivity. Sensory sensitivities are highly variable in autism, from mild to severe. In some children, the sensitivities are mostly auditory; in others, mostly visual. It is likely that many individuals who remain non-verbal have both auditory and visual processing problems, and sensory input may be scrambled. Even though a pure tone hearing test may imply normal hearing, the child may have difficulty hearing auditory details and hard consonant sounds.

Some children have very high pain thresholds (i.e., be insensitive to pain), whereas others have very low pain thresholds. Interventions designed to help normalize their senses, such as sensory integration, Auditory Integration Training (AIT) and Irlen lenses, will be discussed further in this section.

What is the difference between Asperger's Syndrome and Autism?

Asperger's Syndrome is usually considered a subtype of high functioning autism. Most of those with Asperger's Syndrome are described as "social but awkward." That is, they want to have friends but they do not have the social skills to begin and/or maintain a friendship. While high functioning autistic individuals may also be "social but awkward," they are typically less interested in having friends. In addition, high functioning autistic individuals are often delayed in developing speech/language. Those with Asperger's Syndrome tend not to have speech/language delays, but their speech is usually described as peculiar, such as being stilted and perseverating on unusual topics.

Medical testing and treatments

A small but growing number of physicians (many of them parents of autistic children) are involved in trying safe and innovative methods for treating the underlying biomedical basis of autism—the Defeat Autism Now! (DAN!) program. Parents and physicians can learn about this approach by attending DAN! conferences (audio and videotapes are also available), visiting the Autism Research Institute's website <www.AutismResearchInstitute.com> and studying the DAN! manual. The manual, entitled *Biomedical Assessment Options for Children with Autism and Related Problems*, provides a comprehensive discussion of laboratory tests and interventions. A listing of doctors who subscribe to the DAN! approach to autism can be found on the ARI website. A related description of medical testing and treatment is also available at <http://www.eas.asu.edu/~autism>.

Routine medical tests are usually performed by traditional pediatricians, but they rarely reveal problems in autism that can be treated. Genetic testing for Fragile X syndrome can help identify one possible cause, and this testing is typically recommended when there is mental retardation in the family history. Many physicians do not conduct extensive medical testing for autism, because they believe, incorrectly, that the only useful medical treatments are psychiatric medications to reduce seizures and behavioral problems.

Some of the major interventions suggested by DAN! practitioners include:

- Nutritional supplements, including certain vitamins, minerals, amino acids and essential fatty acids

- Special diets *totally* free of gluten (from wheat, barley, rye and possibly oats) and free of dairy (milk, ice-cream, yogurt, etc.)

- Testing for hidden food allergies and avoidance of allergenic foods

- Treatment of intestinal bacterial/yeast overgrowth

- Detoxification of heavy metals

Psychiatric medications

The various topics covered in this overview paper for parents of young autistic children represent, for the most part, a consensus of the views, based on research and personal experience, of all four authors. However, the authors differ in their opinions on the role psychoactive drugs should play. We will present you with the conflicting opinions, so that you can decide for yourself.

In summary, Dr. Grandin has a relatively accepting position on the use of psychiatric medications in autistic children. She feels that it is worthwhile to consider drugs as a viable and useful treatment. Dr. Rimland and Dr. Edelson, on the other hand, are strongly opposed to the use of drugs except as a possible last resort. They feel the risks are great and consistently outweigh the benefits. Dr. Adams has an intermediate view.

Dr. Grandin

There are no psychiatric medications for "autism," but there are many psychiatric medications used for treating specific symptoms often found in autism, such as aggression, self-injury, anxiety, depression, obsessive/compulsive disorders and ADHD. These medications generally function by altering the level of neurotransmitters (chemical messengers) in the brain. There is no medical test to determine if a particular medication is called for; the decision is based on the psychiatrist's evaluation of the patient's symptoms. This is a "trial and error" approach, as dosages need to be adjusted to suit each person, and one medication may be ineffective or have negative effects while others are helpful.

For some classes of drugs the doses that successfully reduce symptoms such as aggression or anxiety are much lower for those with autism than for normal people. For the SSRI drugs, such as Prozac (Fluoxetine), Zoloft (Sertraline), and other and other antidepressants, the best dose may be only one-third of the normal starting dose. Too high a dose may cause agitation or insomnia. If agitation occurs, the dose must be lowered. The low dose principle also applies to all drugs in the atypical or third-generation antipsychotic drug class, such as Risperdal (Risperidone). The effective dose will vary greatly between individuals. Start low and use the lowest effective dose. Other classes of drug, such as anticonvulsants, will usually require the same doses that are effective in normal individuals.

Psychiatric medications are widely used to treat the symptoms of autism, and they can be beneficial to many older children and adults. However, there are concerns over their use. There is relatively little research on their use for children with autism. There are almost no studies on the long-term effects of their use, especially for the newer medications, and there is a concern that their long-term use in children may affect their development. They treat the symptoms but not the underlying biomedical causes of autism. One must balance risk and benefit. A drug should have an obvious positive effect to make it worth the risk. In order to observe the effect of a drug, do not start a drug at the same time as you start some other treatment.

Drs. Rimland and Edelson

The Defeat Autism Now! (DAN!) approach to autism described above was developed by a group of advanced physicians and scientists (including a number of parents of autistic children) because the treatments offered as standard practice by traditional pediatricians, child psychiatrists and child neurologists is far from satisfactory. For the most part, traditional, non-DAN! doctors rely on psychoactive drugs, such as Ritalin, Risperdal and Prozac. None of these drugs are approved by the FDA for autistic children and, like all drugs, may have serious side effects, including death. DAN! doctors rarely use drugs, relying instead primarily on nutritional supplements—safe substances that the human body routinely depends upon to keep the brain and body functioning smoothly and safely.

The Autism Research Institute has collected data from many thousands of parents about their experiences with psychiatric medications and other treatments. In general, parents report that the medications are about equally likely to cause problems or to help, with some being worse than others. This is in contrast to other treatments for which the ARI has collected data, such as nutritional supplements, special diets and heavy metal detoxification, which were more likely to help and very rarely caused problems. The results of this ongoing collection of parent survey data is available at <www.AutismResearchInstitute.com>.

Here are the parent ratings of the three of the most often used drugs and the three of the most often used nutrients:

Three most used drugs	Got Worse	No Effect	Got Better	Better: Worse	No. of Cases
Ritalin	45%	26%	29%	0.7:1	3650
Benedryl	24%	51%	25%	1.1:1	2573
Risperidal	19%	28%	53%	2.8:1	401

Three most used vitamins	Got Worse	No Effect	Got Better	Better: Worse	No. of Cases
Vit. B6 & Mag.	4%	49%	46%	10:1	5284
DMG	7%	51%	42%	5.7:1	4725
Vit. C	2%	58%	39%	16:1	1408

Note: These data pertain only to *behavioral* effects. The drugs, but not the vitamins, often cause significant *physical* problems.

We feel that psychoactive drugs should not be used at all on your children and should be used only as a last resort, not as an initial treatment, on autistic teenagers and adults. ARI has collected information from parents of autistic children on their evaluation of various treatments, including drugs, since 1967.

Some adolescents and adults are helped by antipsychotic drugs, such as Risperdal, or antidepressants, such as Tofranil, but the risk of side effects is significant. Drugs should be the last resort, not the first choice. When psychoactive drugs are used with autistic teenagers or adults, it is often found that a very low dose, perhaps one-fourth or one-fifth of the normal dose, is sufficient.

Dr. Adams

Psychiatric medications are not well tested in young children with autism, especially for long-term use, and often have significant side effects. DAN! approaches (nutritional support, diet changes, detoxification) are significantly safer and address core problems rather than symptoms. So, I think DAN! approaches should be tried first, especially in young children. However, there are some children and adults who have benefited from psychiatric medications. So these types of medications are reasonable options to consider after DAN! approaches have been tried. In young children, they should be used only very cautiously, and beginning with low doses.

Educational/behavioral approaches

Educational/behavioral therapies are often effective in children with autism, with Applied Behavioral Analysis (ABA) usually being the most effective. These methods can and should be used together with biomedical interventions, as together they offer the best chance for improvement.

Parents, siblings and friends may play an important role in assisting the development of children with autism. Typical preschool children learn primarily by play, and the importance of play in teaching language and social skills cannot be overemphasized. Ideally, many of the techniques used in Applied Behavior Analysis, sensory integration and other therapies can be extended throughout the day by family and friends.

Applied Behavior Analysis

Many different behavioral interventions have been developed for children with autism, and most of them fall under the category of Applied Behavioral Analysis (ABA). This approach generally involves therapists who work intensely, one-on-one with a child for 20 to 40 hours/week. Children are taught skills in a simple step-by-step manner, such as teaching colors one at a time. The sessions usually begin with formal, structured drills, such as learning to point to a color when its name is given. After some time, there is a shift towards generalizing skills to other situations and environments.

A study published by Dr. Ivar Lovaas at UCLA in 1987 involved two years of intensive, 40 hour/week behavioral interventions by trained graduate students working with 19 autistic children ranging from 35 to 41 months of age. Almost half of the children improved so much that they were indistinguishable

from typical children, and these children went on to lead fairly normal lives. Of the other half, most had significant improvements, but a few did not improve much.

ABA programs are most effective when started early, (before age five years), but they can also be helpful to older children. They are especially effective in teaching non-verbal children how to talk.

There is general agreement that:

- Behavioral interventions involving one-on-one interactions are usually beneficial, sometimes with very positive results.

- The interventions are most beneficial with the youngest children, but older children can benefit.

- The interventions should involve a substantial amount of time each week, between 20–40 hours, depending on whether the child is in school.

- Prompting should be used as much as necessary to achieve a high level of success, with a gradual fading of prompts.

- Proper training of therapists and ongoing supervision is beneficial.

- Regular team meetings should be held to maintain consistency between therapists and check for problems.

- Most important, keeping the sessions fun for the children is necessary to maintain their interest and motivation.

Parents are encouraged to obtain training in ABA, so that they provide it themselves and possibly hire other people to assist. Qualified behavior consultants are often available, and there are often workshops on how to provide ABA therapy.

Sensory integration

Many autistic individuals have sensory problems, which can range from mild to severe. These problems involve either hypersensitivity or hyposensitivity to stimulation. Sensory integration focuses primarily on three senses—vestibular (i.e., motion, balance), tactile (i.e., touch), and proprioception (e.g., joints, ligaments). Many techniques are used to stimulate these senses in order to normalize them.

Speech therapy

This may be beneficial to many autistic children, but often only 1–2 hours/week are available. So it probably has only modest benefit unless integrated with other home and school programs. As mentioned earlier, sign language and PECS may also be very helpful in developing speech. Speech therapists should work on helping the child hear hard consonant sounds such as the "c" in cup. It is often helpful if the therapist stretches out and enunciates the consonant sounds.

Occupational therapy

This can be beneficial for the sensory needs of these children, who often have hyposensitivities and/or hypersensitivities to sound, sight, smell, touch and taste. This may include sensory integration.

Physical therapy

Often children with autism have limited gross and fine motor skills. So physical therapy can be helpful. This may also include sensory integration.

Auditory interventions

There are several types of auditory interventions. One with significant scientific backing is Berard Auditory Integration Training (called Berard AIT or AIT), which involves listening to processed music for a total of 10 hours (two half-hour sessions per day, over a period of 10–12 days). Many studies support its effectiveness. Research has shown that AIT improves auditory processing, decreases or eliminates sound sensitivity, and reduces behavioral problems in some autistic children.

Other auditory interventions include the Tomatis approach, the Listening Program and the SAMONAS method. Some empirical evidence supports their efficacy. Information about these programs can be obtained from the Society for Auditory Intervention Techniques' website <www.sait.org>.

Computer-based auditory interventions have also received some empirical support. They include Earobics <www.cogconcepts.com> and Fast ForWord <www.fastforword.com>. These programs have been shown to help children who have delays in language and have difficulty discriminating between speech sounds. Earobics is much less expensive (less than $100) and appears to be less powerful than the Fast ForWord program (usually over $1,000). Some families use the Earobics program first and then later use Fast ForWord.

Computer software

There are many educational programs available for typical children, and some of those may be of benefit for autistic children. There is also some computer software designed specifically for children with developmental disabilities. One major provider is Laureate <www.llsys.com>.

Vision training

Many autistic individuals have difficulty attending to their visual environment and/or perceiving themselves in relation to their surroundings. These problems have been associated with a short attention span, being easily distracted, excessive eye movements, difficulty scanning or tracking movements, inability to catch a ball, being cautious when walking up or down stairs, bumping into furniture, and even toe walking. A one- to two-year vision training program involving ambient prism lenses and performing visual-motor exercises can reduce or eliminate many of these problems. Visit <www.AutisticVision.com>. More information on vision training can be found on Internet website of the College of Optometrists in Vision Development <www.pavevision.org>.

Irlen lenses

Another visual/perceptual program involves wearing Irlen lenses. Irlen lenses are colored (tinted) lenses. Individuals who benefit from these lenses are often hypersensitive to florescent lights, bright sunlight or other types of light, or certain colors or color contrasts, and/or have difficulty reading printed text. Irlen lenses can reduce sensitivity to these lighting and color problems as well as improve reading skills and increase attention span. See <www.Irlen.com>.

Relationship Development Intervention (RDI)

This is a new method for teaching children how to

develop relationships, first with their parents and later with their peers. It directly addresses a core issue in autism, namely the development of social skills and friendships. Visit <www.connectionscenter.com>.

Preparing for the future
Temple Grandin

As a person with autism I want to emphasize the importance of developing the child's talents. Skills are often uneven in autism, and a child may be good at one thing and poor at another. I had talents in drawing, and these talents later developed into a career in designing cattle handling systems for major beef companies. Too often, there is too much emphasis on the deficits and not enough emphasis on the talents. Abilities in children with autism will vary greatly, and many individuals will function at a lower level than me. However, developing talents and improving skills will benefit all. If a child fixates on trains, use the great motivation of that fixation to motivate learning other skills. For example, use a book about trains to teach reading, use calculating the speed of a train to teach math and encourage an interest in history by studying the history of the railroads.

Developing friendships

Although young children with autism may seem to prefer to be by themselves, one of the most important issues for older children and adults is the development of friendships with peers. It can take a great deal of time and effort for them to develop the social skills needed to be able to interact successfully with other children, but it is important to start early. In addition, bullying in middle and high school can be a major problem for students with autism. The development of friendships is one of the best ways to prevent this problem.

Friendships can be encouraged informally by inviting other children to the home to play. In school, recess can be a valuable time for teachers to encourage play with other children. Furthermore, time can be set aside in school for formal "play time" between children with autism and volunteer peers—typical children usually think that play time

is much more fun than regular school, and it can help develop lasting friendships. This is probably one of the most important issues to include in a student's Individualized Education Program (IEP, or education plan for the child). Children with autism often develop friendships through shared interests, such as computers, school clubs, model airplanes, etc. Encourage activities that the autistic individual can share with others.

State services

Most states will provide some services for children with autism, primarily funded by the federal Medicaid program. Many states have waiting lists for a limited number of slots. The quality of services varies widely state to state. Most states have one set of services for children under three years old (early intervention) and a second set of services for older children and adults.

State services for developmental disabilities

Typical state services for people with autism include respite, habilitation, speech therapy and occupational therapy. To qualify for services, children or adults must be diagnosed with autism (not PDD or Asperger's Syndrome, which do not qualify) by a licensed psychiatrist or psychologist with training in childhood development. Furthermore, the applicant must meet three of seven functional limitations:

- Self-care
- Receptive and expressive language
- Learning
- Mobility
- Self-direction
- Capacity for independent living
- Economic self-sufficiency

Contact your local ASA chapter to obtain more information about the developmental disabilities services in your community.

Once a child is determined to be eligible, he/she may be awarded service hours. Many states have waiting lists for services, but some states provide services to everyone who qualifies. It is then up to the parent to choose a provider agency for each type of service. Speech therapists, occupational therapists and physical therapists are in high demand, and the state pays only modest rates. Thus, it can be a challenge to find them. Similarly, it can be very challenging to find respite and habilitation providers (for an ABA program), and an even greater challenge to train and retain them. Often parents need to advertise for therapists and then bring them to a provider agency for hiring. Often parents need to hire behavior consultants to train their habilitation (ABA) workers; this is very important and highly recommended if the parents can afford it.

School programs

For children younger than three years old, there are early intervention programs. For children over three years of age, preschool and school programs are available. Parents should contact the local school district for information about local programs. In some cases a separate program for special needs children may be best, but for higher-functioning children integration into a regular school setting may be more appropriate, provided that there is enough support (a part or full-time aide, or other accommodations as needed). It is important that parents work with their child's teacher on an Individual Education Plan (IEP), which outlines in great detail the child's educational program. Additionally, meeting with the child's classmates and/or their parents can be helpful in encouraging other students to interact positively with the autistic child.

In some states, home therapy programs (such as ABA and speech therapy) may be funded by the school district, rather than through the state. However, it may take considerable effort to convince the school district to provide those services. Check with your local ASA chapter and other parents about how services are usually provided in your state.

Social Security assistance

Families with limited incomes (under about $25,000–$35,000/yr., depending on family size and assets) can apply to the Social Security agency to obtain monies to help children with a disability. For more information,

contact your local social security office by calling 1-800-772-1213.

Special needs trusts

Children who have assets over approximately $2,000 are ineligible to receive state and federal services. They must spend their money first. However, most states allow "special needs trusts" to be set up for children with disabilities. These are irrevocable trusts in which a guardian decides how to spend the money on the child. They are the best way for relatives to leave funds to the child, because these monies do not count against the child when determining their eligibility for government services.

For more information, contact a lawyer who specializes in special needs trusts. In addition to working out the financial details, it is very useful to write up a description of suggestions of how you want your child cared for and/or supported. MetLife also has a special program for children with developmental disabilities.

Long-term prognosis

Today, most adults with autism are either living at home with their parents or living in a group home. Some higher-functioning people live in a supported-living situation, with modest assistance, and a very few are able to live independently. Some are able to work, either in volunteer work, sheltered workshops or private employment, but many do not. Adults with PDD/NOS and Asperger's Syndrome generally are more likely to live independently and are more likely to work. Unfortunately, they often have difficulty finding and then maintaining a job. The major reason for chronic unemployment is not a lack of job skills but rather their limited social skills. Thus, it is important to encourage appropriate social skills early on, so they are able to live and work independently as much as possible.

Some of the most successful people on the autism spectrum who have good jobs have developed expertise in a specialized skill that often people value. If a person makes himself or herself very good at something, this can help make up for some difficulties with social skills. Good fields for higher functioning people on the spectrum are architectural drafting, computer programming, language translator, special educator, librarian and scientist. It is likely that some brilliant scientists and musicians have a mild form of Asperger's Syndrome (Ledgin, 2002). The individuals who are most successful often have mentor teachers either in high school, college or at a place of employment. Mentors can help channel interests into careers. Untreated sensory oversensitivity can severely limit a person's ability to tolerate a workplace environment. Eliminating fluorescent lights will often help, but untreated sound sensitivity has caused some individuals on the spectrum to quit good jobs because ringing telephones hurt their ears. Sensory sensitivities can be reduced by auditory integration training, diets, Irlen lenses, conventional psychiatric medications and vitamin supplementation. Magnesium often helps hypersensitive hearing.

It should also be pointed out that the educational, therapy, and biomedical options available today are much better than in past decades, and they should be much better in the future. However, it is often up to parents to find those services, determine which are the most appropriate for their child, and ensure that they are properly implemented. Parents are a child's most powerful advocates and teachers. With the right mix of interventions, most children with autism will be able to improve. As we learn more, children with autism will have a better chance to lead happy and fulfilling lives.

National societies

Autism Research Institute

Directed by Bernard Rimland, a parent of an autistic adult and a leading advocate of research on autism. Publishes a quarterly newsletter summarizing current research on autism and maintains a website full of relevant information about autism. ARI also sponsors the Defeat Autism Now! approach to autism. DAN! conferences, held biannually, are the leading conferences on biomedical treatments for autism.
Visit <www.AutismResearchInstitute.com> or fax: 619-563-6840.

Autism Society of America

Publishes a newsletter, sends monthly e-mails, hosts a national meeting and maintains a good website. Most important, it is the major lobbying body for people with autism, including efforts to increase research on autism and educational opportunities and to generally improve the lives of people with autism. Parents should be encouraged to join and support the ASA.
Call 1-800-3-AUTISM
or visit <www.autism-society.org>.

Families for Early Autism Treatment (FEAT)

Provides valuable information regarding Applied Behavior Analysis. Visit <www.feat.org>.

Internet

There are hundreds of web sites and news sources to explore. An excellent newsletter starting point is the Schafer Autism Report (SAR). Visit <www.sarnet.org>.

Suggested reading

Books with an asterisk are available from the Autism Research Institute
(4182 Adams Ave.
San Diego, CA 92116
fax: 619-563-6840
<www.AutismResearchInstitute.com>)

* *Facing Autism* by Lynn Hamilton. This is one of the first books parents should read. It tells how one mother helped her child recover from autism and it gives a good overview of testing, treatments and resources.

* *Children with Starving Brains*, by Jacquelyn McCandless, MD. This is probably the best book on the medical conditions of people with autism and how to treat them. Available from <www.amazon.com>.

* *Biomedical Assessment Options for Children with Autism and Related Problems* by Jon Pangborn, Ph.D. and Sidney Baker, MD. Recommended series of tests and treatments for autistic individuals and those with related disorders. Available from the
Autism Research Institute
4182 Adams Ave.
San Diego, CA 92116
<www.AutismResearchInstitute.com>
fax: (619) 563-6840.

* *Biological Basis of Autism* by William Shaw, Ph.D.
Available from
Great Plains Laboratory
(913) 341-8949
<www.greatplainslaboratory.com>.
Covers many biological issues and treatments, including yeast/bacterial infections and casein-free/gluten free diets.

* *Let Me Hear Your Voice* by Catherine Maurice. A story of how one mother helped her autistic child with ABA.

* *Unraveling the Mystery of Autism & PDD: A Mother's Story of Research and Recovery* by Karyn Seroussi. Discusses one mothers successful search for interventions for her child, with a focus on wheat-free, dairy-free diets.

* *Special Diets for Special Kids,* by Lisa Lewis. Recipes for wheat-free, dairy-free foods.
Available from <www.autismndi.com>.

* *Emergence: Labeled Autistic* by Temple Grandin and Margaret M. Scariano (contributor).

* *Thinking in Pictures: And Other Reports from My Life With Autism* by Temple Grandin.

Relationship Development Intervention with Children, Adolescents and Adults by Steven E. Gutstein, Ph.D. and Rachelle K. Sheely. An excellent book on developing social skills.

Autism, Handle With Care by Gail Gillingham. This book deals with the sensory issues often seen in people with autism.

"Little Rainman" by Karen L. Simmons.

What to do next?

Take one or more of the following steps:

1. Attend one or more parent support groups: Parents can be a wonderful source of support and information. There are over 200 chapters of the Autism Society of America, over 70 chapters of FEAT, and other informal parent support groups. Consider joining at least one.

2. Contact your state's Developmental Disabilities program and apply for services. Be persistent.

3. Contact your local school district and ask about school programs. See what they have to offer.

4. Find a local physician, preferably one who is familiar with the Defeat Autism Now! Protocol, and plan a series of medical tests and treatments. Some physicians will be open to medical testing and biomedical treatments, but others will not—find one who is willing to help your child, as opposed to just monitoring the severity of your child's problems. Do not take your child to a physician who does not support you or respect your viewpoint.

5. Attend local and/or national autism conferences.

6. Make sure you still find some time for your other children and spouse/significant other. Having a child with autism can result in many challenges, and you need to be prepared for the long term.

7. Continue trying to learn all you can.

Good luck!

When parents first hear the diagnosis of autism . . .

Contributing Author Thomas McKean is an author and advocate currently living in Virginia. He wrote Soon Will Come the Light: A View From Inside the Autism Puzzle
Resources and links—Thomas A. McKean suggests visiting his Autism Today website to learn about his other products and services: Visit <http://mckean.autismtoday.com> today! (*Please note, don't put in the www.)*You can contact Mr. McKean at <Tmckean@aol.com>.

Introduction

When parents first hear the diagnosis of autism for their child, there is often fear and confusion. Fear from wondering what lies ahead, and confusion from not knowing the next steps to take to protect the child.

In the midst of grieving, there are four things you can do at first to be sure you are doing the right things later. These first four things will lead you in the direction you need to go to meet your own individual needs:

Go to the library

The first thing you need to do is get educated not only on what autism is, but also what it is NOT. For this, you will need to read. And read. And read some more.

But in your reading, be sure you do not make the mistake a lot of parents make. Be sure you check the copyright date on the books. Reading a book that is older may have information that, if acted on, could actually harm you or your child. Some books to start with:

- *A Parents Guide to Autism,* by Charles Hart
- *Thinking in Pictures,* by Temple Grandin
- *Autism Treatment Guide,* by Elizabeth Gerlach

Autism biographies can also provide valuable information that you won't find elsewhere.

Sensory integration therapy

Find an occupational therapist trained AND CERTIFIED in sensory integration technique, and have your child evaluated and treated. Autism is a neurological/sensory disorder and early intervention is crucial to the future of the child.

Find a local support group

Support Groups are great for parents. They can help parents learn more about autism and can recommend good doctors—something you will need. And they can help support you when you need to know you are not alone.

Attend a few conferences

Yes, they can be expensive—but here is where you will learn the latest in autism theory and treatment. And you can network with people who are going through the same thing you are.

Conclusion

This is something that you never wanted, never planned on, never knew very much about. But by following these first four steps, you will gain the knowledge and the courage you need to move forward and give your child the best quality of life possible.

Where do I begin if someone I know has been diagnosed with autism?

Contributing Author Daniel Hawthorne is a diagnosed High Functioning Autistic. He is the author of *Child of the Forest* and *Guidelines to Intervention in Autism*, and webmaster and author of the award winning site <www.autismguidelines.com>. He has degrees in Communication and Business Administration, most recently through the University of Arkansas. He does numerous speaking engagements to autism support groups and to special schools, in addition to managing an online resume posting business.

Resources and links—Daniel Hawthorne suggests visiting his Autism Today website to learn about his other products and services: Visit: <http://hawthorne.autismtoday.com> today! *(*Please note, don't put in the www.)* He enjoys corresponding with parents, teachers, and others in the autism community, and may be contacted at <daniel@autismguidelines.com>.

I would think that you should speak with the doctor who made the diagnosis and with people associated with autism support groups in the area to get their ideas and perspectives. This, I think, would provide a basis for a good general understanding about autism and specifically how being autistic can and does affect the person who has been diagnosed.

Then, whenever one is around that person, observe him. Let him show you what his needs and preferences are. See if these observations make sense in terms of what one has already learned about the typical physiological differences of an autistic individual. Also, keep in mind that every autistic person is different. Autism affects different people to a different extent and in different ways.

Whenever a person gets diagnosed, the perception of that person by others may change, not the person. If in the days and months following the diagnosis the autistic individual needs structure in his life and an absence of crowd noise, one can be sure that he needed them before being diagnosed.

The main problem with an autistic child is that the child often has difficulty expressing his or her needs. As a result, those around him or her may well have had no way of knowing that his or her needs were any different from theirs. The diagnosis does not cause the child to have special needs; it only reveals needs that were there all along. So, after the diagnosis is a time for gaining better understanding.

In addition, keep in mind that those with autism are individuals with their own sets of strengths and weaknesses. Such an individual may excel in such things as sorting and filing things, proofreading documents and caring for animals—but not be as good at such things as synthesizing information from lengthy Sociology reports.

The color of autism

Contributing Author Toni Flowers is an award-winning educator whose work with autistic children won her the Autism Society of America's coveted Teacher of the Year award in 1989.

Resources and links—Toni Flowers suggests visiting her Autism Today website to learn about her other products and services: Visit: <http://flowers.autismtoday.com> today! (*Please note, don't put in the www.*) You can write to Ms. Flowers at <tflowers@jcs.k12.in.is>.

My book, *THE COLOR OF AUTISM*, is the result of almost 20 years of teaching individuals with autism. It incorporates experiences that I learned in the classroom, as well as knowledge gained from numerous conferences, visits with friends with autism and the relationships that I have maintained with former students and their families.

Work in the field of autism is often slippery. Nevertheless, I would like to share a few constants that I have found over the years:

- There is not one way to teach, reach or live with a person with autism. It is an individual journey, and each person with autism needs individual goals.

- The educational journey of a person on the autism spectrum does not follow a printed map. The journey takes detours, and you need to follow these detours—sometimes following, sometimes leading, but never giving up.

- Your vision of the finish line will not be the same vision as the vision of the person with autism.

- You need to focus on the individual's ability, not the disability.

- Many things I have learned about autism are not universal; they are pertinent to one person's autism.

- Nothing is wasted on a person with autism. It is better to try something than to do nothing. You can step back and adjust later.

- I have found that the more I discover about autism, the more there is to learn. As I fill in the blanks, the canvas grows larger.

Open *THE COLOR OF AUTISM* and use what works. Tweak the suggestions. Refine them. Rework them. Learn to continually look beyond the autism and see the child's individual strengths and concerns, interests, personalities, hopes and dreams.

Respect people with autism as individuals and challenge them to do their best. You will not be disappointed.

THE COLOR OF AUTISM has nine chapters. Their titles are as follows:

- Chapter One—Challenges and Expectations . . . The child with autism can learn
- Chapter Two—So Many Words—So Little Time . . . Change your way of Communicating.
- Chapter Three—I Never Met a Person with Autism I Didn't Like . . . The Importance of Bonding.
- Chapter Four—The Classroom . . . Designing a Place to Learn.
- Chapter Five—Schedules . . . Making Sense of the School Day.
- Chapter Six—The Fine Art of Cueing.
- Chapter Seven—To Self Stim or Not to Self Stim.
- Chapter Eight—School and Beyond . . . Homework.
- Chapter Nine—Activities . . . The Daily Grind.

Each chapter offers true stories of my experiences with individuals with autism that capture the essence of that chapter.

Helping a parent cope emotionally with a child's autism diagnosis

CHAPTER 9

The difference between heaven and earth

(Originally published in the column Postcards from the Road Less Traveled,
Autism/Asperger's Digest, www.autismdigest.com, *May-June 2005)*

Contributing Author Ellen Notbohm—Author of *Ten Things Every Child with Autism Wishes You Knew*, winner of iParenting Media's Greatest Products of 2005 Award, and co-author with Veronica Zysk of *1001 Great Ideas for Teaching* and *Raising Children with Autism Spectrum Disorders*, winner of Learning Magazine's 2006 Teacher's Choice Award. She is a regular columnist for Autism Asperger's Digest and Children's Voice, and is a contributor to numerous magazines and websites. She is the mother of sons with autism and ADHD. Your thoughts and comments are welcome at <ellen@thirdvariation.com>.

Resources and links—Ellen Notbohm suggests visiting her Autism Today website to learn about her other products and services: Visit <http://notbohm.autismtoday.com> today! *(*Please note, don't put in the www.)*

"The difference between heaven and earth is not so much altitude but attitude."

Ken Keys Jr, *The Power of Unconditional Love*

Mother's Day and Father's Day aren't big events in our house. My husband years ago declared himself allergic to Hallmark-induced holidays. It's enough for me to be a mother on Mother's Day. Although the challenges of raising atypical children can seem staggering, it has been my privilege to have them as mine and to love them unconditionally. It has taught me profound lessons about how excruciating it can be to keep that kind of love in the crosshairs at all times. You too? Rising above and firmly pushing aside our own fears, disappointments, expectations and lost dreams can seem like a mission of overwhelming enormity. Your child's limitations become your limitations—the places you can't take him, the social settings he can't handle, the people he can't relate to, the food he won't eat. Yeah, it can be a long list.

It takes great courage to admit that you are scared, feel cheated, heartsick, depleted. Wanting out of that matrix and not knowing how to start. Here's how you start: by knowing you can do this. It's already in you.

In the beginning, as I contemplated what Bryce and my family's lives would be like with autism in our midst, I could not deny the fact that *it could be so much worse*. All around me were people who had confronted just that. Close friends had lost their precious two-year-old daughter to a heart defect. It was a life-shattering event and it was much, much worse than anything autism ever threw at me and my family.

Bryce taught me that happiness does not come from getting what you want, but from wanting what you already have. It is the greatest gift I have ever been given. A friend once asked me: But how do you get there? What do you think is the secret of your success?

It's no secret. It is just this: as much as possible, accept your situation *without bitterness*. Play the cards you drew with grace and optimism. Bitterness can be a formidable foe; overcoming it can be a daily exercise. Some of us make it; some of us don't.

I once spent some time with a father whose mantra was, "Because of autism, I can't have a relationship with my son. How do you think I feel knowing that he'll probably end up in prison?" I talked and reasoned and pleaded away the afternoon begging him to see that he was setting up a self-fulfilling prophecy. Couldn't he take one baby step out, imagining a different outcome for his belligerent but very bright child—10 minutes of floor time, coming to school once a month, finding a restaurant only the two of them liked? I think he loved his son but to the child it no doubt felt conditional, dependent upon a certain kind of behavior, even if there were organic reasons why he could not comply. In the end, they both lost out. This dad could not move beyond his bitterness and grief. Grief is real. But getting stuck in that grief—that is the true tragedy, not the fact that your child has autism.

Directing the focus of autism's difficulties away from yourself and walking with your child in his shoes will liberate both of you. For me, understanding sensory integration propelled me out of my own fears. I was horrified by the knowledge of what Bryce was living with: his prison of environmental hostility, having no "normal" basis of comparison, never knowing that life can be something other than a bombardment of unpleasant sensations. He was very young, without life experience and without means of communicating his misery. I could not turn away from the raw truth, which was this: if I do not swallow my own anguish and be the one to step up for him, who will?

For some cosmic, not-to-be-understood reason, I was blessed with the serenity to bypass the denial and the anger and the self-pity that frequently come unbidden and unwelcome when we learn our child has a disability. But that is not to say that I don't endure my own bouts with melancholy. I never, ever fail to be deeply hurt by what I call the "Knife to the Heart" moments. These are the times when the rest of the world seems intent on letting you know that your child is different and apart. Usually there's no conscious malice; it just happens because the "typical" population is steaming about their business in "typical" fashion that doesn't or can't include your child. The offhand child-cruel remark, the birthday party that everyone else is invited to, the snubs on the bus, the questions he asks you as he begins to figure out that he is different. I always thought that if I endured enough of these moments, I would develop scar tissue or the ability to laugh them off. I haven't. But as both my boys move with increasing grace toward maturity and independence, these moments become fewer, more time passes between them and they become more fleeting. The power I allowed them to have over me has weakened over the years.

Unconditional love requires that you work hard to look beyond what seems like limitations in your child and find the gifts autism has given him. Your daughter doesn't share your passion for skiing, but you can still have fun even if it's just moving the snow from one place to another—like the folks who masterminded the pyramids. Your son won't play the family piano, but his fascination with plumbing is going to save you thousands of dollars!

Loving Bryce unconditionally required making peace with our reduced social opportunities, with the fact that he didn't seem to want conventional friendships, play dates and sleepovers, wasn't interested in the usual after school activities like soccer or choir. Curiously, I can't say I "missed" these things because he plainly was happy. Our psychologist had once told me, "All children, all people, unfold in their own time. This may just not be his time. His time will come."

And I was determined to let him unfold in his own time. Those times did come as he grew older and played Little League, swam on a swim team, became a rather accomplished actor in community theater, enjoyed Cub Scout activities, read Harry Potter— several years behind the "typical" timeline, but just as successfully.

Every day of Bryce's life I have told him that he is the best kid who ever lived, that I am the luckiest mommy who ever lived, that he is great just the way he is. In the beginning, I believed it enough to start saying it, but as time went on a wonderful thing happened. I came to believe it body and soul. More importantly, he came to believe it. And because he believes it, he has grown into a young man with remarkable aplomb, self-confidence, empathy and work ethic—not necessarily the typical hallmarks of autism. He has marvellous self-esteem; he likes himself and is comfortable with who he is. It was contagious. I began to actively look for things about him to articulate: I told him I was proud of how readily he shared treats and privileges with others, how I admired his devotion to his school work, how much I enjoyed the clever associations he made as he pulled minute details out of movies and related them to his real life. How much I could trust him because he never lied, how nicely he took care of himself with healthy food choices and good hygiene.

Think of it as affirmative brainwashing—the more you tell your child he's the greatest, the more both of you are going to believe it.

If you can get to a place where you believe, accept and put true unconditional love into practice, you will find yourself infused with an incredible energy on behalf of your child. It's that powerful. Without it, you are going to be running this race with a fairly nasty pebble in your shoe. It may be a $100 shoe, but that pebble will ensure that your focus is on the ever more painful wound to your extremity rather than on the span of the road ahead or the beauty of your surroundings. It's a pretty simple choice: let the irritant remain until it cripples you or remove it and head for the horizon.

I actually did get a pretty groovy Mother's Day gift last year, a DVD of my all-time favorite movie, *The Wizard of Oz*. Of course, the lesson of this film is unmistakable. The Scarecrow, Tin Man and Lion had the brains, heart and courage they yearned for all along. So do you. Click your heels together three times and believe it.

Helping a parent cope with a child's diagnosis of autism

(The terms "parent" and "spouse" are used in this chapter for the sake of simplicity. Their use is not meant to exclude single parents, caretakers, guardians, or significant others and partners.)

Contributing Author Karen Siff Exkorn is a consultant who works with families of newly diagnosed children with autism. She is the author of *The Autism Sourcebook: Everything You Need to Know—From a Mother Whose Child Recovered,* published by ReganBooks/HarperCollins in October 2005 with a Foreword by Dr. Fred Volkmar, of the Yale Child Study Center.

Resources and links—Karen Siff Exkorn, BA., MA suggests visiting her Autism Today website to learn about her other products and services: Visit <http://exkorn.autismtoday.com> today! (*Please note, don't put in the www.)*

Every 20 minutes, a parent in the United States hears the words: "Your child has autism."

Over 48 million parents all over the world have heard these words.

I was one of those parents.

When your child is first diagnosed, you receive a lot of expert advice about which treatments to choose and how to exercise your legal rights to obtain those treatments—all crucial elements in helping to support your child. But what the experts don't tell you is how to support yourself. Because at the time your child is diagnosed, you're not even thinking about yourself. If you're like most parents, all of your focus and energy is going into helping your child and his or her needs, with little left over for you, your marriage, and your friendships.

The emotional impact of a diagnosis of autism can be devastating. It can be a shock even for parents who suspected there was something wrong with their child in the first place. Our son Jake had some of the classic signs of autism. He reached all of the developmental milestones by age 17 months—he was a happy, healthy, talkative toddler—before we began to notice a decline in his development. Over a period of months, our energetic and vibrant son became a lethargic, disconnected little boy. By age two, Jake stopped speaking entirely. He stopped responding to his name, pointing to objects and relating even to us, his parents. During the months leading up to Jake's second birthday, I argued with our pediatrician that

something wasn't right with our son. He regularly reassured me that Jake was fine. "Boys develop later than girls," he'd say, reminding me that I was a typical first-time mother who worried too much.

When I finally took Jake to another doctor, I thought I'd be relieved to learn that there was a name for Jake's condition. I wasn't.

When the doctor told me that Jake had autism, I did what many parents do. I cried for a while and then discovered the door that opened into the world of denial—a lovely place where I didn't have to feel the deep hurt that I'd experienced upon hearing the news of the diagnosis. But my visit was short-lived and after a week I surfaced, only to find myself plummeting into worlds of anger and then depression that lasted for months. The emotional roller coaster also included other strong feelings often connected to the stages of grieving. It was a long road to reach that last stage of acceptance.

All parents experience and express a range of emotions in response to a child's diagnosis. Because individuals process their feelings in their own ways and in their own time, one parent may remain in the denial stage while the other is struggling with depression. Both parents may get stuck in the anger stage. Coping with a spouse's feelings in addition to your own is not easy. On top of this, the balance in the relationship may change. If one parent chooses to devote all of his or her time to the child with autism, resentment can build on the part of both spouses.

Some parents report that they become so involved with their child's life that they lose sight of themselves as individuals.

Keeping a marriage healthy during this time can be a challenge. In addition to the usual day-to-day issues that most married couples face, parents of children with autism find themselves dealing with situations that most parents of typically developing children don't have to deal with—like deciding which treatments are right for a child and determining a child's special education plan. In an attempt to make the right decisions, parents often lose sight of the fact that they are partners on the same team.

If you find yourself still trying to sort out your feelings about your child's diagnosis and the impact of the diagnosis on the rest of your life, you're not alone. Don't lose hope. There are effective techniques to help keep both your marriage and yourself together. In fact, there are ways to create an even stronger bond with your partner and reach a stronger place within yourself.

Through my own experience and through consulting with families of newly diagnosed children with autism, I've learned the following invaluable lessons on how to cope with a child's diagnosis of autism and issues surrounding the diagnosis.

Allow yourself to have your feelings

The beginning is the hardest part. Processing the diagnosis, deciding which treatments to choose and adjusting to your new life can seem overwhelming. The worst thing that you can do is to hold in your feelings. Allow yourself to grieve. Honor your feelings—don't judge them. People sometimes have this mistaken idea that crying or expressing sadness is a sign of weakness. If you don't allow your feelings to come out, they will remain inside and fester. Anger turned inward can lead to depression. Unexpressed emotions can lead to stress-related physical and psychological ailments. To avoid this, you need to find a way to get your feelings out in a constructive manner. Screaming at your spouse or other children is not constructive; venting your feelings in a therapy session is. Express your feelings in a journal and talk to a friend and/or a therapist.

Don't isolate

Many parents feel that no one can really understand what they're going through and, as a result, shut themselves off from family and friends. As much as a child's diagnosis is a deeply personal experience, it's not healthy to try to handle it all by yourself. Share your feelings with someone—your spouse, best friend or a therapist. Sometimes parents find that it's easier to self-disclose to a group of strangers who are going through a similar experience and choose to participate in either live or on-line autism support groups. Do whatever you feel is best for you, but make sure to share your feelings with someone.

Respect your spouses' emotional response— mothers and fathers have different reactions to their child's diagnosis of autism

Studies show that mothers respond with more depression and guilt to a child's diagnosis than fathers (Gray 2003). Mothers may become consumed with "shoulds," such as "I should have eaten a healthier diet during my pregnancy," or "I should have noticed my child's symptoms earlier." There is considerable evidence that mothers experience the impact of a child's diagnosis far more than fathers (Sharpley, Bitsika and Efremidis 1997; Seltzer 2001). Mothers also seem to be more open to venting their feelings, while fathers have a tendency to suppress their emotions. As you can imagine, all of this can create enormous stress in a marriage. And while it might be tempting to yell at your spouse for expressing feelings too much or not at all, it is not productive.

To open the lines of communication between you and your partner, psychologists recommend a technique known as "active listening." Active listening involves staying in the moment and listening with no agenda. Instead of formulating your own thoughts or arguments while the other person is speaking, active listening involves focusing on what the other person is saying so that they feel genuinely heard. Don't attack your partner or fall into the blame game. Sometimes, it's helpful to take the other person's point of view.

For example, think about why your spouse might be feeling a certain way. Is his or her denial a self-protection mechanism? Is his or her venting a way to assuage guilt? By taking the other person's perspective, you can be more understanding and compassionate and less resentful. The technique of active listening requires effort, but the payoff can be tremendous. It can help you establish a respectful and loving partnership with your spouse.

Make time for your marriage

Maintaining a strong and solid marriage is not always easy, especially when you have a child with a developmental disorder such as autism. It's up to you to make a conscious effort to work on your relationship, and that includes setting aside time to be with your spouse. Hire a babysitter or enlist the help of a friend or relative to watch your child so that you and your spouse can spend an afternoon or evening together. Go for a walk or out to the movies. It's important to reconnect with your spouse and enjoy time dedicated to just the two of you. Sometimes parents experience feelings of guilt about leaving their child. Your child will be fine without you for a few hours, and those few hours may be crucial to keeping your marriage healthy.

Ask for what you need and want

Often, parents find that they don't want to burden family members and friends with requests for help after their child is diagnosed. They try to do everything themselves, insisting on playing the roles SuperMom or SuperDad. What they don't realize is that it's impossible to do it all—and this is the time when they need to ask for help. In fact, friends and loved ones want to be called upon to help. They often feel just as helpless as parents do after a child is diagnosed. They want to be supportive, but don't always know the right things to say or do. So it's up to you, the parent, to tell them. Ask for help—whether it's in the form of childcare, running errands, requesting a shoulder to cry on, or seeking financial help to pay for doctors' appointments and treatments.

Know that you have the power

Even if you may not be in touch with your personal power right now, it's still inside you. You just need to be able to access it. Most parents don't know a lot about autism when their child is diagnosed, which can lead to feelings of powerlessness. To regain a sense of power, it's important to get educated. Remember the adage, "knowledge is power." This is the time to educate yourself. Learn about the latest research on autism and different treatments for it. Read books, access information on the Internet, and talk to autism professionals and parents of children with autism, so that you can gain a better understanding of how to help your child and yourself. Educate friends and family as well. Being informed can lead you to feeling more confident and powerful.

Remember that you are an expert

When parents are constantly surrounded by "expert" advice and opinions from doctors and professionals in the field of autism, they often lose sight of their own expertise. Remember—you know your child better than anyone. Make sure you value your own opinions about your child as highly as those you receive from the experts.

Take ten

You will probably hear friends and loved ones telling you that you should give yourself a break during the day and take some time for yourself. This will make absolutely no sense to you in the beginning, when the autism immersion process first strikes. Most parents find themselves so consumed with helping their children that the notion of taking time out to go to the gym or to dinner with a friend seems preposterous. So here's what I suggest. Take 10 minutes every day to do something that is not autism-related. Take a walk or a drive, or just sit down and drink a cup of tea. I work with parents who cannot bear the thought of taking even 10 minutes a day away from their mission to help their child. So I remind them that this time will actually help their child. Those 10 minutes can help them clear their heads and refocus. A perpetually stressed-out parent cannot effectively help a child. Eventually, you can extend the 10 minutes to longer, but in the beginning, at the very least, take ten.

Remember the basics

Eat, sleep and take care of yourself. An undernourished or sleep-deprived parent is no good to anyone— including himself or herself! Many parents become so consumed with helping their child that they neglect their own basic needs. They are vigilant about keeping their child's appointments with doctors and specialists, but then miss their own. Mothers cancel mammogram appointments and Fathers cancel physical exams. Parents miss out on sleep because they're staying up too late researching or their stress level prevents them from falling asleep or staying asleep. They skip meals because they're racing to bring their child to a speech therapy session.

It's crucial that you, as a parent, maintain your health—for yourself and your family. Keep healthy foods in the house and make time to eat. If your lack of sleep is stress related, try relaxation techniques or natural remedies such as herbal tea before bedtime. Don't do research on autism right before you plan on going to sleep. If your mind is racing, you may have trouble falling asleep. If you find that you are experiencing chronic insomnia, speak with your doctor about medication.

When you can make the time, add in exercise. Exercise can help relieve stress. If you don't have the time to go to the gym, then take a walk. Many parents find themselves spending a lot of time indoors, especially if they are running their child's home treatment program. Make sure to set aside time to go outside. A walk in the park can help to lift your spirits.

Think positive

During this difficult time, it's especially important to surround yourself with people with positive attitudes. They will be your best allies and will offer you the support and guidance you need. Avoid negative friends and family who might not have worked through their own feelings about the diagnosis and may unnecessarily share feelings of anger and fear with you.

Also, be mindful of your own self-talk. What we tell ourselves gets registered in our unconscious and can manifest itself in the way we feel about ourselves. Self-esteem can be adversely affected by negative self-talk. What messages are you sending yourself? Many parents fall into the trap of telling themselves that they are not doing enough for their children or that what they are doing is never good enough. To avoid falling into this trap, give yourself positive affirmations. Affirmations are statements that are made in the present tense. For example, tell yourself: "I am okay," not "I'm going to be okay," or "I used to be okay." Remind yourself that you're doing the best that you can. Give yourself a pat on the back for the work that you're doing to help your child. Recognize and reward yourself for your efforts.

Try to live in the moment

I purposely use the word "try" in this piece of advice because the notion of living in the moment can often be difficult in this fast-paced, future-focused world in which we live. Sometimes, fears about a child's future can prevent parents from appreciating their child in the present. Parents may get caught up in asking: "What will happen to my child when he or she is five years old, or 12 or an adult?" or focusing on other unknowns such as when their child will speak or learn to relate to others. While it's important to think about and plan for your child's future, you cannot allow it to cloud your vision of where your child is at present. Celebrate your child for who he or she is right now.

You're not alone

As you cope with your child's diagnosis, keep in mind that you are not alone in your journey. Contact other parents who've been through this with their own children. Reach out to your friends and loved ones. Share your feelings in a support group. Find ways to take care of yourself. You deserve the same love and attention that you are giving your child.

References

- Gray, D. (2003) Gender and coping: the parents of children with high functioning autism. Social Science and Medicine, 56, pp. 631–642

- Seltzer, M. et al (2001) Families of adolescents and adults with autism: uncharted territory. In: International Review of Research in Mental Retardation, L.M. Glidden (ed.) San Diego: Academic Press (Available from the National Autistic Society Information Centre)

- Sharpley, C.F., Bitsika, V. and Efremidis, B. (1997) Influence of gender, parental health, and perceived expertise of assistance upon stress, anxiety, and depression among parents of children with autism, Journal of Intellectual and Developmental Disability, 22(1), pp. 19–28.

Family matters—helping siblings & extended families

CHAPTER 10

Helping others understand the one you love

Contributing Author Lisa Simmons is the creator of the <Ideal Lives Online Advocacy & Inclusion Center> and author of the special report, <Disability Awareness: Special Kids Don't Have to Feel Left Out>.

Resources and links— Lisa Simmons suggests visiting her Autism Today website to learn about her other products and services: Visit <http://lsimmons.autismtoday.com> today! (*Please note, don't put in the www.)* You can write to Ms. Simmons at <lisa.simmon@cox.net>.

You are walking through the shopping mall or buying groceries with your family. Suddenly you are approached by a stranger who either stares, pointedly looks away or asks you a point blank question: "What's wrong with your child?" The stranger's look and action show lack of understanding and tolerance.

How do you respond? With righteous anger or compassion?

You will almost certainly feel anger on behalf of your child and family, but giving in to it will leave you drained and frustrated. And what if the person who doesn't understand is actually part of your immediate or extended family? This can cause even deeper emotional wounds.

I want to encourage you to do all that you can to respond with compassion in these situations. You have started on a journey, and so have they. They just don't know it yet!

Make your goals **(A)** awareness, **(E)** education, and **(AC)** acceptance—usually in that order.

Disability awareness

Disability awareness or, in this case, autism awareness is about helping someone make the leap from confusion and fear to acceptance and understanding. Sometimes that leap can be made quickly and sometimes it only happens with lots of encouragement and persistence.

We will start at home and walk through ways you, your spouse and your family can practice this process. Then we will move on to practical ways to move through this process with your child, your child's classmates or peers, and your community at large (including those aggravating strangers at the mall).

Although it may feel counterproductive to start at home when strangers on the street are the ones causing you sleepless nights, I do this because it gives you a chance to increase your personal circle of support and it gives you lots of practice talking about your child's diagnosis, so that you can fine-tune your explanation and provide it in a way that is calm, clear and concise.

Step 1: Start with yourself

If your child has received his/her diagnosis recently, then the first person you need to escort through this process is yourself.

(A) Listen to the stories of other parents raising children with autism spectrum disorders. Do you see yourself and your child? Try not to focus on the stories that scare you. Instead, tuck away helpful hints and jot down names of parents you may want to talk with more, down the road.

(E) Do your homework. Do the symptoms ring true for your child? Do you believe that this is the correct diagnosis for your child? Do you understand the challenges that lie ahead as well as the resources that can offer hope and support to your family?

(AC) Apply what you have learned. Begin to build the network of support that your special child needs (medical treatments, education strategies, personal support). <Click here to read more ideas on how to identify your own personal network of support.>

Step 2: Support your spouse

Often the spouse not involved in primary childcare has more difficulty accepting a diagnosis of autism. This person may withdraw into roles outside the family or even withdraw from the family completely. It's important to do all you can to help your spouse reach acceptance. Your spouse's active participation will make your efforts as a parent, caregiver and advocate much more effective. To get started, think about how your spouse makes decisions and help him/her find the kind of input needed to reach acceptance.

(A) Share the realities of your day. Encourage your spouse to spend time alone with your child and experience his/her care first hand. If verbal discussions become highly charged, try writing a journal or a letter and sharing that.

(E) If your spouse responds to facts, have him/her complete a signs and symptoms checklist for your child. Seeing the results in black and white can be an eye-opening experience. If he/she gives greater weight to the voice of experts, find a parent book on autism for him/her to read or take them along to a therapy session. Is there a need to process in private or in a group? Attending an autism conference where he/she can meet others living your reality can provide opportunities to connect with other spouses. On-line options like <teleclasses and multimedia presentations> can provide all the information of a conference in a much more private forum. The key is to find what works for your spouse and connect him/her with the necessary information.

AC) Involve your spouse as much as possible. Your advocacy efforts will be strongest if you attend school meetings and medical appointments together. This will allow both of you to help establish priorities, contribute to the "the plan of action" and take advantage of opportunities to ask questions. It also ensures that the support you offer your child at home will be a united effort.

Step 3. Support your extended family members

Loved ones who don't see your family frequently may find it easier to see your child's behavioral symptoms as a reflection of your parenting rather than the special needs of the child. *Accept that this is a coping mechanism*, an attempt to block out information these people don't want to receive.

(A) Let family members know about your child's diagnosis as soon as possible. Often writing a letter makes a more lasting impression than engaging in a conversation. Chances are this will be their first introduction to the subject of autism. So try to use your own homework to explain it as simply as possible in words that are familiar.

(E) Not every family member will be open to knowing more, but encourage any that show signs of interest. Loan them your resource books to read. Spend time together with your child or write out a typical day, so they can understand the reality of your child's needs. Print and provide family-friendly information that you find online and let them learn a little at a time.

(AC) Talk about ways individual family members can support your family (coming with you to meetings, babysitting so you can go to a support group or out to dinner, spending time with a sibling who may be feeling overlooked, etc.) By letting them do just a few non-threatening tasks and showing your appreciation you both benefit and your family bond is strengthened.

Step 4: Support your child

Parents go through a range of emotions when a child is diagnosed with autism. Your child also needs to be given information about the diagnosis and support for understanding and coping with this new information. Adults on the spectrum who are successful have learned who they are, and accept and use that information to help themselves become the best they can be in life.

Does the idea of discussing autism or Asperger's Syndrome with your child seem scary or even silly? Lots of parents put this task off. They fear that the child won't understand or that hearing the information will make the child feel bad. Chances are your child won't understand what you have to say the first time, but a journey can't start without that first step. Your child's diagnosis will affect his/her entire life. Problems will occur and the road will have challenges, but correct information about the diagnosis and his/her differences offers the child a better chance of being successful.

Timing: There is no exact age or "right time" to tell a child about the diagnosis. You know your child best and you will need to make a decision based on his/her personality, abilities and social awareness. Look for signs that the child is ready for information. Some children will actually ask: "What is wrong with me?"; "Why can't I be like everybody else?"; or, even, "What is wrong with everyone?" These types of questions are certainly a clear indication. Others, however, may have similar thoughts and not be able to express them. The bottom line: try to offer your explanation before your child has lots of negative experience related to his/her diagnosis. Just as early intervention is the key to effective treatment, early communication is the key to healthy self-esteem and self-acceptance.

So, when you're ready . . .

Set a positive tone and focus on uniqueness as the quality that makes each of us special. Talk about the qualities of different friends and family members, how each has their own likes and dislikes, strengths and weaknesses, and physical characteristics. This makes uniqueness just a matter of course. It also makes it easier to talk about differences related to your child's diagnosis.

Practical tools: (A) When your child is young, read simple stories about autism or other children who have autism spectrum disorders. A book like *My Friend with Autism* by Beverly Bishop is a great choice. It is a coloring book designed to help children ages four to eight understand autism and Asperger's Syndrome. It was created by the mother of a young man with autism and is highly informative. Best of all, it is

simple enough for young children to understand and short enough to keep a younger reader's attention. For an older child try, *Asperger's: What Does It Mean to Me?* by Catherine Faherty. It comes in a workbook format that provides activities that help explain an autism spectrum diagnosis as well as make the information more child specific and concrete. The child and you, as the trusted adult partner, can complete the workbook together.

(E) Check with your state Parent Training & Information Center or your local autism support group. Many have a library of videos that can be checked out for viewing by your family.

(AC) Talk with your child one-on-one. If your child is very visual, videotape them and watch the video together as a conversation starter. Consider your child's ability to process information and try to decide on what and how to give them information. Remember it doesn't all have to happen all in one big session. A series of conversations may meet both your needs better.

Step 5: Inform your child's classmates and teachers

Just as you come to rely on your co-workers as an extended family, so your child will see his/her classmates at school as a primary source of interaction and support. Time spent ensuring that this group is well informed and supportive when your child is young will make the road easier as your child grows.

(A) Volunteer to do an autism awareness presentation for your child's class as soon as school starts. Use strategies and conversations you have already developed with family and friends to explain this complex diagnosis in child-friendly language. The Center for Disease Control & Prevention has a <Kids Quest of Kid-Friendly Facts> that may be helpful. Be sure to personalize your information for your child and cover critical issues like communicating with your child and understanding his/her social signals.

(E) Work with your child's teacher to integrate autism awareness into the class's regular curriculum through stories, empathy building activities and reports.

(AC) Discuss ways to encourage peer friendships for your child through the use of peer mentors or friendship groups, such as a Circle of Friends. Add these items to your child's individualized education program (IEP) to make them a priority. And be sure to focus attention on your child's social responses as well. Utilizing techniques such as social stories, social circles and software programs designed to help children with spectrum disorders recognize and interpret facial expressions can all help your child feel more comfortable and confident in social situations.

Step 6: Build awareness in your community

When it comes to the community at large, you may have great difficulty moving any particular individual through the entire process. Instead, focus on building awareness. Plant many seeds and hope for a beautiful garden of wildflowers.

- Volunteer to give presentations to community organizations. Talk about your family's experience and about your child's particular diagnosis. Most community members will have little or no experience with autism, and you can explain both the joys and the challenges in a uniquely personal way. If there is a way the organization can help, don't be shy about suggesting it. Most civic organizations are constantly looking for ways to improve the community and are very open to ideas.

- Take part in regular autism awareness events/ activities with your support group. Frequently, a group of parents working together to raise public awareness will have a larger impact than an individual can have acting on his or her own. In the United States, April is recognized as National Autism Awareness Month, but for a larger impact, consider working with your group to do small activities throughout the year. Whether you are sharing information or doing a fund-raising event for autism research, let your voice be heard in your community.

- Write letters to the editor giving your perspective on special needs issues. Many sectors in your community will affect your child with autism (childcare, healthcare, education, employment). A simple, personal letter can have great impact. Don't allow your child's options to be limited because you didn't speak out on issues that were close to your heart.

- Remember that calm, clear, concise message you've been working on? Consider that your "elevator speech," and have it polished and ready for anyone who approaches you on the street. Your goal: give your message within 30 seconds.

- <Educational cards>—If you aren't sure you can talk calmly when someone has spoken rudely to you or your child, create a set of educational cards. This allows you to "do your part" for raising awareness by simply handing the individual one card and walking away. Your local chapter of the Autism Society of America may have cards that you can purchase or you can print your own with a personal message. They are usually about the size of a business card.

Now what about that stranger on the street? Try these quick solutions:

- For the person with the awkward question, use a snappy comeback, such as "Kids come in all shapes and sizes."

- If a stranger simply stares, walk away. But as you walk, focus on your child and count five of your child's small, amazing accomplishments. Genuine pride and delight will soon put the smile back on your face.

Siblings of children with autism

Contributing Author Sandra L. Harris, Ph.D., Psychology, Rutgers, The State University of New Jersey—Dr. Sandra L. Harris is Board of Governors Distinguished Service Professor at Rutgers University, and executive director of the Douglass Developmental Disabilities Center, a university-based program for the treatment of children with autism. Her research and clinical interests focus on children with autism and their families. She has written extensively in this area, including several books and dozens of journal articles and book chapters. Dr. Harris consults nationally to schools and organizations that serve people with autism and has served as an expert witness in legal cases concerning the rights of people with developmental disabilities. She is an associate editor of the Journal of Autism and Developmental Disorders, a fellow in the APA divisions of Clinical Psychology and Child and Youth Services and a fellow in the American Psychological Society. Dr. Harris is a licensed practicing psychologist. Dean Harris's book, *Siblings of Children with Autism* received the 1995 Autism Society of America Award for Literary Achievement.

Resources and links—Sandra L. Harris, Ph.D. suggests visiting her Autism Today website to learn about her other products and services: Visit <http://harris.autismtoday.com> today! (*Please note, don't put in the www.*) Parents tell me these books are helpful in understanding the experiences of siblings:

- Feiges, L. S. & Weiss, M. J. (2005). Sibling stories: Reflections on life with a brother or sister with autism. Shawnee Mission, KS: Autism Asperger Publishing Co.

- Harris, S. L. & Glasberg, B. (2003). Siblings of Children with autism. A Guide for families. 2nd ed. Bethesda MD: Woodbine House.

- Siegel, B., & Silverstein, S. (1994) What about me? Growing up with a developmentally disabled sibling. New York: Plenum Press.

You can write to Dr. Harris at <sharris@rci.rutgers.edu>.

For most of us, life is in families. Every child on the autism spectrum has a powerful influence on parents, grandparents, siblings and other caring people who surround the family. When we think about the needs of people on the autism spectrum, we must also think of the needs of the family as a whole. As a parent you have a responsibility to provide the best possible childhood for all of your children. However, you will not be able to meet this challenge unless you also ensure that your life and that of your family is one of substance and value.

Next to their child with autism, most parents worry most about the other children in the family. They worry about whether they are neglecting these children because they are trying to do their best for their child with autism. In any family it is always a balancing act to meet everyone's needs. We all have limited resources and many things to do. But children with autism have exceptional needs and that heightens the stress for parents as they try to meet the needs of other children in the family.

Fortunately, there are things you can do to address your concerns about whether you are supporting all of your children appropriately. One thing is to remember that all of us have had jealous feelings about our brothers or sisters. As children we all felt competitive with our siblings, and there were times when we thought our parents were giving more to a sibling than to us. Those concerns are not unique to parents of children with autism. Remembering that may help you keep your typically developing child's feelings and needs in perspective.

It is also important to remember that children have different needs at different points in their development. The very young child needs a sense of security and safety. That means ensuring they are protected from the tantrums or aggression of an older sibling with autism. As they get older, children are more concerned about issues of fairness. You may not be able to devote exactly the same time or resources to each child, but you can try to ensure that each child has opportunities for your focused attention. Try to provide individual time and attention to each child. As your child grows up, she will be able to understand your explanations about why her sibling with autism needs more from you, but she still needs to know there are times during which she is the focus of your attention.

Many children take a page from their parent's book when it comes to understanding their sibling with autism. If you as a parent have achieved some comfort about such things as going into the community or dealing with your child's problematic behaviors, it is likely that your other children will model your behaviour in these situations. That does not mean they will not have moments of embarrassment, especially when they are in their teens, or that they will never be unkind to their brother or sister on the autism spectrum. Most children, like most adults, say unkind things from time to time. But remember that you are your child's most important role model, and he or she will very likely come to share your perspective over time.

It is also important not to allow brothers or sisters to become auxiliary parents. Although everyone in the family needs to do his or her part in keeping the family afloat from day to day, children should not be asked to take on too much responsibility for the care or supervision of their brother or sister with autism. They should especially not be called on to deal with challenging, hard-to-manage behavior problems.

Finally, it is important to keep in mind that research shows that brothers and sisters of children with autism are pretty much like other people. Most of them cope well with the special demands created by their sibling and have good lives as adults, including an ongoing connection with their adult sibling.

How to deal emotionally with spousal and other relationships around autism

CHAPTER 11

How to deal emotionally with spousal and other relationships around autism

(selection from Maintaining a Strong Parent Team)

Contributing Author Nicholas Martin, MA, Clinical Practices, Psychology Department, University of Hartford—Mr. Martin is a conflict resolution consultant residing near Fort Worth, Texas. He is a very popular conference presenter with a background in clinical psychology and in court and postal service mediation. Among his published works are *An Operator's Manual for Successful Living, Strengthening Relationships When Our Children Have Special Needs*, and *A Guide to Collaboration for IEP Teams*.

Resources and links— Nicholas Martin, MA suggests visiting his Autism Today website to learn about his other products and services: Visit <http://martin.autismtoday.com> today! (*Please note, don't put in the www.*) You can contact Mr. Martin by visiting his web site, <www.4accord.com>.

Ask any parents with experience in the autism world and they are likely to tell you that the first rules of success are: don't go it alone, and don't wait for a crisis before taking steps. Simply stated, among the best things parents can do for themselves and their families is to get connected with support groups and services before they reach a point of desperation.

A proactive position begins with the recognition that having a child with special needs is going to add to the challenges a couple will face. However, many parents and researchers report that, handled correctly, the challenges associated with raising such children have actually strengthened and benefited families in many deep and meaningful ways. But going to bat without adequate preparation can only lower anyone's chances of success. Knowing what you're likely to be up against is half the battle won!

A little bit of research or a few books and articles will quickly bring into focus a handful of the challenges most commonly reported by parents. These include: avoiding blame, finding adequate child care, finding resources for support and guidance, maintaining effective communications, finding time alone and together, managing the extra expenses and maintaining a positive outlook.

Space does not permit exploring these issues in depth, but here are a few suggestions from those who have faced these challenges with success:

Finding time alone:

- Give yourselves permission to take time out for self.

- Make plans for weekly or monthly time alone (schedule it).

- Meet for lunch or arrange a regular hour before or after work.

- For guidance, information and support:

- Let it be known when you need help.

- Connect with other parents facing similar challenges.

- Join a support group right away and get involved in its activities.

- To communicate effectively:

- Recognize how important this is and make an agreement to work on it.

- Use "I" statements and a tone of caring, as opposed to anger, blame and frustration.

- Set aside time on a regular basis to talk; don't wait for a crisis.

- Be patient, and sensitive to your partner's feelings and priorities; ask how best to approach him or her, when would be a good time to talk and how he or she wants to be kept informed.

- Seek professional help if necessary.

Dealing emotionally with relationships around autism

Contributing Author Daniel Hawthorne is a diagnosed High Functioning Autistic. He is the author of *Child of the Forest* and *Guidelines to Intervention in Autism,* and webmaster and author of the award winning site <www.autismguidelines.com>. He has degrees in Communication and Business Administration, most recently through the University of Arkansas. He does numerous speaking engagements to autism support groups and to special schools, in addition to managing an online resume posting business.

Resources and links—Daniel Hawthorne suggests visiting his Autism Today website to learn about his other products and services: Visit <http://hawthorne.autismtoday.com> today! *(*Please note, don't put in the www.)* He enjoys corresponding with parents, teachers, and others in the autism community, and may be contacted at <daniel@autismguidelines.com>.

I am convinced that most people do not have a clue about the immense amount of frustration and anxiety felt daily by those within the autism community. Loving parents, devoted teachers, caring therapists—all feel this same frustration, at varying degrees. Eventually, it affects the health of these people. Of course, the individual with autism, being tormented by sensory overload and sensory confusion, suffers the most.

A lot of times, when hostility is expressed by a spouse having difficulty dealing with the fact that his or her child is autistic, it isn't personal.

Creating positive parent–physician partnerships

CHAPTER 12

A parent–physician team approach

(This section is based on excerpts from *Diagnosis Autism: Now What? 10 Steps to Improve Treatment Outcomes*)

Contributing Author Lawrence P. Kaplan, Ph.D., Health Administration and Research with an emphasis in autism spectrum disorders, Kennedy-Western University—Dr. Kaplan is the Executive Director of US Autism and Asperger Association, Inc., a national association dedicated to enhancing the quality of life of individuals and their families/caregivers touched by autism spectrum disorders by providing educational and family support through conferences/seminars and published and electronic mediums. Dr. Kaplan is the author of *Diagnosis Autism: Now What? 10 Steps to Improve Treatment Outcomes.*

Resources and links— Lawrence P. Kaplan, Ph.D. suggests visiting his Autism Today website to learn about his other products and services: Visit <http://kaplan.autismtoday.com> today! (*Please note, don't put in the www.)* You can reach Dr. Kaplan at US. Autism and Asperger Association by calling 1-888-9AUTISM or by writing <drlkaplan@usautism.org>.

Background

As parents, my wife and I remember our pediatrician explaining that our child would be fine, that he would talk and walk. As our older son and the other twin developed normally, we were advised to be careful not to compare the kids. While it was difficult to refrain from making comparisons, it was obvious that one of the twins was not progressing on the same path as the other boys. This was evident when our son was not walking at 18 months of age, had had episodes when he banged his head on the walls and was very limited in his development.

While we have met many understanding and helpful health-care practitioners, we have also experienced many frustrations of the waiting room: completing lengthy medical forms and enduring the embarrassment as our son screamed and ran throughout the halls while we were looked upon as inadequate parents. Visiting experts resulted in responses of "There isn't anything I can do for you."

Even though my wife and I at times have nearly exhausted ourselves during the past 12 years trying to gain assistance for our son, we continue to persevere and maintain patience. We have been extremely fortunate to have met many individuals who have furthered understanding of this complex disorder. And though there are not any cures, organizations have developed rapidly over the last few years that are dedicated to helping all of our children who fall within the spectrum of autism disorders.

A pediatric partnership

It has taken many years for us to develop a pediatric partnership. While it is not entirely perfect and resistance does exist, we are fortunate to have partnered with a wonderful and caring pediatrician. When I bring our son in for an appointment, she is no longer intimidated by the fact that I am holding a stack of books with the most recent information on autism. At times, there is a role reversal, when the patient educates the pediatrician!

The majority of pediatricians are absolutely wonderful for primary care, but it is a mammoth challenge for a pediatrician, or any physician, to be proficient in all aspects of disease. I challenge you, the parent, and the health care practitioner to empower each other. Form partnerships to investigate the best methods to improve care for your child.

The causes of ASD are a complex maze of hypotheses. The abundance of theories has caused many practitioners to either overlook the disorder or proceed extremely slowly in providing referrals to specialized practitioners. What complicates the issues further is that the diagnosis includes various assessment methods. Different evaluations result in a diversity of intervention and treatment protocols that lead to different paths for different individuals. And these paths can change as the child grows.

Pediatricians who evaluate infants during the first years of life should be able to identify relevant abnormal milestone markers. Once the diagnosis is confirmed, case management should be implemented without delay. Physicians need to integrate all of the information they gather and provide effective patient care. This care includes making the parents aware of the risks and benefits of a proposed course of treatment, and fostering an effective dialogue between the health-care practitioner and parents regarding what action to take. The parents should be just as involved as the physician in the decision-making process.

For example, pediatricians should inform parents of the relevant benefits of vaccinations as well as the possible risks. However, the pediatrician should not simply give the parents this information and ask them for a decision. The parents and pediatrician should engage in a dialogue, where the parents can express concerns and pediatrician can relate her/his personal experiences and discuss ways to help reduce some of the risks of vaccinations.

If the goal is to ensure a successful outcome for your child, how do you begin? You start the implementation process by following the 10-step program from the book <u>Diagnosis Autism: Now What? 10 Steps to Improve Treatment Outcomes; A Parent-Physician Team Approach</u>. The 10 steps apply to partnering with many different types of health care practitioners, not just pediatricians. The following steps occasionally refer to materials found in the book.

Steps to an effective parent–physician team approach

Step 1: Monitor and chart your child's development

The first step toward a parent–physician team approach is to provide your doctor with a thorough record of your child's development. Accurate, up-to-date records of your observations and concerns are essential for accurate diagnosis and early intervention treatment. The preparatory tools for your physician meeting and initial appointment include a *Daily Log*

and a *School Activity Chart* that allow you to monitor and record your child's development at home and at school. As you chart behaviors and reactions of your child in these two logs, the list of *Common Characteristics of Autism Spectrum Disorders* may be helpful in identifying additional traits.

Step 2: Organize information for physician interview

Two steps prepare you for the first appointment with the physician.

1) Gather essential information, including:
   - Your complete *Daily Log* and *School Activity Chart*
   - Health insurance information
   - Your written expectation of achieving the best outcome for your child, including the use of consultants (e.g., DAN! practitioner, neurologist and speech therapist)
   - Medical records from all laboratory tests and diagnostic procedures
2) Recognize distractions in and around the clinic.

Step 3: Develop an assessment and evaluation plan

Studies have demonstrated that early intervention improves a child's behaviors, language skills and cognitive abilities. Using various assessment and evaluation tools may identify areas for additional treatment, increasing the likelihood of successful outcomes. Scales and developmental testing tools commonly used by clinicians are found in the *Assessment, Evaluation, and Testing Tools Chart* of my book.

Step 4: Acquire a knowledge base through research

Acquiring a strong knowledge base on autism spectrum disorders is imperative, and your research should begin before your first meeting with the physician. A considerable amount of material may be obtained from libraries, universities, non-profit organizations and friends in similar circumstances. In my book I introduces five key points for Internet research in Step 4. The *Research Resources Chart* lists links and contacts that may help you as you develop an effective parent–physician partnership.

Step 5: Formulate questions for the physician appointment

It is important that you understand the physician's practice policies and know how the clinic's group of physicians will treat your child. Step 5 in my book provides sample *Questions for Physician Interview.*

Step 6: Initiate treatment and program approaches

Interventions can be divided into three main categories: educational, medical and complementary. Charts in my book include *Educational Therapy, Medical Therapy, Nutritional Supplements Therapy,* and *Dietary Therapy.* According to the *Nelson Textbook of Pediatrics* (2004): "There is compelling evidence that intensive behavioral therapy, beginning before three years of age and targeted toward speech and language development, is successful both in improving capacity and later social functioning." *The Manual of Pediatric Therapeutics* (Graef 1997) supports this. Once the pediatrician has identified the disorder, it is essential to initiate treatment that "consists of a structured program in a supportive special education environment. This includes behavioral treatment for improving social responses and communication, and decreasing inappropriate behaviors; and parent education."

Step 7: Carefully choose your primary physician

One approach is to use a primary care pediatrician for general pediatric visits, and a supplemental practitioner who specializes in autism spectrum disorders. In my book, Step 7 includes recommended options for sourcing a pediatrician and a DAN! practitioner, as well as other health-care practitioners whose skills reflect the health-care needs for your child with ASD.

Step 8: Respect your doctor/earn your doctor's respect

To create a working relationship with your physician, first, respect your doctor. Then, during your interview, you should strive to earn your doctor's respect. Respect refers to your acknowledgement that the doctor is a well-trained professional and your recognition that you both have the same goal: the best outcome for your child.

Step 9: Listen and be open minded

Once you have made your case during your initial appointment, it is the physician's turn to talk. If you want to be a better communicator, learn to listen. Keep your focus on the physician, giving the physician your undivided attention. Try not to be distracted by your surroundings. It helps to have your initial appointment without your child. Step 9 proposes 10 steps leading to effective listening and receiving advice from your physician.

Step 10: Review, negotiate and follow through

Now that you have met the pediatrician or other health care practitioners, it is time to evaluate the interview. In order to effectively assess the initial meeting, list the advantages and disadvantages. Step 10 in my book covers the appointment review, negotiation and follow-through. There is a list of advantages and disadvantages in the *Interview Worksheet.* The *Negotiation Tips Worksheet* offers suggestions on how to negotiate with your doctor.

To acquire an in-depth knowledge on how to successfully achieve a parent-physician partnership, following this link to purchase the book <u>Diagnosis Autism: Now What? 10 Steps to Improve Treatment Outcomes; A Parent-Physician Team Approach</u>.

Helping the child with ASD gain social skills

CHAPTER 13

Social skills training for children with Autism Spectrum Disorders

Contributing Author Jed Baker, Ph.D.—Dr. Baker is the Director of the Social Skills Training Project in Maplewood, N.J. He is on the professional advisory board of ASPEN (an information network for parents of children with Asperger's Syndrome). He is a behavioral consultant for several New Jersey School systems, where he provides social skills training for students with pervasive developmental disorders and learning disabilities. He directs and supervises social skills training for students at Millburn Public Schools. In addition, he writes, lectures and provides training across the country on the topic of social skills training for individuals with Asperger's Syndrome and related PDDs. He has recently published both a manual on social skills training for children with Asperger's Syndrome and a social skill picture book to aid in social skills training.

Resources and links—Jed E. Baker, Ph.D. suggests visiting his Autism Today website to learn about his other products & services: Visit: <http://baker.autismtoday.com> today! (*Please note, don't put in the www.*) For more information about Dr. Baker and the Social Skills Training Project, visit <www.socialskillstrainingproject.com>.

Motivation to socialize

John is three years old, with very limited language skills. When his parents try to sit and play with him he focuses on lining up play letters on the floor, virtually ignoring his parents. They call his name and he does not respond. They show him other toys and he ignores them. His older sister tries to engage him in a game of peek-a-boo and he shows no interest.

Karen is a 12-year-old with Asperger's Syndrome. Her intellectual and language skills are excellent. She is very articulate and understands most anything someone says to her. Often, when she has a project in school, she either refuses to do it or refuses to compromise with peers or teachers on how to do the project.

Her teachers and parents explain that she needs to compromise if she wants to develop friendships with peers and needs to do the work if she wants to get a job later in life. She explains that she has no interest in making friends or ever having a job, and thus there is no need to do the work or compromise with others.

Although very different in their levels of functioning, neither John nor Karen is motivated to learn social skills. Efforts to teach them how to relate to others will be frustrating for all until the issue of motivation is addressed. The table below describes several methods of motivating students to learn social skills and many other skills.

	External/Contrived Motivators	Internal/Naturalistic Motivators
Preverbal reasoner	• Controlled studies demonstrate effectiveness • Discrete Trial Intervention: Lovaas (Rewards are not necessarily logically related to the student's response.)	• Controlled studies demonstrate effectiveness • Verbal Behavior Training: Sundberg & Partington • Natural Language Paradigm and Pivotal response Training: Koegel & Koegel (Rewards are logically related to the student's response.) • Promising but no true controlled outcome studies: Floortime—Greenspan; RDI—Gutstein
Verbal reasoner	• Controlled studies demonstrate effectiveness • Token systems and behavior charts • Increase awareness of assets before describing possible challenges that need to be addressed • Make socializing fun • Have student teach others the social skills	• Promising but no true controlled outcome studies yet • Link skill goals to student's personal goals

The Table on the previous page categorizes methods of motivating students in terms of the language ability of the students (preverbal *versus* verbal reasoner) and the locus of motivation (external/contrived *versus* internal/naturalistic). Preverbal reasoners are students who may have some language but are not yet able to understand "if—then" statements, such as "If you play this with me, then you can have a snack." Verbal reasoners can understand "if—then" statements, so that one can try to motivate them through verbal reasoning. An example: "If you do your math with me, then we can play afterwards."

External/contrived motivation refers to providing students with a reward that may be unrelated to the activity or response they are making. For example, if a student is able to greet others when prompted, an external reward might be a special snack or access to a toy. The reward here is not logically related to the response (i.e., greeting) and is not naturally built into the situation (i.e., the instructor must provide the reinforcement).

Internal motivation refers to situations in which the student's behaviors naturally provide them with rewards because the activity itself is rewarding or because the student's responses bring its own rewards. For example, if a child enjoys playing follow the leader, then playing the game is itself rewarding and there is no need to provide another reward. Similarly, if a student learns to request a toy from others and receives the toy, then the request naturally leads to its own reward, receiving the toy, and there is no need for other rewards.

Motivational strategies for non-verbal reasoners

The motivational methods listed for non-verbal reasoners include strategies often associated with "early intervention." The goals are often to build crucial skills that are prerequisites for later learning in school and social settings. These skills include joint attention (attending to others and attending to what others point out), the ability to label objects, request objects, follow simple directions and answer simple questions. The interventions associated with applied behavior analysis (ABA) have been subjected to the most rigorous controlled evaluations of outcome and demonstrate excellent results in about 50% of autistic students in terms of intellectual, language, adaptive and early social skills.

ABA approaches include Discrete Trial Intervention (DTI) (Lovaas, 2003), Natural Language Paradigm (and its more recent cousin Pivotal Response Training) (Koegel and Koegel, 2005), and Verbal Behavior Training (Sundberg and Partington, 1998). Although these approaches share a basic structure of teaching behavior through cueing, prompting and rewarding students, they differ in their emphasis on teaching in natural environments and utilizing internal/naturalistic *versus* external/contrived motivational systems.

A discrete trial has five components: a cue, a prompt, the student's response, a reward and data collection. Early DTI interventions often emphasized compliance and labeling of objects. For example, if a child was learning colors, the child might get a cue, "Point to the blue car." Then the instructor might prompt the student to touch the blue car. If the child responded correctly he might then get a favored reward, such as a piece of candy. Here the reward is not naturally related to the response. Earlier DTI approaches have been shown effective in improving students' abilities to respond to adult cues, but they are not always as successful in increasing students' spontaneous language or generalizing skills in natural settings.

In contrast, Verbal Behavior Training and Pivotal Response Training occur in more natural settings and capitalize more on the students' own interests. In the first phase of verbal behavior training, the emphasis is on teaching children to spontaneously request, utilizing the students' own interest in activities, food, objects, wanting a break or wanting attention while in a more natural play environment. As such, the students are typically highly motivated, since their responses lead to naturally rewarding consequences (i.e., getting what they requested). Similarly, Pivotal Response Training begins with assessing what the students is interested in and then beginning a discrete trial centered on that interest. For example, if a youngster shows an interest in playing with a car, the adult might hold the car out and cue, "What color is the car?" If the youngster says "car," the adult might cue and prompt, "What color is the car? Is it blue?" And when the child says, "blue car," the child would get to play with the car.

Greenspan's "Floortime" DIR (Developmental Individual-Difference, Relationship-Based) model also capitalizes on the student's own interests, emphasizing following the lead of the youngster as the adult plays with the student in an effort to target various developmental skills (the interested reader should see Greenspan & Wieder, 1998). Although there are some semi-structured play activities in this model, cues, prompts and rewards are not used in the same systematic way as in ABA methods.

Another promising approach is Relational Development Intervention (RDI) (Gutstein & Sheely, 2002). RDI outlines a systematic set of activities that encourage students to want to engage in social interaction because of the joy in the social activity and not because of a contrived/external reward for interacting. Early activities to build joint attention might include imitation games like follow the leader or "follow my eyes to the prize," where students have to look at an adult's eyes to find where the adult hid a prize in the room (the adult is looking in the direction of where the prize is hidden). Although these activities have not yet been empirically tested, the concept is reasonable: engage students in activities that limit over-stimulation and require on attending to others.

Motivational strategies for verbal reasoners

Verbal reasoners understand "if—then" statements. For example, if you learn how to interview for a job, you might get that job. External motivational strategies focus on finding incentives (rewards, privileges) for practicing new skills. Often tokens or points are earned on a behavior chart and exchanged for short and long-term rewards.

For many students, external rewards are not necessary. Internal motivational strategies start with linking social skills training to students' goals. If students want friends, a job, good grades or to be able to engage in an activity (sports, clubs or a birthday

party), then teaching crucial skills can be linked to these goals. For example, if a youngster wants to go to a birthday party, one can motivate him to learn how to play the games that they will play at the party and other crucial skills to maintain himself at the party. Similarly, many adolescents who never wanted to learn social skills suddenly develop motivation to learn certain skills in an effort to help them find a date.

Strategies cannot be so straightforward for the student who seems to have no goals, has become depressed and is withdrawing from the social world entirely. Such students may need to deny a need for skills training. It takes a modicum of self-esteem to tolerate thinking about one's difficulties. One way around such resistance is through counselling that allows them to expand their senses of their talents and strengths before targeting areas that need improvement. For most students, it is helpful to have someone else point out two to three strengths for every difficulty that is highlighted. The student can be asked directly what talents and strengths they have and then the counsellor can add or refine that lists of strengths before suggesting areas in need of improvement. For example, during group sessions I will ask each member what his or her special talents are and corroborate these positive descriptions. Then I might say, "There are some minor issues I want to address with you guys so that you can continue to do as well as you are doing." Then comes the lesson on a skill topic.

There are several more ways to motivate engagement for skill lessons including: using entertaining role-plays and social games; linking skill lessons to fun group activities or projects; and creating skill lessons to teach others. (See Baker 2003; Baker, in press.) This last method involves students creating picture books (See later discussion of making social skill picture books.), videos or live skits, so that they can demonstrate the skills to other students. As such, they can learn a skill in order to "help others" without having to acknowledge that they themselves needed to learn it.

With some motivation to socialize, skills can be more easily taught and generalized. What follows is a description of the components of social skills training, including teaching skills, generalizing skills and targeting typical peers.

The components of social skills training

All social interaction and social problems involve at least two people. A social difficulty can be defined as both a skill deficit for the student with a social disability and a problem of acceptance of that student by peers or the community. Thus intervention must focus on teaching skills for both the student with a disability and typical peers. All too often we strive to "fix" the child with the disability and virtually overlook the "typical" peers who may be ignoring, teasing or rejecting the student. Moreover, including typical peers as a focus for intervention may yield results much sooner, as typical peers may learn to be understanding of the student with a disability more quickly than the child with a disability can learn to interact more appropriately with peers. We might begin to target peers at the age that many students enter school environments and typically begin to interact with peers, by about three to four years of age.

Consistent with this view, I believe effective social skills training for individuals with ASD and their peers consists of at least four components. The student with ASD requires: skills training lessons to teach explicitly the social skills that do not come naturally for ASD students; and activities to promote generalization of skills in the situations where they are needed. Typical peers and the student's community require: sensitivity training lessons, so that they are more accepting of, and engaging with, students with ASD; and activities to promote generalization of sensitivity to ASD students.

Skill lessons

Skill lessons include a variety of strategies geared to the students cognitive/language functioning. For verbal reasoners (i.e., students who can understand verbal explanations), we might break down a skill into its component steps, *explain it, model it and role-play it* until the youngster can demonstrate the skill and understands why it is important. Let's say a student with good verbal skills always wants to do things his way and that conduct gets in the way of developing peer relations. We decide to teach him how and why to compromise. We teach him how to ask what others want, say what he wants and to offer to do a little of both. We explain that when you do a little of both (i.e., compromise) the other person will be happy and may want to play with you again or be your friend. Using this straightforward approach, we have broken down into simple steps over 70 such social skills related to play, conversation, emotion management and empathy in a manual on social skills training for children with social-communication problems. (See Baker, 2003.)

For very young students (three and under) with very little language or ability to attend to others, we might begin with the early intervention strategies described earlier (Discrete Trail Intervention, Verbal Behavior Training, Pivotal Response Training, Floortime—DIR, and RDI). For students who have developed some language but still have difficulty understanding verbal explanations, I have translated a subset of the skills that appear in the manual (Baker, 2003) into picture form. (See the *Social Skills Picture Book,* Baker, 2001.) Instead of explaining skill steps with words, we show a picture sequence. Thus for a skill-like compromise, the pictures demonstrate a student asking to play a game with another youngster who says he wants to play another game. We show them pictures of the students compromising and playing a little of both games with both looking happy. Then we show them pictures of the same people not compromising, not playing with each other, with both looking upset. Of particular benefit is making your own picture books, so that students have pictures of themselves engaged in the right (or wrong) ways to demonstrate a skill. After the pictures are shown, students should still role-play the skill so that they can actually go through the motions of the skill steps.

Another strategy called cognitive picture rehearsal utilizes cartoon-like drawings on index cards combined with positive reinforcement principles (Groden & Lavasseur, 1995). Cognitive picture rehearsal always includes drawings or pictures of three components: the antecedents to a problem situation, the targeted desired behavior and a positive reinforcer. The pictures are displayed on index cards. On the top of each card (or on the back of the card) is a script describing the desired sequence of events. Children are shown the sequence of cards until they can repeat what is happening in each picture. The sequence is reviewed just before the child enters the potentially problematic situation.

For example, a cognitive picture rehearsal was created for Matt, a seven-year-old who would throw tantrums when his teacher told him to get off the computer. Cards 1 and 2 illustrated the antecedent to the problem situation: Matt is playing at the computer and then the teacher tells him it is time to get off the computer. Cards 3 and 4 showed Matt engaged in the desired target behavior: thinking that the teacher will be happy if he gets off the computer and give him a chance to use the computer later, and then saying, "Okay, I'll get off the computer." Cards 5 and 6 show the positive rewards of engaging in the desired behavior: Matt receiving a point on a reward chart and the teacher letting Matt use the computer again later because he had cooperated earlier.

Social Stories™, developed by Carol Gray and colleagues (Gray et al., 1993), uses stories written in the first person to increase students' understanding of problematic situations. Beginning with the child's understanding of a situation, a story is developed describing what is happening and why, and how people feel and think in the situation. While the story contains some directive statements (i.e., what to do in the situation), the focus is on understanding what is happening in the situation.

The following situation provides an example of a situation in which Social Stories™ may help an individual with autism deal with a social problem. Peter was a 13-year-old who frequently got into fights at lunchtime because he believed that other students in the cafeteria were teasing him. He said that several other boys who sat on the other side of the cafeteria always laughed at him. He would give them "the finger" and then they would start a fight with him. When Peter was observed at lunch, it was apparent that the other boys were laughing, but not at him. They were at least 50 feet from Peter, not looking at him, and laughing with each other, presumably about some joke or discussion they were having.

We developed the following social story for Peter, starting with his perspective that others might be laughing at him:

"When I am in the cafeteria I often see other boys laughing and I think they are laughing at me. Lots of students laugh during lunchtime because they are talking about funny things they did during the day, or funny stories they heard or saw on TV, movies or books they read. Sometimes students laugh at other students to make fun of them. If they are making fun of other students, they usually use the student's name, or look and point at that student. If the other students are laughing, but they do not look or point at me, then they are probably not laughing at me. Most students do not get mad when others are laughing, as long as they are not laughing at them. If they do laugh at me, I can go tell a teacher rather than give them the finger."

Like cognitive picture rehearsal, Social Stories™ are read repeatedly to children until they have over-learned them, and are then read again just prior to the problematic situation.

Generalization

Generalization refers to the ability of an individual to use a new skill in situations beyond the training session, and hopefully to use the new skill spontaneously without prompting from others. To achieve this level of fluidity with a new skill, individuals must practice and repeat the skill steps a great deal. As a result, it is unrealistic to think one can generalize many new skills at once. In my experience, true generalization occurs when individuals are reminded about or rehearse no more than one to three new skills every day for several months. Although individuals can learn the concept of many more skills during skill lessons, they may only be able to generalize one to three new skills at a given time. Generalization of a skill involves three steps: priming before the situation in which the skill is needed; frequent facilitated opportunities to practice the skill; and review of the skill after it is used.

Priming involves some reminder to the individual of what the skill steps are just prior to needing the skill. For example, just before going on a job interview, an individual might go over how to answer anticipated questions. Or just prior to starting a frustrating task at school or at work, the individual might review options for dealing with frustrating work. Priming can be verbal and/or supplemented by a visual aide. Verbal priming involves someone verbally explaining the skill steps prior to the situation in which they will be needed. Cue cards, behavior charts, copies of skill lessons (See Baker, 2003.), Social Stories™, cognitive picture rehearsals and social skill picture books can serve as visual aides that depict the skill steps.

If students want to change their behavior but can't remember the skill steps, then cue cards or copies of the skill lessons may be ideal. We might write one to three skills on an index card and laminate it. Then we might ask a parent, teacher, or employer or the student him or herself to review the skill steps prior to the situation in which it will be needed. Although it is ideal for the student to see the skill steps immediately prior to the situation in which they need to use the skill, this may not always be practical. Instead the parent, teacher, employer or student might review the skill once in the morning prior to school or work, once at lunch and then again at the end of the day so that the student at least has to think about the skill three times per day.

If a student has not fully agreed to try a new skill and thus is lacking in "internal" motivation to perform the skill, then a behavior chart can be used in which external rewards are contingent on demonstrating certain targeted skills.

In order to practice the new skills, students need opportunities. Facilitated opportunities involve creating daily situations in which the skills can be practiced and coached. Sometimes those opportunities are naturally built into the day. For example, a student learning to deal with frustrating work may always have his or her share of challenging work to do during the day. Other times, the practice opportunities need to be carefully planned or created. For example, a student who never initiates conversation with anyone may be asked to call someone on the phone once a day or join others for lunch and initiate conversation once during that period.

After situations have occurred in which skills were needed, the student's performance can be reviewed to increase awareness of the skill. If a youngster is on a reward chart, the reason why the student received the reward (or not) should be reviewed with him or her to enhance learning.

Peer sensitivity

Sometimes youngsters with ASD are ignored, yet often they are actively teased or bullied. Students with ASD may do nothing to deserve such teasing and other times they may provoke such reactions with unintentional "irritating" behaviors like perseverating on a topic, making loud noises or having angry meltdowns. When students are harassed, teased or rejected because they look or behave differently, it is crucial to explain to others the unintentional nature of their behaviors and how others can help. We often talk with peers not only about the unintentional nature of their difficult behaviors, but the strengths and talents of the individuals with ASD and about examples of successful, famous figures who may also have had an ASD.

Generalization of peer kindness

We ask peers to do three things to help their ASD classmates and each other: (1) include others who are left out; (2) stand up for those who are teased; and (3) offer help to those who are upset. To help these kind behaviors generalize into the daily routines of the students, we might create a lunch buddy program, where peers volunteer to eat and hang out with the ASD student on a rotating schedule. We might also introduce a reward program to recognize and reward "kind" behaviors towards fellow students. We may also train peers in how to engage ASD students in play, including how to get their attention and what kinds of games to initiate (i.e., games the ASD student can play). Our experience and a growing body of research suggests that including typical peers as targets for training can have profound effects on the development of social skills and overall happiness of ASD students in school environments (Baker 2003; Wagner, 1998).

Baker, J. E. (2001). *Social skill picture books*. Arlington, TX: Future Horizons, Inc.

Baker, J. E. (2003). *Social skills training for students with Aspergers syndrome and related social communication disorders*. Shawnee Mission, Kansas: Autism Aspergers Publishing Company.

Baker, J.E. (In press). *Social skills training for the transition from high school to adult life*. Arlington, TX: Future Horizons, Inc.

Baker, J.E. (In press). *Social skill picture book for teens and adults*. Arlington, TX: Future Horizons, Inc.

Gray, C., Dutkiewicz, M., Fleck, C., Moore, L., Cain, S.L., Lindrup, A., Broek, E., Gray, J., & Gray, B. (Eds.). (1993). *The social story book*. Jenison, MI. Jenison Public Schools.

Greenspan, S. I. and Wieder, S., (1998). *The child with special needs: Encouraging intellectual and emotional growth*. Addison-Wesley, Reading, MA

Grodon, J., & LeVasseur, P. (1995). *Cognitive picture rehearsal: A system to teach self-control*. In K. A. Quill (Ed.), *Teaching children with autism* (pp.287-306) Albany, NY: Delmar Publishing.

Gutstein, S. E. & Sheely, R. K. (2002). *Relationship development intervention with children, adolescents and adults: Social and emotional development activities for asperger syndrome, autism, PDD, and NLD*. London: Jessica Kingsley Publishers Ltd.

Koegel, R. L., & Koegel, L.K. (Eds.) (2005). *Pivotal response treatments for autism: Communication, social, and academic development*. Brookes Publishing Co., Inc.

Lovaas, O.I. (2003) *Teaching Individuals with Developmental Delays: Basic Intervention Techniques*. PRO-ED, Inc., Austin, Texas

Sundberg, M.L. and Partington, J. W. (1998). Teaching language to children with autism or other developmental disabilities. Behavioral Analysts, Inc.

Wagner, S. (1998). Inclusive programming for elementary students with autism. Arlington, TX: Future Horizons, Inc.

Learning styles and autism

Contributing Author Stephen M. Edelson, Ph.D., Experimental Psychology—Dr. Edelson has worked in the field of autism for 25 years. He is the Director of the Center for the Study of Autism in Salem, Oregon, which is affiliated with the Autism Research Institute in San Diego, CA. He is also on the Board of Directors of the Oregon chapter of the Autism Society of America and is on the Society's Professional Advisory Board.

Resources and links—Stephen M. Edelson, Ph.D. suggests visiting his Autism Today website to learn about his other products and services. Visit: <http://edelson.autismtoday.com> today! (*Please note, don't put in the www.*) Dr. Edelson's main autism website is <www.autism.org>.

"Learning styles" refers to the ways people gain information about their environments. People can learn through seeing (visually), hearing (auditorily), and/or through touching or manipulating an object (kinesthetically or "hands-on" learning). For example, looking at a picture book or reading a textbook involves learning through vision; listening to a lecture live or on tape involves learning through hearing; and pressing buttons to determine how to operate a VCR involves learning kinesthetically.

Generally, most people learn using two to three learning styles. Interestingly, people can assess their own interests and lifestyle to determine the ways in which they obtain much of their information about their environment. In my case, when I read a book I can easily understand the text. In contrast, it is difficult for me to listen to an audiotape recording of that book—I just cannot follow the story line. Thus, I am a strong visual learner, and a moderate, possibly poor, auditory learner. As far as kinesthetic learning, I am very good at taking apart objects to learn how an object works, such as a vacuum cleaner or a computer.

One's learning style may affect how well a person performs in an educational setting, especially from junior high on through college. Schools usually require both auditory learning (i.e., listening to a teacher) and visual learning (i.e., reading a textbook). If a person is poor at one of these ways of learning, he/she will likely depend mostly on his/her strength (e.g., a visual learner may study the textbook rather than rely on the lecture content). Using this logic, if one is poor at both visual and auditory learning, he/she may have difficulty in school. Furthermore, one's learning style may be associated with one's occupation. For example, those individuals who are kinesthetic learners may tend to have occupations involving their hands, such as shelf stockers, mechanics, surgeons or sculptors. Visual learners may tend to have occupations which involve processing visual information, such as data processors, artists, architects or manufacturing part sorters. Moreover, auditory learners may tend to have jobs which involve processing auditory information, such as sales people, judges, musicians, 911 operators and waiters/waitresses.

Based on my experiences and those of my colleagues, it appears that autistic individuals are more likely to rely on only one style of learning. By observing the person, one may be able to determine his/her primary style of learning. For example, if an autistic child enjoys looking at books (e.g., picture books), watching television (with or without sound), and tends to look carefully at people and objects, then he/she may be a visual learner. If an autistic child talks excessively, enjoys people talking to him/her and prefers listening to the radio or music, then he/she may be an auditory learner. And if an autistic child is constantly taking things apart, opening and closing drawers, and pushing buttons, this may indicate that the child is a kinesthetic or "hands-on" learner.

Once a person's learning style is discovered, relying on this style to teach can greatly increase the likelihood that the person will learn. If one is not sure which learning style a child has or is teaching to a group with different learning styles, then the best way to teach could be to use all three styles together. For example, when teaching the concept "jello," one can display a package and bowl of jello (visual), describe its features such as its color, texture, and use (auditory), and let the person touch and taste it (kinesthetic).

A common problem of autistic children is that they run around the classroom and do not listen to the teacher. Such a child may not be an auditory learner—and so is not attending to the teacher's words. If the child is a kinesthetic learner, the teacher may choose to place his/her hands on the child's shoulders and then guide the student back to his/her chair, or go to the chair and move it towards the student. If the child learns visually, the teacher may need to show the child his/her chair or hand them a picture of the chair and gesture for the child to sit down.

Teaching to the learning style of the student may affect whether or not the child can attend to and process information presented. This, in turn, can affect the child's performance in school as well as his/her behavior. Therefore, it is important that educators assess for learning style as soon as an autistic child enters the school system and that they adapt their teaching styles to the strengths of the student. This will ensure that the autistic child has the greatest chance for success in school.

Idioms and metaphors and things that go bump in their heads

(This section is expanded from *Idioms and Metaphors and Things That Go Bump in Their Heads*, originally published in the Autism/Asperger's Digest, www.autismdigest.com, January–February 2005)

Contributing Author Ellen Notbohm—Author, columnist and mother of sons with autism and ADHD, Ellen Notbohm is co-author with Veronica Zysk of *1001 Great Ideas for Teaching and Raising Children with Autism Spectrum Disorders*. A columnist for Autism Asperger's Digest, her articles on autism have also appeared in Exceptional Parent, Children's Voice, Language Magazine, numerous parenting magazines and over 100 websites.

Resources and links—Ellen Notbohm suggests visiting her Autism Today website to learn about her other products and services: Visit: <http://notbohm.autismtoday.com> today! (*Please note, don't put in the www.*) Your comments and requests for reprint permission are welcome at <ellen@thirdvariation.com>.

"If the English language made any sense, a catastrophe would be an apostrophe with fur."

Doug Larson's words are steeped in truth, of course. But a woeful truth it is for young children with language deficits. The problems are more thorny than furry.

Vernacular English as we speak it is nuanced to the eyeballs (there's one right there), and if you were to stop yourself throughout your day every time you unthinkingly used an idiom, pun, metaphor, double entendre or sarcastic remark, you would get very little else done.

For our children with autism, it must seem like an impenetrable swamp. With their concrete, visual thinking, their often brilliant associative abilities and their limited vocabularies, the imagery generated by some of our most common idioms must be very disturbing. Ants in his pants? Butterflies in her stomach? Open a can of worms. Cat got your tongue?

Actually, that very imagery they conjure up is at the root of some of our everyday expressions. When you tell him it's pouring cats and dogs, what you really mean is that it's raining very hard. One interpretation of the origin of this idiom—and there are many—goes back several hundred years to the English floods of the 17th and 18th centuries. After these torrential downpours, the streets would be littered with the bodies of cats and dogs that had drowned in the storm. It looked as if they had rained from the skies.

And I am sure this is what a lot of young ones with autism visualize when you say it's raining cats and dogs. Heaven help you if he hears you telling someone it's a dog-eat-dog world or not to throw the baby out with the bathwater.

You wouldn't dream of knowingly issuing instructions to your child in a foreign language, but English can seem that way, even to the unchallenged neurotypicals. A popular Internet essay notes: "Why do we drive on the parkway and park in the driveway? There is no egg in eggplant, nor ham in hamburger; (there's) neither apple nor pine in pineapple. A guinea pig is neither from Guinea nor is it a pig. If the plural of tooth is teeth, why isn't the plural of booth beeth? One goose, two geese. So one moose, two meese? If teachers taught, why didn't preachers praught? We have noses that run and feet that smell. How can a slim chance and a fat chance be the same, while a wise man and a wise guy are opposites?"

When Bryce was quite young, his ultra-literal, concrete thought processes were constantly tripping me up. One day I went into the boys' bathroom and discovered, in the sink, my older son Connor's Michael Jordan action figure with a tub of Danish Orchards Seedless Raspberry Preserves dumped on top. I was truly mystified. What is this? I asked Bryce.

Space Jam, he replied, having just seen the movie. I watched the crimson stain spreading across the sink and oozing down the drain. I truly did not know what the proper response should be. So I did the sensible thing. I nodded and walked away.

The bathroom was in fact the source of more than one run-in with the English language. One memorable afternoon I was helping Connor pack for a weekend trip, gathering up toothpaste, shampoo and soap. Where is your toiletries bag? I called across the loft.

WHAT??!! gasped Bryce.

I'm looking for the blue bag where Connor keeps his toiletries, I explained.

TOILET TREES?! HE'S TAKING TOILET TREES ON HIS TRIP???!!!

Bryce's jousting with the English language grew more sophisticated as he learned to read. At one point he went through a phase where he would become very agitated by the sight of phone booths: "Oh no! Not another one of those!" I eventually found out why—he had recently mastered the fact that "ph" makes an "f" sound, and he found it frankly annoyingly. (Or did he phind that phact phrankly annoying?) Seeing "phone" all around ticked him off. Speaking of which—why isn't 'phonics' spelled the way it sounds?

The bottom line is, communicating with a child with autism is astonishingly easier when we pause to consider our words. It may take a bit of retraining—yours, not his. Reconsider these popular idioms and clichés:

And even when you become aware of the morass of language obstacles your young one faces, you will fall off the wagon occasionally. (See?) When Bryce was about seven, we experienced what I came to call "The Terrible Weary Battle of the Hangnail." It was one of those infamous incidents that escalate inexorably from nothing to warfare before you realize what's happening. And you are left with an episode for which you can be forever un-proud.

He came to me with a tiny hangnail on the index finger. The offending finger was being held immobile by the opposite hand. No big deal, I said, I'll just nip it off with the nail clippers. Nooooooooooooo! He shrieked, gale force. It will HURT!

This child had spent his whole life being impervious to true pain and extreme cold. But for reasons I simply could not imagine, this hangnail was an antagonist of Goliath proportions.

First, the usual rebuttals. It won't hurt. I promise. I'll be very quick. Look the other way. No? Then: OK, you can do it yourself. No clippers? Just bite it off. No. We'll numb it with an ice pack first. No. We'll soften it up with a warm bath. No.

Out came plans B, C, D, E, F and G, like some horrid Cat in the Hat variation. All rejected.

Don't say	Instead say
It's a piece of cake	It is easy to do
Hold your horses!	Please stop (or slow down)
You are the apple of my eye	I love you very much
You have ants in your pants	It's hard for you to sit quietly
I'm at the end of my rope	I'm about to get angry
Stop beating around the bush	Please answer my question
Bite your tongue!	Please don't speak to me like that
You're like a bull in a china shop!	You are being too rough
I have butterflies in my stomach	I'm nervous/anxious about this
The ball is in your court	It's your turn
Let's call it a day	It's time to stop for now
He can't hold a candle to you at chess	You are better at chess than him
Cat got your tongue?	Is there a reason you can't answer me?
I smell a rat	This doesn't seem right to me

Exasperation on both sides escalated sharply.

The evening wore on. Was that me, almost shouting? I knew I was losing it, being sucked in, sucked down, seemingly unable to break the fall. Now two people were miserable instead of one.

Look, I said. Here are the choices: I nip it off. You nip it off. Or you just live with it.

Nooooooooooo! Scarlet face, tears flying, hair matted with sweat.

Bedtime finally came, and with it, a mom with the determination of Houdini. As I bent to tuck him in, so stealthily palming the nail clipper, I grabbed his finger and the hangnail was history. The pure surprise on his face was unforgettable. There, I said. Did it hurt?

No.

The next morning I took him on my lap and told him two things. First, he had to trust me. If I tell him something will not hurt, I mean it. I would always be honest with him if something was going to hurt, like a shot. I respected his preference for the truth, however unpleasant. So when I told him it wasn't going to hurt, it wasn't going to hurt.

Just as important, I told him I really admired his tenacity. I explained that "tenacity" meant that he really stood by what he believed, didn't back down, resisted pressure. That took strength and determination. "You really stuck to your guns," I said, "and that can be a very good thing." The words hadn't even cleared my lips before I knew I had goofed. A dark cloud instantly eclipsed a troubled face.

"I don't want to stick to a gun!" he cried, truly alarmed.

And then: "Are you sure you didn't mean . . . *gum?*"

Common idioms

Our conversation is rife with potentially incomprehensible idioms. How many of these automatically make their way into your speech: catch more flies with honey, bird in the hand, chicken feed, clam up, cold turkey, cook your goose, cry wolf, count your chickens before they hatch, look a gift horse in the mouth, eat crow, fat cat, for the birds, get your goat, high horse, in the doghouse, kill two birds with one stone, let the cat out of the bag, mad as a wet hen, monkey business, pull a rabbit out of a hat, rat race, sick as a dog, get your ducks in a row, snake in the grass, from the horse's mouth, straw that broke the camel's back, wild goose chase, teach an old dog new tricks.

And that's just the animal idioms. How about food idioms? It's cheesy. But that's the way the cookie crumbles. We all know you can't have your cake and eat it too.

Body idioms? Might cost an arm and a leg! But if you learn it by heart, you'll become an old hand, and be able to keep it under your thumb at all times.

Sports idioms, anyone? Hit it out of the park! The ball is in your court now, so if you jockey into position, you'll be able to call all the shots.

It's enough to drive your child up the wall.

Adolescents with autism and Asperger's Syndrome

CHAPTER 14

Preparing for the essential tasks of the real world

Contributing Author Teresa Bolick, Ph.D., Licensed Psychologist—Dr. Teresa Bolick is a licensed psychologist with a special interest in neurodevelopmental disorders, including autism, Asperger's Syndrome, and other autism spectrum disorders. Dr. Bolick graduated from the University of North Carolina at Chapel Hill with a B.A. in Psychology. She holds M.A. and Ph.D. degrees in psychology from Emory University. Dr. Bolick provides evaluation and treatment to children, adolescents and their families. She consults frequently to schools in New Hampshire and Massachusetts. She is an enthusiastic speaker, presenting workshops for parents, paraprofessionals and professionals across the United States. Dr. Bolick is the author of *Asperger Syndrome and adolescence: Helping preteens and teens get ready for the real world*, and *Asperger Syndrome and young children: Building skills for the real world*.

Resources and links—Teresa Bolick, Ph.D. suggests visiting her Autism Today website to learn about her other products and services: Visit <http://bolick.autismtoday.com> today! (*Please note, don't put in the www.*)

What's so special about adolescence?

"The period of life beginning with puberty and ending with complete growth and physical maturation"

—Stedman's Medical Dictionary, 1995

Bookstores and libraries are full of books that try to help parents and professionals understand adolescence. Almost every newspaper or magazine includes a story about yet another challenge that confronts adolescents in the twenty-first century. Why is it that so many of us look to the experts for advice in negotiating this phase of our youngsters' lives when this is the time of life that we remember best? Perhaps it is the complexity of physical, social, and emotional development. Perhaps it is our own memories of "the best and worst of times." Perhaps it is the signal that our children will be adults before we know it. And, although the books and experts may differ in their conclusions and advice, they share at least two conclusions about adolescence in general:

- Adults need to be sharp to understand what's going on. No two adolescents are the same, and there is no one-size-fits-all strategy for parenting or teaching.

- Adolescent brains are undergoing remarkable growth and change. These changes prepare the adolescent for the increasingly abstract and complex demands of the adult world. During this time, even the most typical of adolescents may process information in unique, often perplexing ways.

Is it any wonder, then, that parents and professionals are even more confused by the thoughts, feelings and behavior of adolescents with autism spectrum disorders? This chapter aims to shed light on some of the confusion. By no means, though, can one chapter answer all the questions. Instead, the goal is to provide food for thought and to point parents and professionals in the direction of additional answers. (You will find references at the end of this chapter. My own ideas are expressed in greater detail in my book, *Asperger Syndrome and adolescence: Helping preteens and teens get ready for the real world*.)

Adolescence meets autism spectrum disorders (ASD)

The advantages of ASD during adolescence

Although we don't often think of it, adolescents with ASD often bring with them a host of characteristics that can protect them from some of the social/emotional conflict and chaos of adolescence. These characteristics can also spare parents a few headaches, as they limit exposure to the more reckless aspects of adolescent life. They include:

- **Belief in, and need for, rules,** which allows the adolescent to behave well, at least as long as he/she knows the rules—more about this later.

- **A preference for telling the truth,** which virtually ensures that the adolescent with ASD will confess any transgression.

- **Black and white thinking,** which makes it less likely that the adolescent will try to look for the loopholes in the rules or directions that adults have given.

- **Reduced concern for what others think and popularity,** which can decrease susceptibility to negative peer pressure and fads.

- **Ability to focus on things that matter,** especially one's passions and preoccupations, which can lead to productivity and discovery.

- **Special talents and interests,** which can be sources of new ideas and ways to connect with others, and which can support strategies for coping.

When he or she studies, lives or works with people who understand his/her strengths and challenges, the adolescent with ASD can be an active and exemplary participant. The strategies that the adolescent uses to reduce unpredictability and anxiety also tend to prevent the risky behaviors that tempt typical peers. And, when engaged in a pursuit that interests them, adolescents with ASD are among the most conscientious and productive of workers. As Temple Grandin has often commented, people with ASD get more done because "the rest of you just stand around chatting all the time."

A real-life example: Thirteen-year-old Marc attended a school that placed a high premium on personal and community responsibility. When several of the boys in his grade became involved in a scheme to sell their parents' prescription drugs, most of their friends looked the other way. They didn't want to risk being called a "snitch" (or worse). Marc heard about the scheme and quickly realized that it violated many school and community rules. He immediately went to the school principal and gave names and details of the scheme. Marc's parents and teachers praised him for averting what could have been disastrous for the entire school community.

The disadvantages of ASD during adolescence

While many of the characteristics of ASD make it easier for the adolescent to follow rules and persist in problem solving, each of these characteristics can also have its drawbacks. Black and white thinking may keep a student on the right side of the school rules but doesn't help much in the world of adolescent friendships. Similarly, persistence in pursuing special interests can get in the way of completing schoolwork in other subjects.

In addition, adolescents with ASD typically struggle with one or more of the following concerns:

- **Poor regulation of the Four A's (Alertness/Arousal, Attention, Activity, Affect),** which can lead the adolescent to break many of the rules that he/she holds most dear. For example, when surrounded by lots of people, Sally becomes so "revved" that she can't pay **attention** to the person who is talking with her. She also begins to rock back and forth **(activity)** to help settle down her nervous system **(alertness or arousal)**. If she has to stay in the situation, she's likely to feel increasingly overwhelmed and to display emotion **(affect)** in ways that are not suitable for the situation.

- **Clumsiness,** which can lead the adolescent with ASD to stand too close to others, to display awkward body language and to have trouble negotiating the crowded hallways of school or malls. And in a culture that places extraordinary value upon athletic skills, the

147

adolescent with poor motor skills may not know how to fit in.

- **Difficulties in seeing the forest for the trees,** which can pose the risk that the adolescent will get stuck on details and miss the big picture. It's not at all unusual for a very bright adolescent with Asperger's Syndrome, for example, to recite every detail in a movie without knowing what the movie is about. And, since social interaction is so often a matter of big picture, they are likely to engage in "socially penalizing behaviour," a term coined by Elsa Abele, an expert in social communication.

- **Inefficiencies in social communication,** which are probably universal for adolescents with ASD. These inefficiencies can range from severe challenges in oral expression to milder difficulties in understanding the subtleties of adolescent humor and slang. Regardless of the severity, these inefficiencies make it difficult for the adolescent with ASD to know what other people mean. They can miss the point in academic lessons (and study the wrong things) or fail to heed the indirect directions and warnings of peers and adults (for example, "Don't you think your sister would like a turn on the computer?"). Inefficiencies in social communication are likely to affect every aspect of daily life.

- **Problems in perspective-taking (Theory of Mind),** which tend to go hand in hand with inefficient social communication. How can we make inferences about another person's feelings unless we can read verbal and nonverbal communication? And how can we adjust our own behavior to create a desired impression unless we know something about what the other person likes, dislikes, feels and thinks? Over and over again, I am dismayed by how difficult it is for bright adolescents with Asperger's Syndrome and autism to answer the question, "What is (person's name) like?" Even when the adolescent can describe the person's physical characteristics, possessions and behavior, he/she is unable to predict the person's reaction or preferences. Without adequate Theory of Mind, the adolescent is unable to behave empathically or respectfully.

- **Challenges in problem solving,** which are common, even for the most intellectually gifted individual with ASD. Many of these difficulties are associated with limited ability to identify what is salient (or important) in a situation. Without efficient salience determination, the adolescent is unlikely to know what to look or listen for and, unfortunately, to fail to filter out irrelevant thoughts or actions. Another obstacle to problem solving is poor generalization. Often, the adolescent with ASD does not see the similarity between the current task and previous situations. Instead of applying the skills that worked so well last time, he or she starts over from the beginning.

- **Inexperience in social situations,** which is a frequent contributor to the everyday functioning of the adolescent with ASD. While everyone else learned "playground politics" (Stanley Greenspan's term) in the sandbox at preschool, the child with an ASD had too many motor or sensory challenges to tolerate the playground. While peers had play dates and sleepovers, the child with ASD still communicated too inefficiently for parents to trust him/her with another family. Hanging out at the mall, going to the movies or sitting around gossiping are seldom on the list of favorite activities for children with ASD. Hence, the individual with ASD enters adolescence without the information necessary to manage a growing body, a questioning mind and ever-changing emotions.

A real-life example: For the first time in her life, 17-year-old Anne had some friends. Girls in the art club recognized Anne's drawing talents and were receptive to her lengthy descriptions of animé characters (her special interest). Over a weekend, Anne's parents told her that she had earned the privilege of going to the animé convention in a nearby city. Eager to tell this exciting news to her friends,

Anne went to school on Monday morning and spied her friends at the end of the hall. Two girls were huddled around a third girl, who was obviously upset, according to an observant teacher. Anne was so intent upon her desire to share her news that she totally missed the big picture that a friend was in distress. When she bounded up to the girls and shouted out her exciting news, the other three looked at her with disdain. Why didn't she know that a friend was upset?

Six essential tasks and how to master them

Partnership—a necessary first step

Remember that the one of the tasks of adolescence is to learn to be as independent as possible. Doesn't it make sense, then, that the adolescent with an ASD should be a working partner in the process?

The first step in any intervention program is to ensure that you and your working partner (the adolescent) have a mutual understanding of the goals and how to try to reach them.

Task 1: Adaptive self-management of thoughts, feelings and behavior

Adaptive self-management refers to a person's ability to regulate alertness, attention, activity and affect (emotion) efficiently enough to support active participation in everyday life. As suggested above, poor self-regulation is one of the most common challenges faced by individuals with ASD. Adults with ASD, such as Temple Grandin, confirm that challenges in self-regulation are among significant obstacles to success in the world of work. As she stated matter-of-factly in one presentation, "If you throw your computer monitor out the window when you're mad, you'll get fired." Others, such as Stephen Shore and Jerry Newport, explain that self-regulatory challenges (especially sensory sensitivities) can have a dramatic effect upon dating and relationships.

There is no doubt that adolescents with ASD try hard to manage their sensations, thoughts and feelings. Their repetitive behaviors, need for routine, and single-minded focus on preferred topics are examples of these efforts. The problem is that their self-regulatory strategies are frequently inefficient or inappropriate to the situation.

Many individuals with ASD must deal with extremely high stress levels. The accumulation of sensory assaults, language and social demands, and flexibility requirements taxes the person's capacity to manage. At a certain point, an apparently small thing can lead to a meltdown. Observers often wonder why the person with ASD is over-reacting to something so trivial. It's important to realize that the individual is not reacting to that last event but, more likely, the event is the straw that broke the camel's back.

A real-life example: Rick is a 14-year-old in Grade 8. Although his non-verbal problem-solving skills are quite impressive, his language skills are similar to those of a child in Grade 1. Rick converses well one-on-one with people who know how to adjust their language to his skills. But when another person enters the conversation or when the language level gets too complicated. Rick gets anxious and begins to quote Disney videos. The benefit of Rick's "scripting" is that it takes him away from an anxiety-provoking situation. A disadvantage is that he is unavailable for appropriate interaction with other people. Rick also gets stuck in his scripting and is unable to understand and follow the directions of his parents and teachers. If adults insist on compliance, Rick is likely to yell out "NO! You can't make me!" and run from the room. In other words, Rick's stress levels are so high they have prompted a fight or flight response.

Of course, it's impossible to eliminate all of the stress in life. And occasionally everyone has trouble coping with the last straw. The key to self-management is to reduce stress and strain before it reaches unmanageable levels. This is accomplished by two types of interventions: modifications of environment and routine, and preventive stress management. Over the course of adolescence, it's important to shift more and more of the responsibility for these interventions to the person with ASD. It is this shift that allows the adolescent or young adult to function with maximum independence.

Modifications of environment and routines

- **Create spaces that support the adolescent's sensory needs.** For example, a student with hypersensitive hearing is likely to need a quiet home base or retreat space at school and at home, for study or for regrouping.

- **Carefully consider the sensory load associated with places like the school bus or cafeteria.** The convenience associated with bus transportation or a hot lunch might not be worth the costs of sensory overload or exposure to teasing.

- **Allow access to music, snacks and other sensory tools that enhance concentration and reduce stress.** It may actually help to listen to music while doing homework or to eat a crunchy snack before a class that requires a lot of listening.

- **Experiment with clothing and hygiene routines that reduce irritation but do not create socially penalizing situations.** One adolescent girl was constantly adjusting her bra, drawing stares from other people. At the suggestion of her counselor, the girl and her mother went to a department store with experienced saleswomen. Although the girl detested the hour or so of bra fittings, the result was the discovery of a style that fit comfortably. After several washings, the bras were comfortable and the adjustments ceased. A young man was hypersensitive to the feel of a toothbrush in his mouth. His occupational therapist suggested that he brush his teeth while in the shower. Voila! Problem solved! (By the way, the same young man later discovered that he could shave in the shower with similarly positive results.)

- **Make sure that the adolescent has a sleep routine.** This includes falling asleep at a reasonable time and awakening at the time needed to get ready for school or work. Consult a physician if this is not possible.

Direct teaching of stress management

- **Teach the adolescent to monitor physical and emotional signs of stress.** The Alert Program (also known as "How does your engine run?") by Williams and Shellenberger can teach individuals how to recognize their level of alertness/arousal and choose suitable remedies to perk up or settle down their nervous systems.

- **Experiment with relaxation strategies that fit the adolescent's learning profile.** For example, Cautela's book on relaxation techniques is particularly helpful for adolescents with cognitive challenges. On the other hand, an adolescent with better verbal skills might enjoy meditation or autogenic relaxation training (See the reference by Goldbeck and Schmid, 2003.). For students with adequate imitation skills, yoga can be extraordinarily helpful. A helpful hint: adolescents are more likely to accept these strategies if they are presented to an entire class!

- **Develop a regular exercise routine, adapted to the student's sensory and motor profile.** Adolescents with ASD are often more comfortable with non-ball sports and with exercise that does not require special (uncomfortable) clothing or equipment. Running, swimming, skiing, weight training (for those older than 14) and martial arts (with a sensitive teacher) are examples of exercise regimens that have been successful for individuals with ASD. Remember, research has demonstrated that exercise is superior to medication and other therapies as an antidepressant!

- **Consider involvement in the arts, as a participant or as a spectator.** Music, visual arts and drama have multiple payoffs. From a regulatory status, they can be remarkably efficient. They have the added benefit of exposing the adolescent to other people who tend to be more accepting of diversity.

- **Help the adolescent learn to use special talents and interests as stress management strategies.** For example, an adolescent who likes to make clay figures might add a half-hour of sculpting time to his morning or evening routine.

- **If special interests are not developmentally or socially appropriate, use them as starting points.** For example, one middle schooler was obsessed with PokeMon long after his peers had moved on to other card and electronic games. His school counselor countered the boy's resistance to the other games by setting up an incentive system: for every half-hour spent playing a game of his peer's choice, he earned a half-hour of playing PokeMon with the counselor.

The benefits of music: When I extolled the self-regulatory virtues of music during one workshop, an occupational therapist provided additional information about why playing an instrument (especially a horn) is so efficient. Not only does playing require the individual to breathe in a controlled way but it also requires the musician to use hands together at the midline of the body, an action that we know to be organizing for the nervous system.

Task 2: Functional and portable communication

Functional and portable communication means that the individual is able to convey needs, desires, thoughts and feelings to anyone anywhere. All too often, we hear parents or professionals say, "But I know what he means." That's terrific, but it doesn't do much good if you're not with the individual with ASD. While the type of communication is going to vary with the individual (whether it is speech, gestures or augmentative systems), everyone needs to be able to convey the following communicative intents:

- Joint attention: the ability to share a mutual focus with another person, whether non-verbally or verbally.

- Desire or need for an item or activity.

- Dislike for an item or activity.

- Initiation of social attention or interaction.

- Continuation of social interaction: reciprocity or two-way communication.

- Desire for "space" or to be left alone.

- Request for information or clarification.

- Comments upon the words or actions of others.

- Communicative repair: for example, "Oh, I didn't mean that I wanted you to go away. I just meant that I need to think a minute."

- Negotiation.

- Conflict resolution.

While most of us assume that these skills can be problematic for adolescents with greater communicative challenges, we may not realize that those with Asperger's Syndrome or PDD-NOS typically need just a much help (though perhaps in a different way).

A real-life example: After several weeks of successful employment in a used book store, 19-year-old Sam suddenly stopped going to work. He wasn't ill. He was just too overwhelmed to go. After a lengthy discussion in my office, the problem surfaced. Sam's boss had given him a "punch list" of things to do when there were no customers in the store. When he got to the task of "straighten the books on the shelf," Sam didn't know what was meant. "You can't straighten used paperbacks. They're too floppy," Sam thought. Sam's confusion made him anxious and his anxiety made him flee. Once he left, he was too embarrassed to call his boss. The bottom line: Sam hadn't mastered the communicative skill of seeking clarification. No one had thought to teach him.

By adolescence, individual therapy only within the office of the speech/language pathologist (SLP) is often insufficient. Some of the most effective intervention I have observed occurred when the SLP observed in the real-life setting, practiced the requisite skill with the adolescent one-on-one or in a small group, and then assisted the adolescent in generalizing the skill back to the real-world setting. It's also essential to work first on skills that are critical and/or meaningful for the adolescent's success. Of equal importance is the recognition that communication training is not just the task of the

SLP. Communication needs to happen throughout our waking hours, on good days and on bad.

"Small group conversations make my nerves feel like they are wearing stilts on an icy pavement."(Liane Holliday Willey, 1999, p. 37.) I use Dr. Willey's quote as a way of reminding us that communication puts the person with ASD in a precarious situation. In order to help, we have to approach from two directions: first, by using modifications and accommodations to "dry up the pavement"; second, by teaching the communicative equivalent of "walking on stilts."

Modifications and accommodations (a partial list)

- **Talk with your working partner, the adolescent, about what to tell others about his/her communication.** Then help the adolescent convey these tips to teachers, coaches and peers. (The tips listed below emerged from conversations I've had with adolescents I know.)

- **Always give ample processing time.** Don't ask rapid-fire questions. Don't talk louder. Don't answer for him/her. And don't let him/her off the communicative hook.

- **Respect the adolescent's ability to communicate.** Don't look to the adolescent's parent or assistant for an answer unless the adolescence cues you to do so. And if you're the parent or assistant, don't answer for the adolescent unless he/she requests.

- **Seek clarification when you don't understand.** Don't just provide the "backfill" that allows you to understand what the adolescent means. Other people may not be able to fill in the gaps as efficiently.

- **If the adolescent uses an augmentative communication system, ensure that he/she always has it nearby.** (This is the adolescent's voice.) Then encourage and reinforce the use of the system, including by using it yourself.

- **Use visual and verbal cues.** Visual cues can take many forms—photos, picture symbols, lists or gestures. They help the adolescent understand what you mean. Visual supports can help the student with working memory challenges to remember important information or steps in a process.

- **Coach peers regarding the communication strengths and challenges of the adolescent with ASD.**

Direct teaching of skills

- **Always start with the skills that the adolescent needs or wants most.** For example, 16-year-old Melanie had absolutely no interest in working on social communication until she noticed that the other girls on the track team passed the time between events by chatting. She came to the next session asking for help with learning conversation starters. All of a sudden, she was quite motivated to work on social communication.

- **Teach skills within a meaningful context, whenever possible.** Alex's team wanted him to learn socially appropriate mealtime manners and conversation. Yet his sensory sensitivities were such that he couldn't tolerate the lunchroom, and he ate lunch in the classroom with his assistant. Alex had very little to say until the team decided to bring in peers during lunchtime. All of a sudden, Alex was intrigued with social interaction. And the peers let him know when he "grossed them out" by chewing with his mouth open or belching loudly. They were much more successful in modifying Alex's mealtime behavior than the adults had been.

- **When necessary, teach scripts for specific social situations.** Many of the adolescents I know follow Temple Grandin's suggestion of using "mental videos" to remember what to say in certain situations.

- **Be sure to teach slang, including when to use it and when to avoid using it.** In adolescence, this also includes teaching when/when not to curse.

- **Teach code switching.** In other words, make

sure that the adolescent knows which topics, words and tone of voice can be used in different situations.

- **For students who learn well from videos, use favorite movies or TV shows (on tape) to illustrate target skills.** Videos are particularly helpful in teaching about non-verbal skills, such as body language, facial expressions and personal space. Don't hesitate to videotape peer models engaging in the communicative behaviors that you'd like the adolescent to acquire.

- **Refer to references by Freeman and Dake, McAfee, Garcia Winner, and Gutstein for lesson plans and more ideas.**

Task 3: Social cognition/awareness (or "Theory of Mind")

A real-life example: For what seemed like years, Corey's parents and team had been trying to teach him to be empathic. But he just wasn't able to step out of his own shoes long enough to take another person's point of view. Then, in Grade 8, he came to his therapy session saying that he thought I would be proud of him. He went on to describe a situation at his locker earlier that day. One of the top three girls in the eighth grade had been at her locker a few doors down. When she bent over, Corey was able to see down the neckline of her tank top. When asked what he did next, Corey said, "I turned and went into my classroom." I asked why he had chosen that action. Corey said, "I didn't think she would want to know that I saw."

Understanding of the mental states of others allows us to follow directions, avoid hurt feelings and other interpersonal scrapes, and form friendships and close relationships. Difficulties with social awareness and Theory of Mind also predispose the adolescent to sound rude and disrespectful to listeners who do not understand ASD. Social awareness also underlies the behavioral adjustments that we make from one situation to another and from one person to the next. To parents, poorly developed social cognition/awareness leads to the concern that their child will never develop empathy.

For many individuals with ASD, empathy and social awareness are learned in a logical or scripted format. For example, the work of Simon Baron Cohen (e.g., *How to teach children with autism to mind read*) provides a series of pictures and formulas that explain what makes a person feel a certain way. Parents sometimes say that they don't want their son or daughter to merely behave in a considerate or empathic way but also to feel empathy. I typically reply that I hope that the adolescent will eventually feel empathy, but in the meantime we need to make sure that he or she acts empathically and avoids social penalties

Modifications and accommodations

- **Make sure that peers and adults understand that the adolescent's social errors are likely to be a result of naiveté and social incompetence, not disrespect.** Otherwise, the adolescent with ASD will receive negative disciplinary consequences that follow school policy but do little to teach adaptive replacement behaviors.

- **Use the principles of applied behavior analysis and functional assessment to understand when, where and with whom the adolescent makes social and behavioral errors.** Functional assessment of behavior can point us toward the supports that will increase the adolescent's understanding of the situation and the new behaviors that should be taught.

- **"Make the implicit explicit,"** as my SLP colleague Nancy Cegalis states. Be very clear about behavioral expectations and the social and emotional consequences of the adolescent's actions and words. For example, after overlooking the shrill ear-splitting (but gleeful) repetitive vocalizations of their 13-year-old daughter when she was ill with allergies, Suzy's parents decided they needed to address this socially penalizing behavior once she felt better. They started with a social story that explained that loud shrieks hurt people's ears and made them unhappy. The social story ended with a

153

picture of a person gesturing "Sh-h-h." Suzy was then reinforced each time she responded positively to the reminder of "That hurts my ears. Sh-h-h."

Direct teaching of the "rules of the social road"

- **Teach manners and social conventions.** Even if the adolescent doesn't understand the reasons, make sure that he or she knows how to behave in common situations. Social stories are excellent ways to teach social conventions. Videos are also quite helpful. Alex Packer's book is a humorous guide to manners for all adolescents. Remember, though—no nagging! Adolescents with ASD are as immune to nagging as their typical counterparts.

- **Talk about photos or magazine pictures that illustrate mental states.** Draw arrows to the facial expressions, body language and background details that give clues. Then speculate about the emotions and reasons for it. (Dr. McAfee provides a number of wonderful suggestions about this in *Navigating the social world*.)

- **Make a chart of "passions and peeves" for family members.** Talk about what each person likes and dislikes. Record it on a giant poster board. Then talk about what a person could do to please Mom when she's had a frustrating business trip or what to avoid when Dad is feeling stressed.

- **Teach discretion.** For a more verbal adolescent, use a concentric circles chart (Some call this a Circle of Friends.) with the adolescent at the center to illustrate which topics can be talked about at different levels of closeness. A less verbal adolescent may need a simpler format, such as a two-column chart with headings "Private" and "Public." Then use sticky notes or pictures to document what can be said or done in private *versus* public contexts.

- **Read books or watch movies with the adolescent and talk about the emotions of the characters.** Books or videos are often more helpful than verbal discussions because they can be reviewed again and again to assist understanding.

Task 4: Emotional competence

Emotional competence refers to the ability to recognize, understand, express and modulate (or control) feelings. As discussed above, recognition and regulation of emotion is essential to behavior management. All too often, adolescents with ASD don't recognize their emotions until they have already acted upon them. Another significant challenge for a number of adolescents with ASD is the emergence of anxiety and/or depression. Emotional competence rests upon prevention of anxiety and depression as well as the recognition and understanding of feelings in the moment.

Modifications and accommodations

- **Practice "low and slow."** As soon as the adolescent begins to get agitated, we need to settle ourselves down. Lower the volume and pitch of our voices. Slow down our rate of speech. Allow plenty of processing time. Slow our breathing and actions. Loudness, finger-pointing and threats (such as "Do you want a time out?!") only increase the level of the fight or flight response that the adolescent experiences.

- **Help the adolescent use adaptive self-management strategies preventively.** See the section on Self-management for suggestions.

- **Use visual schedules and sub-schedules to ensure that the adolescence knows what to expect.** These may include pictures, words, and/or high tech (such as a PDA). The key element is that of predictability.

- **Predict glitches (or unexpected events).** Whenever you introduce a schedule of any kind, remind the adolescent that something unexpected may happen. Social stories can help explain glitches.

- **Use social stories and other visual supports to explain a situation and expected behavior in advance.** Provide information regarding what will happen, how other people are likely to feel and act, and how the adolescent can act in order to be most comfortable. For adolescents with substantial regulatory challenges, include a safe exit strategy, such as "If you get overloaded by all the talking, you can go to Uncle John's study and play Game Boy."

- **Consult the adolescent's physician if anxiety, sadness, hopeless or repetitive thoughts and behaviors interfere with daily functioning.** While medication is not a cure-all, it may take the edge off the emotions long enough for the adolescent to benefit from other interventions.

Direct teaching of skills

- **Ensure that the adolescent has a repertoire of remedies for settling down and perking up his/her mind and body.** See the section on Self-management for suggestions.

- **Use a Feelings Chart to help the adolescent make connections between the physical signs of the emotion, the "name" of the emotion, a possible reason for the feeling and an adaptive remedy if needed.** This may start with something like, "You're frowning, grinding your teeth and yelling. You look like you're angry." (For less verbally skilled individuals, present this in photo or picture form.) Avoid asking "why" questions, as these tend to be disorganizing. Instead, for the more naïve adolescent, say something like, "I wonder if you're angry because we ran out of chocolate ice cream." For the more sophisticated adolescent, try, "You're mad because . . . ." and wait. Once the adolescent knows a reason for the feeling, you can move on to, "What can you do about it?" or "You feel angry. Do you want to . . . . or . . . ?" Keep the Feelings Chart and a menu of possible remedies handy for quick reference when a similar situation arises again. See my book for more ideas.

- **For the adolescent with intrusive or repetitive thoughts and actions (obsessions or compulsions), work with the team to complete a functional assessment of the behavior before trying to eliminate it.** Repetitive thoughts and actions often serve a self-soothing function. If we try to take these away without replacing them with an adaptive alternative, the adolescent is likely to develop a new troublesome behavior. Once you know the function of the behavior, you can work with the team to create a positive behavioral support plan.

- **Reinforce every instance of adaptive coping.** For example, Ed had begun to make threatening gestures and comments whenever his mother interrupted his activity with a direction to do something different. Both of them were quite shocked when he actually hit her one day. Ed then agreed that he needed to learn another strategy for coping with disappointment. We agreed that turning around and walking away was a good first step, although his parents hoped that he could eventually follow their directions immediately. In the first phase of teaching coping, Ed's parents noted on a point sheet each time he accepted a direction without threatening behavior (and gave him triple points for complying immediately). They also commented (after he had calmed down) about times when he started to threaten but then stopped himself. Within several weeks, Ed's threatening behavior was eliminated.

- **Help the adolescent use special interests and talents as coping mechanisms.**

A real-life example: Bart had already learned that his interest in music could help him connect with peers in the band. The new peers helped him branch out in his musical tastes, trying types of music that he had previously rejected. Soon Bart learned that he could choose music according to the mood he needed to be in—cool jazz to settle himself down for studying or Canadian Brass to perk himself up when he was dragging. By the way, Bart also parlayed his encyclopedic musical knowledge into a part-time job as a DJ!

Task 5: "Showing what you know"

As a psychologist who evaluates children and adolescents with ASD, I often find that the individual is inefficient at demonstrating knowledge on demand. My own observations of the student or observations by parents and professionals often suggest that the adolescent can provide much more information when the idea "just comes" than when asked directly. But the real world of work and relationships can seldom wait for the solution to "just come." This makes it critical for us to ensure that the adolescent can access information and skills on a bad day as well as on a good day, in an unfamiliar context as well as in a familiar one.

While the specific information or skill to be accessed is going to depend upon the adolescent's cognitive and communicative abilities, there are several strategies that are helpful to everyone.

Modifications, accommodations and direct teaching

- **Remember the Hanes underwear slogan of many years ago: "You can't think right when your underwear's too tight."** Lesson to be learned: our bodies and minds have to be well regulated for us to learn and problem solve.

- **Teach the adolescent how to follow a schedule or list of activities.** Ideally, the adolescent should be able to make a transition from one task or activity to another with a minimum of interfering behavior or redirection.

- **Always identify the purpose of an activity or task.** This will allow the adolescent to focus more easily upon salient aspects and to ignore irrelevant aspects.

- **Whenever possible, help the adolescent activate prior knowledge about a topic or skill.** Individuals with autism often have difficulty with generalization, largely because they don't automatically recognize the similarity between a current situation and one that went before.

- **Use task cards to improve independent functioning.** A task card is like a recipe in that it lists the necessary materials and then the steps required for completing a task. Task cards can employ photos, pictures, words or a combination. Once an adolescent can complete a task with adult supports, gradually withdraw the assistance until the student is entirely independent. Keep a notebook of task cards. After several are mastered, simply list the task on the daily schedule and have the student find the necessary task card and materials.

- **Teach the adolescent how to find information.** Every adolescent should be able to seek information or assistance, whether in a book or online, or from another person. Many teachers use task cards to help the student remember how to seek certain types of information.

- **Use templates to help the adolescent express information.** For a student who is struggling with oral expression, sentence strips such as those in the Picture Exchange Communication System (PECS) assist in the expression of complete thoughts. For more verbal adolescents, use story grammar templates (Who? Where? When? What happened? How did everyone feel?) to remind them what information is necessary when telling someone else about an event. Adolescents with more advanced written expression skills will also benefit from the use of paragraph or essay templates to organize their work.

Task 6: Safety and life skills

Unfortunately, few adolescents with ASD are able to generalize efficiently from skills taught in books to real-world situations. I like to use video modeling, social stories, power cards and task cards to pre-teach rules and skills and then to go with the adolescent into the real world for additional practice.

A real-life example: Stan had two goals that he wanted to achieve by his eighteenth birthday, only a few months away. He wanted to register to vote and he wanted to order his own meal at our traditional birthday lunch at the local house of pizza. For several years, Stan was too anxious to order. More recently, his speech was still unintelligible to "outsiders." For several weeks before his birthday, Stan used the menu to read aloud his selection. He then practiced in front of his mother and in front of me. We role-played what he could do when the restaurant worker didn't understand him. He decided to do a quick relaxation exercise before going into the restaurant. We agreed that writing down his order could be his last resort. After pre-teaching and practice, Stan successfully ordered. Later that day, he also secured his voter registration card!

Teaching safety and life skills to adolescents with ASD is just like teaching anything else: we have to identify the steps, teach each step systematically with visual supports, use task analysis to problem-solve when there are glitches and plan for generalization. There are a number of tools on the market that can save you the effort of reinventing the wheel, including Wrobel's 2003 book on hygiene and personal care. Jerry and Mary Newport's book on sexuality also provides a number of helpful lessons regarding safety in dating and relationships. The most important point is that safety and life skills must be taught directly, even to the most gifted of adolescents with ASD.

A few other important issues
Disclosure and self-advocacy

The decisions about what, when and whom to tell about ASD are ultimately left to the adolescent and his/her family. Individuals who are more severely affected by autism usually face fewer questions about disclosure, because their challenges are more visible. Adolescents with Asperger's Syndrome or PDD-NOS often face a more difficult choice, however.

A real-life example: Madeleine had an Individual Education Plan (IEP) throughout school. When she went to art school for college, she insisted that she wanted to try it on her own. Madeleine did not register with the college learning support center nor did she admit to professors that she had Asperger's Syndrome. Madeleine managed quite admirably with most of her coursework. Two art professors became quite impatient with her slow pace, however. At first,

Madeleine tried to explain it as her "learning style." The professors were not sympathetic, though, and Madeleine fell further and further behind. Finally, Madeleine went to the learning support center with her high school IEP, revealed that she has Asperger's Syndrome and enlisted the assistance of an advisor there. The advisor helped Madeleine explain AS to the professors and their attitudes became more supportive.

Ultimately, disclosure and self-advocacy are tools to secure supports necessary for success in the real world. Early in adolescence, parents and other adults are likely to take the lead in advocating for these supports. Ideally, over the course of adolescence, the individual with ASD becomes more skilled in asking for what he or she needs. This process is described quite eloquently in essays written by individuals with ASD and published in books edited by Dawn Prince-Hughes (2002) and Stephen Shore (2004).

Employment

Employment success for individuals with ASD varies widely, but all too many are under-employed or unemployed. Fortunately, there are some excellent resources about career development and employment. Please refer to books by Meyer (2001) and Grandin & Duffy (2004) for suggestions. But, remember, employment success is likely to rest more upon adequate self-management and communication skills than upon technical skills or information.

Supported living

Certainly we all hope that our adolescents will mature into adults who can live independently. When this is not the case, states and provinces have a variety of programs to assist adults with living as independently as possible. What isn't so well known, though, is that these programs are often overwhelmed with referrals. Don't wait until your son or daughter is an adult to look into this. Talk with your local developmental disabilities agency early in adolescence. It's better to have a spot and not need it than the other way around.

Medication

It is commonly accepted that there is no medication for autism *per se*. It is also accepted that medications are often helpful for some of the troubling aspects

157

of ASD. In adolescence, medications are used most frequently to address anxiety, depression, repetitive behaviors and poor impulse control. Discussion of the use of medication is beyond my expertise. Please refer to books by Tsai (2002) and Volkmar and Wiesner (2004) for comprehensive information.

Psychotherapy and other supports

Many adolescents with ASD are not able to take advantage of traditional insight-oriented psychotherapy, but appropriate services from psychologists, psychiatrists, clinical social workers and other psychotherapists can be very useful in:

- Evaluating and explaining the adolescent's developmental profile

- Developing the working partnership

- Conducting functional assessments of behavior and creating positive behavioral support plans

- Teaching self-management, social cognition and communication skills

- Providing cognitive behavioral interventions to address anxiety, depression, obsessive-compulsive behaviors and other problems

- Providing support for parents, siblings and educational teams

- In addition to the supports derived from psychotherapy, many adolescents with ASD will benefit from social skills groups, occupational and/or physical therapy and recreational therapy. Ideally, each of these interventions will be a part of coordinated program.

One last take-home message

We often worry about what will happen to our children when they grow up, especially when the child has a disability. As we look to the future of our children, though, we must remember the words of Ralph Waldo Emerson (1878): "What is a weed? A plant whose virtues have not yet been discovered."

I wish you the best of fortune in the discovery of your adolescent's virtues.

NOTE: References marked AS-AD are particularly focused upon adolescents with Asperger's Syndrome.

American Academy of Child and Adolescent Psychiatry (1999). Practice parameters for the assessment and treatment of children, adolescents, and adults with autism and other pervasive developmental disorders. *Journal of the American Academy of Child and Adolescent Psychiatry, 38,* 32S-54S.

Andron, L. (2001). *Our journey through High Functioning Autism and Asperger Syndrome: A Roadmap.* London: Jessica Kingsley Publishers. **(AS-AD)**

Attwood, T. (1998). *Asperger's Syndrome: A guide for parents and professionals.* London: Jessica Kingsley Publishers. **(AS-AD)**

Baker, L.J., & Welkowitz, L.A. (2005). *Asperger's Syndrome: Intervening in schools, clinics, and communities.* Mahwah, NJ: Lawrence Erlbaum Associates

Bashe, P.R., & Kirby, B.L. (2001). *The OASIS guide to Asperger Syndrome.* New York: Crown Publishers.

Bolick, T. (2001). *Asperger Syndrome and adolescence: Helping preteens and teens get ready for the real world.* Gloucester, MA: Fair Winds Press. **(AS-AD)**

Bothmer, S. (2003). *Creating the peaceable classroom.* Tucson, AZ: Zephyr Press.

Cautela, J., & Groden, J. (1978). *Relaxation: A comprehensive manual for adults, children, and children with special needs.* Champaign, IL: Research Press Company.

Cohen, D.J., & Volkmar, F.R. (Eds.) (1997). *Handbook of autism and pervasive developmental disorders* (Second edition). New York: John Wiley & Sons. **(AS-AD)**

Cumine, V., Leach, J., & Stevenson, G. (1998). *Asperger Syndrome: A practical guide for teachers.* London: David Fulton Publishers. **(AS-AD)**

Debbaudt, D. (2002). *Autism, advocates, and law enforcement professionals.* London: Jessica Kingsley Publishers.

Ducharme, J.M., & Drain, T.L. (2004). Errorless academic compliance training: Improving generalized cooperation with parental requests in children with autism. *Journal of the American Academy of Child and Adolescent Psychiatry, 43,* 163-171.

Duke, M.P., Nowicki, S., & Martin, E.A. (1996). *Teaching your child the language of social success.* Atlanta: Peachtree Publishers. **(AS-AD)**

Faherty, C. (2000). *Asperger's—What does it mean to me?* Arlington, TX: Future Horizons.

Fouse, B., & Wheeler, M. (1997). *A treasure chest of behavioral strategies for individuals with autism.* Arlington, TX: Future Horizons, Inc.

Freeman, S., & Dake, L. (1997). *Teach me language: A language manual for children with autism, Asperger's syndrome and related developmental disorders.* Langley, BC, Canada: SKF Books.

Fullerton, A., Stratton, J., Coyne, P., & Gray, C. (1996). *Higher functioning adolescents and young adults with autism.* Austin, TX: Pro-Ed. **(AS-AD)**

Gagnon, E. (2001). *Power cards: Using special interests to motivate children and youth with Asperger Syndrome and autism.* Shawnee Mission, KS: Autism Asperger Publishing Co.

Gilpin, R. W. (1993). *Laughing and loving with autism.* Arlington, TX: Future Horizons. (and its sequels)

Goldbeck, L., & Schmid, K. (2003). Effectiveness of autogenic relaxation training on children and adolescents with behavioral and emotional problems. *Journal of the American Academy of Child and Adolescent Psychiatry, 42,* 1046-1054.

Grandin, T. (1995). *Thinking in pictures.* New York: Doubleday. (and other books by Dr. Grandin)

Grandin, T., & Duffy, K. (2004). *Developing talents: Careers for individuals with Asperger Syndrome and high functioning autism.* Shawnee Mission, KS: Autism Asperger Publishing Co.

Gray, C. (2000). *The new social story book: Illustrated edition.* Arlington, TX: Future Horizons.

Gutstein, S. E. (2000). *Autism Aspergers: Solving the relationship puzzle.* Arlington, TX: Future Horizons.

Haddon, M. (2003). *The curious incident of the dog in the night.* New York: Doubleday.

Heinrichs, R. (2003). *Perfect targets: Asperger Syndrome and bullying.* Shawnee Mission, KS: Autism Asperger Publishing Co.

Hoeksma,M.R., Kemner, C., Verbaten, M.N., & van Engeland, H. (2004). Processing capacity in children and adolescents with pervasive developmental disorders. *Journal of Autism and Developmental Disorders, 34,* 341-354.

Howlin, P., Baron-Cohen, S., & Hadwin, J. (1999). *Teaching children with autism to mind-read: A practical guide.* Chichester: John Wiley & Sons.

Jacobsen, P. (2003). *Asperger Syndrome and psychotherapy: Understanding Asperger Perspectives.* London: Jessica Kingsley Publishers.

Kashman, N., & Mora, J. (2002). *An OT and SLP team approach: Sensory and communication strategies that work.* Las Vegas: Sensory Resources.

Klin, A., Jones, W., Schultz, R., Volkmar, F., & Cohen, D. (2002). Defining and quantifying the social phenotype in autism. *American Journal of Psychiatry, 159,* 895-908.

Klin, A., Volkmar, F.R., & Sparrow, S.S. (Eds.) (2000). *Asperger Syndrome.* New York: Guilford. **(AS-AD)**

Kluth, P. (2003). „*You're going to love this kid!" Teaching students with autism in the inclusive classroom.* Baltimore: Paul H. Brookes.

Levine, M. (1990). *Keeping a head in school.* Cambridge, MA: Educators Publishing Service. **(AS-AD)**

Levine, M. (1999). *Developmental variation and learning disorders* (Second Edition). Cambridge, MA: Educators Publishing Service, Inc.

Levine, M. (2001). *Jarvis Clutch, Social Spy.* Cambridge, MA: Educators Publishers Service. **(AS-AD)**

Levine, M. (2002). *A mind at a time.* New York: Simon & Schuster.

LINKS Curriculum. Educational Performance Systems, Woburn, MA.

Maag, J.W. (2004). *Behavior management: From theoretical implications to practical applications.* (2nd edition). Belmont, CA: Wadsworth/Thomson Learning.

Manassis, K., & Young, A. (2001). Adapting positive reinforcement systems to suit child temperament. *Journal of the American Academy of Child and Adolescent Psychiatry, 40,* 603-605.

McAfee, J. (2002). *Navigating the social world: A curriculum for individuals for Asperger's Syndrome, High Functioning Autism, and related disorders.* Arlington, TX: Future Horizons. **(AS-AD)**

Meyer, R.N. (2001). *Asperger Syndrome employment workbook.* London: Jessica Kingsley Publishers. **(AS-AD)**

Moyes, R. A. (2001). *Incorporating social goals in the classroom: A guide for teachers and parents of children with high-functioning autism and Asperger Syndrome.* London: Jessica Kingsley Publishers. **(AS-AD)**

Myles, B.S., & Adreon, D. (2001). *Asperger Syndrome and Adolescence: Practical solutions for school success.* Shawnee Mission, KS: Autism Asperger Publishing Co. **(AS-AD)**

Newport, J., & Newport, M. (2002). *Autism-Asperger's & sexuality: Puberty and beyond.* Arlington, TX: Future Horizons. **(AS-AD)**

Nowicki, S., & Duke, M.P. (1992). *Helping the child who doesn't fit in.* Atlanta: Peachtree Publishers. **(AS-AD)**

Ozonoff, S., Dawson, G., & McPartland, J. (2002). *A parent's guide to Asperger Syndrome and high-functioning autism.* New York: Guilford.

Packer, A.J. (1997). *How rude! The teenagers' guide to good manners, proper behavior, and not grossing people out.* Minneapolis, MN: Free Spirit Publishing. **(AS-AD)**

Prince-Hughes, D. (Ed.) (2002). *Aquamarine blue 5: Personal Stories of college students with autism.* Athens, OH: Swallow Press.

Rourke, B.P.(Ed.)(1995). *Syndrome of nonverbal learning disabilities: Neurodevelopmental manifestations.* New York: Guilford Press.

Rosenn, D. (2002). Is it Asperger's or ADHD? *AANE News,* Issue 10.

Shore, S. (Ed.) (2004). *Ask and tell: Self-advocacy and disclosure for people on the autism spectrum.* Shawnee Mission, KS: Autism Asperger Publishing Co.

Shore, S. (2001). *Beyond the wall.* Shawnee Mission, KS: Autism Asperger Publishing Co.

Tanguay, P.B. (2002). *Nonverbal learning disabilities at school: Educating students with NLD, Asperger Syndrome, and related conditions.* London: Jessica Kingsley Publishers.

Thompson, S. (1997). *The source for nonverbal learning disorders.* East Moline, IL: LinguiSystems. **(AS-AD)**

Tsai, L. (2002). *Taking the mystery out of medications in Autism/Asperger Syndromes.* Arlington, TX: Future Horizons.

Volkmar, F.R., & Wiesner, L.A. (2004). *Healthcare for children on the autism spectrum: A guide to medical, nutritional, and behavioral issues.* Bethesda, MD: Woodbine House.

Wagner, S. (2002). *Inclusive programming for middle school students with autism/Asperger's Syndrome.* Arlington, TX: Future Horizons. **(AS-AD)**

Whitman, T.L. (2004). *The development of autism: A self-regulatory perspective.* Philadelphia: Jessica Kingsley Publishers.

Willey, L.H. (1999). *Pretending to be normal.* London: Jessica Kingsley Publishers. **(AS-AD)** (and subsequent books)

Williams, M.S., & Shellenberger, S. (1996). *„How does your engine run?"* Albuquerque, NM: TherapyWorks, Inc. **(AS-AD)**

Winner, M.G. (2000). *Inside out: What makes a person with social cognitive deficits tick?* San Jose, CA: Michelle Garcia Winner, SLP. <www.socialthinking.com> **(AS-AD)**

Wrobel, M. (2003). *Taking care of myself: A hygiene, puberty, and personal curriculum for young people with autism.* Arlington, TX: Future Horizons.

Web Sites

<www.udel.edu/bkirby/asperger/support.html> (OASIS)

<www.aane.org> (Asperger Association of New England)

<www.asperger.org> (Asperger Syndrome Coalition of the United States)

<http://www.tonyattwood.com.au/> (Tony Attwood's site)

<www.aspie.com> (Liane Holliday Willey's home page)

<www.TheGrayCenter.org> (Carol Gray's site)

<www.faaas.org> (Families of Adults Afflicted with Asperger's Syndrome)

<www.autism-society.org> (Autism Society of America)

<www.researchautism.org> (Organization for Autism Research website—includes a downloadable version of "Parent's Guide to Research)

<www.naar.org> (National Alliance for Autism Research—another source re latest in biomedical research)

<www.aspergerteens.com> (a website created by an adolescent with AS in order to "give something back" to other teens with AS and their families)

Autism coaching—what it is and how it can help you

CHAPTER 15

Autism coaching

Contributing Author Barry Bettman, PCC Professional Certified Coach specializing in Autism Spectrum Disorders and Attention Deficit Disorder—Barry Bettman, an author and workshop leader, and a speaker at international conferences, is designated as a Professional Certified Coach with the International Coaching Federation (ICF) and has served as Chairperson of the Professional Personal Coaches Association. A Professional Co-Active Coach (CPCC) with the Coaches Training Institute, Mr. Bettman brings skills in ADD/ADHD coaching based on in-depth training for the A.D.D. Coach Academy and his lifelong experience with Attention Deficit Disorder. Mr. Bettman has extensive experience with Anthony Robbins Mastery Universities. He holds a BA degree in Business Administration from San Diego State University.

Resources and links—Barry Bettman, PCC Professional Certified Coach suggests visiting his Autism Today website to learn about his other products and services. Visit <http://bettman.autismtoday.com> today! (*Please note, don't put in the www.*) For more information about Barry Bettman's work, visit <www.barrybettman.com> and the Autism Coaching Web Site <www.autismcoaching.com>.

Why read this chapter on Autism Coaching?

There are so many excellent chapters with outstanding expertise in this Official Autism 101 E-Book. You may be curious or asking yourself, why read this chapter on Autism Coaching? This can be answered with 4 simple questions: 1. What is it? 2. How can it help me? 3. Why is it different? 4. Where do I get it?

1. What is it? Autism Coaching is a powerful new method for focusing a client forward to help get results. What types of challenges hinder the autistic person or family? Difficulty with sensory integration or making changes in behavior, complexities parenting a child with autism or being an adult thrown into the over stimulated world of autism, and even the family attempting to understand and cope with the autism spectrum disorder. Autism Coaching can be a highly success resource to your agendas because it empowers you to move forward with action and learning. Autism Coaching is not about "fixing the problem", but rather giving you the momentum and practical steps to living a wonderful life around autism spectrum disorder.

2. How can it help me? Autism Coaching can be of assistance to you whether you are a parent, a teacher, a family member or a professional helping someone on the autism spectrum. With traditional methods of learning, there can often be an increase in comprehen-

sion over ones own baseline knowledge of autism spectrum disorders. Knowledge alone is not enough! Autism Coaching is individualized, personalized, customized and it understands the nature of the difficulties the person(s) on autism spectrum and related issues. Some clients have reported with the addition of Autism Coaching, up to 88% more is achieved for them with practical action plans and a deeper understanding of autism spectrum disorder. In this chapter, there also are three specific examples of Coaching with clients. While education alone can fade, coaching reinforces learned concepts and skills until they become second nature.

3. Why is it different? Autism Coaching allows the client (i.e. parents, educators, professionals, family members) to be naturally creative, resourceful, and who they are in the quest for what they want in their own life. The purpose of Autism Coaching is not to quote "solve the problems of Autism", rather to bring out the greatness of the person. You are just fine and OK the way they already are. Coaching is not consulting, therapy or counseling. Many people in the world of autism may have experienced one or more of these modalities. Autism Coaching can be seen as a different or an effective supplementary service to the other approaches to help people on the autism spectrum. Coaching is focused on action, not healing. It looks at the future, not the past. Why things are the way they are doesn't matter. What matters is how you want them to be. The focus of Autism Coaching is on identifying specific objectives, and developing strategic plans, action steps and thinking processes that will move you toward achieving your desired goals for yourself and the person with autism.

4. Where do I get it? Autism Coaching is available from Professional Certified Coaches with a direct specialization in autism spectrum disorders. The Autism Today community has partnered to bring you the best of autism knowledge / resources with the best of Professional Coaching. Autism Coaching is available on a one-on-one individual basis, in teams of small groups of a couple to few people, or in large team groups, where many people are involved in the coaching at one time. Teleconferencing using the telephone with private conference bridge line allows the Coach and the Client(s) to enter into Autism Coaching anywhere throughout the world. Autism Coaching can make everyday tasks into excitement and progress instead of being challenged by the weight of autism spectrum disorders. An immediate resource for Autism Coaching is the website <www.autismcoaching.com>

Overview

Autism Coaching is a powerful new method for focusing a client forward to help get results. For some people, results might be a specific IAP Plan, clear communications between the support team members for the autistic person, putting into practice specific learning content from a conference or just achieving more balance in life, especially when supporting someone with special needs.

Autism Coaching focuses on allowing the client to be naturally creative, resourceful, and to be the person the client wants to be in the quest to fulfill life goals. Coaching is not consulting, therapy or counseling. Whether you are a parent, teacher, or professional helping someone on the autism spectrum, Autism Coaching can help you help a person with autism, Asperger's Syndrome or ADD. With traditional methods of learning, there can often be an increase in comprehension over ones own baseline knowledge of autism spectrum disorders. Knowledge alone is not enough! Autism Coaching is individualized, personalized,

customized and it understands the nature of the difficulties the person(s) on autism spectrum and related issues. Some clients have reported with the addition of Autism Coaching, up to 88% more is achieved for them with practical action plans and a deeper understanding of autism spectrum disorder. While teaching can fade, coaching reinforces learned concepts and skills until they become second nature. Your coach provides skills training in the "need-to-know" moment that formal teaching misses. He also helps you remember how much you already know. You learn more by discovering answers than by hearing them.

Introduction to professional coaching

Professional coaching is a new powerful way to help people get results. You are probably familiar with sports coaching where an athlete, such as a golfer or tennis player, works with a coach to improve his or her game. Autism Coaching is similar. It is a professional relationship that enhances your ability to learn, make changes and achieve desired goals. Whereas a sports coach helps you with your game, a professional coach helps you clarify what you want in your life and take action in the following ways:

- Clarify what you want to accomplish.
- Set specific goals.
- Make an effective action plan.
- Stay focused.
- Eliminate obstacles.

What is Autism Coaching?

Autism Coaching is a natural extension of professional coaching with specific focus areas around the autism spectrum and goals for people associated with autism and Asperger's Syndrome. Whether you are a parent, a teacher or a professional helping someone on the autism spectrum, Autism Coaching can be of assistance to you. Why is Autism Coaching so powerful? Have you ever read a book, listened to a tape or attended a seminar on the subject of autism, only to leave with a little more knowledge but not a practical game plan to implement or a team to help you get the desired results? Autism Coaching is about changing your behavior to help achieve your chosen goals with the person with autism.

Autism Coaching uses the basic skills of coaching with specific emphasis on addressing the learning style needs associated with autism and Asperger's Syndrome, such as non-verbal cues, attention, behavior, communication, social skills, etc. A regular professional coach can coach anyone toward chosen goals and dreams. An Autism Coach understands the unique talents and characteristics of people with autism and Asperger's Syndrome, their challenges and how these affect the lives of others. With Autism Coaching, you as a client will be coached by a specialist in coaching with special insight and training in autism and Asperger's Syndrome.

Why Autism Coaching? A true personal story

After more than 20 years as a consultant, I thought I was an expert who knew how to help others. Then in 1993 I ran across professional coaching. I didn't think much of it but was intrigued—maybe like you. I considered having a coach guide me toward a more fulfilling life. But why did I need a coach, I asked myself. After all, I am an expert.

Then in 1996, tired of my life's daily struggle, I decided to partner with a highly talented and experienced coach to help clarify my direction, set specific goals and create focus areas. We began to develop my vision and set a game plan to get there.

At this time I met another professional coach who was also a professional organizer. We talked over lunch and seemed to have a lot in common. I began to ask her about difficulty I had organizing my office, specifically the file cabinet. She mentioned something about ADD (Attention Deficit Disorder), about the challenges some people have remaining focused while completing a task. After some self-reflection and reading on the subject of ADD, I was surprised to learn that a neurobiological disorder was standing in the way of my success. I went to a doctor specializing in ADD and confirmed the diagnosis.

As I continued with my own coach, we began to partner for success, even though my ADD was now disclosed to me and the so-called "cat was out of the bag." Over just a few months, I began to see results in my life that I hadn't ever been able to achieve. I had extensively tried other modalities with limited success. But this seemed quite different. As I look back now, I can see the following results of partnering with a coach:

- I gained a clearer direction of what I wanted.

- I partnered with my coach on "my agenda," not what someone else wanted for me.

- I felt understood for the first time in my life, especially around my own special needs of ADD.

- I began to make progress toward my desires.

- I eliminated obstacles that seemed like boulders before.

- I got even clearer on my focus and decided that I could employ the strengths conferred by ADD and my understanding of coaching to help others.

- I raised my standards and went through several coaching certifications.

- I coached clients for thousands of hours to meet the strenuous Professional Certified Coach criteria set by the International Coach Federation.

- I realized that coaching in the special needs arena is a special gift and sought out the additional focus in the autism spectrum.

- I sought out experts in, and knowledge of, autism and Asperger's Syndrome to learn the differences between ADD and autism.

- I partnered with Autism Today to bring the best resources in autism and best of coaching to help people like you make progress.

- I felt very satisfied knowing I am helping people in the area of special needs have a more fulfilling and balanced life.

This is my own (Barry's) personal story of why coaching can be so powerful. I do not claim that coaching is right solution in every case where a person has special needs, whether due to autism, Asperger's Syndrome, ADD or anything else. Expertise, knowledge and resources are key ingredients for success. I just want to acknowledge that having a coach and partnering for success has made a profound difference in my own personal life and I am very grateful for this.

Co-active coaching skills: a foundation for Autism Coaching

Co-active coaching refers to a style of coaching that involves the active and collaborative participation of both the coach and the client. In other words, it brings the resources of client and coach together, and allows the client to take away gems that he/she can put into action.

One of the beauties of the co-active model is that it uses a set of skills that both the client and coach can draw on. These skills are not just for coaching. They are life skills suited to anyone, whether the person has autism, Asperger's Syndrome, ADD or is a neurotypical parent, child, teacher, educator, professional or even a friend.

The four pillars of the co-active coaching model are:

- The client is naturally creative, resourceful and whole.

- Co-active coaching addresses the client's whole life.

- The agenda comes from the client, not from the coach.

- The relationship is a designed alliance between the client and the coach.

As such, the clients have the answers or they can find the answers. From a co-active coach's perspective, nothing is wrong or broken, and there is no need to fix the client. Therefore, the coach does not have the answers. Rather the coach has questions that help the client to inquire within. The client doesn't do all the work. It's a joint coaching effort. The term co-active refers to using the resources of both the client and the coach.

Addressing the client's wholeness, not brokenness, is a real key of co-active coaching. A client may have challenges or difficulties, but the focus is on how the client is naturally creative, resourceful and whole. The client is viewed as being in charge of his/her destiny. The coach's job is to highlight the client's agenda and bring forth his/her client's greatness.

Lastly, a designed alliance is a relationship that is custom tailored. It is built on the communications approach that works best for the client and coach. The clients learn that they are in command of their coaching relationship and ultimately of the changes they make in their lives. The fundamental principle of coaching is that action and learning take place. These two components combined together create change. Forwarding the action and deepening the learning complement each other.

A common misunderstanding about Autism Coaching is that it is all about getting things done. Sometimes coaching has been inaccurately compared to hiring a nagging parent to make sure things get done. This is not coaching! Actually by utilizing the co-active coaching model, deepening the learning is just as important as action.

At the heart of the co-active coaching model are five primary keystones: listening, intuition, action/learning, self-management and curiosity. The coach employs these with the client as part of the designed alliance throughout the coaching relationship. They help the client achieve:

- Fulfillment: what fills the client's heart and soul.

- Balance: how to live within yourself and have natural equilibrium.

- Process: for the coach and client together acknowledge exactly where the client is right now and explore what's really up for the client now in the present moment.

Co-active coaching skills used by the coach and the client include:

- Accountability: What will you do and by when?

- Acknowledgement: Addresses who the client is being, not what the client has accomplished.

- Asking permission: Granting the coaching relationship access to unusual or sensitive areas of focus.

- Brainstorming: Generating ideas together.

- Championing: Standing up for what the client is capable of achieving.

- Clarifying: Articulating clearly what he/she really wants or is thinking.

- Creating trust: Setting up a foundation for mutual safety and trust.

- Intuiting: The process of accessing and trusting one's inner knowing.

- Listening: The coach listens for the client's vision, values and purpose. To "listen for" is to listen in search of want the client wants.

- Powerful questions: Open-ended questions that evoke clarity, action, discovery, insight or commitment. Powerful questions expand the range of possibility, encourage learning and clarify vision.

- Requesting: Based on the client's agenda, requesting is designed to help the client achieve goals.

- Structures: Devices that remind clients of their visions, goals or purpose, or of actions that they need to take immediately.

- Values: Who the client is being right now. These are principles you hold to be of worth in your life.

- Vision: A multifaceted mental image and set of goals that personally define and inspire the client to take action.

Co-active skills give the coach and client a common framework through which to move forward.

Formats of coaching

As a parent and/or professional, coaching unlocks your potential to work with people on the autism spectrum, including those with Asperger's Syndrome. In a coaching relationship, you and your coach prioritize, plan, analyze, troubleshoot and brainstorm. Your coach provides structure, feedback, perspective, skill-building techniques and smart questions. As a coaching team, you evaluate options, make decisions, track progress and, most important, celebrate achievements.

The structure of individual, one-on-one coaching is flexible. You and your coach custom design an arrangement that meets your needs and schedule. The basic design consists of:

- An initial session to create a coaching strategy.

- Special targeted coaching sessions on an as-needed basis.

- Regular ongoing coaching sessions.

Team Coaching is similar to Individual Coaching, but it has a broader focus with one or more topics for several people at the same time. With Team Coaching, individuals are coached while the others deepen their learning by witnessing the coaching. In Team Coaching, an individual often works with a buddy, gaining knowledge and experience in a multi-person setting.

Coaching is often conducted over the telephone. From the convenience of you home or office, anywhere in the world, you or your team can interact with your coach. Sometimes, coaching in person is used, particularly if the client and coach live near one another. Often e-mail can be used to supplement the coaching session with written information. A coaching call sheet provides can help a client or clients prepare and maximize the value of a coaching session. One example of a coaching call sheet is a Success Partnership Form.

Success Partnership Form

*The Success Partnership Form is from the book **Extreme Success** by Rich Fettke 2002 <www.Fettke.com>.*

It has been said that pale ink is better than the best memory. That is why a Success Partnership Form (SPF) can help you stay clear on what you said you would do, what you actually did and what you plan on doing. Each week, either fax or e-mail an SPF the day before you meet with your Success Partner. Whenever I sit down to fill out this form, it allows me to reflect on how effective I'm being during the week and where I can improve. Clients have told me that an SPF has been one of the best tools for enhancing their effectiveness and performance. There are several sections to an SPF. The easiest way to use this form is to create a template, make copies of it and fill one in every week. You can customize the form to meet your needs.

SUCCESS PARTNERSHIP FORM

DATE: _____

MEETING TIME: _____

CHECK IN (HOW WAS THE PAST WEEK):
- _____
- _____
- _____

I WANT TO USE THIS PARTNERSHIP MEETING TO:
- _____
- _____
- _____

RESULTS OF MY GOALS FROM OUR LAST MEETING:
- _____
- _____
- _____

SUCCESSES AND WINS:
- _____
- _____
- _____

CHALLENGES AND OBSTACLES:
- _____
- _____
- _____

MAJOR FOCUS AREAS IN MY LIFE THIS MONTH:
- _____
- _____
- _____

MY GOALS FOR THIS WEEK:
- _____
- _____
- _____

How does coaching differ from other modalities?

Traditional consulting offers solutions and expertise. Coaching facilitates discovery by helping you find your own answers. Your coach provides his/her expertise when it is useful but doesn't do things for you. The primary role of your coach is to listen, question, observe, pinpoint, reframe and articulate what's so. The plans and goals you make are your own.

Coaching reinforces learned concepts and skills until they become second nature. Your coach provides skills training in the "need-to-know" moment that formal teaching misses. He also helps you remember how much you already know. You learn more by discovering answers than by hearing them.

Coaching focuses on identifying specific objectives and developing strategic plans, action steps and thinking processes that will help you achieve your desired goals with your child with autism. Coaching is focused on action, not healing. It looks at the future, not the past. Why things are the way they are doesn't matter. What matters is how you want them to be.

The nature and scope of coaching

The following is from the International Coach Federation. To learn more, visit <www.coachfederation.org>.

The International Coach Federation (ICF) is the professional association of personal and business coaches that seeks to preserve the integrity of coaching around the globe. ICF helps people find the coach most suitable for their needs. It supports and fosters development of the coaching profession, has programs to maintain and upgrade the standards of the profession, conducts a certification program that is the gold standard for coaches worldwide and conducts the world's premier conference and other educational events for coaches. ICF is the largest non-profit professional association worldwide of personal and business coaches with thousands of members throughout dozens of countries in the world. We exist to build, support and preserve the integrity of the Coaching Profession.

Part I: With respect to psychotherapy

Who the client is
The individual coaching client is someone who wants to reach one or more of the following: a higher level of performance, learning or satisfaction. The client is not seeking emotional healing or relief from psychological pain.

The coaching client can take action to move towards a goal with the support of the coach. The successful client is not excessively limited in the ability to take action or overly hesitant to make this kind of progress.

How service is delivered

Coaches and clients arrange the schedule and means of contact (e.g., in person, by phone or via e-mail) that serve them both. They are not constrained to follow a standardized schedule or means of contact.

The relationship in coaching

A coach relates to the client as a partner. A coach does not relate to the client from a position of an expert, authority or healer.

Coach and client together choose the focus, format and desired outcomes for their work. The client does not relinquish the responsibility for creating and maintaining these nor does the coach take full responsibility for them.

Results

Coaching is designed to help clients improve their learning and performance, and enhance their quality of life. Coaching does not focus directly on relieving psychological pain or treating cognitive or emotional disorders.

Time frames

Coaching concentrates primarily on the present and future. Coaching does not focus on the past or on the past's impact on the present.

Coaching uses information from the client's past to clarify where the client is today. It does not depend on resolution of the past to move the client forward.

Emotions

Coaching assumes the presence of emotional reactions to life events and that clients are capable of expressing and handling their emotions. Coaching is not psychotherapy and emotional healing is not the focus of coaching.

Relationship to psychotherapy

Coaching can be used concurrently with psychotherapeutic work. It is not used as a substitute for psychotherapeutic work.

Advice

Advice, opinions or suggestions are occasionally offered in coaching. Both parties understand that the client is free to accept or decline what is offered and takes the ultimate responsibility for action. The coach is not discouraged from offering advice, opinions or suggestions on occasion.

Requesting

A coach makes a request of the client to promote action toward the client's desired outcome. A coach does not make such requests in order to fix the client's problem or understand the client's past.

Part II: With respect to consulting

Definition

In all of the following statements, the word "client" is used to denote the person who is being coached, regardless of who is paying for the service.

Expertise

Coaches are experts in the coaching process and may not have specific knowledge of a given subject area or industry. Where coaches have expertise in other areas, they may use it to facilitate the coaching process. Coaches do not use this particular expertise to diagnose, direct or design solutions for the client.

Relationship

Relationship is the foundation of coaching. The coach and client intentionally develop a relationship which is characterized by a growing and mutual appreciation and respect for each other as individuals. This relationship is not an adjunct to or by-product of the coaching. Nor is it based on the client's position or performance.

Use of information

In coaching, information drawn from the client is used by the coach to promote the client's awareness and choice of action. This information is not used to evaluate performance or produce reports for anyone but the person being coached.

Scope

Coaching has the freedom and flexibility to address a wide variety of personal and professional topics. In any given coaching relationship, coach and client alone determine the scope of their work. Coaching is not necessarily restricted to a narrowly defined issue nor is its scope determined in any other way.

Contribution to results

In coaching, any contribution the coach makes to producing the client's desired outcome is through ongoing interaction with the client. The coach's role does not include producing a contracted product or result outside of the coaching sessions.

Ongoing impact

Coaching is designed to provide clients with a greater capacity to produce results and a greater confidence in their ability to do so. It is intended that clients do not leave coaching with a perception that they need to rely on a coach in order to produce similar results in the future.

What are the benefits of Autism Coaching?

Autism Coaching provides many benefits to clients, whether the client is a parent, teacher or professional helping the person on the autism spectrum, or the client is the person with autism.

Autism Coaching provides the client with forward moving action on autism issues. It offers an excellent way to deepen your learning about autism. When working with an autism coach, together you co-create action plans. The aim is to clarify your intentions and gain success. Of course, the coach won't do the work for you. He/she will guide you, to help you achieve your goals, whether they are to assist a person with autism, gain a better understanding of autism or achieve balance in your life while you support others on the autism spectrum.

Clients of Autism Coaching are often parents, family members, professionals, teachers, educators, people with autism, Asperger's Syndrome or ADD— anyone who wants to move his/her life forward. Areas where Autism Coaching may benefit include:

- Sensory integration
- Behavioral strategies
- Social skills
- Communication strategies
- Biomedical interventions
- Methodology selection
- Parenting a child with autism
- Adults dealing with autism themselves or in the family
- Vaccinations and environmental concerns
- Career planning
- Life estate planning to include care for an Autistic person
- Diet and food sensitivities
- Life skills planning
- ADD and ADHD
- School program planning
- Puberty
- Talents and strengths
- Asperger's Syndrome
- Safety Awareness
- Curriculum development
- Disclosure
- Learning styles
- Emotions
- Making friends
- Transitions
- Life map creation
- Anything else that the coaching client wants (It's the client agenda!)

The benefit of Autism Coaching is to transform challenges into exciting progress. Imagine waking up thrilled because you are on the way to having a more fulfilled life with people on the autism spectrum. Having your own coach takes you to the next level— beyond reading a book or listening to a tape. Autism Coaching helps you practice and achieve actions that develop you and the person with autism.

Coaching versus psychotherapy: the great debate

The following excerpt is from Choice Magazine. To read the entire article, visit <www.autismtoday.com/therall.pdf>.

While therapy and coaching may share a common background, their differences are vast. Therapy is vital for those with psychological problems—what we call pathology. Coaching is for those who are healthy and already self-motivated. Both fields have their place and should not be confused. For advanced therapy patients, coaching can be an additional benefit, but coaching assumes the healing and well-being of its clients as a given. A therapist may add coaching skills to his or her practice, but a coach never engages in therapy. A coach is trained to detect any need for therapy and there are guidelines for when to refer a coaching client to a therapist. . . .

Essentially, a therapist is the professional with the answers to pain and brokenness; a coach is a professional partner to assist in discovery and design for growth. The shift from seeing clients as "ill" or having pathology toward viewing them as "well and whole" and seeking a richer life is paramount to understanding the evolution of coaching. I often say therapy is about uncovering and recovering, while coaching is about discovering.

A good way to view the foundational differences between therapy and coaching is to think of two cars driving along a sandy, wave-washed shoreline. One car hits a log and breaks an axle, sinking deep into the sand. The other car swerves to keep from hitting the log, but in doing so also sinks in the sand. For the first car, the only hope is a tow truck and a week in the shop. It is broken and cannot go further. This is a therapy patient. The second car merely needs a push, a little traction under its wheels, and it continues its race across the sand. This is the coaching client. Unlike therapy, little time is spent in the past with coaching, except for brief "visits" and then the focus is on developing the future. This philosophical shift has taken root in a generation that rejects the idea of sickness and seeks instead wellness, wholeness and purposeful living—both personally and professionally. The coaching relationship allows the client to explore blocks to great success and to unlock his or her biggest dreams and desires.

Three examples of coaching

Johnny the client was having a one-on-one individual coaching session

The Coach asked Johnny what he wanted to focus on today. Johnny said he was having difficulty keeping focused and getting tasks accomplished. The Coach inquired of Johnny: How do you sustain attention to get a task accomplished?

Johnny thought to himself and said, I really don't know how to sustain attention. The Coach explained to Johnny that when we set out to achieve a task or goal, we begin by focusing our attention on the task or goal at hand. Some people have a difficult time sustaining and holding attention long enough to get a specific task accomplished.

Johnny said, I get it. It's like when I am having difficulty getting my checkbook balanced. I begin to place my attention on balancing the check book and then I have to go find the check book and the bank statements. Then I need to open the statements, take a yellow highlighter and mark the sections by deposits, checks and bank charges. Is this holding my attention? Johnny asked the Coach.

Let me ask you a question, Johnny. On a scale of 1 to 10, where 10 being the most and 1 being the least, how does this fit for you on sustaining attention? Johnny proudly perked up. It's about 7 for me. Great, exclaimed the Coach. What would make it a 9 or 10 for you? Johnny pondered this a minute. What if I was to break this down into smaller pieces? The Coach inquired what would those pieces look like. Johnny said, only work on one month of bank statements at a time.

The Coach inquired, What next? I will commit to balancing one statement a week, said Johnny. For how long? asked the Coach. Until all my backlog statements are balanced. The Coach said, So you mentioned that you have 10 months of backlog bank statements to balance, right? Yes, said Johnny. How reasonable is it to get all 10 bank statements balanced over the next 10 weeks, which is about two and a half months? Johnny had an "ah ha!" You nailed it on the head. I bit off more than I can chew. I guess what's realistic here is to commit to balance each current month of bank statement within a week of receiving them. The Coach said, Okay, that takes care of the current statements. What's next for the backlog? Johnny said: I commit to balancing one backlog statement every two weeks.

Is it okay with you if we both write down that the smaller pieces you are committing to are to:

- Balance each current month bank statement within 1 week.
- Balance one backlog statement every 2 weeks.

Johnny says that he feels really good about this. He is excited and looks forward to the smaller steps. Great, says the Coach, I look forward seeing you be successful.

Susan and Bob decided to have Coaching together, in a Team Coaching arrangement

Susan and Bob are partners in an architecture company. They are also parents of two wonderful special needs children.

The Coach asked Susan and Bob: What's most important to you in life? They took out pads of paper and wrote their lists. Susan explained that being listened to by her husband, co-workers and children was at the top of her list. Bob said that seeing the big picture of where they were headed was most important to him.

The Coach asked: Where to you want to be 12 months from now? They looked at each other and said, free of misunderstandings. The Coach inquired: What's getting in the way? Susan said, I keep telling Bob what I want but he doesn't listen. Bob explains that he doesn't think Susan gets the vision.

The Coach asked them about how they process information. Susan and Bob were perplexed. They had never been asked that question, even after raising two children and being in business for over a decade. What do you mean by "process information" they asked?

The Coach explained that people process information in various ways. Most of us have five senses: sight, hearing, touch, smell and taste. A visual person will often say, "I can see what you mean" whereas one who depends more on hearing will say "I hear you loud and clear."

Susan and Bob were astonished—but they understood the point the Coach was making. What did you learn? the Coach asked. That I want to hear what Bob has to say, and he wants to see it from me, she said.

Bob was amazed. I didn't realize until now that I was so visual. I process information in pictures. If I can't see the picture, I just assumed that the other person wasn't communicating to me.

The Coach asked if it was okay to assign some homework. Susan said sure, but Bob asked what it might involve. The Coach explained that homework is practice for between coaching sessions, to foster progress. He then turned to Susan. Susan, he said, your homework is to notice when Bob or anyone else says to you, I can hear what you are saying. Bob, he said, your homework is to notice when Susan or anyone show's you the picture or vision of where they are headed. Each of you, notice when you feel you are being heard and when you are not. Bring your learning with you to the next Coaching call.

Susan and Bob brought excitement and enthusiasm to the next Coaching call, a week later. The Coach asked each of them about what had worked well since the last Coaching call. Bob pulled out a pictorial diagram and showed how he processes information as a visual processor. The chart also showed how Susan listens to information and hears what's happening.

Susan talked about what she learned. I said I hear you—and really meant it. I never realized how hard I listen and had always thought until now that everyone else did this, too. What I got out of our coaching session is that different people process information in different ways.

The Coach asked Susan and Bob to notice their own dominate processing modality and communicate to the other person in their own preferred processing modality. Susan and Bob agreed to this and said they would begin to do it with their children.

The Coach congratulated them on their new-found understandings.

Sharon engaged with an Autism Coach to focus on disclosure of Asperger's Syndrome

During the prior week between coaching sessions, Sharon did some homework on disclosure. She gave thought to disclosure and posed this question at the coaching session: How do I disclose that I have Asperger's Syndrome?

The Coach set up a safe and trusting environment by asking permission to coach her about disclosure.

Sharon appreciated this, saying it is a really sensitive area. The Coach asked that Sharon only share what she felt was applicable. He said she should be aware that she possesses within herself all the resources she needs to be able to disclose when appropriate. Sharon asked the Coach how he knew this. The coach explained that he holds Sharon, the client, as naturally creative, resourceful and whole. Sharon replied that this approach differed from others she had experienced. I have always been told what to do and how to do it. Where do we go from here? she asked.

The Coach asked Sharon about her values concerning disclosure. She thought and then spoke of three values: integrity, trust and clear communications. In what ways are these important for you? the coach asked. Sharon explained that being in integrity with herself and others has her feel congruent with herself. Trust allowed her to feel safe and speak from her heart. Clear communications will minimize miscommunication when I disclose about having Asperger's Syndrome. I can put it right out there and get the word out when I need to. Wow, I just said it, I can put it right out there and get the word out when I need to. That's amazing how easy disclosure seems to be now.

The Coach congratulates Sharon for being brave, courageous and articulate. This reflects her values, integrity, trust and clear communications. Sharon congratulates herself for stepping up to the plate.

Using a skill called Requesting, the coach makes a request of Sharon to set up a meeting with the person she wants to tell about her having Asperger's Syndrome. Sharon, he says, I have a request for you to set up a meeting with Mr. Harris to disclose your situation. Well, maybe, she says. The coach reframes the request, asking, What will it take for you to be prepared for a meeting on disclosure with Mr. Harris? She paused a short while, then said: to be integrity with all the components of disclosure of my Asperger's, trust myself and communication clearly with Mr. Harris. Wow, I am really clear, she replies. What's next, inquired the coach. It will really be helpful for me to write down the specific items to disclose, this way I'll really have a basis for clear communications. Then I'll have to look at my calendar, call Mr. Harris and ask him to check his schedule. Next we will set a time and place to meet. The coach asks an accountability question: How will you know that you have written down your items to disclose, looked at your calendar, checked with Mr. Harris on his schedule, and set a time and place to meet? Sharon explains: That's easy, it will be scheduled on both of our calendars and a reservation for lunch will have already been made for our meeting. And I'll bring the sheet I wrote down the items to disclose with me to the meeting with Mr. Harris. The coach echoed those words of her commitment back to Sharon. The coach acknowledged to Sharon, you are truly living your values of integrity, trust, and clear communications.

I get it, she said. I'll report back at our next coaching call on my progress on disclosure. He asked, when would you like to have our next coaching session Sharon? How's 2:00 p.m. Thursday? Fine, talk to you then, said the Coach. Sharon said thanks! I am off to my calendar and call Mr. Harris now.

Human Software Engineering™: a toolbox of options for Autism Coaching

Human Software Engineering can provide an extra turbo boost to the coaching client's success. In my search for excellent tools to add to the toolbox for Autism Coaching, I have found, experienced and adopted Human Software Engineering™. This is a unique and perfect fit for coaching. Human Software Engineering™ is a revolutionary way of finding and eliminating the causes of obstacles in human life. For example, a computer software analogy is used here with humans to describe a viewpoint of how we are programmed or conditioned.

If a computer is not giving us the desired output, it may need to be debugged or upgraded. The same is true for us. Our Inner Human Software™ is made up of thoughts, feelings and intentions. These control our "output." So if something isn't going right in your life, you could benefit from some debugging and upgrading of your Inner Human Software.

The bugs, or unwanted programs, that we all accumulate through our human conditioning tend to keep us locked in old ways of thinking and acting that can get in the way of what we really want in life. These "bugs" are barriers to your own human success.

You can think of these bugs as self sabotage within our own Inner Human Software. What prevents us from removing these barriers from within ourselves is accessing the patterns of energy that are resonating somewhere inside of us. In simple terms, Human Software Engineering uses the principles of physics, specialized coaching skills, optionally sophisticated electronic technology—the WaveMaker™ (which can cancel the internal energy of internal barriers) and special testing techniques to pinpoint the energy patterns of these Inner Human Software bugs and delete them. What this means to the coaching client, you can begin to live free of the inner barriers which may have stopped you from your own success.

A coaching model called The 12 Core Dynamics to Common Problems™ is used within Human Software Engineering to understand and debug the barriers that get in the way of our own success. The 12 Core Dynamics to Common Problems™ provides a new language and structure for understanding the nature of human conditioning. The Core Dynamics model is a part of an emerging field called Human Software Engineering. The new insights, techniques and skills that are utilized, when learned and used, can help you liberate yourself from the invisible but powerful influences of your early conditioning. Our conditioning has a pervasive and insidious grip on us, controlling our behavior and decision making and keeping us locked into a very limited level of self expression and enjoyment of our lives.

The 12 Core Dynamics to Common Problems™ are:
1. Resisting feeling things fully
2. Ignoring your intuition
3. Being judgmental
4. Avoiding the present
5. Looking for yourself where you are not
6. Mistaking need for love
7. Resisting change
8. Limiting self expression
9. Trying to force an outcome
10. Excluding other perspectives
11. Manufacturing interpretations
12. Over-reacting to circumstances

How are the 12 Core Dynamics to Common Problems™ used in Autism Coaching? A client, who is a parent in this instance, brings to a coaching session a focus area for getting their autistic child to school on time. The Coach asks the client what's getting in the way of getting the child to school on time. The client says he is always late and he is going to make the child be on time. Note that the act of being on time for the child is one focus. The client having internal barriers in their own way is a different coaching focus. The two barriers that are present for the client are Being judgmental and Trying to force an outcome. The parent may be creating an extra demand on themselves by Being judgmental about their child being late and Trying to force the outcome by forcing their child to be on time. The client often reports a physiological sensation or feeling within them when discussing these barriers. This is just energetic resonance within herself of conflicting feeling sensations. Clients already have a sense of this energetic resonance as they tend to notice one or more conflicting feeling sensations within their body.

There are some very excellent coaching techniques to assist the client to eliminate this internal energetic resonance of conflicting feeling sensations. One of them is to ask the client to feel into the core of the energy. Feel the sensations of the energy within themselves that shows up within their body around Being judgmental or Trying to force an outcome. Usually clients report back that once they feel directly into the core of the energy, there seems to be an absence of these core dynamics. In this case, Being judgmental or Trying to force an outcome as barriers begin to diminish and are eliminated. Now the client can work with a coaching structure for the child around being on time without being caught up in the charge of the child being late. The 12 Core Dynamics helps to eliminate barriers to success.

Human Software Engineering can be used as an additional tool for Autism Coaching in assisting to remove bugs or barriers with in ourselves. Just as a computer runs on software and hardware, as a computer analogy so do humans. Our software is our beliefs, values, intentions and conflicting intentions. Our hardware is our bodies, which are sometimes blocked by food sensitivities, toxins such as mercury or other insidious barriers. With the use of highly a skilled Human Software Engineering practitioner with specialized coaching skills, optionally sophisticated electronic technology—the WaveMaker™ (which can cancel the internal energy of internal barriers) and special testing techniques to pinpoint the energy patterns of these Inner Human Software bugs and eliminate them, making it much more easy and effortless for clients to move forward in their lives. You may ask when is it optimal to utilize the Human Software Engineering as part of Autism Coaching? It's simple. When a person has insidious barriers or obstacles to success that don't seem to be addressed in other ways, Human Software Engineering utilizing the 12 Core Dynamics, with or without the WaveMaker technology, can provide an extra turbo boost to their success.

How do I get started with Autism Coaching?

Have your own direct experience! Reading about Autism Coaching is one thing, experiencing first hand is the real thing. Recently, Autism Today has begun a partnership with Autism Coaches that aims to bring together the best of autism knowledge and resources and the best of coaching. Autism Coaching is available on a one-on-one, individual basis, in teams of small groups of a couple of people to a few or in large team groups, where many people are involved in the coaching at one time.

Teleconferencing enables Autism Coaching anywhere in the world. A good way to get started with Autism Coaching is to connect with a coach specializing in autism. One resource is to visit <www.autismcoaching.com>. Another is to call the offices of Autism Today at 866-9AUTISM. Of course you can also ask your friends who they are using for an Autism Coach—or search on the Internet for one. Be sure to find a coach who is certified and who specializes in autism. You will want to find someone whom you connect with, one who fits your own needs for a coach and who understands the uniqueness and strengths of the autism spectrum.

Summary

Autism Coaching is a modern new approach for getting forward-looking results for those with autism. You and your Autism Coach work together to:

- Clarify what you want to accomplish
- Set specific goals
- Make an effective action plan
- Stay focused
- Eliminate obstacles

In a coaching relationship, you and your coach prioritize, plan, analyze, troubleshoot and brainstorm. Your coach provides structure, feedback, perspective, skill-building techniques and smart questions. Together as a coaching team, you evaluate options, make decisions, track your progress and, most important, celebrate achievements.

As a parent and/or professional, coaching unlocks your potential to maximize your own performance for working with people on the Autism Spectrum, including Asperger's Syndrome. With great understanding for what you may be going though around autism, I wish you the very best of success.

References

- The Nature and Scope of Coaching: International Coach Federation <www.coachfederation.org>

- Coaching VS. Psychotherapy, The Great Debate: Choice Magazine <www.autismtoday.com/therall.pdf>

- Success Partnership Form, Book *Extreme Success*: Rich Fettke 2002 <www.Fettke.com>

- Co-Active Coaching: The Coaches Training Institute: <www.thecoaches.com> Co-Active Coaching book 1998 by Laura Withworth, Henry Kimsey-House, Phil Sandahl.

- Human Software Engineering, The 12 Core Dynamics, WaveMaker: Great Life Technologies: <www.greatlifetechnologies.com> <www.experiencethewavemaker.com>

Typical areas of strength, building self-esteem and positive tools for those on the autism spectrum or with ADHD

CHAPTER 16

Genius may be an abnormality: educating students with Asperger's Syndrome or high functioning autism

Contributing Author Temple Grandin, Ph.D., Animal Science, University of Illinois—One of the most world's most accomplished and well-known adults with autism, Dr. Grandin is a prominent speaker and writer on this subject. In her book, *Thinking in Pictures,* Dr. Grandin delivers a report from the country of autism. Writing from the dual perspectives of a scientist and an autistic person, she tells us how that country is experienced by its inhabitants and how she managed to breach its boundaries to function in the outside world. What emerges documents an extraordinary human being, one who gracefully and lucidly bridges the gulf between her condition and our own. Dr. Grandin is also a gifted scientist who has designed livestock handling facilities used worldwide and is an Associate Professor of Animal Science at Colorado State University.

Resources and links—Temple Grandin, Ph.D. suggests visiting her Autism Today website to learn about her other products and services: Visit: <http://grandin.autismtoday.com> today! (*Please note, don't put in the www.*) You can learn more about Dr. Grandin and her work at <http://www.grandin.com>.

Introduction

I am becoming increasingly concerned that intellectually gifted children are being denied opportunities because they are being labeled either with Asperger's Syndrome or with high functioning autism. Within the last year I have talked to several parents and I was disturbed by what they said. One mother called me and was very upset that her six-year-old son had Asperger's Syndrome. She then went on to tell me that his IQ was 150. I replied that before people knew about Asperger's Syndrome, their child would have received a very positive label of intellectually gifted.

In another case the parents of a teenager with Asperger's Syndrome called and told me that they were so concerned about their son's poor social skills that they would not allow him to take computer programming. I told his mother that depriving him of a challenging career in computers would make his life miserable. He will get social interaction through shared interests with other computer people. In a third case, a super-smart child was not allowed in the talented and gifted program in his school because he had an autism label. Educators need to become more aware that intellectually satisfying work makes life meaningful.

I am what I think and do

My sense of being, as a person with autism, is based upon what I think and do. I am what I think and do, not what I feel. I have emotions, but my emotions are more like those of a 10-year-old child or an animal. My life has meaning because I have an intellectually satisfying career that makes life worth living. In my work designing livestock facilities, I have improved the treatment of farm animals and I have been able to travel many interesting places. I have traded emotional complexity for intellectual complexity. Emotions are something I have learned to control.

It is essential that talented children labeled either high functioning autism or Asperger's Syndrome be trained in fields such as computer programming, where they can do intellectually satisfying work. As for many people with Asperger's Syndrome, for me my life is my work. Life would not be worth living if I did not have intellectually satisfying work.

I did not fully realize this until a flood destroyed our university library. I was attending the American Society of Animal Science meetings when the flood occurred. I first learned about it in a story on the front page of *USA Today.* I grieved for the "dead" books the same way most people grieve for a dead relative. The destruction of books upset me because "thoughts died." Even though most of the books are still in other libraries, there are many people at the university who will never read them. To me, Shakespeare lives if we keep performing his plays. He dies when we stop performing them. I am my work. If the livestock industry continues to use equipment I have designed, then my "thoughts live" and my life has meaning. If my efforts to improve the treatment of cattle and pigs make real improvements in the world, then life is meaningful.

I have been reading with great satisfaction the many articles in magazines about Linux free software. People in the business world are not able to comprehend why the computer people give their work away. I am unable to think about this without becoming emotional. It is no mystery to me why they download their intellectual ideas into a vast, evolving and continually improving computer operating system. It is because their thoughts will live forever as part of the "genetic code" of the computer operating system. They are putting themselves into the operating system—and their "intellectual DNA" will live forever in cyberspace. As the program evolves and changes, the code they wrote will probably remain hidden deep within it. It is almost like a living thing that is continually evolving and improving. For both me and for the programmers that contribute to Linux, we do it because it makes our lives more meaningful.

Continuum of traits

There is a continuum of personality and intellectual traits from normal to abnormal. At what point does a brilliant computer programmer or engineer get labeled with Asperger's Syndrome? There is no black and white dividing line.

Simon Baron-Cohen, an autism researcher at the University of Cambridge, found that there were two times as many engineers in the family histories of people with autism. I certainly fit this pattern. My grandfather was an engineer who co-invented the automatic pilot for an airplane. I have second and third cousins who are engineers and mathematicians.

At a recent lecture, Dr. Baron-Cohen described three brilliant individuals with Asperger's Syndrome. There was a brilliant physics student, a computer scientist and a mathematics professor. It is also likely that Bill Gates has many Asperger's Syndrome traits. An article in *Time Magazine* compared me to Mr. Gates. For example, we both rock. I have seen videotapes of Bill Gates rocking on television. Articles in business magazines describe his incredible memory as a young child.

There is evidence that high functioning autism and Asperger's Syndrome have a strong genetic basis. G.R. DeLong and J.T. Dyer found that two thirds of families with a high functioning autistic had either a first or second degree relative with Asperger's Syndrome. In the journal *Autism and Developmental Disorders*, Sukhelev Naragan and his co-workers wrote that educational achievement of the parents of an autistic child with good language skills were often greater than those of similar parents with normal children. Dr. Robert Plomin at Pennsylvania State University states that autism is highly heritable.

In my book, *Thinking in Pictures*, I devote an entire chapter to the links of intellectual giftedness and creativity to abnormality. Einstein himself had many autistic traits. He did not learn to speak until he was three years of age and he had a lack of concern about his appearance. His uncut hair did not match the men's hairstyles of his time. Additional insights into Einstein are in *Thinking in Pictures* and other books in my reference list.

Genius is an abnormality?

It is likely that genius in any field is an abnormality. Children and adults who excel in one area, such as math, are often very poor in other areas. The abilities are very uneven. Einstein was a poor speller and did poorly in foreign languages. The brilliant physicist Richard Feynman did poorly in some subjects.

A review of the literature indicates that being truly outstanding in any field may be associated with some type of abnormality. Kay Redfield Jamison, from Johns Hopkins School of Medicine, has reviewed many studies that show the link between manic depressive illness and creativity. N.C. Andreason, at the University of Iowa, found that 80% of creative writers had mood disorders sometime during their lives. A study of mathematical giftedness, conducted at Iowa State University by Camilla Persson, found that mathematical giftedness was correlated with being nearsighted and having an increased incidence of allergies. I recently attended a lecture by Robert Fisher at Barrow Neurological Institute in Phoenix,

Arizona. He stated that many great people had epilepsy, including Julius Caesar, Napoleon, Socrates, Pythagoras, Handel, Tchaikovsky and Alfred Nobel. For additional information on the links between abnormality and giftedness, refer to the reference list.

Types of thinking

There appear to be two basic types of thinking in intellectually gifted people who have Asperger's Syndrome or high-performing autism. The highly social, verbal thinkers who are in the educational system need to understand that the thought processes of these people are different.

The two types are the totally visual thinkers like me, and the music, math and memory thinkers described in Thomas Sowell's book, *Late Talking Children*. I have interviewed several of these people, and their thoughts work in patterns in which there are no pictures. Sowell reports that in the family histories of late talking, music, math and memory children, 74% of the families will have an engineer or a relative in a highly technical field such as physics, accounting or mathematics. Most of these children also had a relative that played a musical instrument.

Every thought I have is represented by a picture. When I think about a dog, I see a series of pictures of specific dogs, such as my student's dog or the dog next door. There is no generalized verbal dog concept in my mind. I form my dog concept by looking for common features that all dogs have and no cats have. For example, all of the different breeds of dogs have the same kind of nose. My thought process goes from specific pictures to general concepts, whereas most people think from general to specific. I have no vague, abstract, language-based concepts in my head, only specific pictures.

When I do design work, I can run three dimensional, full motion "video" images of the cattle handling equipment in my head. I can "test run" the equipment on the "virtual reality" computer that is in my imagination. Visual thinkers who are expert computer programmers have told me that they can see the entire program "tree," and then they write the code on each branch.

It is almost as if I have two consciences. Pictures

are my real thoughts, and language acts as a narrator. I narrate from the "videos" and "slides" I see in my imagination. For example, my language narrator might say "I can design that." I then see a video of the equipment I am designing in my imagination. When the correct answer pops into my head, it is a video of the successful piece of equipment working. At this point, my language narrator says, "I figured out how to do it." In my mind there is no subconscious. Images are constantly passing through the computer screen of my imagination. I can see thought processes that others have covered up with language. I do not require language for either consciousness or for thinking.

When I learned drafting for doing my design work, it took time to train my visual mind to make the connection between the symbolic lines on a layout drawing and an actual building. To learn this I had to take the set of blueprints and walk around in the building, looking at the square concrete support columns, seeing how the little squares on the drawing related to the actual columns. After I had "programmed" my brain to read drawings, the ability to draw blueprints appeared almost by magic. It took time to get information in, but after I was "programmed," the skill appeared rather suddenly. Researchers who have studied chess players state that the really good chess players have to spend time inputting chess patterns into their brains. I can really relate to this. When I design equipment I take bits of pictures and pieces of equipment I have seen in the past and reassemble them into new designs. It is like taking things out of the memory of a CAD computer drafting system, except I can reassemble the pieces into three-dimensional, moving videos. Constance Milbrath and Bryan Siegal at the University of California found that talented autistic artists assemble the whole from the parts. It is "bottom up thinking," instead of "top down thinking."

Teachers and mentors

Children and teenagers with autism or Asperger's Syndrome need teachers who can help them develop their talents. I cannot emphasize enough the importance of developing a talent into an employable skill. Visual thinkers like me can become experts in fields such as computer graphics, drafting, computer programming, automotive repair, commercial art, industrial equipment design or working with animals. The music, math and memory type children can excel in mathematics, accounting, engineering, physics, music and other technical skills. Unless the student's mathematical skills are truly brilliant, I would recommend taking courses in library science, accounting, engineering or computers. Learning a technical skill will make the person highly employable. There are few jobs for mediocre mathematicians or physicists.

Since social skills are weak, the person can make up for them by being so good at something that they will be attractive as employees. Teachers need to council individuals to go into fields where they can easily gain employment. Majoring in history is not a good choice because obtaining a job will be difficult. History could be the person's hobby instead of the main area of study in school.

Many high functioning autistic and Asperger teenagers get bored with school and misbehave. They need mentors who can teach them a field that will be beneficial to their future. I had a wonderful high school science teacher who taught me to use the scientific research library. Computers are a great field because being weird, or a "computer geek," is okay. A good programmer is recognised for his/her skills. I know several very successful autistic computer programmers. A bored high school student could enrol in programming or computer-aided drafting courses in a local community college.

To make up for social deficits, the autistic person needs to become so good at their work that its brilliance is recognized. People respect talent. They need mentors who are computer programmers, artists, draftsmen, etc., to teach them career skills. I often get asked, "How does one find mentors?" You never know where a mentor teacher may be found. He may be standing in the checkout line in a supermarket. I found one of my first meat industry mentors when I met the wife of his insurance agent at a party. She struck up a conversation with me because she saw my hand-embroidered western shirt. I had spent hours embroidering a steer head on the shirt. Post a notice on the bulletin board at the local college in the computer science department. If you see a person with a computer company name badge, approach him and show him work that the person with autism has done.

Sell your work, not your personality

Since people with autism and Asperger's Syndrome are inept socially, they have to sell their work instead of their personalities. I showed my portfolio of pictures and blueprints to prospective customers. I never went to the personnel office. I went straight to the engineers and asked to do design jobs.

Another approach is to put up a web page that showcases work in drawing or programming. Freelance work is really great. It avoids many social problems. I can go in and design the project and then get out before I get social problems.

There have been several sad stories where an autistic draftsman or technician has been promoted to a management position. It was a disaster that ended up in the person being fired or quitting. Employers need to recognize the person's limitations. An excellent draftsman, commercial artist, technician or computer programmer may lose their career when promoted to management. These people should be rewarded with more pay or a new computer instead of management jobs.

People with autism and Asperger's Syndrome need concrete, well-defined goals at work. For example, the job is to design a better speech recognition program. When one project is finished, they should be given another project with a well-defined goal. If too many projects are thrown at them all at once, they will become confused. Let the person with autism or Asperger's Syndrome finish the first project before he/she is given another. The projects can be really hard but they must have a well-defined goal.

Teaching citizenship

Since people with autism and Asperger's Syndrome are emotionally immature, they must have basic morality reinforced when they are small children. When I was little I was taught in a concrete way that hurting other people, stealing and lying were bad. At age 8, I stole a toy fire engine, and my mother made me give it back. She told me "How would you like it if someone stole one of your model airplanes?" She also told me that you do not hit other kids because I would not like it if they hit me. It was the Golden Rule: "Do unto others as you would want them to do unto you." Some Asperger's Syndrome children and adults have done some bad deeds because the basic rules were not taught to them. I live a rule-based life and I have a rule system I still use today.

Anxiety problems

For many people with autism and Asperger's Syndrome, anxiety and nervousness is a major problem. This is discussed in detail in my book, *Thinking in Pictures*. Anxiety problems worsen with age. My anxiety became unbearable in my early thirties. It was like a constant state of stage fright. At times, my nervous system was so aroused that I felt as if a lion was stalking me, but there was no lion. I have talked to several people with autism who quit good, high paying jobs in graphic arts when anxiety and panic attacks made going to the office impossible.

Many people with autism or Asperger's Syndrome need medication to control their anxiety. I have been taking antidepressants for almost 20 years. My career would have been ruined if I had not started taking antidepressants to control my anxiety. I know many autistic and Asperger adults that are taking Prozac or one of the other Serotonin re-uptake inhibitors. People need to be counseled that medications such as Prozac can improve their lives.

The anxiety is due to biological problems in the nervous system. Recent brain research is showing that there is immature development in certain parts of the brains of people with autism. Autopsies of brains of people with autism show that there are biological abnormalities which occur when the foetus is developing. Antidepressant medication helps reduce anxiety caused by biological problems in the nervous system.

1. Andreason, N.C. 1987. Creativity and mental illness prevalence rates in writers and first-degree relatives. American Journal of Psychiatry 144: 1288–1292.

2. Bailey, et.al 1998. A clinicopatholic study of autism. Brain. 121: 889–908 (Brain Study).

1. Kemper, T., and Barman, M. 1998. Neuropathology of Autism. Journal of Neuropathology and experimental Neurology. July, (Brain Study)

2. Cranberg, L.D., and Albert, M.C. 1988. The Chess Mind, In L.K Obler and D. Fein, Editors. The Exceptional Brain. Guilford Press New York. Pp. 156–190.

3. Delong, G.R., and Dwyer, J.T. 1988. Correlation of family history and specific autistic subgroups: Asperger's syndrome and bipolar affective disease. Journal of Autism and Developmental Disorders 18: 593—600.

4. Gleik, J. 1993. Genius: Richard Feynman and modern physics. Little Brown, New York.

5. Grandin, T. 1995. Thinking in Pictures. Doubleday, New York. Now published by Vintage Press Division of Random House.

6. Grandin, T. 1995. How people with autism think. In: E. Schopler and G.B. Mesibov Editors. Learning and Cognition in Autism. Plenum Press, New York.

7. Grant, A. 1885. Charles Darwin. Appleton, New York.

8. Grant, V.W. 1968. Great Abnormals. Hawthorn, New York.

9. Highfield, R. and Garter, P. 1993. The private lives of Albert Einstein. St. Martin's, New York.

10. Kevin, G. 1967. Inspired Amateurs. Books for Libraries Press, Freeport, New York.

11. Kincheloe, J.L., Steinberg, S.R., and Tippins, D.J. 1992. The Stigma of Genius. Hollowbrook, Durango, Colorado.

12. Landa, R., Piven, J., Wzorek, M.M., Gayle, J.O., Chase, G.A., and Folstein, S.E. 1992. Social language use in parents of autistic individuals. Psychological Medicine 22: 245–254.

13. Milbrath, C., and Siegol, B. 1996. Perspective taking in the drawings of a talented autistic child. Visual Arts Research, School of Arts and Design, University of Illinois, Urbana, Illinois USA. Pp22: 56–75.

14. Myerson and Boyle. 1941. The incidence of manic-depressive psychosis in certain socially prominent families. P. 20. In K.R. Jamison, 1993. Touched with Fire. The Free Press, New York.

15. Narayan, S., Moyer B., and Wolff, S. 1990. Family characteristics of autistic children: a further report. Journal of Autism and Development Disorders 20: 523–535.

16. Pais, A. 1994. Einstein lived here. Oxford University Press, New York.

17. Patten, B.M. 1973. Visually mediated thinking: a report of the case of Albert Einstein. Journal of Learning Disabilities 67: 15–20.

18. Persson, C.B. 1987. Possible biological correlations of precocious mathematical reasoning ability. Trends in Neuroscience 10: 17–20.

19. Plomin, R., Owen, M.J., and McGuffin, G. 1994. The genetic basis of complex human behaviors science, 264: 1733–1739.
20. Sowell, T. 1997. Late Talking Children, Basis Books, Division of Harper Collins, New York.

The Strongest Urge of All

Contributing Author Karen Simmons Sicoli, CEO, Autism Today—Karen Simmons is a mother of six and the author of *Little Rainman,* a story of autism told through the eyes of her son and co-author of forthcoming "Chicken Soup For The Soul" book surrounding exceptional needs. A gemologist by trade, Karen shifted gears to working full time in the autism community after a near-death experience. She is the founder of AutismToday.com and is active worldwide in promoting a deeper and more personal understanding of autism and Asperger's Syndrome. She makes her home in Sherwood Park, Alberta Canada.

Resources and links—Karen L. Simmons, CEO, Author suggests visiting her Autism Today website to learn about her other products and services: Visit: <http://simmons.autismtoday.com> today! (*Please note, don't put in the www*).

Once again, my three-year-old Jonathan refused to walk, and I was forced to drag him across a busy street to keep an appointment with an autism specialist. It was an appointment that I was sure would be a waste of time, as nothing was wrong with my son Jon. As usual, his tantrum was getting unwanted attention from other people, and I was subjected to the stares that implied I couldn't control my child. I was used to people reacting this way to Jonathan's moods. Heaven knows even some members of my own family didn't understand how special he really was and often gave me well-intentioned but useless advice.

Maternal love can often be a blinding emotion. My continued reluctance to accept the fact that there might be something wrong with Jonathan merely added fuel to my frustration. I was confident that he was an exceptionally bright child, as he had begun reading at the young age of two and his first word wasn't the usual "Mommy" or "Daddy," but "recycle."

For an hour, the doctor asked Jonathan a battery of questions and then said he might have Pervasive Developmental Disorder: a fancy name for what would later be termed "autism." Because he was so young, a definite diagnosis would not be possible. The doctor told us to go home and to come back in a year.

A year! Wait for a year? I knew enough about PDD to know that early diagnosis and treatment during the formative years was crucial. So I immediately sought a second opinion. The next doctor gave Jon tests and also observed his actions. Jon would spin around in circles, couldn't sit still, wouldn't follow simple instructions and hummed out loud. This doctor also suspected autism and recommended us to another psychiatrist.

So off we went, and thank God we did. The next doctor recommended and found a placement for Jonathan in an Early Intervention Program. But even so, I still needed reassurance of the diagnosis and went to another specialist just to make sure. It was when the last doctor confirmed the fact that I was finally able to accept the reality of Jonathan's disorder.

It was winter 1993 when I placed him into a neighborhood school Early Intervention Program that is designed to help special needs children during the first years of their lives. Therapies, there, focused on enhancing speech, communications interaction, fine and gross motor movement, sensory stimulation and physical therapy. A bonus of this program was that the ratio of teachers was three for every eight students. Finally, Jonathan was going to get everything he needed, and I could expend some of my energies on other family members.

My husband Jim and I had five children and this made for a busy household and a full life. Kimberly was eight, Matthew seven, Christina six, Jonathan, and baby Stephen who was only 19 months old. And just when you think things have settled down, God gives you another blessing. I became pregnant with our sixth child.

I had never experienced difficulties with any of my previous pregnancies. So I continued on with my hectic schedule. In addition to raising the children,

I had started attending conferences on autism, ever hopeful that somewhere would be a cure and maybe this whole thing would go away. Again, this was my maternal urge and a mother's unrealistic hope for a miracle.

Our son Alex, born on April 18, 1994, wasn't even named for three weeks, but was just known as "Baby Sicoli." That was because I had not recovered well from the birth and spent three weeks in a coma in intensive care, surviving five major surgical procedures and care from 20 doctors. At times there was doubt that I would survive, and I had received last rites. But the doctors' skills, combined with the prayers of relatives, friends and members of prayer groups that I had never met, saved my life.

While it may sound funny, there was another event that gave me that final boost of energy to recover. Jim came into my hospital room and, through a fog, I heard him say, "Don't worry, honey, I'll take care of the kids." How could he do that and manage the family business, not to mention all the things Jonathan required? This time my maternal urge was a positive emotion that drove me up out of that hospital bed. To this day, many people refer to me as the Miracle Lady.

It was a joyous moment when I was able to hold Alex for the first time. All the children came to visit and after their initial awkwardness about all the tubes and the breathing machine, they climbed aboard and I gave them wheelchair rides. They were eager for me to come home and young Stephen even tore the "Sic" off my Sicoli wristband in an effort to show that I was well and ready to leave.

The homecoming was a nervous time for me. I couldn't walk and stairs were out of the question. Six months were to pass before the tube from my kidney was removed. At the same time as this happened, another milestone event slammed into our lives.

My mother had noticed that baby Alex's eyes "jiggled" and she was also worried that he couldn't support his weight on his little legs. I really didn't think it was a big deal but I made an appointment with our pediatrician so that it could be checked. Once again, my maternal urges were protecting me against a possible problem.

Our doctor did a thorough examination including a CT scan and while we were still at the hospital we got the test results. The good news was that it was not a brain tumor; the bad news was Alex had cerebral palsy. I felt like vomiting. No brain tumor? I hadn't even thought of that and had felt sure all the tests were going to be negative. I was in shock about the cerebral palsy, though. Not one but two children with special needs. Life just wasn't fair.

I went home and cried my eyes out. But after a while I realized that for the sake of everyone, I had to get on with things. Even though I couldn't see it, I kept telling myself there's always a good side to everything.

Soon Alex and I began the same journey I had taken with Jonathan: one doctor after another; one test after another. And again, we had more sad news. I had picked up Alex's CT scan from one hospital and carried it with me to a brain specialist the following day. After examining Alex he said, "I don't know why you're here, there doesn't seem to be anything wrong with this child." "Did you see the scan?" I asked. He hadn't. He and an intern then viewed it in the examining room with me and I heard him mumble. "See this groove here, and this one here, you could drive a truck through it." I wondered what on earth he was talking about.

Finally he turned to us and said, "CP is the least of your problems. You will have to watch Alex carefully and you won't be able to be sure till he's five but he may have major delays. It doesn't look good." I was devastated and his style didn't give me any kind of reassurance. I still think some doctors should be required to take a "Bedside Manners When Dealing with Patients and Parents" course. It's a course I know many of us would love to help instruct.

Without my really realizing it, my life had now become very full. In addition to raising the children, I was helping with our family business and attending numerous conferences relating to autism, cerebral palsy and services for children. It was at one of these conferences that a new focus entered my life. What was said by a 12-year-old autistic boy, a speaker at the conference, struck a nerve in both my heart and my soul. "I wish I would've known about my autism earlier. Everyone else knew," he said.

I was filled with resolve that this wasn't going to happen to Jonathan. It was his life, and he deserved to know everything about it. I began to search for a book that would tell him what he needed to know but I came up empty. No such book existed. So with my usual single-mindedness, I proceeded to write one. To my delight a publisher accepted the story and *Little Rainman* was born. It was a surprise announcement for Jim as I had kept that book a secret. He was still having trouble accepting Jonathan's autism. Every day he would come home and say, "Is Jonathan OK?" He kept hoping Jon would just snap out of it one day.

Little Rainman took off and, aside from its originally intended audience (children with autism), it is being read by friends, relatives and teachers of autistic children. The publisher, Future Horizons, says: "*Little Rainman* gives a more simplistic, yet comprehensive explanation of this strange disorder than any other book we have seen." Those kind words mean the world to me. They validated my labor of love for Jonathan.

As I write this, Jonathan is doing fine. Yes, he's still autistic. He goes to a regular school, and we certainly have our moments. His latest "accomplishment" is that he has learned to lie. Most children pick this talent up earlier in life. A recent example was when he told his aide that he had a tummy ache and didn't want to go play. Then he went to his teacher and said, "I told my aide I had a tummy ache so I wouldn't have to go play." The teacher told the aide what he had said. She said, "Jonathan, a little 'birdie' told me that you didn't want to go play, so you told me you had a stomach ache. Is this true?" Jonathan said, "Teacher doesn't have feathers!" With true mother's bias, I view this as an example of wit and humor.

In a couple of months, Alex is going into the same Early Intervention Program that Jonathan attended. At his orientation day, the teacher was so impressed with his progress that she suggested he might be able to start in the advanced class. This made me very happy and made the time I have spent enriching his program over the last two years very worthwhile. He is just beginning to speak and we call him our little miracle baby. He walks, runs and even climbs all over everything. Not that I would ever complain about his high level of activity, I consider it a blessing. He had his first seizure last winter and it scared the living daylights out of us. I pray that it will not be repeated.

Alex's doctor says his brain scan shows the typical image of someone who is severely crippled and most likely has been confined to a wheelchair. Not that that life is always dreadful. I have the good fortune of knowing a local newspaper writer who has cerebral palsy and his life is very rich. I was thrilled when he took the time to write a delightful article about *Little Rainman*.

I never anticipated the overwhelming response to my book and I have been told that it is changing the way autistic people are viewed. It demonstrates that they too, want and need to be loved. They do appear distant and uncaring at times, but this is because autism is a sensory and communication disorder. The very thing they have a hard time with, communication and their lack of social skills, blocks the amount of love they receive. But love, once given, is returned a hundredfold. It would be my hope that these words will be the spark to ignite other mothers to write and share their life experiences as they deal with their children and their own strong maternal urges.

In July of 1996, before the book was printed, I started the Key Enrichment of Exceptional Needs Foundation (KEEN), in Sherwood Park, Alberta. The purpose was to assist people with exceptional needs to become the best that they can be. To this end we provide funds towards existing programs, equipment, services, and therapies. An important intent of the foundation is to help enrich the lives and minds of parents, siblings, educators of special needs children and of course . . . special needs children.

In my own case, taking the knowledge I have gained from Jonathan and Alex and applying it to others has certainly enriched my life. I am now thrilled to be distributing all Future Horizon's books on autism across Canada in the hope that this will raise autism awareness and promote diagnosis at the earliest possible age. This, along with many public speaking engagements to different groups about autism and special needs, continues to keep my life full and meaningful.

I thank God daily for my life and for my loving and compassionate husband, parents and friends. He has given me six wonderful children, including the two who have special needs. My own words are inadequate to describe all they have taught me about love and acceptance. Who would have guessed, a single gemologist jeweller, in ten short but full years, would become a mother of six, almost die, write a book and start a foundation. My life, although chaotic at times, is really about living with what God has given me. They say that view of life determines whether your glass is half empty or half full . . . like my maternal urges and love, my cup runneth over!

I Am . . . for Mothers of Children with Disabilities

Contributing Author Michelle M. Guppy is listowner and facilitator of Texas Autism Advocacy at <www.TexasAutismAdvocacy.org> Michelle is an inspirational writer who currently writes a "Life Lessons" article for Special Education Today—a publication of LifeWay, Inc. Michelle lives in Houston, Texas with her husband Todd and two sons, Matthew and Brandon. Brandon has autism. Michelle has teamed up with Steven Knox of Boundless Creations to sell disability/autism awareness notecards and prints featuring the poem "God's Beautiful Butterfly." They can be ordered by contacting <BoundlessCreations@yahoo.com> or through the website <www.BoundlessCreations.biz> (Click on "Notecards with Poetry.")

Resources and links—Michelle M. Guppy suggests visiting her Autism Today website to learn about her other products and services: Visit <http://guppy.autismtoday.com> today! (*Please note, don't put in the www.*) You can contact Ms. Guppy at <MichelleMGuppy@yahoo.com> or at her web site for parents in Texas: <www.TexasAutismAdvocacy.org>.

I am the mother of a child who has special needs. I am the little engine that did. When on my journey in life my tracks led me to a mountain—a diagnosis of autism, or CP, or MR, or a similar disability—I have looked at it with defeat, thinking there was no way I could climb over it. I then pondered the obstacle before me, and I then said to myself over and over, "I think I can, I think I can . . . ." Then I slowly started climbing the mountain. saying to myself over and over, "I know I can, I know I can . . . ." and I made it over that ominous diagnosis and continued my journey. I am the little engine that did.

I am more devoted than Noah's wife. I sometimes feel overwhelmed in my "houseboat," 365 days and 365 nights a year, constantly working with and teaching my child. But when the storms of isolation and monotony become most unbearable, I do not jump ship. Instead I wait for the rainbow that is promised to come.

I am Xena, real life warrior goddess of Autism. With my steel-plated armor I can battle anyone who gets in the way of progress for my child. I can overcome the stares and ignorance of those with no experience of disability in their lives and educate them as to why my child is the way he is and why he does the things he does. With my sword of persistence, I can battle the schools to have them properly educate my child. Yes, I am Xena—and I am prepared for any battle that might come my way.

I am beautiful. I have hairy legs because I get no time alone in the bathroom. I have bags under my eyes from staying up all night with my child. The only exercise I get is the sprint from my house to my car, to take my child to therapy. "Dressed up" to me is, well . . . just that I had a moment to get dressed! They say that beauty is in the eye of the beholder. So even on the days when I don't feel very beautiful, I will know that I am beautiful because God is my beholder.

I am the Bionic Woman. With my bionic vision, I can see through the disability my child has, to see the beauty in his soul, the intelligence in his eyes, when others can't. I have bionic hearing. I can look at my child when he smiles at me, and hear his voice say, "I love you, Mommy," even though he can't talk. Yes, I am thankful to be Bionic.

I am Mary. I am a not-so-well-known mother of a special needs child who was brought here to touch the souls of those around him in a way that will forever change them. And it started with me by teaching me things I would never have known, by bringing me friendships I never would have had and by opening my eyes as to what really matters in life. He has shown me things like the Joy of just living in the moment, the Peace of knowing that God is in control, never losing Hope, and knowing an unconditional Love that words cannot express. Yes, I too am blessed by a special child, just like Mary.

I am Superwoman. I am able to leap over tall loads of laundry in a single bound and run faster than a speeding bullet, to rescue my child from danger. Oh yes, without a doubt, I am Superwoman.

I am Moses. I was chosen to be the mother of a special needs child. I may at times question whether I am the right person for the job, but God will give me the faith I need to lead my child to be the best he can be. And like Moses, God will give me the small miracles, here and there, needed to accomplish my mission.

I am Stretch Armstrong—the mom who can be stretched beyond belief—and still somehow return to normal. I can stretch limited funds to cover every treatment and therapy that insurance won't cover. I can stretch my patience as I bounce from doctor to doctor in a quest to treat my child. I can stretch what time I have, and share it with my husband, my children, my church—and still have some left over to help my friends. Yes, my name is Stretch. And I have the stretch marks to prove it!

I am Rosa Parks. I refuse to move or waver in what I believe is right for my child in spite of the fact that my views are among those of the minority, not the majority. I refuse to accept the defeatist question, "What can one mother do?" Instead, I will write, call and rally before the government, if I have to, and do whatever it takes to prevent discrimination against my child and to ensure he gets the services he needs.

I am Hercules, the Greek god known for strength and courage. The heavy loads I must carry would make others crumble to the ground. The weight of sorrow, fear of uncertainty of the future, injustice at having no answers, and the tears of despair, would alone possibly be too much, even for Hercules. But then the joy, laughter, smiles and pride at my child's accomplishments balance the load and make it easy to bear.

I am touched by an Angel, an Angel who lives in a world of his own. And it's a fact. He lives in a world of innocence and purity, a world without hatred or deceit. He lives in a world where everyone is beautiful and where no one is ugly, a world where there is always enough time. He lives in a world where he goes to bed with no worries of tomorrow and wakes up with no regrets of the past. Yes, I most certainly am touched by an Angel, and in some ways his world is better.

I am a true "Survivor." I am the mom of a child who has faced, is facing and will face some of the most difficult challenges life has to offer. I am ready for the challenge and have God-given endurance to last until the end, along with a sense of humor to cope with all the twists, turns and surprises along the way. Oh yes, I am a true "Survivor"—and I don't need to win a million dollars to prove it!

I am a mom of a special needs child, all the above, and so much more. Some days I will want to be none of the above and just be a typical mom with a typical child, doing typical things. On those days I will know it's okay to be angry, and to cry and to lean on my family, friends and church for support, because after all most importantly I am human.

And on this day, and any other day I feel the need, I will read this as a reminder of just who it is that I am.

For permission to reprint this article, please contact <MichelleMGuppy@yahoo.com> or call her at 281-686-0103.

Treatment methodologies and therapies

Medication management in Asperger's Syndrome and high functioning autism: General guidelines

Contributing Author Keith McAfee, MD (university)—My comments in this chapter are derived from sections I wrote in a chapter co-authored with my wife Jeanette McAfee, MD, in an upcoming book entitled *A Team Approach to Asperger's Syndrome: A Guide for Parents and Professionals,* edited by Kate Sofronoff and Tony Attwood, to be published by Jessica Kingsley Publishers. Permission granted by publisher.

Resources and links—Keith McAfee, MD suggests visiting his Autism Today website to learn about his other products and services. Visit: <http://kmcafee.autismtoday.com> today! (*Please note, don't put in the www.*)

Introduction

The role of medications must be properly understood in the broader context of the physician's role in caring for a patient with AS/HFA. Indeed, even when used to treat several conditions, medications represent only a small part of the overall management of an individual patient's medical care. In many cases medications are not indicated at all. (Many of my patients with AS/HFA take none whatsoever.) In other situations (as is true of many of my other AS/HFA patients), medications can literally turn a patient's life around for the better. The important point is to see medications as just one tool among many (nutritional, behavioral, social, etc.), and neither to rely too heavily upon them nor refuse them altogether.

In this short chapter, I will first focus on *general guidelines* for the appropriate use of medications in AS/HFA. I will then briefly review the major categories of some of the commonly used medications in patients with autism. A comprehensive review of all available medications is well beyond the scope of this article, but there are several excellent textbooks that can provide that information. Of note, I will not address the issue of vitamins or other alternative approaches in the treatment of autism (such as in the DAN! protocol), as the subject is quite wide-ranging and could not possibly be adequately covered here. I will, however, note that when addressing the perceived controversy between traditional medications *versus* alternative treatments, I personally reject the notion that it should be an "either/or" proposition. A "both/and" approach is far more appropriate and confers the best of both worlds. Nevertheless, since I have been

asked to write about traditional medications, I will confine my comments to that subject.

When discussing the care of patients on the autism spectrum, few issues are as controversial as the use (or not) of medications. Opinions range from an absolute aversion to any medicines whatsoever to the opposite extreme in which every problem should be treated by a "magic pill." Of course, as in most things in life, the truth lies somewhere in between. That being said, there should be an underlying assumption and fundamental bias that medications are *not* to be used unless a condition or behavior arises that truly warrants their use. In other words, the burden of proof should always be placed on the physician to justify the need for any specific medication. On the other hand, if and when such treatable conditions are recognized— as they frequently are—then withholding medications does not serve the best interests of the patient. As in all things, there must be a balance.

Holding the above general ideas in mind, the following is a list of general guidelines regarding appropriate use of medications in patients with AS/HFA.

General guidelines

Medications *do not* treat autism *per se.* Autism spectrum disorders are caused by abnormalities in the structure and function of neurons in the brain—they are *not* primarily behavioral or mood disorders. No medication has yet been shown to correct these structural neurological deficits. As of this date, if you come across a medical provider who tries to treat the core autism deficits with medicines, run for the hills.

Although autism itself is not treated by medications, there are many *comorbid conditions*—the technical medical term for other diagnoses that can coexist with autism in an individual patient—that might be present in a person with autism and are often very responsive to medications. The rationale for treating these coexisting conditions is as follows. Imagine that you are a person on the autism spectrum. You face a formidable task of trying to cope with core deficits in the areas of social, emotional and communication skills, and of learning how to live in an often-hostile world that you do not easily understand. This task is extremely challenging even in the best of circumstances (i.e., if you are in perfect health with nothing else wrong with you) and it uses a remarkable amount of energy even if you have no other diagnosis that would make the task more difficult. Now imagine that you also suffer from significant depression or AD/HD or chronic insomnia or a very suboptimal diet or mood instability, none of which you can control through willpower. Your formidable task now becomes all but impossible and your stress level and sense of discouragement (or even failure) will skyrocket. This is a recipe for disaster. In this context, medications can be remarkably beneficial. If they can eliminate the symptoms of the comorbid conditions (e.g., you are no longer depressed, you can concentrate, you get good sleep, you eat a wide-ranging and healthy diet, you are not tossed around and getting in trouble because of your uncontrollable temper, etc.), then you have a fighting chance of learning to remediate your core autistic deficits. In a sense, then, the medications are simply "leveling the playing field." As such, they can be a tremendous gift.

In keeping with the above, medications should be carefully targeted. When used in "shotgun" fashion, medications can be detrimental. When used like a rifle, they can work well. The key is to target a *specific* medication for a *specific* condition.

The assumption in any use of medications is that there should be no significant side effects.[1] And a patient with AS/HFA should *never* be given medications for the purpose of just "dulling them down" to keep them out of trouble.

Any medication can have potentially serious side effects—some more likely than others—but those serious complications are usually quite uncommon or even rare. (Medications that have frequent serious problems are usually taken off the market or are used only in specialized care centers for the most gravely ill patients.) However, just because a medication *can* cause a significant side effect does not mean that it necessarily *will* cause one. This is a crucial distinction, and I have personally heard even some influential leaders in the field of autism not recognize the difference. As an example: certain mood stabilizers can cause weight gain and can even lead to diabetes (but only if not adequately monitored by a physician—and it takes at least many months for this to happen). Preventing this complication is quite easy if the patient is seen at regular intervals with weight checks, possibly with lab tests, etc. So the problem should not happen if the physician is doing his or her job well. In terms of benefit to the patient, those medications can have powerfully positive effects in stabilizing (i.e., improving and giving the patient control over) otherwise uncontrollable mood swings. I have witnessed some very dramatic improvements in the lives of some of my patients from these medications, with exuberantly grateful parents complimenting the medication's worth. And if, as rarely happens, early signs of trouble become evident (e.g., weight gain, etc.), then the medication can be stopped without problem and another medication or approach can be taken. However, to not even consider such medications because someone assumes that they "will" cause rather than "can" cause diabetes would be to miss a potentially life-changing treatment. In similar fashion, just because driving a car "can" lead to an accident does not mean that it "will." If you need to get somewhere and if it is worth the small risk (and it usually is), then drive on. Just be careful.

When deciding on medication doses, "start low, go slow" should be the rule. Individuals with AS/HFA can be quite sensitive to medications, and lower doses are frequently indicated. However, rules in medication management are rarely absolute, and higher doses can be necessary.

Use as few medications as possible. However, two or three medications targeted to specific symptoms and given at the lowest effective doses are usually better than one medication at a higher dose, since lower doses often yield excellent results with fewer side effects.

193

Comorbid conditions that can be associated with AS/HFA and that are amenable to medication usage

(Not an exhaustive list)

- Insomnia
- Appetite problems: excessive, lack of, restricted
- Anxiety
- Depression
- Attention deficit/hyperactivity disorder (AD/HD)
- Obsessive Compulsive Disorder (OCD)
- Bipolar disorder
- Psychosis
- Tic disorders (e.g., Tourette's)
- Seizure disorder

Frequently used medications for comorbid conditions in patients with AS/HFA

It is not feasible here to provide a comprehensive review of all relevant psychotropic medications or of their varied indications,[2] risks, drug interactions, side effects, etc. Moreover, given the rapid development of newer treatment regimens, such a review would soon become obsolete. However, a brief summary of the major medication categories (at least those available in the United States) and of their usefulness in AS/HFA is in order. Remember that medications do not treat AS/HFA per se and should only be used to treat specific symptoms belonging to specific comorbid diagnoses.

One further note: within each category there are usually several medications from which to choose. For the most part (with a few exceptions), the medications within each category are relatively similar in efficacy. Which medication to select is therefore often based upon its desired side effects. To illustrate, let's assume that an AS/HFA patient has marked mood instability. If that patient happens also to be underweight from a poor appetite or have chronic insomnia, the physician will select a medication that will not just work on the mood disorder but will also cause improved sleep and better appetite. If, on the other hand, that patient tends to sleep too much or be overweight, then a mood stabilizer that does *not* cause those side effects will be chosen (ideally one which might even energize the patient or cause less of an appetite). This choice of medications can be as much an art as a science and necessitates a familiarity with the various options, since each individual patient can respond so differently, unpredictably and even paradoxically to any one medication.

SSRI's (selective serotonin reuptake inhibitors)

These include citalopram, escitalopram, fluoxetine, fluvoxamine, paroxetine, and sertraline. Very useful in depression, OCD, and other anxiety disorders, these medications are commonly used in patients with AS/HFA. Efficacy is generally comparable within the class as a whole.

SNRI's (serotonin-norepinephrine reuptake inhibitors)

These include venlafaxine and duloxetine. Mirtazapine, although not strictly an SNRI in the same way as the other two drugs, also has dual effects on serotonin and norepinephrine. These three medications share the advantages of SSRI's in terms of serotonin effects to improve depression and anxiety, but also have norepinephrine effects that can treat fatigue, lack of motivation and anhedonia.

Tricyclic antidepressants (TCA's)

Although no longer first line because of their side effect profiles and potentially dangerous cardiac toxicity, TCA's occasionally can be very helpful in certain situations (e.g., clomipramine for OCD). Used judiciously in select patients, TCA's can work very well. Some physicians would classify TCA's as older versions of SNRI's.

Bupropion

A norepinephrine-dopamine reuptake inhibitor used mainly for depression, but with special effectiveness against anhedonia (lack of motivation and interest) and fatigue, this is also helpful in some patients with AD/HD.

Stimulants

These include methylphenidate, *d*-amphetamine and *l*-amphetamine compounds. Contrary to their undeserved reputation from some quarters, these medications are very safe and can be remarkably beneficial in AS/HFA patients with concomitant AD/HD. Stimulants completely leave the body by the end of the day (if not sooner), so there is no residual medication around by the next morning to help with getting ready for the day. This can be advantageous for those who worry about drug accumulation, but it can be frustrating for those who need medication just to get organized. In a sense, you have to start all over again, each and every morning.

Atomoxetine

Very useful in AD/HD. Because of its longer duration (usually 24-hour effectiveness), it avoids the typical "peaks and valleys" of the stimulants. Can be used simultaneously with stimulants (a fact often overlooked). Although sometimes not sufficiently potent as a solo medication for AD/HD, atomoxetine can be excellent as a first line AD/HD drug. If stimulants are needed concomitantly, much lower doses of stimulants are generally required. (For instance, imagine that atomoxetine is only 50% effective in treating the hyperactivity or poor concentration of a child with AD/HD. Then only about 50% as much stimulant medication will be needed the next day—thus avoiding a big "peak and valley" effect that day—and the person with AD/HD will have at least a moderate amount of organizational skills each morning with which to start the day. This can be a distinct advantage, especially for families with multiple children getting ready for school.)

Alpha 2 adrenergic agonists

These include clonidine and guanfacine, both of which have some benefit in the inattentive component of AD/HD. Clonidine can also help with insomnia.

Atypical neuroleptics (atypical antipsychotics)

Called "atypical" *pharmacologically* because they are serotonin-dopamine antagonists (rather than dopamine antagonists alone) and *clinically* because they have a low incidence of causing extrapyramidal symptoms (involuntary movement disorders from the medications). This class includes aripiprazole, clozapine, olanzepine, quetiapine, risperidone and ziprasidone. (Clozapine, with its serious side effect profile, is essentially never used.) These medications represent a very effective class of medications, having many advantages. They are particularly helpful in comorbid bipolar disorder, in mood stabilization in general, in reducing impulsivity and aggressive or self-injurious behavior, and in psychosis. The atypical neuroleptics can also augment other agents in treatment-refractory OCD or anxiety. In addition, some of their side effects can actually be advantageous. For example, the sedation and appetite stimulation of olanzepine and risperidone can be helpful in patients with insomnia and restricted food intake. (Both symptoms are common in AS/HFA.)

Lithium

Well-documented efficacy as mood stabilizer, but with higher incidence of potentially serious side effects. Therefore, not generally first line.

Anxiolytics

The SSRI's and SNRI's are now considered first-line agents for anxiety disorders. Mirtazapine, with its serotonin and norepinephrine effects, has similar efficacy. Tiagabine, a GABA reuptake inhibitor is also very helpful. Benzodiazepines, although very effective, are not as commonly used because of their potential for addiction, and they generally should not be first line agents.

Sleep medications

"Sleep hygiene" should always be the first treatment for insomnia, but it is often insufficient. In terms of medications, trazodone is very helpful, although it can cause morning sedation (and priapism in males). Zolpidem and zaleplon are shorter acting (which is sometimes a disadvantage) and are very effective. Eszopidone is the newest member of this category, lasting slightly longer than Zolpidem and zaleplon. Clonidine, mirtazapine and some of the atypical neuroleptics have sedation as a side effect and, if appropriately indicated for other symptoms, can be used for insomnia.

Anticonvulsants

These include valproic acid, carbamazepine, lamotrigine, gabapentin, and topiramate. Obviously indicated if a seizure disorder is present. Quite diverse and varied in their usefulness for other issues. Gabapentin can help with insomnia (actually is one of the medications with the least detrimental effect on the sleep cycle). Valproic acid is very effective for mood instability, insomnia and poor weight gain. Lamotrigine and topiramate can help stabilize mood, with topiramate having the beneficial side effect of weight loss in some patients (or, at least, stopping weight gain if other appetite-stimulating medications are unavoidable).

Notes

[1]Any medication (even Tylenol) can have some sort of side effect in someone somewhere. The ideal when treating a patient, of course, is to not cause any side effect at all, and that is often achievable. However, if a comorbid condition is significant enough to really interfere with an autistic person's ability to function and learn, then a minimal amount of side effects (such as, for example, a slightly faster heart rate or perhaps slight hand shaking) might be worth tolerating. I have had many patients and their family members who have emphatically requested that a medication be continued despite mild side effects, because the patient's life was so dramatically improved with that medication.

[2]Most psychotropic medications, with few exceptions, have not been extensively studied in children and have not received official indications for pediatric patients from the governing medical authorities for the treatment of the comorbid diagnoses discussed in this chapter. Even for adults, these medications have only certain limited official indications. Further complicating the situation, the allowed indications often vary between countries. Consequently virtually all psychotropic medications, by necessity, regularly are used "off-label." My discussion in this section is not intended as a recommendation for any specific medication for any particular condition, but rather is meant to reflect current common medical practice.

As an example, fluoxetine (called Prozac in the USA) tends to be taken in the morning because it is generally an "activating" medication. However, when my HFA daughter took it years ago, she had to take it in the evening because it made her so sleepy. Of note, she suffers from severe and chronic insomnia, so the sedation from fluoxetine was a welcome side effect at the time.

Evaluating the effects of medication

Contributing Author Temple Grandin, Ph.D., Animal Science, University of Illinois—One of the most worlds most accomplished and well-known adults with autism, Dr. Grandin is a prominent speaker and writer on this subject. In her book, *Thinking in Pictures,* Dr. Grandin delivers a report from the country of autism. Writing from the dual perspectives of a scientist and an autistic person, she tells us how that country is experienced by its inhabitants and how she managed to breach its boundaries to function in the outside world. What emerges documents an extraordinary human being, one who gracefully and lucidly bridges the gulf between her condition and our own. Dr. Grandin is also a gifted scientist who has designed livestock handling facilities used worldwide and is an Associate Professor of Animal Science at Colorado State University.

Resources and links—Temple Grandin, Ph.D. suggests visiting her Autism Today website to learn about her other products and services. Visit <http://grandin.autismtoday.com> today! (*Please note, don't put in the www.)* You can learn more about Dr. Grandin and her work at <www.grandin.com>.

When a medication is being evaluated to modify the behavior of a person with autism, one must assess the risks *versus* the benefits. The benefits of the medication must outweigh the risks. Some medications can damage the nervous system and other internal organs, such as the liver. These risks may be greatest in young children because an immature nervous system may be more sensitive to harmful side effects. A good general principle is that the use of powerful drugs should be avoided in young children when the risk is great. The younger the child the greater the risk. For example, it would be justified to give a young child Prozac to stop severe self-injury, but it would probably not be justified if the only effect was that it made him slightly calmer. If a medication improved language, its use would probably be recommended.

The brain of a teenager or an adult is fully formed, so that medications pose less risk. Many teenagers and adults with autism may benefit from Prozac or Zoloft. (See my book, *Thinking in Pictures,* or other papers I have written for the Internet web site <www.autism.org>.) There is a possibility in some cases that if too many drugs are given to young children they may not work when the child needs them when he becomes a teenager. This may be a problem especially with drugs such as Haldol or other neuroleptics. Practical experience has shown that the nutritional supplement DMG is safe for young children.

A medication that works to change behavior should have an obvious and dramatic effect. One of the best ways to evaluate a medication is a blind evaluation. A simple way to do this is to start the medication and do NOT tell the teacher at school. If the teacher says "Wow, your son's behavior has improved remarkably," then you know that the medication works. To evaluate a medication, it is important that the other therapies are not changed at the same time. Change only one thing at a time, so that you can see the effect of what you have changed. A new medication cannot be properly evaluated if the child goes to a new school around the same time that the medication is tried. If a medication does not show enough benefit to outweigh the risk, you should discontinue using it. Medications should work. If the change is not obvious and is not dramatic, it probably is not worth giving the medication. It is also important to start only one medication at a time so that its effects can be evaluated.

Many people with autism are taking too many different medications. If the person has been on a medication for a long time, it must never be abruptly stopped. The dosage should be reduced slowly. If you try a new drug for a few days or weeks and decide you do not like it, you can usually stop it, but it is best to check with your child's doctor.

There are many different brands of medications. For example, Prozac, Paxil and Zoloft are very similar, but there is just enough difference between them that some people will do better on Prozac and others will do better on Zoloft. If you do not like one then try another. If you are using a generic, do NOT switch brands. Find a brand that works and stay with it.

People with autism have very sensitive nervous systems. Some individuals may require much lower doses of medications than people with a normal nervous system. This will vary from individual to individual. If some individuals are given too high a dose of either an older tricyclic antidepressant or one of the newer medications, such as Prozac or Zoloft, there may be side effects. Antidepressants have a dosage window. Too little will not work and too much causes side effects. The first sign of too high a dose of an antidepressant is (seen at) early morning awakening. This can usually be corrected by lowering the dose. If the excessive dosing continues, the person will escalate into insomnia, irritability, agitation and aggression. To determine the correct dose, you must be a good observer. Enough must be given to be effective but too much can have almost the opposite effect. Both parents and doctors have reported that when the antidepressant was first given, the person became calmer and then about two weeks later, he went berserk. This is due to a slow buildup in the system. This is especially a problem with Prozac. The dose must be lowered at the first indication of insomnia.

In this article I have not discussed the full range of medications that can be used for autism. The basic principles of assessing risk *versus* benefit and using a blind evaluation should be used with all types of medications which are used to improve a child's behavior and/or language development.

Navigating the sea of approaches for working with children on the autism spectrum

Contributing Author Stephen Shore, M.Ed., Boston University—Diagnosed with "Atypical Development with strong autistic tendencies," Mr. Shore was viewed as "too sick" to be treated on an outpatient basis and recommended for institutionalization. Nonverbal until four, and with much help from his parents, teachers and others, he is now completing his doctoral degree in special education at Boston University with a focus on helping people on the autism spectrum develop their capacities to the fullest extent possible. In addition to working with children and talking about life on the autism spectrum, Mr. Shore presents and consults internationally on adult issues pertinent to education, relationships, employment, advocacy and disclosure, as discussed in his book *Beyond the Wall: Personal Experiences with Autism and Asperger's Syndrome*, the recently released *Ask and Tell: Self-advocacy and Disclosure for People on the Autism Spectrum*, and numerous other writings. A board member of the Autism Society of America, he serves as board president of the Asperger's Association of New England as well as for the Board of Directors for Unlocking Autism, the Autism Services Association of Massachusetts, MAAP, and the College Internship Program.

Resources and links—Stephen Shore, M.Ed., suggests visiting his Autism Today website to learn about his other products and services: Visit <http://shore.autismtoday.com> today! (*Please note, don't put in the www.*) For more information, visit Mr. Shore's web site, <www.autismasperger.net/>.

Introduction

The autism bomb hits the mark, and life is never the same again for the person on the autism spectrum or for the family members, educators, doctors and others who provide support. The first questions that bubble up are: "What should I do?" and "What is the best intervention for my child with autism?" During the mid-1960s there were very few choices for a child who became non-verbal, had tantrums and very little body-to-environmental awareness. At that time an autism diagnosis was considered as a sentence to a life of dependency with either family members or in an institution. Perhaps, with luck and a lot of hard work, employment in a sheltered workshop was a possibility.

Interventions

There are now myriad interventions, approaches and techniques for working with children on the autism spectrum. Many parents and others who support people with autism wonder which one is the best? Is it Applied Behavioral Analysis (ABA) as originally developed by Ivar Lovaas? What about the Treatment and Education of Autistic and related Communication handicapped Children (TEACCH)? Is Developmental Individual-Difference Relation-Based intervention (DIR), often referred to as "Floortime" better than Relational Developmental Intervention (RDI)? And then there is Daily Life Therapy (DLT), developed in Japan, and available in the Boston area for the past two decades. There's also the Miller Method (MM), which has been developed over the past 40 years.

I haven't even gotten to techniques such as Powercards, Sensory Integration, Picture Exchange System. What about all those biomedical interventions, such as Gluten/Casein Free diets, chelation and other heavy metal detoxifications?

Reframing the quest for the best methodology to "Which methodology is best *for this person at this time?*" will be much more helpful. Although all well-designed approaches and techniques should be considered when supporting a person with autism, for purposes of space I shall concentrate on the educational/behavioral methods and save the others for future exploration.

Six educational approaches

We shall look at six promising methodologies for working with children on the autism spectrum as mentioned above: ABA, TEACCH, Daily Life

Therapy, DIR, the Miller Method, and RDI. When implemented by competent professionals well versed in both the method and the characteristics of the child they are working with, all of these approaches can offer great benefit. The challenge is to match the method to the child's needs as close as possible. This decision has to be made by the parents and/or other significant caretaker along with others who are familiar with both the child's needs and the methods available.

Given that autism initially was thought to be behavioral in nature (Rutter, 1999), the behavioral method is the oldest of approaches. The ease of measuring and assessing physical behavior also contributes to the popularity of this method. Although commonly thought of as a method even though it is not, the Treatment and Education of Autistic and Communication Handicapped Children (TEACCH) places its main thrust on preparing the person with autism to function in the typical community and work environment. A third approach, Daily Life Therapy, as developed by Dr. Kiyo Kitahara (1984), of Tokyo, takes a more Platonic (1968) view by stressing an order of the physical, emotional and intellectual parts of the child. Further, the pharmacological approach sees autism as stemming from chemical imbalances that can be corrected *via* medication. An offshoot of this approach is the use of medicine to address secondary psychological issues such as excess anxiety and depression that can arise from being on the autism spectrum. The developmental models more closely address the developmental delay aspects of the autism spectrum. Believing that those with autism get stuck at a particular developmental level, progress is encouraged by techniques to spur development on. Developmental Individual-Difference Relation-Based intervention (DIR), of which Floortime is a part, as developed by Stanley Greenspan, stresses building an emotional bond (Greenspan & Wieder, 1998) with the child, whereas the Miller Method, while sharing a developmental component with DIR, takes a more cognitive-systems approach with the implementation of elevated structures.(Miller & Eller-Miller, 1989; 2000) RDI takes many concepts of the Miller Method for developing fluency in experience sharing activities and relationships with others.

The behavioral approach

The behavioral approach, Applied Behavioral Analysis (ABA), is based on operant conditioning that is originally derived largely from the work of Pavlov and Skinner (A. Miller, personal communication, July, 1999). Heavily influenced by the work of these behaviorally oriented psychologists, Dr. Ivar Lovaas began work in the 1960s (Sallows & Tamlynn, 1999) and developed a variant of this behavioral method that is sometimes referred to as the Lovaas Method.

The behavioral methods are concerned with examining and shaping the visible actions of the person being worked with. In the strictest sense, the brain is viewed as a black box with inputs (antecedents) that result in behaviors that are either reinforced or extinguished by ignoring unwanted behaviors or providing negative consequences. The work of the behavioral-cognitivists such as Edward Tolman (1960) expands the behavioral model to include more cognitive-developmental and environmental aspects of a person's existence.

A very useful concept developed and used extensively by practitioners of the behavioral methods is the concept of Antecedent, Behavior, and Consequence when conducting a Functional Behavioral Analysis.

Treatment & education of autistic and communication handicapped children

A program known as the Treatment and Education of Autistic and Communication Handicapped Children (TEACCH) is often erroneously thought of as a method. However, it is a public health program of services that is available in North Carolina for autistic people. It makes use of several techniques and methods in various combinations depending upon the individual person's needs and emerging capabilities (Trehin, 1999). Like other reputable approaches to working with people on the autism spectrum, TEACCH does not claim to cure autism but strives to allow them as much independence as possible in the world around them. Concentrating on the strengths of a person with autism, as opposed to the person's weaknesses, the major thrust of TEACCH reaches toward the improvement of communication skills and autonomy to the maximum of the child potential (Trehin, 1999). Education is used as the medium to achieve that goal. Although the shaping of behavior is an important aspect of the program, behavior is not treated directly as in behavior modification. Rather, TEACCH strives to understand and deal with the underlying causes for any aberrant behavior (Trehin, 1999).

Daily Life Therapy

Daily Life Therapy was developed by Dr. Kiyo Kitahara of Tokyo in the 1960s. Originally a regular kindergarten school teacher, she derived her method from working with a child with autism who was included in her classroom (Kitahara, 1984). Placing heavy emphasis on group dynamics, the method incorporates physical education, art, music and academics, along with the acquisition and development of communication and daily living skills (Boston Higashi School, 1999). Specifically, Dr. Kitahara's method focuses on social isolation, anxiety, hypersensitivity and hyposensitivity, and the apparent fragility of children with autism.

According to Dr. Kitahara (1984), stability of emotions is gained through the pursuit of independent living and development of self-esteem. Mastery of self-care skills allows for the development of self-confidence and a desire to attempt other adaptive skills. The second focal point, extensive physical exercise, is used to establish a rhythm of life. Many of the exercises are founded upon principles of sensory integration and vestibular stimulation that lead to coordination and co-operative group interaction. Vigorous exercise releases endorphins, which help reduce anxiety. In addition, exercise has been found to reduce incidences of self-stimulatory behavior and aggression (Allison, Basile, & MacDonald, 1991; Elliot, Dobbin, Rose, & Soper, 1994; Koegel & Koegel, 1989), along with hyperactivity and night wakefulness while increasing time on task. Children also learn how to control their bodies as they master riding a bicycle, rollerblading, the balance disk and other Higashi exercises. Physical education is carried out in different-sized groups, thus serving as a bridge to social development. Stimulation of the intellect

with academics, including language arts, math, social studies and science is compatible with typical school curricula to prepare each student for inclusion opportunities. In the Higashi program, medication is not recognized as a therapeutic technique for working with children on the autism spectrum. Finally, art and music provide opportunities to gain mastery and appreciation for aesthetics.

Developmental Individual-difference Relation-based intervention

Developed by Stanley Greenspan, "*Floortime*"—which is a part of DIR—is an interactive-developmental approach for working with children with autism. As indicated in *The Child with Special Needs* (Greenspan, 1998), *Floortime* is based on heavy parental involvement. The method strives to bring the child through the six developmental milestones of self-regulation and interest in the world, intimacy, two-way communication, complex communication, emotional ideas and emotional thinking through ever-expanding circles of communication.

This intensive one-on-one method involves a three-part therapeutic approach. The parents are employed to help their child master developmental milestones. The entire program revolves around this component. The second leg consists of specialists, such as speech pathologists, occupational and physical therapists, educators and/or psychologists, who use Floortime techniques to deal with specific challenges and to facilitate development. The third part relates back to the parents who work on their own responses and styles for working with the child.

Floortime is similar to ordinary play with the child, except that the child's partner plays a very active developmental role. The parent or professional in a Floortime session takes the child's lead but does so in a way that encourages the child to interact. The parent or clinician actively follows the child by building on what the child does. It is structured in such a way that the child needs to communicate with the other person.

The Miller Method

The Miller method, which embodies developmental, cognitive and systems components, builds on the work of Heinz Werner, Jean Piaget, Lev Vygotsky and Ludwig von Bertalanffy (Miller & Eller-Miller, 1989). The developmental aspect of the approach looks at children with autism spectrum disorder as being completely or partially stuck at earlier stages of development and therefore structures its interventions to spur on development. The cognitive aspect strives to promote cognitive development by structuring the environment so as to be conducive to increased cognitive development. This emphasis on thought processes contrasts with other, more behaviorally oriented approaches, which devote most of their focus to stimuli and response as the explanations of the way child with autism functions in the world. Finally, the systems address the roles systems play in restoring normal development in two ways. The first is to build on the repetitive behaviors (systems) the children have managed to achieve. A system is defined as a coherent organization (functional or non-functional) of behavior involving an object or event (A. Miller, personal communication, July, 1999). Systems range from quite small (mini-systems) such as flicking light switches on and off to quite elaborate such as taking groceries from a bag and putting them where they belong in cupboard or refrigerator (A. Miller, personal communication, July, 1999). The hallmark of a successfully formed system is a desire in the child to continue the activity after it has been interrupted. The second way is to teach children certain behaviors by introducing repetitive activities. These activities or systems are designed to teach behaviors to a child who has not been able to otherwise develop them spontaneously by him or herself. (Miller & Eller-Miller, 1985)

Use of elevation

The use of elevation in working with children on the autism spectrum is a technique unique to the Miller Method. Dr. Miller has created a series of devices designed to make it possible for very disordered children to function in a goal-directed manner unavailable to them on the ground. When obstacles and sign language are introduced with these structures, they make it possible for disordered children to understand and use signs and spoken words for the first time. (Miller & Eller-Miller, 1985)

The idea of using elevated structures was discovered by accident after Dr. Miller observed some children on the autism spectrum playing on a construction site. A child known for rocking and being relatively unaware of his environment was seen moving from rock to rock in a goal-directed manner across a ditch. Upon reaching one side, he would turn around and go back to the other side. Struck by the contrast between the child's encapsulated rocking and the goal-direct manner of crossing the ditch, Dr. Miller and his wife placed a plank across the ditch and guided the child gently across it.(Miller & Eller-Miller, 1989) The two were amazed as this deeply involved child with autism crossed the ditch with the same directed intensity he exhibited while working his way from rock to rock across the ditch a few moments before.

Shortly thereafter, they started working with children as they stood on and walked across planks set up between tables. The Millers noticed an increased "awareness and sudden increase in intention" (p. 23) as the child proceeded across the board. This awareness seemed to be as a result of an edge experience that occurs when people find themselves in a precarious situation.

Body-world relationship

Another unique feature of the Miller Method is that it works in a way that honors the need for repetitive actions and routines and issues of sensory sensitivities affecting the child with autism. Maintaining that "each child, no matter how disordered, is still trying to make sense of the environment" (Miller, <http://www.millermethod.org>, 1999) even the smallest piece of functioning will be exploited to lead the child from a reliance on ritualistic behaviors to developing a set of functional repertoires. In addition, the method appears well suited for working with the diverse range of presentation that exists within the autism spectrum.

Relational Development Intervention, by Stephen Gutstein

Relational Development Intervention is a six-stage model treatment approach designed to teach people with autism to participate in experience-sharing interactions, as opposed to being solely restricted to instrumental social interaction.(Gutstein, 2000) Instrumental social interaction relies on rote scripts and is conducted to obtain a specific endpoint. In other words, people serve as "instruments" or the means to an end in order to obtain something we want, like information, money, food or any other commodity. One such example is ordering a hamburger from a McDonald's cashier. The challenge is to lead this population towards experience sharing interaction where people are related to as ends unto themselves, in order to create common experiences. Experience sharing interactions introduce novelty and variety in our lives. An example of such an experience might be two friends deciding to take a walk in the woods for the sheer beauty of seeing the trees.

Conclusion

I have only barely begun to scratch the surface in describing some of the salient aspects of six methodologies for working with children on the autism spectrum. Additionally, there are many other approaches for helping those with autism. It is only with complete and unbiased information that parents, educators and others who support people on the autism spectrum can make informed decisions on the best approach or combination of methods for educating persons on the autism spectrum.

It is also important to realize that no matter how effective these methods are for developing ways for people on the autism spectrum to function in society, there will always be residuals of the autistic condition that make their presence known. Some examples include difficulty with subtle social situations, such as office politics, facial recognition, sensory issues, and using multiple modalities simultaneously when taking in information and dealing with tasks that involve unstructured information such as remembering directions to a location or a shopping list of items.(Grandin, 1995; Williams, 1992)

Our goal should be to help persons with autism understand and use their strengths to work around any presenting challenges so they, just like everyone else, has an equal chance at living a fulfilling and productive life.

References

Allison, D.B., Basile, V.C., & MacDonald, R.B. (1991).Brief report: Comparative effects of antecedent exercise and larazapam on the aggressive behavior of an autistic man. *Journal of Autism and Developmental Disorders*, 21, 89–94.

Boston Higashi School. (1999). Daily life therapy. *In Daily life therapy guidelines* (p. 23). Randolph, MA.

Elliot, R.O., Jr., Dobbin, A.R. Rose, G.D., & Soper, H.V. (1994). Vigorous, aerobic exercise versus general motor training activities: Effects on maladaptive and stereotypic behaviors of adults with both autism and mental retardation. *Journal of Autism and Developmental Disorders*, 24, 565–574.

Grandin, T. (1996). *Thinking in pictures: And other reports from my life with autism.* New York: Vintage Press.

Greenspan, S. & Wieder, S. (1998). *The child with special needs: Encouraging intellectual and emotional growth.* Reading, MA: Addison Wesley.

Gutstein, S. (2000). *Autism Aspergers: Solving the relationship puzzle: A new developmental program that opens the door to lifelong social & emotional growth.* Arlington, TX: Future Horizons.

cont'd on next page

Kitahara, K. (1983). *A method of educating autistic children: Daily life therapy: Record of actual education at Musashino Higashi Gakuen School, Japan.* Brookline, MA: Nimrod Press

Koegel, R. L., & Koegel, L. K. (1989). Community-referenced research on self-stimulation. In E. Cipani (Ed.), *The treatment of severe behavior disorders. Behavior analysis approaches* (pp. 129-150). Washington, DC: American Association on Mental Retardation (Monograph No. 12).

Lovaas, I. O., & Simmons, J. Q. (1969). Manipulation of self-destruction in three retarded children. *Journal of Applied Behavior Analysis*, 2, 143–157.

Miller, A. & Eller-Miller, E. (1989). *From ritual to repertoire: A cognitive-developmental systems approach with behavior-disordered children.* New York: Wiley-Interscience.

Miller, A. and Eller-Miller, E. (November, 2000). ʺThe Miller Method: A Cognitive-Developmental Systems Approach for Children with Body Organization, Social and Communication Issuesʺ. Chapter 19. (pp 489–516) in (Eds.) Greenspan, S & Weider, S. *ICDL Clinical Practices Guidelines: Revising the standards of practice for infants, toddlers and children with developmental challenges.*

Plato. (1968). *The republic of Plato*, (2nd ed). Translated by Allan Bloom. Reading, MA: Basic Books.

Rutter M. (1999). ʺThe Emanuel Miller Memorial Lecture 1998. Autism: Two-way interplay between research and clinical work.ʺ *Journal of Child Psychology and Psychiatry and Allied Disciplines*, 40, 169–188.

Sallows, G., & Tamlynn, D. (1999). Replicating Lovaas' treatment and findings: Preliminary results. In Autism 99 Conference. Available: <www.autism99.org/html/pmpapers/Frames/fr_nav_mainpage_to.cfn.>

Tolman, E. (1960). *Purposive behavior in animals and men.* In Century Psychology Series. New York: Irvington Publishers.

Trehin, P. (1999) *Some Basic Information about TEACCH.* Available: <web.syr.edu/~jmwobus/autism/papers/TEACCHN.htm#Section_0.1.>

Williams, D. (1994). *Nobody nowhere: The remarkable autobiography of an autistic girl.* London: Jessica Kingsley Publisher

The Miller Method®: A cognitive-developmental systems approach for children on the autism spectrum

Contributing Author Arnold Miller, Ph.D. is with the Language & Cognitive Development Center in Newton, MA

Resources and links—Arnold Miller, Ph.D. suggests visiting his Autism Today website to learn about his other products and services. Visit <http://miller.autismtoday.com> today! (*Please note, don't put in the www.*) For more information, visit <www.millermethod.org>, write to Dr. Miller at <ArnMill@aol.com>, call 1-800-218-5232 or write to the Language & Cognitive Development Center, Inc., Suite 5, 154 Wells Avenue, Newton, MA 02459.

What is the philosophy behind The Miller Method®?

We maintain that each child—no matter how withdrawn or disorganized—is trying to find a way to cope with the world. Our task is to help that child use every capacity or fragment of capacity to achieve this.

Because the ability to assess and respond to the outside world is essential for survival, we have developed specialized training systems and instructional equipment to help make this possible. Because the ability to understand others and to express oneself is fundamental, we have developed methods for teaching communication through signed and spoken language. And because a disordered child affects all around him, we work closely with parents and families to create a supportive but sufficiently demanding home life so that new capacities to cope that have begun to flourish at the Center may generalize to home and elsewhere.

The Miller Method addresses children's body organization, social interaction, communication and representation issues in both clinical and classroom settings. Cognitive-developmental systems theory assumes that typical development depends on the abilities of the children to form systems—organized "chunks" of behavior—that are initially repetitive and circular but which become expanded and complicated as the children develop. As the children become aware of the distinction between themselves and their immediate surroundings, their systems, previously triggered only by salient properties of the environment, gradually come under their control. Children then combine their systems in new ways

that permit problem-solving, social exchanges and communication with themselves and others about the world.

In contrast, developmentally challenged children become stalled at early stages of development and progress to more advanced stages in an incomplete or distorted fashion. Many on the autism spectrum present an impairment in the ability to react to and influence the world. Lacking a sense of the body in relation to the world, salient stimuli drive them into scattered or stereotypic behavior from which, unassisted, they cannot extricate themselves. This results in aberrant systems involving people and/or objects as well as a hardening of transitory formations found in normal development, e.g., hand inspection and twiddling, or intense object preoccupation.

The Miller Method uses two major strategies to restore typical developmental progressions: One involves the transformation of children's aberrant systems (lining up blocks, driven reactions to stimuli, etc.) into functional behaviors; the other is the systematic and repetitive introduction of developmentally relevant activities involving objects and people. Activities are chosen to fill developmental gaps. This process is facilitated by narrating the children's actions while they are elevated 2.5 feet above the ground on an Elevated Square and similar challenging structures. Elevating the children enhances sign-word guidance of behavior and body-other awareness as well as motor-planning and social-emotional contact. It also helps children make the transition from one engaging object or event to another or from object involvement to representational play.

Parents play an integral role in the program by generalizing the children's achievements at the Center to the home and elsewhere.

How do you assess the children?

We assess the children in two ways. First, with the Miller Diagnostic Survey (MDS) which is completed by parents and transmitted to us. This provides a broad overview of how the parents see their child in their everyday life. Second, with our Umwelt Assessment, which carries the assessment a step further by determining not only what the child does but how close the child is to achieving the next stage in development. The Umwelt Assessment examines the unique way in which each disordered child experiences reality. We observe the manner in which the child reacts or fails to react to different parts of a situation. Figure 1 below indicates what we mean.

What do you do about more limited reality systems once you discover them?

We expand and transform limited reality systems and we enrich the child's repertoire by introducing new ones through spheric activity. When, through their work at the Center, the children learn to tolerate "stretching" their reality systems or to accept new ones *via* repetitive spheres of activity, and can make transitions from one event to another without distress, their abilities to cope with different life situations improve dramatically.

For example, for the child in Figure 1b whose reality includes the ball but not the adult, we find ways to include the adult within the child's object system or change it from a child-object system to a child-adult-object system. For the child in 1c we try to find out what gets in the way of the child's

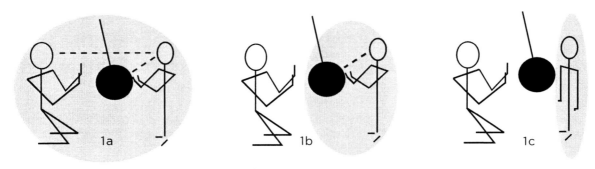

Figure 1: Child's variable engagement with suspended ball

1a represents a child enjoying a repetitive pushing-ball game in which adult and child push a swinging ball back and forth. The dotted lines to both ball and adult indicate that the child's reality system includes awareness of both the ball and the adult.

1b, as the dotted line indicates, reflects a more limited reality system which includes the ball—as shown by his or her pushing it whenever it arrives—but not the adult.

1c shows an even more circumscribed reality system, since here the child fails to react even when the ball bumps into him or her.

failure to react to the ball even when it hits the child. We determine if there are circumstances where the child can become aware of the ball. Some disordered children, for example, become more aware of an object when it approaches very slowly, others when they have repeated opportunity to push the ball.

For children whose reality does not include simple systems such as climbing up stairs to go down a slide, we introduce a repetitive sphere of activity that guides the child up the steps, to sit and to slide down and repeat the sequence. To help the child succeed we may pace the activity quite rapidly so that the child can connect one part of it with another and, eventually, own the system.

How do you help the children generalize what they learn at the Center to the home?

We build in the ability to generalize learning by the way we teach particular functions. For example, suppose a child is being taught to put cups on cup hooks. First, the worker helps the child put the cup on the hook by working hand-over-hand until the child can do this without support. Then, the worker moves about a foot or two away from the child so that the child must turn toward the adult to get the cup and then turn toward the cup hooks.

Ultimately, the child learns to perform the cup-on-hook task while accepting cups of varied shapes and colors from different locations, presented in different positions, and presented by different people. This learning—occurring with the help of at least one parent—makes it possible for the child to perform such tasks at school, at home and elsewhere.

How do you deal with tantrums and other asocial behavior?

We view tantrums as a failure in the child's ability to cope with people or things in his or her surroundings. We try to understand the meaning of the tantrum—since this varies from child to child. For one child it may come about because he or she cannot cope with the shift from one situation to another and needs help with this. For another, it may stem from a feeling of loss triggered by a teacher turning to another child. Whatever the source of the tantrum, we do not deal with it by "time out" (placing the child in a space removed from teacher or other children). Instead, we try to meet the need being expressed, to signal transitions from one activity to another more clearly, and to use repetitive (and often reassuring) rituals to help the child reorganize. If all else fails we hold the child while talking to him or her calmly about what is happening in the classroom, what will happen next, etc.

What is different about how you teach language?

We find—in accord with other developmental theorists—that language begins with directed body action toward or with objects and events. We also find that when PDD children are placed on elevated boards two to four feet above the ground they become more aware of their bodies, better focused and far more able to cope with obstacles or demands directly confronting them. Our research has shown that many children who cannot follow directions on the ground can do so in these elevated board situations. When we place obstacles in their paths and "narrate" what the children do as they climb over, in, through, across these obstacles, the children develop a repertoire of meanings which can readily be transferred to the ground. Since these "narratives" are accompanied by manual signs and words related to their actions the children soon become sign and word guided in these activities.

Goals of the Miller Method®

The goals of the Miller Method are to:

- Assess the adaptive significance of the children's disordered behavior.

- Transform disordered behavior into functional activity.

- Expand and guide the children from closed ways of being into social and communicative exchanges.

- Teach professionals and parents how to guide the children toward reading, writing, number concepts, symbolic play and meaningful inclusion within typical classroom.

The Berard method of auditory integration training (AIT) improves learning, language and social skills

Contributing Author Sally Brockett, M.S., Southern Connecticut State University—Ms. Brockett is the Director of the IDEA Training and Consultation Center in North Haven, Connecticut. She founded the Center in 1992 to focus on interventions for developmental disabilities after 12 years as a special education teacher with all categories of disabilities. After training in France with Dr. Guy Berard, the Berard method of auditory integration training (AIT) and consultation became a special focus of her work. Ms. Brockett is a founding member of the Society for Auditory Intervention Techniques (SAIT) and has served on the Board of Directors since its beginning. She is the current president of the society. Ms. Brockett is a frequent presenter at state and national conferences. Ms. Brockett is on the Professional Advisory Board for the Developmental Delay Resources, and president of the Autism Society of Connecticut South Central Region.

Resources and links—Sally Brockett, MS suggests visiting her Autism Today website to learn about her other products and services. Visit: <http://brockett.autismtoday.com> today! (*Please note, don't put in the www.*) For more information, visit <www.IdeaTrainingCenter.com> or write to Ms. Brockett at <sally@IdeaTrainingCenter.com>.

Berard Auditory Integration Training

Individuals with auditory and sensory processing problems have difficulty interpreting daily experiences. Their capacities to hear and communicate are compromised. Behavioral issues and social skills are often affected as a result.

The Berard method of auditory integration training helps reorganize the brain to improve auditory and sensory processing capabilities. Participants use headphones to comfortably listen to AIT auditory stimulation. This reorganizes the dysfunctional sensory center so that the brain no longer gets overloaded with disorganized information.

Language, learning and social abilities develop more normally and participants are better able to excel as a result. Participants often benefit from just 10 days of AIT training, with two 30-minute sessions a day.

This method of auditory training was originally developed by Dr. Guy Berard—a French ear, nose and throat physician—who successfully used this technique with thousands of people in Europe.

The Berard system of AIT has since become regarded as the most effective approach available for enhanced listening skills, language, learning and sound tolerance.

Indications an individual could benefit from AIT

The following difficulties may present the opportunity to benefit from AIT:

- Poor attention
- Slower thinking and processing
- Difficulty listening, understanding and remembering
- Incorrectly understanding and following directions
- Brain "traffic jams" when processing sensory information
- Hindered ability to put ideas in sequence
- Sound hypersensitivity and hyposensitivity
- Low tolerance for distractions

Why is it important to retrain the system?

Dr. Guy Berard developed AIT as a procedure to retrain a disorganized auditory system that prohibits the efficient processing of information. AIT is relatively quick to administer, readily accepted by the individual and requires minimum follow-up by other professionals. Berard AIT has important relevance for parents and educators of young children because the focus of this intervention is on retraining the system to improve its performance rather than teaching compensating strategies to help children manage better with an inefficient system. By improving the performance of the auditory processing system, individuals benefit more from the support services provided and their rate of progress is increased.

Dr. Berard believes that hypersensitivity, distortions, sequencing problems and delays in auditory signals contribute to inefficient learning. He states that AIT is a method of retraining the ear to listen and to process sounds in a more normal manner, without distortions and delays. How we listen and process sounds affects our alertness, attention span, concentration, information processing and the way we express ourselves verbally and in writing. When the listening process is not working properly, it can interfere with our entire system and its ability to function.

All of these auditory problems contribute to the cognitive fatigue and variable performance that is so common among individuals with learning disabilities and ADHD. These individuals expend much energy trying to decode or translate the scrambled and distorted messages they receive. Their performance will depend upon the amount of energy, interest and motivation they have at any given time. Other variables such as voice quality, pitch and rate of speech delivery of the speaker, background noises and visual cues also impact the performance of these individuals.

Is there data to document results?

The Attention Deficit Disorders Evaluation Scale was used to monitor progress with 48 children who participated in AIT. Rapid improvement was seen in the first three months, with the median percentile reaching the 50th percentile, a gain of 24 percentile points.

A pilot study was conducted at IDEA Training Center, in North Haven, Connecticut, with a group of 14 children with varied diagnoses, but all with identified sensory integration difficulties, to see if the anecdotal reports of sensory improvements could be quantified.

The children participated in a standard program of AIT. Parents completed a sensory checklist prior to AIT, and then at one month, three months and six months post-AIT.

The checklist contained items typically seen on sensory integration checklists and included areas such as vestibular hypersensitivity, vestibular hyposensitivity, tactile discrimination, self-regulation, play interactions, etc.

At the end of six months post-AIT, the median percent of improvement was a 79% decrease in sensory problems. This means that half of the children achieved even better than 79% improvement and half of them did not achieve that much.

What do participants say about their experience with AIT?

Comments from clients who have either directly participated in auditory integration training or whose children have received AIT can provide insights about the results. This information helps others who are interested in AIT to understand more about it and what changes might be produced.

- "I can understand what you say when you say it now, without having to think about it."

- "I can read longer now because I don't get tired. I no longer have to reread what I just read, because I understand it now when I first read it."

- "I can focus on and understand the conversation going on at my table now. I can filter out the background noises."

- "I actually read an entire book and was able to understand what I read with all the background noise of my kids, husband and the TV! In the past, I would have to read in complete silence."

How can I find a Berard AIT Practitioner?

To learn more about whether AIT may be a useful intervention for someone you care for, visit <www.IdeaTrainingCenter.com> or contact Ms. Brockett to discuss your situation. To locate a Berard AIT practitioner, visit <www.Dr.GuyBerard.com>. This site provides a list of International Instructors and AIT Practitioners available around the world.

Pacific Autism Center: Applied Behavioral Analysis

Contributing Author Laura Cook, President, Pacific Autism Center—The President of Pacific Autism Center, Laura Cook, is dedicated to providing only the highest quality ABA services. Mrs. Cook is a parent of an autistic child who is fully mainstreamed in a regular education classroom with no additional support. After five years of intensive treatment, her child is considered to be on the cusp of full recovery. Mrs. Cook's leadership in the autism community and personal insight into understanding the road to recovery through quality programming and provider skill development makes her a valuable asset to this organization.

Resources and links—Laura Cook suggests visiting her Autism Today website to learn about her other products and services. Visit <http://cook.autismtoday.com> today! (*Please note, don't put in the www.*) You can contact the Pacific Autism Center by calling (808)523-8188 or writing <pacificautismcenter@hawaii.rr.com>. The Pacific Autism Center is located at 670 Auahi Street, Suite A-6, Honolulu, HI 96813

Research has shown that the use of applied behavioral analysis (ABA) is effective for reducing maladaptive behaviors and increasing communication, learning and social behavior.

A well known study of ABA was done at UCLA by Dr. Ivar Lovaas (1987). In the study there were three groups of autistic children. The first group received 40 hours of 1:1 behavioral intervention. The second group received 10 hours of the same interventions. The third group received 10 hours of interventions but at off-site locations with independent providers. The study showed that 47% of the group that received 40 hours of 1:1 behavioral interventions reached normal intellectual functioning and were able to be mainstreamed into classrooms with their peers without any assistance.

Our treatment philosophy is to follow what the research has shown. Although there is no guarantee of recovery, we can assure parents that children will improve significantly utilizing ABA depending upon the age when the child starts services. Our behavioral treatment model addresses developmental milestones and each child's strengths. Our model utilizes an interdisciplinary team approach focusing on the acquisition of newly developed skills and the generalization and maintenance of newly acquired skills.

The effectiveness of our services is highly dependent on the early identification of autism. We believe that with early intervention a child will need less intensive and restrictive services in the future. This is the reason for our focus on the preschool age child. With early interventions there is an increased chance that a child will reach the potential of becoming indistinguishable.

Parents should know that recovery from this very debilitating disorder is possible for some children with the appropriate ABA program. An appropriate program has three main components:

- Duration (commitment to several years of implementing the treatment);

- Intensity (30–40 hours a week of ABA services); and

- Quality (provided by well trained, well supervised and well managed staff who are sharp enough to understand the ABA principles and who care enough to follow through with them)

Pacific Autism Center (PAC) has taken steps to ensure the highest quality programs are available through their preschool and elementary learning center. They have partnered with the Center for Autism & Related Disorders, one of the world's leading organizations effectively treating children with Autism Spectrum Disorders. PAC has contracted with CARD to provide program consultation and ongoing staff training. PAC selected CARD because of its strong history in the field of ASD, its experienced and educated staff, and its reputable curriculum that, when implemented effectively, leads to long-term successes and in some cases recovery.

Following the principles of ABA, a scientifically researched and empirically validated treatment method, CARD will work with PAC to develop individualized treatment plans. These plans will cover two areas: Behavior Management and Skill Repertoire Building. The blend of these allows clients to continuously progress and add new abilities as appropriate behaviors are acquired.

The SCERTS Model™: A comprehensive educational approach

Contributing Author Barry M. Prizant, Ph.D., CCC-SLP—Dr. Prizant is the Director of Childhood Communications Services; an Adjunct Professor at the Center for the Study of Human Development, Brown University; and a Fellow of the American Speech-Language-Hearing Association. He has more than 30 years experience as a clinical scholar, researcher and consultant to young children with ASD and other communication and socioemotional disabilities and their families. Dr. Prizant has published more than 90 articles and chapters on autism spectrum disorders and children with language and communication disabilities, serves on the advisory board of five professional journals, and has presented more than 500 seminars and presentations nationally and internationally. He is co-editor (with Amy Wetherby, Ph.D.) of the book, *Autism spectrum disorders: A developmental, transactional perspective.* (2000) Baltimore, MD: Paul Brookes Publishing Company. The SCERTS Model, a new intervention model he has developed with colleagues, is his most recent accomplishment. A videotape series about the SCERTS Model is currently available and the SCERTS Model Manual will be published in two volumes in the Summer of 2005 by Paul Brookes Publishing Co. SCERTS Model Collaborators: Amy Wetherby, Ph.D., Emily Rubin, MS, Amy Laurent, OTR/L, Patrick Rydell Ed.D.

Resources and links—Barry M. Prizant, Ph.D. suggests visiting his Autism Today website to learn about his other products and services. Visit <http://prizant.autismtoday.com> today! *(*Please note, don't put in the www.)* For more information, write to Dr. Prizant at <bprizant@aol.com> or 2024 Broad Street, Cranston, RI 02905. For further information about upcoming SCERTS Model seminars, visit <www.ccseminars.com>.

What is the SCERTS Model?

The SCERTS Model is a comprehensive, multidisciplinary approach to enhancing communication and socio-emotional abilities of young children with ASD. The acronym "SCERTS" refers to Social Communication (SC), Emotional Regulation (ER) and Transactional Support (TS), which we believe should be the priorities in a program designed to support the development of children with ASD and their families. In the SCERTS model, it is recognized that the most meaningful learning experiences in childhood occur in everyday activities within the family and at school. Therefore, efforts to support a child's development should occur with a variety of partners (e.g., parents, other caregivers, brothers and sisters, and other children) in everyday routines in a variety of social situations, and not primarily by working with children or "training skills" outside of these natural and more motivating contexts.

The SCERTS framework has been designed to enhance abilities in social communication and emotional regulation by providing transactional supports throughout a child's daily activities and across social partners. The SCERTS model is best implemented as a carefully coordinated multidisciplinary approach that respects and infuses expertise from a variety of disciplines, including regular and special education, speech-language pathology, occupational therapy, psychology and social work, in a collaborative partnership with parents and family members. The SCERTS Model is designed to have broad application in educational and clinical settings and in everyday activities at home and in the community. The model is applicable for children at different developmental levels, including beginning preverbal communicators through children who are conversational. It is grounded in explicitly stated core values and principles that guide educational efforts.

SCERTS Model statement of core values and guiding principles

1. The development of spontaneous, functional communication abilities and emotional regulatory capacities are of the highest priority in educational and treatment efforts.

2. Principles and research on child development frame assessment and educational efforts. Goals and activities are developmentally appropriate and functional, relative to a child's adaptive abilities and the necessary skills for maximizing enjoyment, success and independence in daily experiences.

3. All domains of a child's development (e.g., communicative, socioemotional, cognitive and motor) are interrelated and interdependent. Assessment and educational efforts must address these relationships.

4. All behavior is viewed as purposeful. Functions of behavior may include communication, emotional regulation and engagement in adaptive skills. For children who display unconventional or problem behaviors, there is an emphasis on determining the function of the behavior and supporting the development of more appropriate ways to accomplish those functions.

5. A child's unique learning profile of strengths and weaknesses plays a critical role in determining appropriate accommodations for facilitating competence in the domains of social communication and emotional regulation.

6. Natural routines across home, school and community environments provide the educational and treatment contexts for learning, and for the development of positive relationships. Progress is measured with reference to increasing competence and active participation in daily routines.

7. It is the primary responsibility of professionals to establish positive relationships with children and with family members. All children and family members are treated with dignity and respect.

8. Family members are considered experts about their child. Assessment and educational efforts are viewed as collaborative processes with family members, and principles of family-centered practice are advocated to build consensus with the family and enhance the collaborative process.

Domains of the SCERTS Model: Social Communication

The social communication domain addresses the over-riding goals of helping a child to be an increasingly competent and confident communicator, and an active participant and partner in social activities. This includes communicating and playing with others in everyday activities and deriving joy and pleasure in social relationships with children and adults. In addressing this goal, we believe children must acquire capacities in two major components of social-communicative functioning: *joint attention abilities* and *symbol use*. With increasing capacities in joint attention, children become more able to share attention, share emotions, as well as express intentions with social partners in reciprocal interactions. Capacities in joint attention enable children to attend to and respond to the social overtures of others and, ultimately, to become a partner in the complex "dance" of *reciprocal social communication*. At more advanced levels of ability, the capacity for joint attention supports true social conversation by fostering a child's awareness of a social partner's emotional state, attentional focus, knowledge and preferences.

With increasing capacities in symbol use, children develop more sophisticated and abstract means of communicating and playing with others. One aspect of symbol use is the means that children use to communicate or "how" children communicate, also referred to as *communicative means*. Communicative means may include presymbolic behaviors, such as the use of gestures or objects to communicate, or symbolic behaviors, including signs, picture symbol systems and/or speech ranging in sophistication from single word utterances to complex expressive language used in conversation. *Multi-modal communication* is valued and targeted in the SCERTS Model. Children are more effective communicators when they have a variety of strategies, so that if one strategy does not work (e.g., speech), a child may shift to another (e.g., pictures or gestures). In fact, a high level of *communicative competence* is defined, in part, by the degree of flexibility a child has available in the means used to communicate, rather than having to rely on only one way to communicate.

We also believe that children are more competent communicators when they are able to communicate for a variety of purposes or functions in everyday activities, such as expressing needs, sharing observations and experiences, expressing emotions and engaging others in social interactions. Children who communicate for a limited range of functions (e.g., primarily for requesting and labeling), tend to be less socially engaging and less desirable social partners.

With increasing abilities in social communication, a child is better able to participate with shared attention in emotionally satisfying social interactions, which are the foundation for developing relationships with children and caregivers. Research as well as clinical experience has demonstrated that with increased social communication abilities, behavioral difficulties may be prevented or lessened. Put simply, if a child has socially acceptable non-verbal or verbal means to make choices, to protest and to get attention, there is less of a need to express strong emotions or attempt to exert social control through socially undesirable behavior.

Social communication and language abilities also are essential for learning in educational settings and everyday activities, and have wide-ranging effects on a child's understanding of daily experiences and growing sense of competence and self-esteem. The great majority of opportunities for learning in childhood occurs through symbolic activities such as language use and pretend play, as well as through non-verbal communication. Therefore, the more competent a child is in language and communication abilities and symbolic play, the more opportunities that child will have for benefiting from learning experiences.

Emotional Regulation

The emotional regulation domain of the SCERTS Model focuses on supporting a child's ability to regulate *emotional arousal*. Emotional regulation is an essential and core underlying capacity that supports a child's "availability" for learning. In order to be optimally "available," a child must have the capacities and skills: (1) to independently remain organized in the face of potentially stressful events (referred to as *self-regulation component*), and (2) to seek assistance and/or respond to others' attempts to provide emotional regulatory support (referred to as *mutual regulation component*), when faced with stressful, overly stimulating or emotionally dysregulating circumstances. A child must also be able to "recover" from extreme states of *emotional dysregulation*, (referred to as *recovery from extreme dysregulation*), through mutual and or/self regulation.

A plan for enhancing capacities for emotional regulation may occur at three different developmental levels and include (1) sensory and motor level strategies, such as providing opportunities for movement or sensory experiences that are organizing or calming, and (2) language level strategies, such as providing information that reduces anxiety or using visual supports to help a child understand expectations for participation in an activity. The third level, when a child is aware of different regulation strategies and can choose the most appropriate strategies, is referred to as a "meta-cognitive level." Approaches are individualized and goals are targeted based on assessment of a child's emotional regulation profile and developmental abilities.

Many factors may be the source of emotional dysregulation: physiological, cognitive, sensory, motor, interpersonal or social. Physiological factors may include illness, allergies or sleep disturbances. Cognitive factors may include language processing difficulties, memories of negative emotional experiences associated with an activity or place, violations of expectations or an extreme need to have events occur in a particular sequence or manner. Sensory factors may include a hyperreactive response bias to sensory input, which may include auditory, visual, tactile or olfactory stimuli. Motor factors may include motor coordination and motor planning difficulties impeding goal directed behavior and resulting in frustration. Interpersonal factors may include partners who do not read or who misread a child's signals of dysregulation, and who therefore are not able to respond in a supportive manner. Social factors may include social activities and social environments that are confusing and anxiety arousing.

Therefore, the ultimate goal of the ER domain of the SCERTS Model is to support a child in adapting to and coping with the inevitable and uniquely individual daily challenges the child will face in maintaining optimal and well-regulated states of arousal most conducive to learning, relating to others and experiencing positive emotions.

Transactional Support

Transactional support is the third and final domain of the SCERTS model. Most meaningful learning occurs within the social context of everyday activities and within trusting relationships, therefore, transactional support needs to be infused across activities and social partners.

Transactional support includes the following:

(1) Interpersonal supports, including the

adjustments made by communicative partners in language use, emotional expression and interactive style that are effective in helping a child with ASD process language, participate in social interaction, experience social activities as emotionally satisfying and maintain well-regulated states. Interpersonal support also includes support from other children, which provides a child with positive experiences with children who provide good language, social and play models, leading to the development of positive relationships and friendships.

(2) Learning and educational supports,

including: the ways settings and activities are arranged to foster social communication and emotional regulation; *visual supports* for social communication and emotional regulation, which may be implemented in educational settings as well as in everyday activities; and *modifications and adaptations* to academic curricula to support success in learning when a

child is less able to succeed within the regular school curriculum.

(3) Support to families, including: *educational support,* such as the sharing of helpful information and resources, or direct instruction in facilitating a child's development; and *emotional support* to family members, which is provided to enhance skills for coping and adapting to the challenges of raising a child with ASD.

(4) Support among professionals and other service providers, including opportunities for enhancing educational and therapeutic skills, and for providing emotional support, to cope with the challenges of working with children with ASD.

In summary, the ultimate goals of the TS domain of the SCERTS model are to coordinate efforts among all partners in using interpersonal supports, in providing learning experiences with other children leading to the development of meaningful peer relationships and in providing the necessary learning and educational supports. Additionally, families must be supported with educational resources and emotional support, and professionals and other service providers need to be supported through professional growth opportunities, as well as opportunities to support each other emotionally.

In the SCERTS Model, it is recognized that when professionals and other caregivers begin to work with a child with ASD and with each other, they enter into complex and dynamic relationships with the child, parents and other caregivers and service providers. Important qualities of all these relationships that must be nurtured include trust, respect and empowerment for the child and family to be competent and independent. Furthermore, these relationships must change and evolve over time, as children grow and develop, and as parents become more knowledgeable about ASD, more confident in supporting their child's development and more clear about their priorities for both the child and the family. As parents change and family needs change, professionals must be flexible and responsive to such changes, and respectful of family decisions.

The whole is greater than the sum of the parts

Although we just have discussed SC, ER and TS as separate entities, they are by no means mutually exclusive in theory, in how children develop or in educational practice. Here are but a few brief examples we have observed repeatedly in youngsters we have known:

(1) Increased abilities in social communication prevent or lessen behavioral difficulties. Social communicative abilities allow children to seek assistance from others (e.g., requesting help), to express emotions (e.g., communicating anger or fear) and to have social control in socially acceptable ways (e.g., choosing activities). By communicating in these ways, a child's emotional regulation is supported.

(2) When communicative partners sensitively adjust levels of language and social stimulation, or use visual supports in daily activities, a child's ability to process and respond to language and to stay engaged in a social activity with focused attention is enhanced.

(3) If a student is given opportunities to engage in organizing or emotionally regulating movement activities, and is provided with a visual schedule (transactional support) to clarify the transition from a school bus to the classroom in the morning, the student is more likely to be able to participate successfully in social classroom activities rather than needing more "settle-in" time.

The SCERTS model reflects our conviction that by prioritizing social communication, emotional regulation and transactional support, educators, parents and clinicians are best able to have a positive impact on a child's development and quality of life. We believe that the focus on these domains is supported by research on core challenges in ASD and priorities and concerns as expressed by parents as well as persons with ASD who have written about and speak about their challenges. We also believe that these capacities are essential for children to succeed

academically and to support optimal learning of functional skills, such as self-help and adaptive living skills. Finally, SC, ER and TS are lifespan abilities. Our initial work on the SCERTS model has focused primarily on children in the preschool and elementary school years. However, professionals and parents to whom we consult or who have attended seminars on the SCERTS model have provided feedback that it is not a model just for children, but that it is a "lifespan" model and, as such, is relevant for persons from childhood through adulthood. The SCERTS Model manuals include a detailed curriculum-based assessment in the domains of SC, ER and TS, and numerous reproducible forms for data collections and tracking progress, and for gathering information from parents and other caregivers.

In summary, we believe multiple sources of information, including research on children with ASD and priorities expressed by parents support the need for an educational model that focuses on social communication and emotional regulation, with the strategic implementation of transactional supports. Furthermore, the very process of enhancing social communication abilities and supporting emotional regulation is an essential part of "connecting" with a child leading to long-term trusting relationships.

See SCERTS Model resources on next page

1. Prizant, B., Wetherby, A., Rubin, E., Rydell, P., and Laurent, A. (2005) THE SCERTS Model Manual: A Comprehensive Educational Approach. (Volume I Assessment: Volume II Educational Programming). Baltimore, MD: Brookes Publishing <www.brookespublishing.com>

2. Prizant, B. M., Wetherby, A., Rubin, E., Rydell, P., Laurent, A. and Quinn, J. (January, 2003). THE SCERTS Model. Jenison Autism Journal (can be ordered from www.thegraycenter.org).

3. Prizant, B.M. , Wetherby, A., Rubin, E., Rydell, P., and Laurent, A. (2003). THE SCERTS Model: A family-centered, transactional approach to enhancing communication and socioemotional abilities of young children with ASD. Infants and young children, 16, 296-316. (may be downloaded at International Society for EI website: <http://depts.washington.edu/isei/>.

4. Prizant, B.M. (2004) Autism Spectrum Disorders and the SCERTS Model: A Comprehensive Educational Approach. 3 part videotape series. Port Chester, NY: National Professional Resources. (www.nprinc.com) and Paul Brookes Publishing: Baltimore, MD

5. Wetherby, A.M., & Prizant, B.M. (Eds.) (2000). Autism spectrum disorders: A developmental, transactional perspective. Baltimore, MD: Paul Brookes Publishing Company

Diet therapy

(This excerpt is printed with the permission from the Winter 2002 issue of Living Without, a lifestyle guide for people with allergies and food sensitivities.)

Contributing Author Lisa Lewis, Ph.D., Biological Anthropology, New York University—Dr. Lewis is the mother of a child with autism who has benefited greatly from dietary intervention. She is a co-founder of ANDI, the Autism Network for Dietary Intervention. ANDI publishes a quarterly newsletter on the subject of diet and autism and serves as a clearinghouse for diet-related information. Dr. Lewis wrote *Special Diets for Special Kids* and *Special Diets for Special Kids Two*. She regularly contributes articles to The Autism and Aspergers Digest and Sully's Living Without magazine and she contributed to the book *Biological Treatments for Autism and PDD*, which was edited by Dr. William Shaw. Dr. Lewis often speaks to school districts and parent-run organizations, and she has presented workshops all over the United States and Canada. In New Jersey, she has given presentations and workshops at COSAC and the State Department of Education.

Resources and links—Lisa S. Lewis, Ph.D. suggests visiting her Autism Today website to learn about her other products and services. Visit <http://lewis.autismtoday.com> today! (*Please note, don't put in the www.*)

Not long ago, I questioned something my doctor was about to do because it seemed unnecessary. He gave a wry smile and replied, "At Johns Hopkins I learned not to let common sense stand in the way of medical dogma."

My doctor was, of course, being facetious. Unfortunately, many doctors actually do fail to let their own observations and logic override what is the accepted and standard medical paradigm in which they were trained.

Historically, this tendency has had devastating effects on the families of children diagnosed with autism. For the first 20 years after this complex disorder was described, it was attributed to bad mothering. It was not until the mid-1960s that psychiatrists finally loosened their grip on the diagnosis and acknowledged that the disorder has biological and not psychological origins. The blame was shifted from "refrigerator mothers" to an unknown genetic defect buried deep in the biochemistry of the brain.

This is now the accepted medical dogma, and the current medical paradigm suggests no possibility for improvement, let alone recovery. But, fortunately, this dismal "no hope" view is changing—ever so slowly. The long overdue shift corresponds with the explosion in the number of cases of autism diagnosed all over the country.

Autism used to be considered a rare disorder. When our son, Sam, was diagnosed in 1991, the incidence was approximately 1 in 5,000. Now the rates are closer to 1 in 500 (Elsewhere, authors are using 1:166). This means that doctors who treated patients for years without seeing an autistic child may now have several in their practice. It also means that some young doctors are finding out that their own children are on the autistic spectrum. Many of these physician-parents are pioneering new therapies and accepting new ideas—and seeking the same miraculous cure as the rest of us.

Perhaps this is the reason that many doctors are finally listening to scientists and parents who insist that dietary changes really are helping children with autism. The information has been available for a long time, though it is only in the last five years that a large percentage of parents began hearing about it shortly after receiving diagnoses.

At first, it may seem odd that removing specific foods would help people with developmental disabilities. The clues, however, have been there all along.

Chronic constipation and diarrhea are common in autistic spectrum children. Sadly, these symptoms were often simply dismissed as part of the autistic disorder and rarely, if ever, were the underlying causes thoroughly investigated. Not even the fact that celiac disease is fairly common in the relatives of autistic children led to a closer look at intestinal health.

The addicted child

As early as 1979, researcher Jaak Panksepp noted the similarity between characteristics of autistic children and the effects of endorphins (naturally occurring substances) and opiate drugs. Intrigued by Panksepp's observation, Norwegian physician Karl Reichelt recalled previously published work suggesting that diet could be implicated in some cases of schizophrenia. He set out to look for evidence of opioids in autistic children, choosing to study urine samples that could be collected with minimal disruption to his young subjects.

Not only did Reichelt find very elevated urinary peptides, his work was later replicated by Paul Shattock in England and then by American Robert Cade. Reichelt began recommending the removal of gluten and casein from the diets of these children as early as 1981. Shattock and his colleagues at England's University of Sunderland wrote extensively on their findings throughout the 1990s, and in 2000 American Robert Cade published similar findings in the United States.

These findings led to the "opioid excess theory" of autism. The theory holds that a metabolic defect leads to the incomplete breakdown of gluten and casein proteins. Proteins are composed of amino acid chains; in the normal course of digestion, the proteins are broken down into their constituent amino acids. At some point during this process, short chains of amino acids remain. These chains are known as peptides.

It has long been known that gluten and casein have opioid characteristics if incompletely digested. The fact that autistic children often have "leaky guts" (through which incompletely digested proteins could pass to the blood) lends further support to the theory. Undigested peptides that cross from the intestine to the blood will be, for the most part, dumped into the urine, and that is where scientists have found them.

Some peptides will cross into the central nervous system, according to the theory, and affect the brain by mimicking neurotransmitters (the chemicals that deliver messages between nerve cells by sending or inhib-

iting nerve impulses). It is now known that everyone has some level of peptides in the gut, but far greater numbers of peptides are found in the urine of people on the autistic spectrum. This means there is likely a concomitant increase in the number that reaches the central nervous system. The increased permeability (leakiness) of the gut worsens the problem.

In 1998, a researcher at Johnson & Johnson decided to see if he, too, could find the elevated urinary peptides. The father of an autistic child who recovered after restricting dietary protein intake, Alan Friedman was using equipment far more sensitive than previous researchers could access in their university-funded laboratories. In addition to verifying the presence of opioid peptides in the urine of autistic children, Friedman also found another extremely unusual compound. Identified as dermorphin, this chemical is a hallucinogenic far more powerful than LSD. No wonder so many autistic children seem as if they are on a "bad trip!"

Friedman theorized that an impaired or insufficient production of a particular protein might be the cause for underlying metabolic defects found in these kids. This protein, dipeptidyl peptidase IV, has many functions in the body. It is involved in the immune system because it signals lymphocytes to reproduce themselves. It is the protein that breaks down opioids. It has been suggested that the mercury preservatives found in several required childhood vaccinations have inhibited the enzyme.

Tummy troubles

Recently, several pediatric gastroenterologists in England have begun a serious study of the GI problems in autistic children. They acknowledge what many parents have known for years—gastrointestinal illness plays an important part in the cause and expression of autism. Autistic spectrum individuals also frequently have complex immunological abnormalities along with their other symptoms. Just this year, these British gastroenterologists have pointed out several commonalities in patients with liver disease and a subtype of autism in which regression follows a period of normal development. In both these conditions, abnormalities in opioid biochemistry is common, and this lends further support to the theory that opioid peptides are involved.

Fortunately, there are doctors and researchers attempting to find the primary problems that underlie this baffling and devastating disorder. In the meantime, there is little doubt that removing gluten and casein from the diet is helpful for a large percentage of those who have tried it.

In 2001, Dr. Ted Kniker from the San Antonio Autistic Treatment Center began a small study (n=28). Because his subjects were in residential treatment, he was able to control their dietary intake. Kniker and the study team collected baseline data that included medical histories and urine peptide profiles. The Autism Treatment Evaluation Checklist was filled out for each subject, and behavioral information was collected. During the first phase of the experiment, milk and dairy and grain products were eliminated from the diet for three months. After three months, data collection was repeated. Dr. Kniker explained that 10 of the 28 participants changed dramatically. Five others deteriorated, but Kniker explained that "the deterioration experienced . . . may be explained if the removal of these foods unmasked negative effects of other foods that they may not ordinarily consume." Because dietary responders are so often allergic to other foods, this is not a very surprising finding.

Kniker is continuing his study, and other studies of dietary intervention are also underway. It is generally accepted that the younger the child when intervention is started, the more dramatic the result. It is therefore encouraging to note that Kniker saw dramatic results in so many of his subjects, none of whom were small children.

While this research supports the importance of the link between behavior and bowel dysfunction, it is still impossible to know whether the bowel problems are a primary cause of autistic traits or symptomatic of a broader immunological dysfunction. We do know that removal of gluten and casein often leads to formed stools in children who have had chronic diarrhea for one or more years. For many parents, relief of this symptom alone makes the diet worth the trouble.

It is hoped that in the near future these questions will be resolved. For now, however, these researchers have one thing in common: all recommend that gluten and casein be removed from the diet of autistic spectrum children. Until we know with certainty why these proteins are not digested fully, removing them from the diet remains the only way to prevent further damage.

Where are we now?

Despite the mounting evidence, many physicians still dismiss dietary intervention in the treatment of autism. Some suggest that "diet won't hurt," but they do not encourage dietary trials. Others continue to discourage parents from trying a gluten-free and casein-free (GF/CF) diet. Some parents are made to feel that removing milk is tantamount to child abuse. The fact that a large percentage of the world's population does not consume milk once babyhood has passed is ignored.

Some children who were diagnosed with autism and began the diet before the age of two have lost their labels and no longer require special education. For children who started the diet at a later age, recovery is probably out of reach.

Even so, dramatic improvement has been achieved after implementing a GF/CF diet. Parents around the world have reported significant changes in bowel function, behavior, attention, language and sociability once gluten and casein have cleared the system.

For a large number of autistic spectrum children, the diet seems to be a critical piece of the puzzle. For others, the results might be less dramatic. In a minority of cases, diet does not help at all. Screening usually shows vitamin, mineral and amino acid deficiencies in this population. Spectrum children typically eat terribly unbalanced diets, often accepting fewer than five foods. We must improve their nutritional state if we are to see good results from any biological intervention. Amazingly, these notoriously picky eaters often will increase the number and type of foods they eat once gluten and casein have been removed. The search for answers continues, but for now removing gluten and casein from the diet remains one of the safest, least invasive interventions available.

Whether or not the diet will need to be life long is still unclear. If scientists have correctly pinpointed the enzyme that is deficient, it may be possible to "fix" this problem in the future using supplementation or even gene therapy. If the metabolic problem is merely a symptom of a greater immunological dysfunction, it may be that the immune system can be healed. For now, our children join the ranks of celiacs and other gluten-intolerant people and do their best while "living without."

The yeast connection

As if the situation were not complicated enough, it turns out that many people with autism are infected with Candida albicans. Why? The gut has a living environment, or flora, of microorganisms. Yeast is but one organism that lives in the gut. A healthy immune system keeps the various organisms in balance, but an infection occurs when the balance is thrown off and the yeast population dominates other flora residents.

This can happen any time the immune system is depressed, either through illness or because a person is taking antibiotic medication for a bacterial infection. A person may be genetically predisposed to improper immune responses, and there is also evidence that the immune system is being damaged by an environmental toxin. For whatever reason, any time a bacteria, fungus or parasite dominates the intestinal flora, "gut dysbiosis" results.

According to chemist William Shaw, the waste products excreted by excessive yeast may be absorbed from the gut and wreak havoc on the brain by mimicking neurotransmitters. Further, yeast infections can damage the muscle lining of the gut and lead to increased permeability. Of even greater concern is the ease with which yeast can become systemic and perhaps increase the permeability of the blood brain barrier.

When yeast is a problem, the diet must be restricted even further. In addition to removing gluten and casein, all sources of sugar must be avoided, because yeast feeds on sugar. Fermented and potentially moldy foods must also be restricted. Often a non-systemic antifungal medication, such as Nystatin, is used. But for extremely persistent yeast infections, doctors often must prescribe stronger medications.

Fortunately, yeast infections can usually be cleared up within a few months. Many children on the autistic spectrum have shown great improvement in bowel and behavioral symptoms once yeast infections are cured.

Autistic or addicted?

Autistic children have many traits in common with people addicted to opioid drugs, including:

- Self-absorption—being in one's own world.
- Inappropriate affect—giggling, crying for no reason.
- Stereotyped behavior—rocking, "stimming" (slang for certain behaviors that include hand flapping, finger movement, vocalizations or other actions that are used repetitively for soothing or self-stimulation).
- Bizarre preoccupations.
- Gastrointestinal problems.
- Insensitivity to pain.

When addicts go off drugs, withdrawal can be intense and includes physical symptoms as well as emotional pain.

Parents often report similar withdrawal when children go off gluten and casein. Behavioral regressions can be severe, as can physical symptoms. Parents have reported fevers, diarrhea and vomiting when the children have gone "cold turkey." For this reason, it's advisable to remove the foods gradually over a period of a few weeks. Even with a gradual removal of these proteins, parents often report an immediate improvement for a few days, followed by a very difficult period. In very young children, the negative effects usually pass within a week. For older children and adults, withdrawal can last from 10 days to 3 weeks.

Autism and nutrition: resources available

Contributing Author Laurence A. Becker, Ph.D., Creative Learning Environments, The Union Institute and University.

Resources and links—Laurence A. Becker, Ph.D. suggests visiting his Autism Today website to learn about his other products and services. Visit <http://becker.autismtoday.com> today! (*Please note, don't put in the www.*) For more information, write to Dr. Becker at <rbecker64@aol.com> or 507 Park Blvd., Austin, Texas 78751, or call (512) 454-4489.

First, let me introduce myself. I am an educator and networker through whom information flows across many different disciplines. I am not a medical doctor. My Ph.D. is in Creative Learning Environments from the Union Institute & University. I have worked since 1977 with Richard Wawro, an internationally known autistic savant artist from Edinburgh, Scotland. In 1983, I produced With Eyes Wide Open, an international, award- winning documentary film about his life and art. Since 1996, I have shared the work of Christophe Pillault, another autistic savant artist from France. I have also worked since 1992 with a young man who cannot speak, cannot walk and cannot feed himself. He is not autistic; he is not a savant. He is a prodigy, and his physical condition is, as of now, still largely undiagnosed. Marshall Ball is an amazing writer and thinker. *Kiss of God: The Wisdom of a Silent Child,* a collection of his writings, was published in 1999 and in the first three months sold over 200,000 copies. I wrote the Foreword for the book.

I have had the opportunity to speak at many conferences over the years and have shared with many parents and researchers my experiences directly related to the fields of autism, disability, and creativity. I was the keynote speaker at the 10th Annual Texas State Conference on Autism in 2001. The title of my presentation was "Seeing: Beneath and Beyond." I looked at hope, faith, destiny, openness to new learning, nutrition, creativity and art. My wife, Rosanne, and I have been involved with nutrition since 1974, and in 2001, we became Directors of our business within the Shaklee Corporation. In 1981 and 1982, I was part of the design team for the largest conferences ever held on nutrition and behavior.

(Autism was not considered at those conferences.) Speakers included Dr. Doris Rapp, Dr. William Crook, Dr. Linus Pauling and Dr. Bernard Rimland.

Since that time I have shared the work of Dr. Rimland, founder and director of the Autism Research Institute. (See <www.autism.com/ari>.) His *Autism Research Review International,* a quarterly publication, reviews biomedical and educational research in the field of autism and related disorders. In 2003, Dr. Rimland edited with Dr. Stephen Edelson *Treating Autism: Parent Stories of Hope and Success,* one of the most important, readable and useful books I know about. In addition to 30 chapters written by parents of autistic children, many of whom are medical doctors, telling of their success in treating their children, the book also contains a chart that shows the results of 22,300 responses to a survey on the treatment effectiveness of drugs, supplements, diets and miscellaneous therapies or conditions. What an incredible source of information for parents and doctors! Write ARI to obtain a copy of the survey and the results or to order a copy of the book. One example of the data in the survey: "Bar graphs depicting the rating of 49 drugs and 8 nutrients by thousands of parents of autistic children note that Ritalin, the most frequently used drug, helped only 29% of the children, while making 44% worse (based on 3082 parent surveys)." Compare that with the ratings of nutrient therapies.

One of the most significant books to enter my life has been Karyn Seroussi's *Unraveling the Mystery of Autism and Pervasive Developmental Disorder: A Mother's Story of Research & Recovery.* It brought together some of the people and information that

I had gained in the conferences in 1981 and 1982 and connected them with autism. It also reaffirmed Dr. Rimland's statement: "In the past 40 years the most significant research in the field of autism has not been done by men in white lab coats, but by mothers!" I cannot tell you how important this book is. Each appendix is filled with resources. Page 262 has information about the Autism Network for Dietary Intervention. Both authors frequently speak at the DAN! conferences. (See <www.autismNDI.com>.) At a Future Horizons conference I received Vol. 1 No. 1 of *Your Life* by the Living Sensibly Foundation, a newsletter with articles by Karyn Seroussi and Lisa S. Lewis, Ph.D., author of *Special Diets for Special Kids*. Write Future Horizons at 721 W. Abraham Street, Arlington, TX 76013 or call (817) 277-0727 for information about this resource and a list of publications.

In 2003 I met for the first time Raun Kaufman, subject of *Son Rise: The Miracle Continues, 1994*. I had first encountered Son Rise in 1978 while living in rural Maine and was introduced to the word "autism" for the first time. The book documents the development of the Option Institute and the Son Rise approach to treatment. (See <www.son-rise.org> or e-mail <sonrise@option.org>). An excellent VHS produced by the BBC, *I Want My Little Boy Back,* is a stunning presentation of the method of treatment. The second person I met was Annabel Stehli, author of *The Sound of a Miracle,* which describes her journey with her autistic daughter Georgie. They found the miracle that transformed Georgie through the work of Guy Berard, MD, who developed Auditory Integration Training. The book is an incredibly moving account of Annabel's journey to find the key to unlock her daughter's prison. For more information, call (860) 355-1545, visit <www.georgianainstitute.org> or write <georgianainstitute@snet.net>.

New on the conference scene and joining the acknowledged scientific leader DAN! conferences, founded by Dr. Bernard Rimland, is the Center for Autism Spectrum Disorders (CASD) Conferences. Organized by Kazuko A. Irie-Curtin, the CASD conferences have in a very short time brought together some of the leading researchers in the field of autism. To learn more, visit <www.casdweb.org>, write

<kazuko@grandecom.net> or call (512) 565-4828. To learn more about Dr. Amy Yasko, visit <www.holistichealth.com>.

I hope these resources will provide you with valuable new information in your own journey to, as Karyn Serrousi says, "track down and slay the beast that has invaded my child's body." According to its book jacket, Karyn Seroussi's book looks at: new research identifying autism as an immune system disorder, immediate interventions that can change the course of the disease process, the role of vaccines, food intolerances and yeast, and detailed directions and recipes that may be key to your child's recovery.

Resources for art and autism include:

- Sandy McMurray at <www.autismarts.com>, e-mail <autismarts@cs.com>

- Karen Simmons at <caretoday@shaw.ca> or 1-877-482-1555, who is the author of *Surrounded by Miracles* and who produced *Artism, Art by Those with Autism* and a CD *Peace of Mind for Autism*

- Lecia Macryn at <www.mindscapeproductions. com>, telephone (248) 288-2242, who produced the *CD Living in the Spectrum vol 1: Autism & Ausperger's*

- Richard Wawro at <www.wawro.net>.

- M.I.N.D. Institute at <www.mindinstitute. org>, which has published a book of its permanent art collection. This wonderful book contains a biography of each artist and a full-color reproduction of the art.

- Dr. Darold A. Treffert at <www.savantsyndrome.com/>, for the work of Chirstophe Pillault and many other savant artists.

- Ping Lian at <www.pinglian.com/>, an 11-year-old artist from Malaysia

As you discover new and helpful resources, I hope you will share them with me. This listing of resources is constantly being updated. I look forward to adding yours.

This statement, intended to point people in the right direction, does not talk about specific nutritional supplements to use with children who have autism spectrum disorders. It does provide a broader context of the research and knowledge in the field. Some of the nutrients mentioned in the Parent Survey used by Dr. Rimland are Calcium, Folic Acid, Vitamin A, Vitamin B3 & B6, Magnesium, Vitamin C, Zinc, Digestive Enzymes, Fatty Acid, and St. John's Wort. The parent survey gives parents a broad knowledge of what a large number of other parents have tried and the behavioral changes that they have experienced. Shaklee nutrition can be used to provide the supplements used in the survey in a number of instances. (See <www.shaklee.com> or our web site at <www.shaklee.net/labco>).

The little booklet *Healthy Kids,* by Betsy and Ginny Vaughn, has also been making a significant impact on the lives of children and families. (Now also available are *Healthy Women* and *Healthy Men.*) Since receiving a copy from a friend, I have ordered and shared over 200 additional copies. Healthy Kids contains 130 accounts by parents, nurses, and doctors, who share their experiences of using nutritional supplements, instead of drugs, to bring health and well being to countless children and their families. The introduction is by a pediatrician, Linda P. Rodriguez, MD, who has been using this approach for over 20 years in her medical practice. The complete index for the booklet lists all of the articles that relate to a specific childhood health problem and also lists the specific nutritional supplements that were used in each account. It has been such a joy for us to share this valuable resource with so many people. Copies of the book may be obtained by calling us at (512) 454-4489, by calling 1-800-669-8162 or by e-mail <vaughng@mindspring.com>.

One other resource needs to be mentioned: *The Wildest Colts Make the Best Horses,* by John Breeding, Ph.D. According to the book jacket: "This timely book calls for a halt to the epidemic drugging of young people in our society today for so-called ADHD. John Breeding is a clear, strong advocate for young people and a great ally to parents wanting support to resist pressure to label and drug their children. He offers a wealth of information and guidance to concerned adults on biopsychiatry, on schools, and on counseling children." Dr. Breeding lives in Austin, Texas and can be contacted at <www.wildestcolts.com>.

Thank you for giving me the opportunity to share some of my experience with you. Please feel free to duplicate this information.

Peace and calm for Special Needs

Contributing Author Gwen Randall-Young—Gwen Randall-Young is an author and Chartered Psychologist in private practice.

Resources and links—Gwen Randall-Young, MEd Cpsych suggests visiting her Autism Today website to learn about her other products and services. Visit: <http://young.autismtoday.com> today! (*Please note, don't put in the www.*) For books, tapes or CDs, visit <www.gwen.ca>.

Peacefulness and calm are not typically associated with autism, Asperger's Syndrome or ADHD. In fact, children with these disorders often have a very difficult time relaxing. One of the tools we can utilize in assisting them is to train them in techniques of relaxation and even meditation.

Teach them how to relax

I have had success with many young clients as I helped them to understand and *feel* the difference between muscles that are tense and those that are relaxed. Starting with an arm, I ask them to pretend that arm belongs to a rag doll. I hold the arm up by the wrist and ask the client if the arm is as relaxed as they can make it. After an affirmative response, I release the wrist, only to find the arm remaining in its position in mid-air! Many children do not know how to relax their bodies. We can tell them to relax but to them that means "settle down and behave." We must *show* them how to be relaxed.

I help them to imagine a rag-doll arm and demonstrate by having them support my wrist with a hand. I then ask them to remove the hand and demonstrate that a relaxed arm is floppy and will fall without support. We work with the arm some more, until they are able to release all tension, so the arm is completely relaxed.

This becomes a game, and we have fun with it. We go on to the next arm, and the game consists of my testing to see if the arm remains floppy. Next we do the legs. I have the child lie down and I support the leg just under the knee, not too far from the floor. When I release my hand, the leg should drop. It is easy to tell when the child is "making" the leg drop, rather than "allowing" it just to fall.

Finally, we work on the neck. We want the neck to be loose, so I can move the head easily from side to side. While doing this, I do a "sneak check" to see if the arm is still floppy. The child, of course, does not want me to "catch" a tense limb, so maintains a very relaxed body.

Once the child understands the concept of a relaxed body and knows what a relaxed arm feels like, we are ready to use this knowledge as a tool. I instruct them that when they want to fall asleep, they can relax the entire body as we have practiced.

If they are in school, or other situations where they need to sit still, and are having difficulty doing so, I instruct them to concentrate on relaxing one arm. While looking at, and listening to the teacher, they are to keep that arm as relaxed as possible.

What I know, but they do not, is that if one arm is relaxed, the entire body settles down, because you cannot be tense or agitated and relaxed at the same time. However, it is easier for a child to focus on one arm, or even a hand, than to try to relax the whole body at once. It is also a simple strategy for them to remember.

Meditation

If the child has learned to relax the body, it is then possible to begin to teach meditation. For a child, meditation can be taught simply as a process o f "not thinking about anything." We can teach them to "listen" to the silence. They may hear the hum of a refrigerator, a computer or a furnace, and as long as they are just listening to that, they are not thinking about other things.

Another approach to meditation is to get them to focus on their breathing: counting in as they inhale to the count of "five", hold for "five" and exhale to the count of "five." You can do this with them. Again, while they are focusing on the breathing, they are not thinking about other things. While relaxation teaches them to quiet the body, meditation teaches them to quiet the mind.

A great process is to start with the body relaxation and, once the body has slowed down, to move into the meditation practice. These two processes will bring lifelong benefits, and should be practiced daily.

Working with the subconscious mind

For children who cannot settle enough to do the activities I've just described—or to enhance the effectiveness of the above—we can use a guided meditation/hypnotic technique. I have developed compact discs which combine soothing music and quiet, gentle talking to ease the mind and body into a state of peaceful relaxation. While listening to the music and the words, it is hard to be running other thoughts through the mind.

The energy of the voice and music combined is extremely calming and there is a hypnotic effect. There is nothing mysterious about a hypnotic state—children go into trances all the time when they watch television. A trance state is simply a very focused state. Unlike television, the messages in the CDs are designed to calm, to build self-esteem, to make the listener feel valued and cared for. This approach is ideal when a child is having a difficult day. Putting on the headphones while having a time out can completely calm and refresh the individual.

Listening each night at bedtime not only makes for restful sleep but reinforces daily at a subconscious level the desirable behaviors we wish to reinforce.

My Special Friends is a CD designed for children 8 years of age and younger. For older children, *Releasing Stress, Raising Self-Esteem,* and *Releasing Anxiety* are helpful. New titles are being developed regularly.

These three approaches to create inner peace and calm have proven very successful, either as an adjunct to medication or, in many cases, as an alternative.

Music therapy and autism

Contributing Author Jennifer Buchanan is an Accredited Music Therapist (MTA) from Calgary, Alberta, and Past President of the Canadian Association for Music Therapy. She is a frequent guest lecturer at national conferences, universities and association meetings as well as an author. Ms. Buchanan has inspired and developed many music therapy programs in schools, universities, health care facilities, and private and government centres, through her long established company, JB Music Therapy. To learn more about JB Music Therapy, visit <www.jbmusic.ca>.

Resources and links—Jennifer Buchanan, BMT, MTA suggests visiting her Autism Today website to learn about her other products and services. Visit <http://Buchanan.autismtoday.com> today! (*Please note, don't put in the www.)* The training of a music therapist involves a full degree curriculum of music classes, along with selected courses in psychology, special education and anatomy, with specific core courses and field experiences in music therapy. Following coursework, students complete a clinical internship and a written accreditation file or board exam. Registered music therapy professionals must then maintain continuing education credits to remain current in their practice. For more information in Canada, visit <www.musictherapy.ca>. For more information in the U.S., visit <www.musictherapy.org>.

He stares at his hands as they twirl his favorite toy. His Mom looks at him with love in her eyes and begins to move closer to him as the music builds in rhythm and verbal cuing. Repetitive words are sung such as "Joshua is moving, his Mom is moving, their hands are touching and they start dancing." The Mom reaches for her son's left hand as he continues to manipulate his toy in his right hand. Her hand begins to move to the improvised song that continues to mimic the couple's every move, including the emotion that is so evident. Suddenly her son drops his toy, clasps both of his Mom's hands and begins to jump up and down around the entire living room. Fleeting moments of eye contact ensue between the two. Later the Mom comments that this would be one of the few close interactions they would experience that day. A neighbor looking through the window would see an energetic child and a smiling Mother.

Research has shown that music can be an engaging and attractive stimulus for children with autism. Several studies have documented music therapy as a successful treatment modality to engage the child in social, emotional, cognitive, communication and motor learning activities. People with diagnoses on the autism spectrum often demonstrate a natural affinity to music, making it an excellent therapeutic tool to develop all areas of self.

The above music therapy session is but one example of a family being affected by the relational qualities of music. Music therapists around the world are facilitating sessions in a variety of styles with the same primary aim: that individuals with autism may experience a heightened opportunity for learning, community contribution and personal growth. Some therapists, like in the first case scenario, strongly support the entire family unit by encouraging family members to participate in the weekly sessions. Other music therapy opportunities include peer group therapy and individual sessions. Music therapy, once a "fringe" form of care for persons with autism, is becoming ever more viable and popular with this population group.

Although music therapists around the world use different methods, there are some universal themes in their approach when working with individuals with autism. They consistently emphasize two main areas of importance in their work: the use of improvised music and the relationship between the therapist and the client through a shared musical experience. Within these broad goals, music therapists work in a variety of ways, often influenced by theoretical models of music therapy and related professions.

The music therapist uses improvised music to reflect back and build on sounds and movements made by the child, much the same way a parent communicates with their infant child. Therapists also initiate and direct through improvised and pre-composed music interventions that support speech development, including, vowels, speech blends and phrasing. Call and response is also a popular technique as music naturally supports inflection to indicate questions posed and answers.

Some music therapists highlight active music making as the main therapeutic agent leading to changes in the child's emotional state: "The emotional life of a child is reached directly by music . . . if he stands at a drum, is given sticks and asked to beat to the music, then immediately, as he becomes active, he becomes directly, personally involved in rhythmic activity and in musical experience. . . . As the child becomes actively engaged in such music he experiences its emotional content closely." (Nordoff, P. and Robbins, C. (1971). *Therapy in Music for Handicapped Children.* Page 50.)

Other music therapists believe that the therapy is "in the music," and that the relationship between client and therapist is solely a musical one. While others still see music not as the therapy itself, but as a means to a therapeutic end: "The act of playing is not the focus . . . . The focus is the relating and its meaning. The relating goes on whether there is playing or not, and the clue to the meaning is not hidden somewhere in the music, but in the shared experience of the therapist and patient." (John, D. (1995). *The therapeutic relationship in music therapy as a tool in the treatment of psychosis.* In: Wigram, T., Saperston, B. and West, R. (eds.) *The Art and Science of Music Therapy: A Handbook.* Page 160.)

No one model of working can be applied to every child, as each child responds in his own way. Work with one child may require a sessions that focus on the child's emotional state, while work with another child may require a more structured, activity based approach.

For 30 minutes a week six young boys come together for music therapy. Starting in child-sized chairs and sitting next to their aides the boys begin their familiar musical greeting that welcomes each other by name, signaling the beginning of the session. They soon move into speech vocalizations and phrasings, concentrating on extending the breath. The aides encourage each child independently in a style that best suits the child, such as the use of PECS, face-to-face

imitation or quiet gestures. The music therapist continues to facilitate several interventions, including instrument improvisation, and vocal and verbal practice through inflection, melody and rhythm.

The boys each have different responses. For some, success is that they have stayed within a group context for five minutes. For others, it is that they have answered a closed question with no prompting or that they have selected an instrument and shaken it three times before passing it back to an aide. And for others it is that they have selected an instrument, traded it with another child, then sat back in their chair indicating that they love music and their friend by their positive, smiling affect. The fact that many individuals with autism can participate successfully and often with others, in music activities, contributes to music therapy's value as an effective therapeutic tool for the child.

The following examples of music therapy interventions address key goals.

Speech/language development

Singing and speech share many similarities, yet are accessed differently by the brain. Language skills such as asking and answering questions, maintaining a conversation and using new vocabulary are embedded in song lyrics that are repeated session to session. Practicing oral-motor imitation exercises, to strengthen functional use of the lips, tongue, jaws and teeth, are repeated through vocalization exercises (singing single or combinations of vowels and consonants, with proper inflection and breath support). Lining out a song (leaving out the last word or few words in a song sentence) supports memory development, comprehension and sentence completion.

Social and emotional development

Every instrument possesses a personality and, depending on how it is played, can reflect or demonstrate many emotions. A percussion instrument may also provide a point of mutual contact between the therapist and the child when other attempts at social interaction are rejected or unnoticed.

229

Cognitive development

Songs aid in memory of new or challenging academic concepts by organizing information into smaller pieces, making them easier to translate and retain. Music engages children in an optimal learning environment especially those who may be easily distracted. Educational research supports the idea that our ability to learn and later use new concepts and information is strongest when we are motivated by meaningful material presented to us. Melodies and rhythm are useful in teaching language concepts, body image and self-help skills.

Motor development

Research is highly conclusive in supporting rhythm as an external timekeeper for movement. Music therapy is often recommended as a direct intervention for students with severe physical impairment or basic goals such as imitating movement. In these cases, musical instruments are used with song cueing to target various grasps, improve coordination and increase duration of participation.

They are swaying again. Not to a greeting this time but to the closing melody. A personalized song that says, "You are wonderful, amazing, beautiful and I am so lucky to be with you." The music therapist adds a special line today: "and together we find happiness, we are happy together and Mommy loves you so much."

Reaching the child with autism through art

Contributing Author Toni Flowers is an award-winning educator whose work with autistic children won her the Autism Society of America's coveted Teacher of the Year award in 1989.

Resources and links—Toni Flowers suggests visiting her Autism Today website to learn about her other products and services. Visit <http://flowers.autismtoday.com> today! (*Please note, don't put in the www.*) You can write to Ms. Flowers at <tflowers@jcs.k12.in.is>.

I wrote the book *Reaching the Child with Autism through Art* to help general education art teachers include students on the autism spectrum in their classes. Too often children on the autism spectrum are "left out" of art class because they are difficult to reach. The lessons in this book have been "autism tested" and given the "lick, sniff, twiddle" seal of approval by children with autism everywhere.

From the introduction

Art is a feeling, an aura, a pleasant memory.

Art is an expression of self. A state of mind. An act not always recorded.

There should be no failure in art—only the release of creativity.

All children benefit from art, but children on the autism spectrum in particular, who may experience difficulties with communication, social interaction and sensory perceptions, can benefit from the creativity and good feelings art produces.

Art leads the child in a positive direction.

Art helps in the development of a positive self image.

Art also helps to develop:
- Figure–ground discrimination.
- Concept development.
- Spatial relationships.
- Form discrimination.
- Sequencing.
- Fine motor skills.
- Directionality.
- Cause and effect.
- Body in space.
- Perceptual motor skills.
- Tactile/kinesthetic awareness.
- Attention span.
- Pride in accomplishment.
- An appreciation of beauty in the environment.

Art as I perceive it does not always have to result in "something to take home." When there is a finished product, it is for the pride of both the adult and the child. The act of doing is for the enjoyment and development of the child alone.

While in college, I was fortunate enough to have an art instructor who did something all the students thought radical. He took away the brushes and canvas and made us use everyday objects in the creation of our art projects. There was resistance from the students at first. Then we started having fun.

There was competition to see who could create the ugliest piece, and I won. I concocted a collage of cooked and uncooked popcorn, paint and plastic bubbles on a background of fungus-ridden wood.

My mother, however, thought this was a beautiful piece of art. She displayed it proudly in her living room for years, until her house burned down. When the "work of art" was destroyed, you would have thought that she had lost a masterpiece. (When there is a finished product, it is for the pride of the parent.)

Although the class set out to outdo each other in grossness, something strange happened. This approach to art released such a creative surge that I went on to make some hauntingly beautiful pieces using pictures of my grandmother's birthplace combined with string, sandpaper and paint.

I got an A in the course, but I'll never forget my professor's comments as he surveyed my work. He said, "I don't know if this is the biggest collection of trash that I have ever witnessed, or if it is the birth of an artistic genius."

I don't think this teacher ever knew the full impact of his course on me. Trash or artistic genius did not matter. The enjoyment and growth I experienced in that course changed the way I looked at the world around me. I began questioning and I began trusting my abilities and instincts, instead of reaching for comfortable truths.

Through my long and varied positions within education, I have found art to be a valuable component of many a child's education because they are all children first and foremost, not this disability or that. Always teach to the child's ability, not their disability.

Experiencing art should lead to an unfolding awareness of self and the environment.

To grow,

To expand,

To begin building trust within yourself,

And to have fun doing it,

To me, that is ART!

Reaching the Child with Autism through Art is divided in collage, painting, play and sculpture experiences.

Each experience is in an easy-to-read format with Objectives, Choices, Suggested Directions and Notes. Many optional suggestions are included to take into account a child's individual needs. For example, if a child is tactile defensive and doesn't want to engage in messy activities, he or she can wear rubber gloves while finger painting.

The simple but most overlooked solution to your child's reading problems

Contributing Author Pat Wyman, M.A—Pat Wyman is known as America's Most Trusted Learning Expert. She is a university instructor of Education, Reading Specialist, and author of several books, including the *Instant Learning*™ series, *Learning vs Testing, What's Food Got To Do With It? 101 Natural Remedies for Learning Disabilities,* and a noted expert who testifies on vision screen legislation. She has developed the Eye-Q Reading Inventory, the I Read I Succeed Program and is the founder of a non-profit organization dedicated to helping all children read at or above grade level at <www.ireadisucceed.org>. Ms. Wyman is an expert on the <www.autismtoday.com> website, a frequent guest on radio and television, and has been interviewed on reading improvement, learning and learning styles in magazines such as Nickelodon's Nick Jr. Family Magazine and Family Circle Magazine. Ms. Wyman is the founder and CEO of the award winning website, <www.howtolearn.com>, where you can give your child her Personal Learning Styles Inventory and find out more about her mission to help children succeed in reading, learning, and life.

Resources and links—Pat Wyman, MA suggests visiting her Autism Today website to learn about her other products and services. Visit <http://wyman.autismtoday.com> today! (*Please note, don't put in the www.*)

Is this your child?

If your child has been diagnosed with autism/Asperger's Syndrome/PDD, will you take just a moment and reply to the questions below?

Is your child disruptive or does he or she try to avoid near point tasks? Does he or she have illegible handwriting, write uphill or downhill on paper? Does your child seem to have no depth perception or frequently bump into things? Does your child avoid all eye contact, choose not to look at the blackboard, have a stiff legged walk, appear to over-use peripheral vision or poke at the sides of the eyes? Does your child seem unable to catch even a large ball or appear to have other eye-hand coordination problems? If your child is reading, has he or she child complained that words on a page jump around, or skip lines when reading aloud? Does your child skip over the punctuation at the end of a sentence? Does your child seem to know a word on one page and not recognize the same word on the very next page?

If you answered yes to several of these questions, then your child may have an undetected visual/perceptual problem that may have been mistaken for normal "autistic" behaviors. However, as you read on, you will most likely discover that these problems can be easily corrected with the proper diagnosis and visual activities treatment. If you have taken your child for a regular eye exam, you may have been told that your child has 20/20 vision and naturally assume that he or she has the ability to read easily or can participate in sport activities with no problems. In addition, you may think that all of the other behaviors listed above are simply "autistic" in nature and must require behavior modification or can be taught with numerous repetitions. This may not be the case at all.

Why 20/20 eyesight is not good enough for your child

You may be surprised to learn that your child's 20/20 eyesight diagnosis (even with corrective lenses) is completely unrelated to reading or eye-hand coordination activities at near point. When your child covers one eye during an exam and reads a chart with letters at 20 feet away, he or she is using an outdated chart from the 1800s, known as the Snellen Chart, which simply says that your child can see a certain size letter from 20 feet away! This chart only measures clearness and sharpness of eyesight using a stationary target.

As soon as parents and teachers hear this, they always ask the same questions. How many children read books from 20 feet away, and isn't there more to reading and sensory motor activities than distance eyesight at 20 feet away?

Eyesight and vision myth

It is important to know that your child needs both eyesight and strong vision to be able to read and perform everyday activities. Yes, few parents or teachers realize that eyesight and vision are very different skills. Eye doctors who specialize in learning-related vision disorders tell us why and how a treatment known as "vision therapy" can make a world of difference for your autistic child.

Eyesight, or the ability to see, is present at birth. Vision has to be learned as your child grows. Eye doctors who specialize in learning-related vision screenings tell us that vision is so complicated it involves about 20 visual abilities and more than 75%–90% of all pathways to the brain. Visual skills allow your child to comprehend and make meaning from what he or she sees. In addition, medical research has shown that supplementing your child's diet with the "smart fats" known as omega 3 oils will help develop your child's vision, improve memory and facilitate faster thinking. (See www.howtolearn.com/omega3.html.)

When a child does a variety of activities, such as coloring, jigsaw puzzles, building blocks, playing with jacks, running, jumping, playing baseball or basketball, riding a bike, building forts, skating and many more, he or she is learning skills that will make him or her a great reader later on.

Today, however, millions of children are doing very different things from those you did when you were a child. You are correct if you think they are indoors more of the time. They are sitting in front of a computer screen at a very young age, (sometimes as early as age one), watching thousands of hours of television (studies show that children watch anywhere from three to seven hours of television a day), and playing video games for hours on end. Your autistic child may be hyperfocused on small things for untold hours.

While these indoor activities may have some value, turned to excessively they actually limit your child's visual development and will cause reading problems in the future. The human visual system is not designed for constant nearpoint activities. Your child may develop so much visual stress, he or she will have to work twice as hard to get the same results as

other kids. In addition, your child won't learn how to develop eye movement skills like tracking (so they can read smoothly and not skip a line), eye-focusing skills, eye-aiming skills, visual perception, peripheral vision, eye-hand coordination (involved in playing sports, copying from the book to the paper or from the board to the paper), right-left directionality (know the difference between a b and d, p and q), and much more.

When your child enters school or is reading at home, his or her visual problems may actually worsen. Children are required to read far more material than you ever had to as a child. The demand on their visual systems is much heavier than it was for you. Since visual skill testing is limited or absent, and your child may not be able to verbalize what he or she is feeling, you also have no way of knowing whether there is further stress on the visual system like eye turns or lazy eye, both of which make reading and other activities very painful and difficult.

Thus, if you have an autistic child, "normal" autistic behaviors such as looking through or beyond objects, aversion to light, lack of reciprocal play, fear of heights, poor reading skills or inability to participate in sports activities may all be related to a weak visual system. This system is so critical to behavior and reading that it can impact nearly every activity your child does.

The following chart shows the relationship between vision skills and everyday tasks your child performs.

Vision skills needed for typical reading, classroom and other tasks

Classroom Tasks ↓	Tracking	Visual Memory	Figure Ground	Eye Movement Control / Fixation	Simultaneous Focusing At Near	Simultaneous Focusing At Far	Sustaining Focusing At Near	Sustaining Focusing At Far	Eye Teaming/ Sustaining Alignment At Near	Eye Teaming/Sustaining Alignment At Far	Central Vision	Peripheral Vision	Depth Awareness	Color Retention and/or contrast	Gross Visual Motor	Fine Visual Motor	Visual Perception / Directionality/Closure	Eye Hand Coordination	Simultaneous Alignment At Near	Simultaneous Alignment Far
Reading	x	x	x	x	x		x		x		x	x		?		x	x		x	
Copying (CB to desk)	x	x	x	x	x	x					x	x			x	x	x	x	x	x
Copying (at desk)	x	x	x	x	x		x		x		x	x			x	x	x	x	x	
Writing	x	x	x	x	x		x		x		x	x		x		x	x	x	x	
Discussion	x	x	x			x					x	x					x			x
Demonstration	x	x	x	x		x					x	x	x	?	x		x			x
Movies, TV	x	x	x	x		x		x		x	x	x		?			x			x
P.E., Dancing	x	x	x	x	x	x		x	x	x	x	x	x		x		x	x		x
Art, Crafts	x	x	x	x	x		x	x	x		x	x	x	x		x	x	x	x	
Play	x	x	x	x	x	x	x	x	x	x	x	x	x	x	x	x	x	x	x	x
Computers	x	x	x	x	x		x	x	x		x	x				x	x	x	x	
Taking notes	x	x	x	x	x		x				x	x				x	x	x	x	

Why your child must have a comprehensive learning-related vision exam and follow-up vision therapy activities, if prescribed

Since eyesight and vision are at the very core of your child's ability to read and learn many activities, it is critical that you provide your child with a comprehensive, learning-related vision exam before embarking on other therapies. A substantial number of "autistic" symptoms may simply be a vision problem in disguise. Specially trained optometrists, known as developmental or behavioral optometrists, can properly diagnose and treat your child. Once your child has this exam, he or she may be prescribed a very specific series of exercises and visual activities, and you may be very surprised to discover that many of the behaviors you thought were "autistic" in nature, improve or disappear altogether.

For more information on vision therapy, download the Eye-Q Reading Inventory at <www.howtolearn.com/ireadisucceed.html>, administer it to your child and visit the website listed on the Inventory to find a doctor in your area who can give your child the comprehensive, learning-related vision exam he or she deserves. If you choose to do some of the vision activities at home, you can find out more by taking a look at the I Read I Succeed Program, already proven to help thousands of autistic children improve their reading and behavioral abilities.

"Live simply, laugh often, love deeply."

Scotopic sensitivity syndrome and the Irlen lens system

Contributing Author Stephen M. Edelson, Ph.D., Experimental Psychology—Dr. Edelson has worked in the field of autism for 25 years. He is the Director of the Center for the Study of Autism in Salem, Oregon, which is affiliated with the Autism Research Institute in San Diego, CA. He is also on the Board of Directors of the Oregon chapter of the Autism Society of America and is on the Society's Professional Advisory Board. His main autism website is <www.autism.org>.

Resources and links—Stephen M. Edelson, Ph.D. suggests visiting his Autism Today website to learn about his other products and services. Visit <http://edelson.autismtoday.com> today! (*Please note, don't put in the www.*) Helen Irlen has trained people throughout the world in the use of her methods. For more information, write to Irlen Institute/PLD, 5380 Village Road, Long Beach, California 90808, U.S.A. or <Irlen_Institute@compuserve.com>, call (562) 496-2550 or fax (562) 429-8699.

There is growing evidence, based on both research and personal reports, that many autistic individuals see their world in a maladaptive, dysfunctional manner. Researchers at UCLA and the University of Utah have found evidence of abnormal retinal activity in autistic individuals. Additionally, there are many visual problems which are often associated with autism, such as reliance on peripheral vision, tunnel vision, hypersensitivity to light, and stereotypic (repetitive) behavior near the eyes, such as hand-flapping and finger-flicking. Donna Williams, an autistic adult, has written several books about her life and has often commented on her vision. She once wrote: "Nothing was whole except the colours and sparkles in the air . . . ." and "I had always known that the world was fragmented. My mother was a smell and a texture, my father a tone, and my older brother was something which moved about."

Scotopic Sensitivity/Irlen Syndrome is a visual-perceptual problem that occurs in some people with learning/reading disorders, autism and other developmental disorders. People with Scotopic Sensitivity/Irlen Syndrome experience "perceptual stress" that can lead to a variety of perceptual distortions when reading and/or viewing their environment. Scotopic Sensitivity is triggered by one or more components of light, such as the source of the light (e.g., fluorescent lighting, sun), luminance (e.g., reflection, glare), intensity (i.e., brightness), wavelength (i.e., color), and/or color contrast. As a result, the person may experience:

- Light sensitivity: bothered by brightness, glare, types of lighting

- Inefficient reading: letters on page move, dance, vibrate, jiggle

- Inadequate background accommodation: difficulty with high contrast

- Restricted span of recognition: tunnel vision or difficulty reading groups of letters

- Lack of sustained attention: difficulty maintaining attention

The Irlen Lens System, developed by Helen Irlen, was designed to treat Scotopic Sensitivity/Irlen Syndrome. Helen Irlen has developed two methods to treat Scotopic Sensitivity: the use of colored transparencies or overlays to improve reading; and tinted glasses to improve one's visual perception of his/her environment.

Transparencies

Transparencies or overlays are used to reduce perceptual stress while reading. For some people, letters/words on a page are not perceived clearly and/or not perceived in a stable manner (i.e., letters and words appear to move). The white background may overtake and dominate the person's perceptual system, and the black print of the text may fade into the background. Other symptoms may include having difficulty reading

237

for relatively long periods of time, developing headaches and feeling dizzy. It is possible that, for some, the high contrast between black print on a white background provides excessive stimulation to the visual system and thus interferes with the reading process.

In the Irlen Lens System, colored transparencies are placed over printed text with the result that these problems may be reduced or eliminated. A colored overlay, such as a light blue transparency placed over the text, will reduce the contrast between black and white as well as reduce the dominance of the white background. The optimal color of the transparency required depends upon each person's unique visual-perceptual system.

Glasses

In addition to reading problems, people with Scotopic Sensitivity/Irlen Syndrome may have difficulty perceiving their surroundings. Many autistic individuals wear tinted glasses, which were prescribed by Helen Irlen or at one of her 76 worldwide diagnostic clinics. They have reported rather remarkable benefits. After wearing her glasses, Donna Williams wrote: "These [Irlen] glasses would have changed all that. Faces and body parts and voices would have been whole and understood within a context of equally conjoined surroundings." Other autistic individuals report seeing better, feeling more relaxed, being less bothered by sunlight and/or indoor lighting, and have fewer perceptual distortions which can affect small and gross motor coordination.

Helen Irlen has developed effective methods for determining if a person suffers from Scotopic Sensitivity/Irlen Syndrome. She has also designed a standardized set of procedures that can be used to determine the correct color prescription for the transparency and the tinted lenses.

Planning for the future

CHAPTER 18

Life Map

Contributing Author Anne Addison, MBA, Kellogg School of Management, Northwestern University—Ms. Addison worked for nearly 10 years in marketing management at several Fortune 100 companies before she launched her own management consulting practice. When her son was diagnosed with Attention Deficit Hyperactivity Deficit at the age of three and, later, with Asperger's Syndrome, she made a life-changing decision to close her consulting company and turn her business skills towards managing her son's case. Through her effective personal style and her ability to successfully manage a health care and education team, Ms. Addison helped her son navigate the last heart-wrenching, sometimes overwhelming, ten years— through educational failures, medication disasters, and more. Today, her son is a strong student in a typical fourth grade classroom. He's involved in outside sports, church choir, and music. Ms. Addison's book, *One Small Starfish: A Mother's Everyday Advice, Survival Tactics & Wisdom for Raising a Special Needs Child,* won the Publishers Marketing Association's Ben Franklin Award, which recognizes excellence in independent publishing.

Resources and links—Anne Addison, MBA, NHA suggests visiting her Autism Today website to learn about her other products and services. Visit <http://addison.autismtoday.com> today! (*Please note, don't put in the www.*) Ms. Addison is an Autism Today expert. You can reach her through our website.

Introduction

For typical children, moving through the cognitive, emotional and physical developmental stages of life is a natural progression. With the right people and experiences put in their path, they continue to move along. But if we want children with special needs to become responsible, capable and happy adults, we need to chart a path from where they are today to where we—and they—hope they will end up.

To determine who you want to become and what you want to do in life you need to know yourself, what you like and don't like, what you can and can't do. You also need a certain amount of social smarts—because, like it or not, the road of life is paved with relationships and interactions. How absolutely unfortunate, then, that some children with special needs have trouble in both of these areas— introspecting and relating to others. They don't think much about their inner selves at any given moment, never mind thinking ahead a month, a year or a lifetime. And they pretty much live in the moment in a state of social confusion. Their hearts are in the right places, but their social senses are not.

If your child is going to make it in life, there is a greater chance that he will do so if there is a roadmap to guide him, one that draws on his strengths and minimizes his challenges. You will have to be intentional about his future. You will also need to teach him to be intentional, being mindful of what he needs to be successful and being able to access the tools to get there.

The Life Map can help define a vision and goals for your child's future and provide the tools to achieve them. Depending on your child's cognitive and emotional abilities, you will need to figure out how much he can participate in the Life Mapping process. As he matures, his role in this process should increase until he is eventually able to take the lead in creating his own Life Map.

The Life Map is a framework for helping a child reach his potential and become the best he can be. If it's a clerk at the local grocery store, let's help him become the one with the biggest smile and the largest helping hand. If it's a herpetologist, let's figure out how to teach him effective listening skills so that he can be part of a research team.

Supporting your child with the skills that he needs does not mean that you are defining his dreams for him. If your child is high functioning, he will have his own dreams. Your role is to look at the competencies he needs to achieve them and help him get there.

Competencies go beyond technical skills. In fact, technical skills are probably the least of your worries.

If your child is succeeding in school, he will probably be able to get through the necessary technical training and education to reach his goals. You need to think about the social, relational, emotional and practical skills he will need—defining what they are and creating opportunities to practice, practice, practice them so that they become competencies.

Following is an excerpt from a letter that we received from Jack's teacher and advisor several weeks after Jack began middle school:

> "Jack really is beginning to show his personality, and as we have a great abhorrence of cookie-cutter kids, we like the fact that he is so independent and outspoken. For instance, in class today I was explaining that academic competitiveness at the school is not really encouraged. That we judge each student by his or her individual progress, not by how they measure up to other students.

> "Having said that, I handed out the vocabulary workbooks, where each student works at his own level. Of course, they started comparing their levels immediately. I went through the explanation again. Jack raised his hand and said, 'I don't go for all that mind-control stuff. Of course, it is better to be in a higher book.' Inside I was chuckling (thinking, there's my little rationalist), but I tried to assure him that I don't play 'mind-control' games and am as honest as I can be, given the circumstances."

You've got to love a kid like that. Carving a path, being conscientious and careful to match your child's temperament and personality to the environment and culture, whether it is school, an activity, or the structure of your home, pays off. You'll see it the minute your child's tent starts unfolding.

What is Life Mapping?

Life Mapping is a process used to realize a person's fullest potential by drawing on his strengths and interests and working on his challenges. Companies go through processes like this all the time. They identify their competitive edge, take a look at what barriers are in the market and come up with goals and a way of reaching them that will satisfy both consumers and stockholders.

This process can also work for individuals. In fact, maybe you've done Life Mapping (although you probably haven't called it that) for yourself—getting to know who you are and what you're good at, setting goals that relate to that and then establishing a way to accomplish them. I'm not suggesting that you won't have a perfectly satisfactory and fulfilling life if you don't do Life Mapping. But for children with challenges, being intentional and thoughtful about who they are and what they need throughout their life will improve the odds that they will live a satisfying life.

Pretend that it is your friend's birthday and you have offered to throw her a party. You ask her who she would like you to invite and what she would like for dessert. Tossing Dr. Atkins to the wind, she says breathlessly, "Triple chocolate mousse cake with extra filling—and don't skimp on the frosting." Determining what you need to do to put the party together, from invitations to cake, is the plan.

Having your friend enjoy a wonderful party and that delicious cake is your ultimate goal, vision, dream, and desire. To make the cake, you look in your kitchen cabinets and see that you've got a couple of eggs and some vanilla. That's the starting point. You go to the grocery store and buy the rest of the ingredients and then proceed to make the cake. From finding out what ingredients were on hand to spreading the last of the butter cream frosting on the cake is process. In fact, all of the actions that you take between coming up with the party idea to holding the event are part of the process. The actual party is just the endpoint, the goal.

The people are everyone involved in the event, from the birthday girl to the clerks at the stores where you shop to the guests and yours truly. They are the ones that carry out the process.

The birthday party could be thought of as a mapping experience: making a plan, using a process that leads you toward the goal and working with people in the process. These three things are at the heart of Life Mapping.

The three elements of Life Mapping

Let's take a closer look at the elements behind Life Mapping: the players, the process, and the plan.

The players

The child, the parents and those who regularly work with your child make up the foundation of the Life Mapping model. At the center is the child. That probably seems obvious. You might even say to yourself, "Of course, it is all about him. I spend half of my waking minutes thinking, worrying, making calls, setting plans, and fussing about him." It is a full-time job, no doubt. But doing the work without understanding the child is not enough. Life Mapping will only be as strong as the foundation. And the foundation starts with the child. Understanding your child means more than knowing what the doctors have told you that he "has." It means knowing many different aspects of him. By nature of his challenges, it is often hard to get close to or understand your exceptional child. But you need to keep trying, because the more you understand your child, the better you'll be able to develop a Life Map for him.

The next part of the foundation is the parent(s.) You're the one(s) who provide the overall support for your child. You might think this support focuses on how your child functions at home, but since you are his coach, mentor and case manager, your influence extends into every part of his life. You have a huge impact on the success of your child's Life Map. So it's vital to understand yourself. The more you know yourself and are aware of how your behavior and attitudes impact your child, the more effective you can be.

The folks who support your child make up the final piece of the foundation. We have all been on teams that are effective and teams that are not. Effective teams can move mountains, let alone move toward goals. The dysfunctional team cannot. The better the team functions, the more your child will benefit. We will look more closely at the nature of the players and their roles in Part II.

The process

In Life Mapping, there are many factors that influence, impact and drive the process. But for our children, the two primary factors are the parent(s) and the team that supports the child. These individuals work closely and on a regular basis with the child. Their interactions with the child may be positive, negative or neutral, but they all have a huge impact.

The plan

Defining goals and having a plan to reach those goals provide a structure for helping you stay focused and mindful that what you are working on are the things that you should be working on; that is, those that will make the greatest impact and difference in your child's life.

It doesn't matter how good a job you do if you are doing the wrong job. And in the case of helping a child reach his potential, you have to know what specifics, when added together, constitute that potential. If you want your child to reach his highest potential, you need to define what that might look like and then develop the steps that are needed to achieve it.

Planning for the future

Contributing Author Sharon A. Mitchell, BA, B.Ed., MA, McMaster University, University of Saskatchewan, San Diego State University—Ms. Mitchell has been involved in the field of special education for over twenty-five years as a Resource Room teacher, counsellor and consultant. She's also worked in a hospital setting doing neuropsychological assessments. Her current position is as a Special Ed Consultant and Coordinator in an amalgamated school district. As well, she is seconded by the provincial department of education to present workshops on working students with autism spectrum disorders. Parents, school personnel, social workers, day care staff, occupational therapists, speech/language pathologists, psychologists, and counsellors attend these workshops.

Resources and links—Sharon Mitchell, BA, BEd, MA suggests visiting her Autism Today website to learn about her other products and services. Visit <http://mitchell.autismtoday.com> today! (*Please note, don't put in the www.*) You can learn about Ms. Mitchell's work by visiting her website, <http://www.sasklearningvillage.ca>. Alternatively, you can write to her at <mitchell.sharon@gmail.com>. To aid in your search for ways to help your child, Ms. Mitchell recommends a visit to <http://www.angel-images.com/adhd&as.htm>, a site run by a woman whose son has Asperger's Syndrome and ADHD. For a free e-book on ASD, visit <http://www.pediatricneurology.com/autism.htm>. For a free e-book on ADHD, visit <http://www.pediatricneurology.com/adhd.htm>. For a free e-book on learning disabilities, visit < http://www.pediatricneurology.com/learning.htm>.

Why think about the future now?

It comes up on us fast, this future thing. Often we are so busy trying to make it through the day-to-day events of our lives that we give little heed to what's down the road. But think about the length of time it takes for your child to acquire a new skill. How quickly does he adapt to a new teacher, a new classroom or to other of life's transition?

Now is the time to begin thinking long term. What skills might he or she need? How do you begin to teach them? And how will you find the time to even think about such things?

Where do you want your child to be in five years? Ten years?

To know how to begin, you need some idea of where you might see your child in five, 10 or 15 years. What is the life you'd hope for him? What are his interests? His talents? Can these be turned into useable skills out in the world? Where might he live? With you? With family? Independently? Sharing an apartment with a friend? In a group home setting? Will he be spending his days in a special class at school, in an integrated classroom, in post-secondary school or at a job placement?

Habits—start early with changes and preparations

It's likely that your child does not take readily to change. He needs time to adjust to the change and to acquire any new skills the situation requires.

Life can be going along fine, when a change is foisted on us. We have to move for a new job. Your child's age requires that he move on to the next classroom or school. A beloved teacher assistant is transferred.

While such change can be hard on all of us, for the person with an ASD such transitions can be especially upsetting. Yet, do we do the child a favour by not introducing change into his life? To help him prepare for change, try bringing in smaller changes while things are going well for him. I know it's hard to think about upsetting the apple cart when you think you are going through a peaceful spell, but it's as necessary to "teach" change as it is any other skill.

Being smart is not good enough

Sometimes we watch our children with Asperger's Syndrome struggle with life. While so much seems hard for them, they do have one strength—they're smart. As parents, it's tempting to focus on the positive. Yes, he's having trouble with this and this and this, but look at his Science marks.

While those marks are nice, keep in mind that being smart isn't good enough. There are many very bright ASD people who are unemployed or seriously under-employed because their lack of social skills keeps them from holding down fulfilling occupations.

Over-helping

In our desire to assist and protect, sometimes we "over-help." This occurs when we do for a child what he could do for himself. Yes, we can do it better ourselves or the child can do it better with our help, but is this what we want? It's faster to do Johnny's coat up for him, true, but in doing so we deny him the pleasure and pride of learning to do for himself.

Be reasonable in your expectations, but pick a skill you would like him to have. Break the task into parts by walking yourself through it, step by step. What does he need to be able to do before he can tackle the task? Demonstrate, practice and hone that skill. Build in increments until he can handle it first with assistance, then on his own. Then build on that success with another skill.

Determine the level of assistance that your child must have and offer no more than that. Re-evaluate this level often and wean off when possible.

There are many ASD children who graduate from high school only to bomb in post-secondary or the world of work. Might they have become too reliant on the assistance of a teacher aide? In schools we adapt and accommodate to meet a child's needs and help them achieve success. The world rarely proffers such understanding and the transition can be daunting for the young person.

Yes, with TA assistance, your child with Asperger's Syndrome might be a straight A student. But are the marks the important thing or is learning how to handle yourself in class the key? It might be better for the student to take those steps toward managing on his own while under the shelter and guidance of his school rather than at college or in the work place.

What is realistic?

While we know that everyone grows and changes, just how much do you realistically think your child will change between childhood and adulthood? It might surprise you. Many of us think of those toddler years and wonder how we survived. Looking back, our children grew and prospered, albeit at their own pace, but they did learn and mature.

Be hopeful but realistic in your plans. Keep in mind the child's talents, special interests and the things he or she will find hard in life. Listen to the opinions of others, but know in your heart that you know your child best. Read what adults with ASD have to say about their years growing up and how life is for them now. We can learn much from their willingness to share the commonalities that make up autism spectrum disorders.

Here are some useful sites:

- www.aspires-relationships.com/jerry_and_mary_newport.htm

- www.aspie.com/pages/1/index.htm

- www.donnawilliams.net/

- www.grandin.com/inc/mind.web.browser.html

- www.isn.net/~jypsy/

- www.askanaspie.com/ This site is run by students from the University of Chicago who have autism. Here is part of what they have to say: "When it comes to information about autism, there are a lot of resources written by professionals for parents. There are a lot of support groups by parents for parents. But how much information out there aimed at parents was written by autistics? It can be hard for a neurotypical parent to understand how an autistic child sees the world, especially when that child has trouble communicating. We are a group of students at the University of Chicago who have Asperger's Syndrome and High Functioning Autism, and we're here to provide a window into the autistic worldview. We can provide information from our own personal experience, point you towards information in the thriving online autistic community, or give you a

245

history of Middle English Pronouns. We're aspies. Between us, we know a lot of random stuff."

- www.autistics.org/isnt/ When we focus too much on the deficits of ASD or think that our way of perceiving the world is the *only* way, pay a visit to this website. Take the test to see if you are "on or off the spectrum."

Build on your child's interests

Having special interests is a feature of ASD. These interests may change over time, but chances are your child will always have a special interest.

Rather than trying to fight the preoccupation, go with it. Use it to your advantage. Build lessons around it. Practice "First . . ., then . . . " where your child must first complete the assigned task before spending time on his area of interest. Allow time for him to indulge his interest, but you will likely need to limit the where, when and how long. Ask yourself: Can this interest or talent be used as a teaching tool? Is there a way to turn it into a life skill? Can he engage in his interest while performing a service to or with others?

Life is a group process

We know that social skills are a troublesome area in ASD. We know how Theory of Mind weakness makes it harder for these children to put themselves in someone else's place. The sensory sensitivities and tendency toward rigidity can make being with others difficult.

But life is a group affair. Almost anyplace we go, we have to interact with others. And, for the most part, like it or not, the world does not bend for us; we need to fit into the world to the degree that we are able.

If you see your child remaining at home with you always, then your adult child will need to be able to function within the parameters of family encounters within your home. If your child will be in a work situation, he will need to tolerate the proximity of others and abide by rules and imposed timelines. If he goes to college, again, handling proximity and time, along with a host of other features will be paramount to success.

At no matter what level your child functions, he will spend large portions of his life as part of a group. Work on the skills he'll need to survive and survive well with other people.

Quality of life goals

There are things we want out of the good life, and these same things we want for our children.

- We want to be happy.
- We want to have friends.
- We want to love and be loved.
- We want to feel useful.
- We want work we enjoy.
- We want variety.
- We want to laugh.
- We want to have fun.
- We want a safe and stable place to live.

Here's a visual example of planning for these valued life outcomes: www.state.vt.us/educ/new/pdfdoc/ pgm_alternate/portfolio/high_priority_021005.pdf.

Which skills can you begin teaching now so that down the road your child can enjoy "the good life?"

By and for people on the autism spectrum

CHAPTER 19

My mother nearly died from German Measles

Contributing Author Veronica York is a female with Asperger's Syndrome. She was born and raised abroad and now lives in the USA. Her diagnosis was given to her when she was 37 years old, opening the doors for her to harmoniously try to channel her autistic journey which began so long ago. She wanted to bring the fragmented part of herself to a whole, and in the process had to learn to recognize her weaknesses, her strengths, and the part of her that links both.

Resources and links—Veronica York suggests visiting her Autism Today website to learn about her other products and services. Visit: <http://york.autismtoday.com> today! (*Please note, don't put in the www.*)

My mother nearly died from German measles, in Chicago, when she was three months pregnant with me, hoping to end an untimely conception. I was born with Infantile Autism. She told me, and I remember, screaming, wailing without consolation, from an onslaught of environmental offences, clothing, light, noise, touch and her mother's milk. You may not believe that I could remember, but I do, especially the white cap of the nurse who peered over the portable basket, lifting my tightly swaddled body, cooing into my face, nose to nose in an effort to calm me, her face devoid of features, the sounds emulating from the triangular hat.

My mother sought a neighbor's advice, a squarely built women who knew how to raise farm animals. "Wrap her up real tight in a flannel-blanket, then keep her warm in a cardboard shoe box, and don't disturb her for three hours at a time." My mother placed me in the kitchen next to the oven door, then, did as she suggested, drip fresh goat's milk down my throat from a glass bottle with a hard rubble nipple. "She's just like the dear little animals that aren't quite finished developing their nervous system." She told my mother. Thanks to her, I survived, but my nervous system remains sensitive, overloading when I receive too much stimuli, such as, riding a tram, eating in noisy restaurants, attending sporting events, and at celebratory parties, causing my arms to ache, nausea and a disorientation of time and space.

High Functioning Autism, a category, niche, diagnosis that gives me a mailbox for many of my defining characteristics, some positive, even extraordinary, my sense of color and smell, awareness of environmental emotions, like the visceral awareness of angry, happy, or, sad energy permeating a space, even when no one else is present in the room. And then, other, challenging aspects of my being; my tactile defensiveness, when someone approaches me from behind, with a highjack response to plant my elbow in their Solar Plexus. I have a photogenic recall of spaces with a keen observation of changes in the décor, any changes, mentally editing the film that replays in my head from the previous time that I was there. Then, there are my problems with sensory overload from florescent lights, noisy fans, obnoxious odors, that are painful and distracting. I scan the room to locate a safe space from the offensive elements, allowing me to calm my sensory system enough to process visual and auditory information again. And, the biggest challenge, hiding my discomfort, if I am with strangers. Appearing calm, moving my body gracefully, responding appropriately, to social overtures.

The friends I have, today, are understanding, perhaps, even cherishing, my unusualness, allowing me transition time, even helping me find my comfort zone in social situations. Maybe, it is my playful nature and oblique sense of humor that I share, when I am relaxed, that helps maintain our relationship. I see and experience the world from a unique perspective, as you may say, as *all* of us do. I believe that this is a major communication gap between those of us who are aspies, and those who are considered to be neuro typical. What I mean to convey, is the *degree* of uniqueness that we experience. I agree with the father, of a son, who is diagnosed with Aspergers, who said, "Differences for my son are more like ten thousand times-normal." He said ten thousand, not ten or one hundred times. It is the difference between carrying an empty backpack on the hike of life, and one filled, with boulders.

When asked, "Would you like to get rid of your autism, I said "No." I am who I am, and accept myself. However, I am willing to change. I continue to modulate sensory overload, avoiding some situations all together, and learn to ask for accommodations in a friendly way. I value the fresh approach and unique perspective that defines my autism. Like adjusting a camera angle, I celebrate the differences between my view and others. Viva la differ ace! Ultimately, we are all part of the great human condition and in the magnificent scheme of all things, we are interconnected and the *same*.

Hi Stephen, how do you do?

Here is my first essay that I am sending you and hopefully it is OK.

If I need to make changes to it, please let me know. I do have one request only. I would not want my real name to be place in the link.

I have chosen Serendip as my pen name, if it could be use I will certainly appreciate it.

Please let me know if this is possible or not.

I have two more letters—*as I call them*—that I would like to post if they fit what they (Autism Today) are looking for.

One talks about ways of communicating between two people in the spectrum and outside the spectrum too. The other one talks about what I feel the experts are missing about us and how their labels bring a shadow to many lives.

Send my regards to your wife and will pray for you and your trip to Lincoln, Nebraska.

Autism and I

I am a female with Asperger's Syndrome, I was born and raised abroad and now live in the USA.

My diagnosis was given to me when I was 37 years old, opening the doors for me to harmoniously try to channelize my autistic journey which began so long ago. I wanted to bring the fragmented part of me to a

whole, and in the process I have learn to recognize my weakness, my strength and part of me that links both.

Autism, my weaknesses and I

Control of one self and the emotions I feel are perhaps one of my biggest challenges in my life with autism. I did not know-- *before I was diagnosed that--* what I felt at times could be an obstacle in my life.

I did not know how some of my flows could impaired my interaction with others.

There are times in which it is hard for me to control emotions of frustration and of sadness, and they both pose a threat to the way I communicate with others.

Ambiguities are not my fort and when I have no control of what goes on around myself I feel anger, and frustrations that show. If at times I have plans and they do not go my way, I have a hard time adapting to what is to happen next. I worry, I get confused, I might withdraw and I wish I could shut off and to retrieve into my world to find peace in my secure refuge.

Those are things that I have to combat in my daily life. Things that I have leaned to recognized and I am trying to understand. Life is not easy for me, having to constantly battle the way I feel, trying to gain a more even control of me. Molding myself to a more assertive being in order to interact with others in better ways and be able to achieve a simple dream.

Autism, my strengths and I

One of the biggest strength I have is that I persevere in what I believe and that I never cease to try to achieve a better way to communicate and a better way to adapt to the world.

Even though, I am an Aspie and naturally resist change, I have a brain with the capability of reasoning and of learning new ways. I learn from my failures more than from anything else, so every time I have failed, at the end I fight to transform it into gain. I have read many books in search for new ways to help myself understand the mechanics of what is called Emotional Intelligence; and I have learned to_rethink a previously *set thought*.

Changes are not easy for anyone in the spectrum, but they can beachieved; specially if there is a third person who could guide us more to learn to interpret the outside world. I was raised in an extended family setting, and in a way that helped, I was guided by family all the time in the things I should do or say.

The social world was a lot more complex than what I thought and I failed a lot, but with the pass of time I gain knowledge by practicing—*role play*— and at the end I was able to adapt better to change.

Life continues to be a challenge in the social world, but it is not an impossible task anymore. It takes time, it takes energy and it takes a lot of prayers from me to be able to go out there and relate.

I thanks my upbringing for the way I have turned out to be, but most of all I thanks God for helping me.

I am still having many problems communicating with others in the outside world, specially when people behave in unconventional manners. However, I do no longer try to impose my orthodox ways, I just try to understand the mechanics of their thoughts so that I can help bring down a the barrier and thus communicate. I believe in self improvement, perseverance and progress; every time I am out there I think of better ways to help myself and my Aspie friends to overcome the fears and ambiguities of the social world. In time all will fall into place, but until then I continue in the search for ways to communicate.

Linking my weakness and my strength

When I am in the outside world, I have to control and channelize my emotions and my belief in order to be able to communicate effectively with people in different types of settings.

I have to remember that my orthodox ways are not the rule and that I have to adapt to what is the norm. It is then when I have to make a great effort to change from my true self to my pretend self.

I have to come to terms with the fact that in order for me to better communicate I must learn to decipher others peoples ways. I am scared in a way-- *after failing so many times*-- of the ambiguities that I might find when I am among others; However, I am mostly

prepared to face them with the knowledge that using less emotions and more logic is the way to go.

Emotional intelligence plays a great role in how I communicate with others as much as thinking of me in a third person does—*my pretend self*—and not my true me.

When I link past experiences, knowledge and self control of my emotions and beliefs I am better prepared to have a more successful way of dealing with social situations of any type. Knowing my weaknesses and my strengths is a plus, since I can use both of them to make life easier for me and for others around me as well.

Communicating effectively will always be a challenging task for me, but it achieved by means of perseverance, control of emotions, knowledge and practice.

I was 37 when I discovered why a part of me was fragmented, I cried, I raged, I calmed down and I learned to understand my weakness and strength; so that I could try to rebuild my fragmented self and turn it into a whole.

The journey has been long, at times I leave pieces of my heart on the road, at times I pick a rose; but throughout it all I know that I am not alone, that there are many fellows Aspies like me on the road . . . And so I continue to persevere in ways to learn to communicate so that others can hear my inner voice.

— Veronica York,
GA, USA

And then, they'll see my mother

Contributing Author Jessica "Jazz" Summers was born in Arkansas in 1990. Diagnosed as mentally retarded at age three and autistic at four, she is the daughter of Lynley Summers. Jazz is the youngest member of Bobbi McKenna's Write Your Own Book Club, a club intended for adults, and will release a book next year. She speaks in her community to increase autism awareness. Having skipped 6th grade, she is an honor student at Mills University Studies High, ranked #20 in the nation by Newsweek.

Resources and links—Jessica "Jazz" Summers suggests visiting her Autism Today website to learn about her other products and services. Visit <http://summers.autismtoday.com> today! (*Please note, don't put in the www.*)

Autism: the word once rang of despair for a lot of mothers who only hoped that their children's actions would be controlled by, perhaps, a behavioral medication. The word once rang of loneliness, for the children on the spectrum had become lost to their own void, their own world, and the mothers and children who had become outcasts to the society to which the mothers once belonged. The word also once rang of defeat, for the mothers broke down, losing all hopes that their lives would ever be the same again, and sometimes leaving their children to try to fight the darkness alone, only to fail and lead a life with no purpose whatsoever. This was the word's definition 11 years ago, when I and many like me had no hope. This was its definition before my mother, Lynley Summers, came and inspired a different meaning behind my once terrible world.

True, I was only four years of age in 1994, but that didn't stop the doctors from trying to trap my mother in the same kind of depression that had ensnared the other mothers of autistic children. They ran diagnostics and IQ tests, among other things. But what they were telling my mother was so much worse: "Your daughter has an IQ of 50. Normally, that is considered "mental retardation.'; "Your daughter will probably never be able to speak English."; "Here's how it works: when Jessica gets a little older, she will have to start wearing a helmet. There is always the option of a group home, full of other people like her (and other misfits to society). Any questions?"

Had I understood what the doctors were saying of me at the time, I most likely would have broken down and gone even further into my own void. My diagnostics had clearly explained to my mother why other people labeled me as a "freak," and why our own family—YES! OUR OWN family—had abandoned us as though I had the plague and like Mom caught it. My autism was something that neither of us could control at the time. However, if my mother had been like the other moms out there at the time, I would not have turned out the way I ended up. And, lucky for me, my mother still isn't the type to give up without a fight.

We went through therapy after painstaking therapy, and sure enough, one year later, I was able to walk into the world again. They had considered me a genius for my age, though I do not remember how high my IQ was after that one year of therapy. I still acted autistic but I was still getting some more of my mother's Chaos Theory Therapy in the meanwhile, to help me "act" normal. There were major setbacks at times. After all, kids will still be kids.

I was still acting sort of "funny" when I entered kindergarten, and so the other kids harassed me. They framed me for almost everything, and the teacher believed every single one of the kids but me—just because I was different. She didn't know what autism was and didn't seem to care what it was. Before I knew it, that lady put me in a remedial class part-time, and the kids made fun of me there, as well. My mother tried to set things straight after she caught one of the kids framing me again. Guess what the lady said: "I've been around your kid more than you have and I can tell that she's nothing but trouble . . . ."

Mom was madder than I'd ever seen in my life. Not only did she move me away from that school, she started doubling our therapy sessions, making sure that I'd never have to deal with anything like that ever again. Before I knew it, after school I was coming to the college where Mom worked and practicing what we had learned in therapy. Sometimes, Mom was interviewing college students while I was in the other room, practicing what I had learned by myself. Other times, my mom and I hung out together with some of her friends while we practiced some more therapy.

Most of the friends that I had in first, second and third grade were my Mom's friends: adults. They understood me; I understood them; all was right with the world, and we could have had a party celebrating our friendship. That's how happy I was, despite the fact that I was still in therapy. And my adult friends liked me so much that I was recruited as the first Junior Member of Alpha Psi Omega, the college's drama fraternity. Even when I went to Japan with Mom for two years, most of my friends were adults and a lot of them even hung out with me during my therapy.

By the time I went into junior high and high school, when I came back to America, you could hardly tell that I was autistic at all. My mother's love had already brought me out of the void that I was in. And people just didn't care anymore. Autism had become just another condition, just another bump in the road, so to speak—much like near-sightedness. I found friends who were my peers. Sure, I was teased every once in a while, but that's just what it was: teasing. So it wasn't a big deal to me. However, every once in a while I end up wishing that I could tell the world some very major points that could probably turn their lives around.

Mothers, please: DO NOT GIVE UP ON YOUR CHILDREN! Although the world might be sunny and bright outside, the void is a dark, lonely place to be, filled with your children's fears, anger and sadness. I know because I've been in that horrible place. If anything besides my mother's therapy regimen can bring your children out of the void, it is your love, faith, understanding and guidance. You have to believe in them. That's all it will take to bring them out of the void.

It's always easier to be lazy about it. It's always easier to think that all is lost or that nothing can

be done. You'd probably hear a person after the diagnostics, crying, "Oh, no! He has autism! All is lost! Alas!"

But that's the thing: all is not lost. That is the mistake that some parents with autistic children made. They give up on them, and allow them to sink deeper and deeper into the void. Most of them expect their kids to learn all they need to know at school. What a joke. Parents leave their kids alone too much. They don't get involved. They let their kids be raised by the television or by the Internet, or they expect everyone else to do it for them. Then, they blame it all on the autism. And one of these days, they're going to sit on a chair, missing their precious children, wondering where they are now. And then they'll realize; they're right where they left them: lost in the void, some of them perhaps in a home where they have few opportunities.

I shudder to think of my "self," left shackled by a "disability," helpless. Some parents may say to themselves, "What have I done? What have I done that made my child deserve this treatment? Why should he have to suffer for the fact that I abandoned him in his time of need? Why didn't I fight for him? He was my child. Why did I have to give up on him?"

And then, they'll see my mother: not the woman who defeated autism, but rather embraced it and formed it to her liking. I was only the clay to the potter and I was shaped into person I am today not only by experience but by love itself. My mother had so much faith in me that it helped me to carry on in life. Yes, there are times when I feel desperate and weak and as though I might falter to the mission in which I must succeed, but my mother is the one who gets me back up on my feet with her faith and love, as she tells me, "You can do it, Jazz; I know you can . . . ."

Every once in a while, at Mills University Studies High School, the school I go to now, when I tell people about Autism, some people already know about it or know someone with it. That, I believe, is progress on our part. However, some of the other people I tell do not know about it or making fun of it afterwards. Like I mentioned before, that's just how kids are. One of the more infamous, but hurtful, jokes goes something like this:

"Why did the Autistic girl cross the road?"

"Well, I don't know. Why?"

"I don't know, either. Why wasn't she in the asylum?"

Like I said: hurtful. It sounded a lot like they were laughing at me, but the truth of it is that they had no clue what it was really about. They didn't even know I was autistic and when I told them that I was they automatically kept their mouths shut about the "autistic girl joke." I also meet people who have absolutely no clue what autism is. I tell them a little about it, and usually I get: "Autism? What is it, like mental retardation?" People should learn that being autistic just means you're a little bit more special than some of the normal kids.

To be perfectly honest, I really don't think that anyone is truly "normal." The only people who really are "normal" are the really boring adults and the really mean kids. Other than that, everyone has their own special qualities. Just like there are special shapes and sizes; everyone is going to be different from you. Different is a good thing; America is a land of diversity, after all.

My point is that you shouldn't shun people just because they're different. According to a song in Schoolhouse Rock, we are said to be the Great American Melting Pot. The way I see it, we, the autistic, are just one more ingredient to this delicious country that we call America. Just because we're different doesn't mean we're defective. It just means that we make America all the more unique.

My Story

Contributing Author—Daniel Hawthorne is a diagnosed High Functioning Autistic. He is the author of *Child of the Forest* and *Guidelines to Intervention in Autism,* and webmaster and author of the award winning site <www.autismguidelines.com>. He has degrees in Communication and Business Administration, most recently through the University of Arkansas. He does numerous speaking engagements to autism support groups and to special schools, in addition to managing an online resume posting business.

Resources and links—Daniel Hawthorne suggests visiting his Autism Today website to learn about his other products and services. Visit <http://hawthorne.autismtoday.com> today! (*Please note, don't put in the www.)* Daniel Hawthorne may be contacted through his website: <www.autismguidelines.com>.

I: The journey begins

It was one of the last things my Dad said to me in our final conversation prior to his death last December, at the age of 82. "You know, I never did understand why you were always so different from other kids. You were just different, is all I know how to put it. No one else in my (extended) family ever had that problem learning how to talk." He went on to tell me how it was both a surprise and a mystery for him. I seem to recall my Mom, prior to her succumbing to Alzheimer's, telling me the same kind of thing. I took it was a mystery to her as well, though she did tell me she was immensely relieved when the doctor said that whatever was causing my speech delay, it was definitely not due to any kind of cancerous tumor on my vocal chords. According to the doctor, in that respect, I was completely healthy.

You see, all my life I've been on a journey, even before I realized I was on one. Even in college, others realized it before I did. One acquaintance remarked, "My goodness! I just realized the truth about you. You're in a search for yourself and you're lost in the woods." Then he shook his head some more and walked away. Now, after so many years, I finally understand what he meant. Truly, I was different from other people, had compulsions and habits others did not have. The same sporting events that others seemed to enjoy so much, complete with all the crowd noise, repelled me. What especially bothered me was how my level of functioning kept changing for no apparent reason. Some, with contempt in their voice, openly labeled me "retarded"; others, with an unmistakable air

of amazement, expressed how much they admired my intellect. An enigma indeed.

My journey toward self-discovery began in earnest in the spring of 1995 with work at a local print shop. The work, being fairly routine, suited me well. One day, I went to the break room as usual, but this time I noticed a religious newsletter on the table. I put my bologna and cheese sandwich aside and picked up the colorful magazine. A front page article entitled, "What is Autism?" captured my attention. I had heard the term before but was not quite sure what it meant, if anything. Inside the brochure, I found the various identifying traits of the condition.

I gasped in shock. It was like looking in a mirror. It was me, all me—the delayed speech, the rituals, the rigid thinking, the difficulty grasping abstract concepts. A storm of mixed emotions stirred inside me. I felt elated and yet I also felt violated. I was elated because now, for the first time in my life, my sensory related difficulties felt real. I could now grasp them in ways I couldn't before. I felt justified in believing they were real. Yet at the same time I was shocked that the whole article of information redeeming my belief system came from a person or people whom I had never met, who didn't know me. They somehow knew my deepest secrets, things I'd never told anyone.

I threw the offending paper back onto the table and rushed out of the break room, resolved not to ever research the subject. It was too disturbing.

Late that evening, I went to the grocery to attempt to shop. As I entered the store, I noticed that few other shoppers were around and the Muzak heard over the intercom was even soothing. I took a deep, satisfying breath; I could shop with little or no torture this time. I grabbed a cart, careful not to make any more noise than necessary. As I glanced up, a child in another shopping cart caught my attention. Though I had never seen this boy before, he seemed so strangely familiar. The boy had a fixed stare at the wall, almost like a statue. The mother, standing to his side, raised her hands and began speaking through sign language. Without ever turning around, he signed in response.

My hands felt cold and clammy. Chills ran down my back. I tried to get a breath, and couldn't. An image began to form from the distant, intentionally forgotten memories of my childhood. This boy was like me as a child. Then a storm of memories flooded my psyche. I drew back, unsure what to do next, or how to assess what had just happened. Slowly, I looked back at where the boy and his mother had been. They were gone.

Some days later, my professor told us to research a list or newsgroup. After a quickly prepared, tasteless supper, I went to the local computer lab to do the assignment. After a while, I glanced up at the clock, and rubbed my aching eyes. It was 2:00 a.m., and I sat alone in the campus computer lab—except for a lab technician who was busy running programs. Bleary-eyed and tired, my only thoughts were of how I should be in bed instead of torturing myself at this computer station. After all, it was only worth 10 points.

Yet, I felt compelled to continue. Though having seemingly accomplished little, I still felt unable to quit for the night, unable to fathom such a change in gears. I just couldn't decide on which article to print. There were so many. Moments later, I came across a list that included an autism discussion group. My heart pounded. I couldn't sit still. I was convinced that if I didn't open this door right then, the matter would forever haunt my nightly dreams. I closed my eyes and took a deep breath. No matter what I might find, I knew I had to know more. What about the condition I had read about in that newsletter? Could there really be other people out there like me? I felt compelled to know one way or the other.

I rushed home, too excited to sleep. I poured myself some hot tea and thought about my discovery. Could I really be autistic? What does it mean to be autistic, anyway? In the days and weeks that followed, I spent countless hours at the university library delving into the matter, and taking meticulous notes about what I found. A few months later, after rigorous testing and a seemingly endless number of interviews, I received my diagnosis. For me, the diagnosis was a relief. I was finally on the verge on understanding myself.

In the process of this journey, I've learned many things about myself. Autism is not just something I have, in the sense that one may have high blood pressure. It is something that I am, in that it affects every facet of my life. It affects the way I think, the way I perceive the world, and the way I respond to it.

II: The basic traits

One way the autism affects me is that I tend to think in much more tangible terms than do most people. In order to grasp abstract terms, I think of them in terms of what I can see, hear, touch. I think in illustrations and analogies, a trait medical experts often think of as mental rigidity.

To an autistic individual, mental rigidity is more than mere words printed on the pages of some psychiatric journal; it is the source of much of his being and who he is. It determines, to a great extent, how he learns about and responds to his environment. It is the reason autistic individuals tend to be so literal in their thinking and why figures of speech often confuse them.

To someone within the spectrum, abstract concepts of any kind are learned only with great difficulty, and realness is a constant issue. It has also been my experience that things I have not seen or touched in a while tend to lose their realness to me. For that reason, I have always had this affinity for nouns, and a certain dislike for verbs. Especially as a child, I had to go around the classroom touching the walls in order to feel comfortable being there. Things have to be tangible to me to seem real. The problem is that if they don't seem real, my mind tends to automatically reject them. Concepts that I reject, I soon forget as well.

For the autistic, learning must relate to something tangible. For myself, the actual learning is not as important as the learning how to learn. So much of what I was expected to learn was abstract, and yet this was the very thing I had trouble grasping. I was puzzled when, in my senior year of high school, my fellow classmates voted me "most studious.' I figured it surely could not be true because I didn't even know what that meant, exactly. Being studious was just another concept that I had difficulty grasping.

Thus, I had my own way of learning how to learn. For instance, the word "running" would conjure up for me an image, a memory of someone hurrying to the bus stop to catch the bus, breathing heavily, with me cheering them on.

Doing this not only made it more tangible, but easier to remember as well. Why visual imagery? I think perhaps so many people within the autistic spectrum are visually oriented because the other senses are even more vulnerable and thus more problematic.

I also discovered that the best time to learn was while I considered myself at play. I would make the learning situation into a game. I would be relaxed and comfortable, and learning became much easier. Experience has shown me that concept learning is best done when the child is relaxed, especially while the individual is at play—not during periods of high-pressure drills. It is my belief that such drills produce masses of memorized statements, but little more.

Another aspect of mental rigidity involves the need for routines and rituals. Everyone has at least some need for a sense of order and, with it, daily routines. Just imagine how hectic life would be without those daily routines, if one had to decide every morning how to get out of bed, what to eat for breakfast, what route to use to get to work, and so forth. Indeed, our lives are filled with enough stress as it is, without making it exponentially more so with constant decision-making, as would be the case if one had no daily routines.

Thus, we all need at least some sense of routine and purpose, but children especially need it, and autistic children need it most of all—simply because of the mental rigidity that comes with the disorder.

That mental rigidity is a major trait of autism that has been known for a long time. One of the implications of this is that autistic children, living in a chaotic world as everyone does, must find ways to impose on their environment a sense of order. Life never comes completely scripted, so far as I know, anyway. As much as I might like sameness, life still

goes on. Since none of us live on a desert island, there are always changes in the way we go about our lives from day to day. I have found that if I know in advance what to expect and that there is a valid, important reason for this change, then I can usually accept the change on an emotional and cognitive basis. But if the change is a total surprise, and seems arbitrary at that, then I have difficulty mentally accepting it's realness.

For the autistic individual, virtually everything about life is not only frustrating but is so in the extreme. The rituals serve a useful purpose in that they impose a sense of order for those who need it. Otherwise, they are forced to cope with the continuously high level of frustration in other, less appropriate ways. Thus, a ritual is a vital technique for coping with a confusing, often disorderly world.

Especially during childhood, all the time I feel either very comfortable and secure, or else very uncomfortable and insecure. Back then, it was always either one extreme or the other. I recall many times things during childhood that when things were not exactly explained to me, and especially not in tangible terms, it caused me to feel mentally frustrated and quite insecure.

Thus, as one might expect, I found ways to cope, including rituals. Some of my rituals were common, such as not stepping on cracks in the sidewalk. But I also felt compelled to tap my teeth together a certain number of times and in a certain manner. Or tap my thumbs with my forefinger in perfect geometric patterns.

During meals, I ate in "rounds." That is, I would take one bite of everything on my plate, then start again. If I disliked an item on the tray, I simply removed it. Since it no longer belonged with my meal, I felt no obligation to eat it—and the sense of order that my psyche required was maintained. My drinks had to be placed on the tray so that they could be included in the meal.

Another ritual involved the way I walked the half mile home from the bus stop. I had a compulsion to walk with my right foot on the road and my left foot on the grass. Any deviation from this and I had to walk it over. Also, I could not enter a bathtub without first rubbing my feet three times each. At the front door, I would knock three times, turn around three times, and shuffle my feet three times before entering. At school, I had to go to my desk, shuffle my books, go touch the teacher's desk, then return to take my seat.

In time, as I developed and as I learned to cope in other ways, my need for rituals decreased.

Truly one of the beautiful aspects of classic autism is the sense of innocence. Autistic individuals tend to be playful, optimistic and a bit mischievous. We tend to want to project good feelings toward others and expect that in return.

Out of this sense of innocence comes a sense of wonder that pervades every day. No matter how often I have experienced it before, it is always as if it is the first time. I am amazed at the way honeysuckles manage to fill a whole neighborhood with their fragrance. I look up at trees reaching up to the sky, and marvel at their magnificence. I see streams bubbling and wonder about that too.

III: Sensory difficulties

For all the inherent difficulties affecting those within the autism spectrum, I would have to say that, by far, the one that causes the most suffering and torture is the tendency toward Sensory Dysfunction, also called Sensory Integrative Disorder.

There are several sensory-related issues that, for someone who is autistic, cause the disorder to be much more troublesome than need be. Indeed, it is the tendency toward sensory difficulties that makes autism so difficult to deal with.

Also called sensory defensiveness, the worst part is that it tends to go in an unending cycle and worsens as it continues—until abated. Parents and teachers may observe it as negative behaviors or as an extreme reluctance to do certain things. But what is really going on is that the child is suffering from sensory distress. Being unable to talk, as is the case so often in classic autism, the child is unable to express what it is that is torturing him or her.

The sensory dysfunction and overload tend to lead to a heightened level of frustration and anxiety. As the nervous system becomes increasingly stressed, the sensory dysfunction worsens, causing harsh sounds and rough textures to become even more irritating

than ever. The sensory dysfunction, as it worsens, leads to yet more anxiety and frustration. The cycle continues until interrupted. As one can see, the well of sensory-related suffering goes deep.

Nature intended us, for our own survival, to have sensory defensiveness. A certain amount of touch sensitivity is necessary to warn us of dangers. Have you ever been out in the yard or in the garden, and felt this spider crawling up your arm? Or tried to read with a fly annoy you? When a sensory system dysfunctions so greatly as it frequently does in autism, the tactile system is especially affected. The skin itself becomes hypersensitive.

So, what does a light touch feel like? The best way I can describe a light touch from the point of view of someone with sensory problems is that it is like having bugs crawling all over you. Believe me, it is quite annoying. This can be anything with a rough, abrasive texture, like certain foods. This would especially apply to polyester-based clothing. Stiff, roughly textured blankets can be just as annoying. I often wonder why manufacturers ever make blankets scratchy like that.

Tactile sensitivity is one of the main reasons individuals with autism so often have trouble sleeping through the night. After all, who can sleep with that kind of stuff going on? No wonder I had so much difficulty sleeping through the night for most of my life.

A second way this hypersensitivity affects is me visually. I often have to keep my computer screen dim to avoid high contrast and the brightly colored, animated advertisements that decorate most web pages. Such harsh glare tends to make me instantly nauseous. On my really bad days, even ordinary fluorescent lights seem to resemble strobe-like floodlights. I may not see the flickering, but I can certainly feel it.

For me, the worst part of going to the dentist was never the shots or the drilling; it was the glare from the lamp. More than once, I wanted to tell the dentist what he could do with his evil lamp. Unfortunately, I couldn't talk for having to hold my mouth wide open.

Noise can be a problem. Hearing sensitivity is especially troublesome for me because it is difficult to protect myself from. Unlike visual distress, it doesn't help just to turn the other way. Actually, turning my head so that one ear is facing away from the noise, just makes the pain worse. It seems that both ears must hear the sounds to a similar degree for my brain to process it adequately. The two types of noise that bother me most, though in vastly differently ways, are sharp, explosive sounds and crowd noise.

Sharp or sudden noises may include such things as metal banging on metal, pencils tapping against a desk, chalk squeaking along a chalkboard, tires squealing, metal forks touching ceramic dishes, as happens at mealtime, car horns blowing and car doors shutting. Leaf blowers, sirens and vacuum cleaners are also major offenders.

What's worse is that the sound does not even have to be loud to be irritating. Water coming out of a faucet, a toilet flushing, the hum of a dishwasher or an air conditioning system all bothered me.

It feels like electrical shock waves beginning at my ear, and being especially bad there, but also traveling along every nerve fibre of my body.

The other type is crowd noise. Our senses are like windows to the world. Information is uploaded to the brain for processing. Nature knew that our brains' processing ability needed protecting. Thus, during periods of loud crowd noise and such, most people are able to block out irrelevent noise. As noted earlier, it's the specialized cells known as Purkinje that do the magic. Unfortunately, without them in sufficient quantity, sensory information overload becomes a big problem for those of us who are autistic. Without this protection, we remain so vulnerable.

Crowd noise can be found everywhere, and even a small amount hurts me. So most of my life has been filled with torture. All too often I find myself in a social setting, filled with people innocently talking— and I am totally unprepared for the unwelcome bombardment of meaningful noise on my senses. Unable to simply ignore it, I find myself forced to listen in on and try to make sense of every single conversation going on in the room. At such times, I feel as if I were a fortress under siege from both meaningful and meaningless sensory data. Mentally, I may know what noise is relevant and what isn't, but my senses don't know. So my senses pick up every bit of available information. Because speech is meaningful noise, my mind wants to somehow grasp it all, to somehow comprehend everything being said.

For the first few seconds, I feel my head filling up, as it were, and being overwhelmed by all the sensory data coming my way, and I cannot ignore it. At first I am acutely aware of the neural pressure, like one feels the pressure of the water when diving into several feet of water. I am also acutely aware of how uncomfortable it is, how much it hurts. I feel the shock waves start at the ears and travel through every nerve fibre in my body. It feels like an electrical jolt surging through my entire nervous system.

Then, as the sensory overload sets in, I become dazed and have difficulty functioning. I can't focus my thoughts. My brain gets overwhelmed to the point that conscious thought is difficult. Mental fog sets in. I begin to feel mentally and physically numbed and disoriented. If I stay there long enough, I feel an aura coming on, leading to yet another seizure.

Later, after some rest, mentally I may feel I have recovered somewhat, but physically I feel bruised. I ache and sting all over as if my entire nervous system were in rebellion.

After repeated assaults, my senses would indeed become confused. I would get dazed and numb. I could have an ache without grasping where I feel the ache, or even whether I feel, hear or see it. At times my senses have gotten so confused and all I have known is that it was torment of some kind and it was real. As anyone who has ever been to a dentist can verify, after being numb a while one begins to crave a sense of feeling in the anesthetized area. Now imagine if one's entire body remained numb over a long period of time. For most, the craving would be unbearable, and so it often is for the autistic individual. Thus, the level of frustration remains high and the quality of life low.

As a child, and even now at times, I have had a continuous feeling that my arms and legs were no longer attached. I have felt compelled throughout the night to continuously rub my joints and wiggle my toes, without ever actually gratifying the strange need I had to touch, to feel something, anything at all. It has caused me a lot of insomnia.

I once fell off the cab of a truck and completely broke my wrist, but felt no pain or other discomfort at all from it. My body was that numb. As I looked down, the sight of my limp hand looked odd, but it did not hurt. I could not feel any physical sensation at all. I realize now I was fortunate not to have gotten hurt more than I did throughout my childhood, as things for me could have been much worse without my realizing it.

But there is a craving that often goes along with this kind of numbness. If one has ever been to a dentist and had one's gums and jaw numbed so the dentist could do a root canal, one may understand just how annoying numbness can be, no matter what the cause. After a period of such numbness, one starts craving some kind of physical sensation in the area that got numbed. Now imagine if one felt that same numbness all over one's body. Imagine, too, that this numbness is not only continuous but lasts for an indefinite length of time. This could be months, even years. After a while, one gets desperate to feel something, anything at all, even if the means to that end is inappropriate.

IV: Some final thoughts

Do I feel cheated not to be like other people? Not at all. I like and accept who I am and I have a passion for life. I am who I am and would not want to be anyone else, even if I could.

The difficulties of my life have made me more appreciative of the beauties of life, and tend to make me appreciate the value of friendships I have made along the way.

Light at the end of the tunnel

Contributing Author Terri Robson is an adult with Asperger's Syndrome. She is the controller at Autism Today. She has a Bachelor of Education with a Music Major and an English Minor. As well, she has a Music Merchandising Diploma and is a Certified Journeyman Partsman. She is pursuing a designation as a professional accountant. She loves great music, good wine, reading, camping and spending time with her partner of 10 years, family and friends. She has 2 purebred dogs (1 of whom is a Canadian and American Champion) that she calls her children. Terri loves being an "Aspie" and wouldn't want to be any other way.

Resources and links—Terri Robson suggests visiting her Autism Today website to learn about her other products and services. Visit <http://robson.autismtoday.com> today! (*Please note, don't put in the www.)*

I debated with myself during the writing of this as to when (in the course of the article) to disclose that I have Asperger Syndrome. Should I come right out with it or should I build the suspense until the end. Needless to say I came right out with it (a very special co-worker suggested I fill you in at the beginning).

I have spent most of my life wondering what was wrong with me and why I was so different. For the longest time I didn't have any answers and neither did anybody else. Not that many people wanted to know. It seemed that no one wanted to get to know me or understand me. But I must say I didn't know or understand myself either. I didn't have any friends. Sometimes that really hurt yet at other times it didn't bother me at all. I was quite content to do my own thing. What a strange contradiction.

There were many issues with family members. I remember my aunt telling me (within the last few years) that she would have her version of a pep talk with my cousins before we went for a visit. It went something like this: Okay boys, your Auntie Marilyn and the kids are coming for a visit. We all know how Terri can be so we need to tread lightly. This isn't an exact quote but you get the gist of it. I'm still amazed that even in my late 30's these words had the power to devastate me. At times they still do.

There were good things about me, special gifts if you will, yet not many seemed to notice. I excelled at academics, music and sports but people only seemed to see my "obnoxious and socially unacceptable" behaviours. I wanted to shout "there is a fun and enjoyable person in here" but I couldn't because more often than not I wasn't even aware of it myself. I was ostracized and bullied in school even though I was bigger than most of my peers. It wasn't "easy being green."

So I did my own thing and got in trouble a lot because I didn't conform to the norm. Just what is the "norm" anyway? It took me many years to develop coping skills and techniques to be able to do the things I wanted and knew I was capable of doing. Yet there were 2 or 3 people who loved me unconditionally. For that I feel very blessed.

My music and my love of reading helped through the tough times (of which there were many). When I was playing my trumpet, and later the euphonium, I was able to put all the hurt, anguish and joy into my music and no one was intimidated or repulsed. What an experience. There was joy in my life; I just wasn't able to realize it then.

My diagnosis of Asperger Syndrome came late in my life; well, at the time I thought it was late. I was in my early thirties. Initially the diagnosis was ADHD yet that didn't ever seem to fit. My spouse and friends didn't agree with the diagnosis because I met very few of the criteria. However, that's all I had so I went with it. A few years later my psychiatrist mentioned Asperger's Syndrome and he believed I should be the recipient of such a delightful diagnosis. Lucky me, I'm an Aspie!!

Actually, he was bang on. As I started reading more and more literature I realized I could have been (and still should be) the poster child for Asperger Syndrome. What an incredible relief. I finally had something to hang my hat on. For those of you who are reluctant to label your child (or yourself) I encourage you to go for it. There was a reason I did all those strange and wonderful things as I was growing up. I wasn't just a big freak who didn't fit in anywhere and nobody liked. Now I'm a big freak with a label and I love it.

I have come to a place in my life where I love and respect who I have become and who I am. I still don't always fit in, but that's okay because I have my own space. I don't always say the right thing in public but when my family and friends need my support I somehow figure it out. I'm honest to a fault and I'll be there for you through thick and thin. Once you've climbed my walls and seen through my behaviours and mannerisms that offend you will have a very special place in my heart and I in yours. Love me for who I am and the rewards are tremendous (so are some the challenges but hey, that goes with the territory).

Take the journey with your child, family member or friend as you both grow and learn. Remember, there is light at the end of the tunnel. I have found mine.